THE LEGAL LANDSCAPE

THE LEGAL LANDSCAPE

Richard C. Smardon • James P. Karp
with graphic assistance from Scott S. Shannon

KF
5605
.S63
1993
West

VNR VAN NOSTRAND REINHOLD
New York

Copyright © 1993 by Van Nostrand Reinhold

Library of Congress Catalog Card Number 92-9295
ISBN 0-442-23536-4

All rights reserved. No part of this work covered by
the copyright hereon may be reproduced or used in any
form by any means — graphic, electronic, or
mechanical, including photocopying, recording, taping,
or information storage and retrieval systems — without
written permission of the publisher.

Printed in the United States of America

Van Nostrand Reinhold
115 Fifth Avenue
New York, New York 10003

Chapman and Hall
2–6 Boundary Row
London, SE1 8HN, England

Thomas Nelson Australia
102 Dodds Street
South Melbourne 3205
Victoria, Australia

Nelson Canada
1120 Birchmount Road
Scarborough, Ontario MIK 5G4, Canada

16   15   14   13   12   11   10   9   8   7   6   5   4   3   2   1

Library of Congress Cataloging-in-Publication Data

Smardon, Richard C.
    The legal landscape : guidelines for regulating environmental and aesthetic quality/ Richard C. Smardon, James P. Karp.
        p. cm.
    Includes bibliographical references and index.
    ISBN 0-442-23536-4
    1. Landscape protection — Law and legislation — United States.
    2. Land use — Law and legislation — United States.   3. Environmental law — United States.   4. Landscape
architecture — United States — Case studies.   5. Landscape assessment — United States — Case studies. I. Karp, James.
II. Title.
    KF5605.S63   1992
    346.7304′5 — dc20
    [347.30645]   92-9295
                                                                                                    CIP

The following have been reprinted with permission of John Wiley & Sons, Inc. From *1986 Foundations for Visual Project Analysis*, by R. C. Smardon, J. F. Palmer, and John P. Felleman. Copyright © 1986: Tables 2.1, 2.2, 2.3, 2.4; Figures 2.2, 2.5, 8.5, 8.9, 9.2, 9.3, 9.17, 10.4, 10.7; and text from pp. 23–24, 26, 30–34, 145–147, 151–155, 164.

Pages 16–24 in Chapter 3 of *The Legal Landscape* from James P. Karp, *The Evolving Meaning of Aesthetics in Land Use Regulation*, Columbia Journal of Environmental Law (1990).

Figure 10.10 a, b, c, d, e, f has been reprinted with permission of EDAW Inc., San Francisco, CA.

Contents

Chapter 4   Current Status of Aesthetics, State by State   25

II   CONSTRAINTS APPLIED TO COMMUNITY ISSUES

III   FEDERAL AND STATE AESTHETIC REGULATION

Chapter 14   Facility Siting   245

IV   Law and Aesthetics in Practice

Chapter 15   Litigation and Aesthetic Analysis   261

Preface

The purpose of this book quite simply is to present legally defensible mechanisms for maintaining and protecting aesthetic quality in the landscape, and to show how appropriate analyses of landscape character and values can be appropriately integrated into these legal mechanisms.

There has been a great deal of controversy over appropriate mechanisms for land-use control and/or project review which have had as their major or partial purpose protection or maintenance of landscape aesthetic quality. This is true for local land-use control as well as federal project/activity review. Seldom have courts and hearing officers been so confused or hesitant to engage such issues when asked to review decisions or process. Such actions are sometimes pushed to the Supreme Court because of alleged conflicts with the first, fifth, and fourteenth constitutional amendments.

Although there have been many law journal articles reviewing such cases, and some technical planning literature that reviews legal mechanisms for aesthetic land-use control, there has not been a major work that coalesces legal application, critical review of such, and appropriate baseline landscape analyses.

In December 1978 Smardon prepared a manuscript for the USDA Forest Services' Pacific Southwest Forest and Range Experiment Station in Berkeley, California entitled "Land And Aesthetics or When is the Pig in the Parlor? A Legal/Policy Overview of Legal Factors Influences on Visual Landscape Policy." This unpublished report was intended to be an in-depth survey of legal factors consideration affecting visual resource management by federal agencies and was subsequently used and referred to by resource professionals in the USDA Forest Service, USDI Bureau of Land Management, and USDA Soil Conservation Service. A few excerpts of this manuscript appeared as papers or were published, but the bulk of the manuscript has never been published.

The revision, updating, and broadening of this manuscript to a format suitable for a book was our objective. Another objective was to broaden the scope of the book specifically to include aesthetic control issues that relate to local governments' jurisdiction, as well as state and federal agencies.

The audience for such a book includes both legal and resource professionals, e.g., environmental and land-use lawyers, planners, landscape architects, and architects; planning para-professionals such as planning board members of local governments; agency personnel from federal and state agencies; and students and professors of planning, landscape architecture, architecture, historic preservation, and environmental law. Lastly, but most importantly, the book can serve as a reference and handbook for citizens who care about maintaining and preserving their own community landscape.

Richard C. Smardon &
James P. Karp
July 1992
Syracuse, New York

Acknowledgments

This book had a long gestation period but a quick final delivery which was painful to some including our families and those who needed our attention in 1991/1992. There are many who contributed valuable bits, including the case study material and some of the graphics. Thanks go to Dr. James Palmer of SUNY/ESF for material relating to the Dennis and Juneau case studies; Peter Bosselman from the University of California Environmental Simulation Laboratory for material for the San Francisco case study; Mary Burgoon of Reimann-Buechner Associates for material for the North Syracuse case study; Dr. Richard Chenoweth of the University of Wisconsin for material and graphics for the Alpine Lakes case study; David Blau, Vice-president of EDAW for the graphics for Mono Lake; Daniel Hamson and Toni Ristau of the National Park Service for the material for the Death Valley case study; Gary Kell of the U.S. Forest Service for the material related to the Allegheny Forest case study; Carl Petrich of Oak Ridge National Laboratories for the material for the Greene County Nuclear Power Plant case study; and Bruce Murray and Bernard Neimann of the University of Wisconsin for the material for the Ice Age National Monument case study.

Scott Shannon from the Faculty of Landscape Architecture provided the computer graphic key images at the beginning of each chapter and some of the line graphics. Various photos were provided by SUNY College of Environmental Science and Forestry faculty including: George Curry, Peter Black, Chad Dawson, Art Eschner, Jim Palmer, and Mathew Potteiger. Parts of various chapters were typed or retyped by our secretaries Pat Gibealt and Sue B. Dean. Dr. Karp's graduate assistant, Laurie also helped us check out some of those pesky citations. Omissions and mistakes are clearly the responsibility of the authors.

I
Introduction
and Constraints

Chapter 1

The Nature and Sources of Law

LAW AND LEGAL PROCESS

In order to function free from the tyranny of the largest numbers, the straightest shooters, or the most cunning schemers, society needs rules for conduct. Rules can create stability and safety so that social existence takes on an aura of predictability. Rules for social governance emanate from society's needs and evolve into a set of social values or ethics. At some stage in human social existence, some of these values or ethics are formalized into rules called law.

Law provides a framework for social action. If an individual knows the rules, and is guided by them in decision-making, he or she can better assess the risks of that action. A person knows that if you build a house on your residentially zoned land, there is little or no risk that society will demand that you take it down. Conversely, if you build an office building on residentially zoned land, there is a significant probability that society through the law will demand that you take the building down, or that you be punished in some manner for ignoring the law.

In the United States there are several distinct sources of law. The sources are briefly recited here, and are discussed in an applied fashion in Chapter 3. Some legal rules, such as the power of eminent domain and the right of the state government to regulate conduct so as to protect the public health, safety, and welfare, are deeply rooted in Anglo-American legal history. These powers of government are held to be inherent in the nature of sovereignty.

Most bodies of rules in our legal system are easier to trace. The federal Constitution is the product of a compact among the states to surrender some of their sovereignty to a central government so that they could func-

tion as an economic, political, and legal unit. It contains the most fundamental attributes of our governmental structure, and of our social beliefs. The roles of the legislative, the executive, and the judicial branches of the federal government are detailed therein. Basic beliefs, like freedom of speech, of religion, and of the press, and the broadly applicable concepts of due process and equal protection of the law are contained in the Constitution. Each of the states has a constitution that to some degree mirrors federal provisions and is applicable solely within the state.

With the constitutional framers having determined the basic structure and principles of the legal system, law-making was turned over to the three branches of the government. The Congress (and the state legislatures) is assigned the basic responsibility for converting desired public policy into written rules or statutory laws. State legislatures delegate some of their constitutional law-making powers to local governments through "enabling acts." For example, state enabling laws authorize municipal governments to adopt zoning codes, to enact laws to protect natural resources located in the community, and to regulate in order to preserve the aesthetic qualities of the area.

Frequently, legislation does not provide the many details necessary to implement the policy underlying the intent of the legislators. The job of filling in the details, or putting the flesh on the legislative skeleton, is given to an administrative agency. Usually, administrative agencies are created by the legislature, and are part of the executive branch of government. Theoretically, agencies do not create law in an original sense. It is undeniable, however, that the modern legislative practice of adopting skeletal legislation allows agencies

3

a great deal of latitude in fleshing out the law. Within the framework of the legislation, the agencies are very important lawmakers.

Courts make laws, too. As with administrative agencies, when courts interpret the constitution or legislation or administrative regulations, they are not making law in an original sense. It is difficult, however, to underestimate the importance of the U.S. Supreme Court in determining the meaning of fundamental but vague constitutional concepts like due process and equal protection of the law. Insofar as there is ambiguity in the federal and state constitutions, legislation, and administrative regulations, the courts play a critical role in making the law.

The courts make law in an original sense, too. The common law is judge-made law. Under our legal system, judges are free to make new laws in areas not regulated by existing constitutional provisions or legislation. For example, many areas of law that affect land use, such as nuisance, trespass, and negligence, are primarily products of the common law. Once a court makes a common law ruling, it establishes a precedent in that jurisdiction for future cases. Common law rules an area until superseded by subsequent legislation or, less frequently, constitutional change.

Confluence of State and Federal Law

As indicated previously, sovereignty, or supreme lawmaking power, is divided under our form of federal government. The federal government is sovereign in areas expressly or implicitly covered in the federal Constitution. All other areas of sovereignty are retained by the states. In areas of federal sovereignty, conflicts between state and federal law are resolved in favor of the federal law under the Supremacy Clause in the federal Constitution.

Regulation by the federal government in an area, such as aesthetics, does not automatically preclude the states from regulating it. The Supremacy Clause prohibits state regulation only when the area of regulation is preempted by the federal government. Preemption occurs when the federal legislation expressly excludes state activity, or when the federal government has so pervasively regulated in the area that it clearly intends for the states to be excluded, or there is a conflict between state and federal law. For instance, the National Environmental Policy Act (NEPA) requires the preparation of environmental impact statements (EIS) under certain circumstances. Many states have similar statutes, some requiring broader coverage in their EIS. There is no conflict between such laws. An EIS can be written that contains the federal requirements, and more inclusively, discusses the additional concerns mandated under state law.

As noted earlier, federal and state constitutions generally contain many of the same basic protections. A state or local legislative enactment or an administrative regulation, for example, one protecting a scenic vista, may be challenged in court as a violation of similar provisions in both the state and federal constitutions. If the law is found unconstitutional under the interpretation of either constitutional provision, it is invalid. Due to the vague nature of certain constitutional protections, such as due process and equal protection of the law, reasonable courts may disagree as to whether a law violates the constitution. As a result, a law may be held constitutional by a federal court applying federal law, but still be held unconstitutional by a state court applying the state constitution.

This principle has importance in the land use area today. The U.S. Supreme Court is dominated by judicial conservatives who have a tendency to defer to the decisions made by the legislature. Some state high courts are less judicially conservative and are more likely to overturn legislative enactments on constitutional grounds. When a case is litigated and appealed in one of these state courts, the courts are inclined to declare a law unconstitutional solely on state constitutional grounds. It is irrelevant therefore that the U.S. Supreme Court might have found to the contrary under federal law.

Classifications of Law

There are some basic legal classifications that need to be understood in dealing with lawyers and legal matters.

Civil versus Criminal

When used in the context of civil versus criminal law, civil law refers to the rules that determine the rights and duties of private individuals engaged in a transaction or a dispute. For example, rules dealing with contracts or property rights are part of the civil law. The term "civil law" is, however, sometimes used, especially in many foreign countries, to refer to code or statutory law.

Criminal law refers to the legal rules that pertain to protecting society's interest from antisocial behavior, such as murder, arson, and rape. A criminal wrong is considered to be a wrong against society; it is then prosecuted by a public official (e.g., the district attorney) and the punishment is public in nature (e.g., fine and/ or imprisonment). A civil wrong by contrast is brought to court by a private party alleging the wrong and the penalty benefits the private individual (e.g., money damages or an injunction).

Procedural and Substantive Law

Procedural law refers to the rules for administering the law. It does not pertain to the legal rights and duties themselves. Procedural rules deal with how a defendant must be served with process, or the period of time the defendant has to respond to the plaintiff's complaint. Procedural rules can affect rights. For instance, if the victim of a civil wrong fails to file suit prior to the expiration of the statute of limitations, the person loses the right to assert the claim.

Substantive law is the law pertaining to the legal rights and duties of the parties. For example, an applicant seeking a variance from the setback requirements of the zoning code must prove, among other things, that denial of the variance will create an unnecessary hardship. Both the setback requirement in the zoning code and the need to prove unnecessary hardship are substantive rules.

LEGISLATIVE PROCESS

As discussed previously, courts are lawmakers. Their law-making is passive in nature in that they must wait for disputes to come to them, and they are constrained by constitutional, legislative, and prior-case language in creatively resolving a current dispute. By way of contrast, legislatures are self-activating lawmakers. Legislatures can convert desired policy into rules of law. Congress is confined in large measure only by the U.S. Constitution. The state legislature is limited by its constitution, and the need to have a public health, safety, or welfare purpose. Municipal legislatures are constrained by state enabling legislation that grants them their powers. Within these broad boundaries, legislatures are free to make law on their own initiative.

The Congress enacts laws by obtaining bicameral approval of both houses and the signature of the president upon presentment of the bill. The president does not have to sign the bill and may choose to veto it. If the president vetoes the bill, the Congress can override the veto by an affirmative vote of two-thirds of each house.

State legislatures have a very similar procedure. Municipal legislatures, which adopt much of the aesthetic-based regulations, often have a simpler procedure. Any policy proposal within the purview of their state-granted powers can be made law by the approval of the majority of a unicameral legislative body, which includes the chief executive (e.g., mayor, supervisor).

Since legislatures often deal with complex policy considerations in seeking a legislative solution to social problems, there is seldom a clear, correct legislative path to take. For example, the legislature may face the dilemma of whether to restrict development along its beautiful beachfront in order to protect the public's interest in it, or to leave the beach unregulated to allow private property rights and free market forces to control its destiny. If it decides that the public interest demands some regulation, should it ban development, or limit density, or simply require greater setbacks to protect the dunes from erosion? There is no right answer to these questions, but the legislature is the one empowered to select among the options available.

The controls on legislatures and their decision-making are twofold: political and legal. Voters can exercise political control by refusing to reelect legislators with whom they have policy differences. Citizens can exercise legal control over legislatures by asking the courts to declare laws invalid. Citizens will not be successful in court if their basis for attacking a law's validity is that they disagree with the policy underlying it. Courts do not, or at least they claim they do not, review the wisdom of the law. The grounds for courts exercising legal control over legislation are that it lacks constitutionality, that the legislature failed to observe standards of fairness in adopting the law, or that the manner selected to address the problem was not among the array of *reasonable* alternative methods. The burden of proving invalidity of legislation is a heavy one and rests on the person attacking its validity.

Complex social problems require equally complex legislative solutions. It is difficult for a large, politically sensitive body to draft legislation that anticipates and makes provision for all situations. In recent years it has become popular for the U.S. Congress and state legislatures to enact skeletal legislation and to create administrative agencies to do the detail work and carry out enforcement. Agencies are confined to the "four walls" of the legislation in adopting their regulations, but with skeletal legislation there is generally a significant opportunity for agency creativity or law-making within the bounds of the legislation.

ADMINISTRATIVE PROCESS

Although they can be created by executive order, administrative agencies are generally the product of legislation. Broadly speaking, their function is to implement and enforce the mandate of the legislation assigned to them. More specifically, they exist because they perform certain functions more efficiently than a legislature. They have or can acquire technical expertise in their area of specialization; they are relatively speedier; they can provide oversight for activities that have a relatively small impact on individuals but a large aggregate social impact (e.g., regulating the octane rating in gasoline); and they protect weak enterprises from the predatory practices of stronger enterprises (e.g., antitrust laws).

Administrative agencies have three categories of powers. They have investigative powers that allow them to gather facts to carry out their substantive functions. Their investigations may take the form of mandating reports or production of records, carrying out inspections, and conducting hearings to inquire into issues. Legislatures, like administrative agencies, generally have investigative powers but courts do not.

Agencies often have rule-making powers. Rules or regulations provide the details and specifics necessary to implement the policy contained in legislation. They add the flesh to the legislative skeleton. Administrative rules must be confined to matters contained within the four walls of the legislation. Federal rules must be published in the Federal Register prior to taking effect in order to provide the public with notice.

Some agencies have adjudicatory powers. These agencies have powers similar to trial courts in that they conduct hearings to determine facts so that they can decide the legal rights and duties of the parties. Since they perform the function of trial courts, the party who loses at the administrative hearing stage and wishes to appeal takes the appeal to an appellate court, not a trial court.

Controls of administrative agencies, like the controls of legislatures, are political and legal in nature. Since administrators are not elected, political control is indirect and limited. Generally, political pressure must be brought on the chief executive or authority who appointed the administrator, rather than directly on the administrator. The party aggrieved by an administrator's action can seek legal recourse in the courts. A complex set of rules has evolved governing the rigorousness of judicial review of administrative decisions. A brief but limited insight into the process of judicial oversight of administrative actions is that courts will closely scrutinize an agency's conformity to procedural requirements but grant significant deference to decisions on substantive matters within the expertise of the administrator.

JUDICIAL PROCESS

When disputes arise between parties over their legal rights and they cannot resolve them, they have access to the courts. Trial courts hear the facts in a case, apply the legal rules to the facts as the judge determines them, and decides the case. The losing party has access to one or more appellate courts. The appellate court reviews the trial decision and determines whether or not the trial judge made a mistake in applying the law, and then either reverses or affirms the lower court's decision.

Just as the bodies of law are bifurcated into state and federal, so are the courts that resolve disputes arising under those laws. For purposes of this book it is unnecessary to delve too deeply into the functioning of the court systems, but some basic explanation is in order.

Federal Courts

The federal government has a three-tier system of courts. The federal district courts are the trial courts. The least populous states have a single federal district court for the entire state. States with larger populations may have up to four district courts operating regionally throughout the state. For instance, Pennsylvania has an Eastern District Court sitting in Philadelphia, a Central District Court in Harrisburg, and a Western District Court in Pittsburgh.

The federal district courts have jurisdiction over cases involving federal law and cases involving diverse citizenship. A plaintiff may *opt* to sue in a federal court even though the dispute concerns state law if the parties are from different states (e.g., the plaintiff is from Ohio and the defendant is from Virginia) and the amount in controversy exceeds $50,000. Once the suit is filed in federal court, the trial is held there and appeals are made through the federal court system.

Initial appeals go to regional courts called courts of appeals. These three-judge panels will listen to the argument of counsel for each side and decide whether or not the federal district court judge made a legal error in deciding the case at trial. The party losing at this intermediate appellate court may seek review from the nine-member U.S. Supreme Court. Today, the U.S. Supreme Court, a court of last resort on questions of federal law, determines its own docket and can decide to grant a writ of certiorari (hear the appeal) or deny the writ (refuse to hear the appeal). All appellate courts rule by majority vote.

State Courts

A description of the state court systems is more problematic because there are fifty separate court systems with some variations from state to state. In addition to having the three-tier structure of trial court, intermediate appellate court, and court of last resort, the states generally have a fourth, lower tier that deals with both minor civil and minor criminal matters.

There is also considerable variation in names among the state courts. The lowest-level courts are usually justices of the peace or municipal courts. The trial courts for important matters are called circuit courts, courts of common pleas, or county courts. The intermediate appellate courts are generally named superior courts or courts of appeals. The highest courts are predominantly called supreme courts. The vast majority of disputes involving state law is resolved by these state courts.

References

Altshuler, B., and Sgroi, C. 1992. *Understanding law in a changing society.* Prentice Hall.
Carter, L. 1984. *Reason in law.* Little, Brown.
Fisher, B., and Phillips, M. 1989. *The legal environment of business.* West Publishing.
Spiro, G. 1992. *The dynamics of law.* Harcourt Brace Jovanovich.

Chapter 2

Managing the Community Landscape[1]

The importance of scenic resources is deeply ingrained in cultural values. In fact, the basic argument in legal circles about definition and standards for regulating scenic resources revolves around this issue of determining cultural landscape values. In traditional societies, the visual harmony between development and context was made possible through widely shared traditions, and the resulting similarity of project types and forms extended over long periods of time (Figures 2.1 a, b, c, d). This is commonly known as vernacular design. Such internal cohesiveness is not possible in modern society. Technological advances have created projects and materials never seen before. The rapid growth of communications and transportation has led to potential development pressures on even the most remote locations, while escalating real estate markets make feasible the development within urban areas of previously impractical sites.

These forces have placed many of our culturally valued scenic resources in jeopardy. Why else would there still be such an outcry about outdoor advertising, historic community preservation, agricultural land preservation, highway strip landscapes, park preservation, and other scenic resource issues? What legal tools do we have available to protect and manage these scenic resources? How do we link these tools with analyses of our scenic resources? Chapter 1 presented basic legal structure as it related to land use regulation. The focus of this chapter is to present an overview of landscape analysis that is applicable at the community scale and where we are in the evolution of community landscape analysis.

REGULATORY STANDARDS

If no legal procedural problems are found during a court challenge to a local aesthetic zoning ordinance or other mechanism, then the court may examine issues of reasonableness. These may include the extent and accuracy of the data utilized, the adequacy of analytical methods, and the incorporation of study findings in the ultimate management or regulatory decision. Courts overturn actions that are arbitrary and capricious, or unreasonable.

Obviously, the resolution of these questions is partially determined by the specificity of the administrative procedure or regulation. In general, three groups of controls can be identified (Smardon, Palmer, and Felleman 1986, p. 25): consideration, specification, and performance. Some procedures and regulations merely list aesthetics as one of many factors to be considered in a decision process. This would be the consideration situation. Professionals or others operating in this situation are provided with little guidance in developing an analytical approach.

Specifications, on the other hand, can include data and results. For example, the New York Public Service Commission requires power line applications to include views from selected viewpoints. But note that there is no specification of viewshed delineation method. The

[1]Portions of this chapter are adapted from R. C. Smardon, J. P. Felleman, and J. P. Palmer, Chapter 2, "Decision-Making Model for Visual Resource Management and Project Review." In Smardon, Palmer, and Felleman (1986).

a.

b.

c.

d.

FIGURE 2.1 a, b, c, d   Landscape scenes from typical communities. *Photo Credit: R. C. Smardon*

Adirondack Park Agency protects scenic shorelines by prohibiting development closer than a specified distance. In this form of regulation, one or more of the project's form parameters are given, even though a project so many feet away may be highly visible and another the same number of feet away may be hidden.

The most sophisticated control approach is to establish performance standards and let the project proponent substantiate conformance. The U.S. Forest Service's (USDA, 1974) visual management classification system yields localized performance objectives (see Smardon, Palmer, and Felleman 1986 for a detailed review). There is also an example of a sign ordinance performance-based system presented by Ewald and Mandelker (1977) in their famous book *Street Graphics.*

CONTEXT FOR COMMUNITY LANDSCAPE ANALYSIS

Before a specific community landscape analysis process is presented, the reader should be familiar with the different scales and applications for which landscape analysis is used.

Visual resource inventories and analyses have been done for large landscape areas. In Table 2.1 the reader can see examples of national, subnational/regional, statewide, regional, and site scale analyses. We would like to focus our attention on those analyses done specifically for town, regional/town, linear corridor, and site/project scales (see Figure 2.2).

At the town or citywide scale, a number of studies

TABLE 2.1   Generic and Project Impact Assessment Studies

Scale	Decision Needs/Processes
National Scale	• national landscape inventory/priority
Subnational/Regional Scale	• multiple river basin water resource planning studies
Statewide Scale	• statewide landscape inventory for land use planning
Regional Scale	• inventories and assessments for land use planning • multiple resource planning studies for national forests • river basin planning • shoreline and coastal zone planning
Town Scale/Areawide	• visual inventory and analyses for land use planning; urban renewal; urban design and image assessment
Regional/Town Scale (Linear Corridor)	• transportation and river planning
Regional to Site Scale	• generic impact assessment for linear and point phenomena, location and general project planning for forestry activity • national recreation areas • coal development • power plants • power transmission lines • LNG off-loading terminals • scenic river management policies
Site/Project Scale	• detailed visual impact assessment of alternatives in environmental assessments or EIS's.

have included visual inventory and analysis for land use planning, urban renewal, urban design, and image assessment. Most of these studies were done in the sixties and seventies in the United States under the Department of Housing and Urban Development planning assistance program and were highly varied in quality and approach.

A particular kind of study that merges regional and site scales is the linear or scenic corridor study. These studies are usually for highway visual quality or scenic rivers. All of the previously mentioned studies were performed by private firms and government agencies to inventory, classify, analyze, and identify existing levels of landscape quality. These are the first steps that a community should undertake if it wants to develop defensible aesthetic control mechanisms and standards. This creates the baseline for aesthetic evaluation of proposed changes in the landscape that may be caused by new development.

The remaining analyses cited in Table 2.1 are examples of generic and project-specific visual impact assessment studies. These analyses attempt to predict change in landscape quality due to proposed development activities. Existing community landscape inventories, classifications, analyses, and designation of locally significant landscapes make visual impact assessments more meaningful and accurate.

Chapter 11 describes the types of treatments of aesthetic impacts within environmental impact statements. As stated elsewhere (Smardon, Palmer, and Felleman 1986; Andrews and Waits 1978), visual considerations as treated in EIS's have rarely met the requirements stated in NEPA. Also, the treatment of visual and aesthetic considerations has not advanced, with a few notable exceptions. The most notable exceptions often utilize forms of visual simulation in order to better portray visual impacts for professional analysis, and to better communicate them to affected publics. Many design and planning firms now have computerized image-processing capabilities for doing accurate and realistic visual simulations of proposed landscape changes.

COMMUNITY PLANNING CONTEXT

The previously described visual analyses are in response to three regulatory situations: (1) public land management and planning, (2) public projects involving private lands, and (3) public regulation of private projects (Smardon and Felleman 1982). Parts of this book will consider all three regulatory situations, but the emphasis will be placed on public regulation of private lands because that is where the legal action is.

Also, as pointed out by Palmer (1983) in an overview of visual quality and visual impact assessment, we will be proposing methods of integrating landscape analyses with legal tools at four stages of environmental decision-making: (1) environmental inventory, (2) policy formation, (3) program planning or project design, and (4) postimpact evaluation. The overall emphasis in this book will be on the first two stages.

To facilitate our discussion of "appropriate fit" of either landscape analyses or legal tools we need some basic framework. In our focus on the community landscape — a midscale landscape context with emphasis on preparation of landscape inventory and analyses suitable for building defensible legal landscape-control measures — we need a framework for community landscape decision-making. A general community decision-making framework is thus described in the following section.

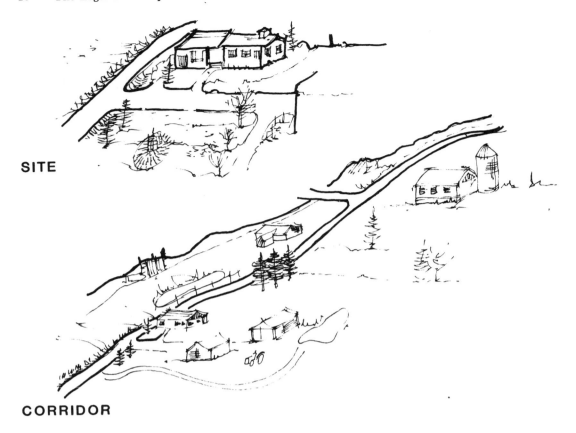

SITE

CORRIDOR

CONTINUUM

ENVELOPE

FIGURE 2.2   Scales of aesthetic analysis. *Source: John Wiley & Sons*

COMMUNITY LANDSCAPE DECISION-MAKING FRAMEWORK

In previous works (Smardon, Palmer, and Felleman 1986; Smardon et al. 1988) we have developed a four-phase framework for landscape assessment and evaluation. The general phases and structure are useful for the community context as well. The phases are: (1) de-fining landscape resources that are significant and likely to be affected by landscape change, and develop-ing an evaluation framework; (2) inventorying aes-thetic resources, which includes surveying existing conditions and forecasting with and without aesthetic regulations/controls; (3) assessing effects on the land-scape of (a) development alternatives or (b) the imple-mentation of aesthetic controls/regulations; and (4) appraising effects via public evaluation in terms of the significance (of impact) and/or mitigation of visual impact.

Each of the phases is described in more detail below utilizing Table 2.2 as a guide:

A. **Define Resources:** This phase is performed to identify aesthetic or visual resources that should be evaluated.

    1. Identify Aesthetic Resources: This is accomplished by reviewing existing information (by local groups or professionals) to identify aesthetic resources that are: (a) significant because of institutional, public, or technical recognition; and/or (b) likely to be affected by landscape impacts or policies.

    Institutional, public, and technically significant aesthetic resources can be defined as follows:

    Institutional recognition: The aesthetic attribute is acknowledged in the laws, adopted plans, and other policy statements of public agencies or private groups.

    Public recognition: Some segment of the public recognizes the importance of an aesthetic attribute or resource.

    Technical recognition: The importance of the resource is based on scientific or technical knowledge or judgment of critical resource characteristics.

    Interrelated aesthetic resources having more than one aesthetic attribute should be considered; for example, a salt marsh yielding sound, smell, and sight sensations. As such, many aesthetic resources will be deemed significant by more than one criterion.

    2. Develop Evaluation Framework: The appropriate attributes to be assessed should be arranged in the evaluation framework. Note that such attributes are primarily visual but may include other senses. Although such attributes may be partially embodied in physical landscape attributes, the most appropriate aesthetic indicators relate to levels of enjoyment or pleasure experienced by people exposed to the resource. For indicators of the presence of aesthetic resources, one can rely on subjective judgments of local people in the community, professionals, or both.

B. **Inventory Resources:** An inventory process collects or develops information that is useful for assessing the effects of alternative plans or policies; it employs the evaluation framework to determine the data useful for specific indicators as well as units of analysis.

    1. Survey Existing Conditions: This activity involves an inventory of existing landscape conditions utilizing inventory and classification systems for such phenomena as landform, land cover, and cultural land use patterns. There are many different landscape inventory and classification systems (see Smardon, Palmer, and Felleman 1986).

    2. Forecast of Conditions without Plans/Policies/Regulations/Controls: A forecast should propose the most probable conditions of the future landscape at the projected timeline. Of particular importance, for example, would be the possible creation or loss of significant vistas, change in landscape quality due to vegetative growth or succession, or change in land use patterns and historic architecture.

    3. Forecast with Alternative Plans/Policies/Regulations/Controls: Alternative plans/policies should be described in a manner consistent with the chosen landscape classification systems and scales used in steps B.1 and B.2. The condition of the landscape under each alternative plan or policy should be described. Secondary effects of proposed projects such as generation of new land development, or of policies such as elimination of ugly signage, should be included.

C. **Assess Effects:** The purpose of this phase is to identify and describe effects of alternative plans/policies/regulations or controls on aesthetic resources.

    1. Identify Effects: The affected area from which the project/plan is visible should be determined using visibility analysis. Significant places in the affected area should then be identified based on exposure, use, or other indications of culturally significant aesthetic values. Simultaneously, the potential impact of the activity should be analyzed by identifying project characteristics that affect specific parts of the landscape, such as fills

TABLE 2.2   Community Landscape Decision-making Framework. Source: John Wiley & Sons

Planning Process:	Aesthetic Resource Study:
1. Specify Problems and Opportunities	Red Flag Criteria
2. Inventory and Forecast Resource Conditions	Phases of 1. Define resources 2. Inventory resources
3. Formulate Alternative Plans	Design Prototypes and Impact Mitigation Through Design!
4. Evaluate Effects	Phases of 3. Assess effects 4. Appraise effects
5. Compare Alternatives	Weigh Aesthetic Criteria Against Other Appropriate Criteria
6. Select Plan	Implement Recommendations in Final Design, Construction, and Management Activities

affecting landform, vegetation cuts, or new structures or activities. Identifying effects of proposed landscape regulations or policies is more difficult if effects are areawide or in isolated pockets. However, viewpoints could still be selected, exposure estimated, and type of effect characterized.

2. Describe Effects: Significant visual effects can be described with respect to critical viewpoints in the affected area. Critical viewpoints can be based on such considerations as highly frequented viewpoints, culturally significant views, and representative views of landscapes. For each vista or viewing mode, a representation or simulation of the scene is needed both with and without the project or proposed policy to describe potential effects. The potential effects also need to be traced back to the causal attributes of the project, activity, or policy.

3. Determine Significant Effects: This step includes the assessment of professional findings or public preferences concerning the aesthetic impacts of project or policy alternatives. Public preferences and evaluative appraisals are needed to determine the degree of significance of potential effects on the landscape.

D. **Appraise Effects:** This phase is performed to identify the appropriate weight of significant effects on aesthetic resources, individually or collectively, for each alternative plan/policy/regulation or control. This is the phase in which aesthetic resources are compared to other resources in terms of the importance of effects, and decisions are made concerning the proposed project or policy.

1. Appraise Significant Effects: The significant effects of each alternative should be appraised. Such an analysis may lead to modifications or mitigation of effects if causal linkages are known through steps C.1 and C.2.

2. Judge Overall Effects: Judgment of the overall effect on environmental quality of each project alternative or policy is the final step. The visual analyst represents the visual resource in this process and advises the final decision-maker.

A community may not want to follow this whole process but utilize pieces of it depending on local aesthetic management needs. To review: The basic steps in community landscape aesthetic decision-making include: defining aesthetic landscape resources locally, inventorying such resources in systematic fashion, assessing effects of alternative plans or policies in comparative fashion, and appraising trade-offs of such plans and policies on aesthetic and other resources.

PLAN OF THE BOOK

At this point it may help the reader to outline the content and organization of the book. These first two chapters review very basic concepts of legal land use principles and the planning processes. They constitute the basic building blocks of the book. The third chapter is a brief history of how aesthetics has been treated in regard to land use law and explores a few principles for aesthetic standards that could be used as a basis for use of aesthetic land use control. The fourth chapter is a state-by-state review of key court cases that indicate whether aesthetics can stand alone as a rationale for use of the police power for local land use control.

The second part of the book contains four chapters that are applicable to local community aesthetic land use control and regulation. Each chapter contains a synthesis of relevant legal history, key tests for sustaining ordinances, current developments, and a case study that illustrates how aesthetic analysis can be used to develop or test the local aesthetic control. These chapters include: Chapter 5, Zoning and Land Use Control; Chapter 6, Architectural Regulation, Preservation, and Design Review; Chapter 7, Outdoor Advertising and Sign Control; and Chapter 8, Scenic View Protection. These four chapters are the basic tool kit that local government needs to begin aesthetic community planning.

The first two parts of the book provide the foundation of key legal concepts and of aesthetic control from a community perspective. Part III has a wider, federal and state perspective but includes issues of interest to local government as well. The six chapters include: Chapter 9, Wilderness and Natural Area Preservation; Chapter 10, Regulation of Environmentally Sensitive Areas and Resources; Chapter 11, Aesthetic Project Review; Chapter 12, Surface Mining; Chapter 13, Timber Harvesting and Vegetation Protection; and Chapter 14, Facility Siting. Each chapter includes a summary of relevant federal and state laws and procedures, a summary of aesthetic impact issues, and a case study that illustrates the application of analyses that address the aesthetic impact within a legal context.

The last part of the book contains two chapters: Chapter 15, Litigation and Aesthetic Analysis; and Chapter 16, The Legal Landscape: Issues and Trends. Both are syntheses in different ways. The chapter on litigation is a practical tactical guide to how to prepare, conduct, and use aesthetic analyses in courtroom and hearing contexts. Chapter 16 is a philosophical look at major trends in aesthetic analysis and regulation with some observations on the roles of different players and their respective contributions.

Each of Chapters 5 through 14 has a landscape graphic that relates each legal landscape control mech-

FIGURE 2.3   Generic landscape. *Credit: Scott Shannon*

anism to an idealized prototypical landscape and serves as context and orientation (Figure 2.3). This figure is a computer graphic which will be altered to display the visual theme of each chapter.

References

Andrews, R. N. L., and Waits, M. J. 1978. *Environmental values in public decisions: A research agenda.* School of Natural Resources, University of Michigan.

Ewald, W. R. Jr., and Mandelker, D. R. 1977. *Street graphics.* The Landscape Architecture Foundation, McLean, Virginia.

Palmer, J. F. 1983. Approaches for assessing visual quality and visual impacts. *Social impact assessment methods.* ed. K. Finsterbusch, L. G. Llewellyn, and C. P. Wolf, pp. 263–283.

Smardon, R. C., and Felleman, J. P. 1982. The quiet revolution in visual resource management; a view from the coast. In *Visual resource management in the coastal zone: the move from procedure to substance,* special issue, ed. R. C. Smardon and J. P. Felleman. *Coastal Zone Management Journal* 9 (3/4): 211–214.

Smardon, R. C., Palmer, J. F., and Felleman, J. P. eds. 1986. *Foundations for visual project analysis.* John Wiley & Sons.

Smardon, R. C. et al. 1988. *Visual resources assessment procedure for US Army Corps of Engineers.* Instruction Report EL-88-1, USCOE, Waterways Exp. Stn., Vicksburg, MS.

Chapter 3

The Evolution of Law and Aesthetics

APPLICABLE LAW

As seen in Chapter 1, law comes from different origins, and there are several sources of law that have either directly or indirectly provided the foundation for aesthetic regulation. Powers inherent in the sovereign, the constitution, legislation, and court decisions have each had input into the body of aesthetic law.

Powers Inherent in the Sovereign

Eminent Domain

The sovereigns under American law, the federal and state governments, have the inherent power of eminent domain, that is, to condemn or take private property. The power did not arise from an express grant. It emanated from a legal philosophy that was formulated by scholars in England and the United States over the last several centuries.

The provisions in the Fifth Amendment to the federal Constitution, and similar clauses in the state constitutions, do not grant to the governments the power of eminent domain, but rather establish limitations on its exercise. The widely adopted limitations are that the taking of land must be for a public use, and that the landowner must be paid just compensation. The clearest example of a taking involves a physical invasion of the land by the government.

A recent U.S. Supreme Court case stated that public use is coterminous with the concept of public purpose under the police power. As a result, the power of eminent domain can be exercised for any public health, safety, or welfare reason. As will be discussed later, one public welfare reason for regulation in the land use area is aesthetic. If the government is willing to take land for aesthetic reasons, it must be willing to pay just compensation. Just compensation means paying fair-market value for the land. If the government perceives the land as important enough to pay fair-market value, it has the authority to take the land from the private owner. The problem is that governments are usually unwilling or unable to pay just compensation for land sought for aesthetic purposes.

Police Power

American legal theory holds that state governments have another inherent power, called the police power. They can regulate in order to protect the public health, safety, and welfare of their citizens. Through their constitutions or through legislation, states can delegate the police power to local governments. As stated above, the notion of public welfare is broad enough to encompass regulations for aesthetic purposes.

The federal government does not have the police power. Authority for federal regulations must be found in the enumerated powers of the Constitution, or it must be one of the so-called unenumerated or implied powers within the federal Constitution. All powers not expressly or implicitly granted to the federal government by the Constitution are reserved to the states by the Tenth Amendment. The police power is not granted expressly or implicitly in the federal Constitution.

Regulation under the police power is a more frequently used technique for preserving aesthetic qualities than is eminent domain. Under police power regulations, governments do not physically take the land from its private owner. They merely restrict the use that a landowner can make of the property. As a result, the government does not have to pay just compensation, so that regulation is a much more financially attractive method than eminent domain for protecting the aesthetic qualities of the land.

Constitution

Although the federal Constitution does not address the issue of aesthetics, numerous state constitutions do have provisions that deal with it. Some state provisions are narrowly circumscribed and explicit, like Article 50 of the Massachusetts Constitution, which gives the legislature the express authority to regulate outdoor advertising based on aesthetics.

In a few states, whose economies rely heavily on tourism, the constitution may provide for protection of the natural beauty upon which tourism is based. The Hawaii Constitution gives the legislature the power to regulate in order "to conserve and develop its natural beauty, objects and places of historic or cultural interest, sightliness and physical good order." This broad language justifies any reasonable regulation based on aesthetics.

Several other states, caught up in the winds of environmental protection in the early 1970s, amended their constitutions to grant their citizens a constitutionally protected right to an unpolluted environment. The Montana Constitution, Article II, Section 3, declares that every citizen has an inalienable right "to a clean and healthful environment." This language is broad enough to include aesthetics, and provides a basis for state legislation passed in the name of protecting the aesthetic features of the physical environment. Similarly, in 1972 Massachusetts adopted a broad aesthetics-based provision to its constitution. The Massachusetts Constitution establishes as a state policy its citizens' right to the "natural, scenic, historic and aesthetic qualities of their environment."

Legislatures acting in any area must find authorization to do so either in the inherent powers of the state or in the state constitution. Legislation must be legitimated by one of these sources of law.

Legislation

State legislation pertaining to aesthetics can take one of several forms. One form is a direct imposition of restrictions to retain or create aesthetic quality. The Minnesota Legislature adopted a statute declaring that

"to conserve the natural beauty of areas adjacent to highways, it is necessary to reasonably and effectively regulate . . . advertising devices." The legislature can then set up specific criteria for regulating advertising devices along highways.

Alternatively, as is more often the case, the legislature merely frames the outline of a regulatory program and turns the specifics over to an administrative agency. The legislature may prohibit signs in some areas, but allow signs in "business areas." It is up to the appropriate administrator to define "business areas" and thereby determine the exact extent of the prohibition on signs for aesthetic purposes. In this way, administrators participate in the business of aesthetic regulation.

Much land use regulation is done at the local, not the state level. State legislatures, through enabling legislation, delegate to local governments their police power to regulate land use. The enabling legislation is generally fairly inclusive so as to encompass aesthetics. The Massachusetts enabling legislation delegates authority to regulate in order to preserve and increase amenities. Language such as protecting amenities implicitly permits local governments to regulate for aesthetic reasons.

Common Law

The common law does not directly regulate aesthetics. Judges make law pertaining to aesthetics when they interpret and apply the constitution, legislation, administrative regulations, and the police power in cases raising aesthetic issues. However, the ties between the common law and aesthetics go deeper.

The legal remedy provided under the concept of nuisance has its origins in the common law. A nuisance is a substantial and unreasonable interference by a person with an owner's use of land. A use can become a nuisance, or a noxious use, where it interferes with the orderly development of a healthy, safe, and attractive neighborhood—the proverbial pig in the parlor. Aesthetics, at least where it can be tied to a common law nuisance, has long been recognized as fodder for a lawsuit. It is, however, a bit of a stretch to relate occasional, individual private lawsuits to a systematic approach to land use regulation for aesthetic purposes. Even the concept of a public nuisance, which has criteria similar to a private nuisance but involves a wrong to the public, does not constitute a methodical regulatory system. It is important to note that most of the area of police power regulation historically, and to a lesser extent today, has its foundation in the notion of nuisance or prevention of harm. It would be useful at this point to examine the historical evolution of aesthetics as a basis for land use regulation.

JUDICIAL HISTORY OF AESTHETICS-BASED REGULATION[1]

The history of aesthetics-based regulation involves a movement in the courts from general skepticism to a search for theories to uphold expansions of this type of regulation into new areas. State legislatures have in some cases made the courts' task easier by enacting constitutional provisions expressly authorizing aesthetics-based regulation, but only a small minority of states has such provisions as yet. However, while courts have struggled with this type of regulation, its forms have proliferated both on the state and local levels.

The Birth and Infancy of Aesthetics in Land Use Regulation

Until approximately the mid-1930s, aesthetics was considered an inappropriate basis for regulating land use under the police power.[2] Despite the breadth of the concept of public health, safety, and welfare, courts held that there was no room for protecting aesthetics. Courts gave several reasons for invalidating regulation for aesthetic purposes. One reason was judicial concern for protecting private property rights from public invasion.[3] An early case noted that, "aesthetic considerations are a matter of luxury, an indulgence rather than necessity, and it is necessity alone which justifies the exercise of the police power to take private property without compensation."[4] The only recognized "necessity" was preventing a harm to members of society. Protection of aesthetic values was viewed not as preventing public harm but as a legislative attempt to confer a benefit on the public at the expense of a private landowner without paying for it.[5]

An even more important reason for judicial hostility to regulation for aesthetic purposes was the subjective nature of aesthetics. It was argued that if aesthetics was kith and kin to beauty—an accepted premise prior to about 1925—then regulation of it was too arbitrary.[6] The importance and content of beauty are considered highly controversial matters, and the courts, demanding the comfort of objective criteria, found themselves without satisfactory standards when dealing with aesthetics-based regulations.[7] Courts were not concerned about whether aesthetics was a more inclusive concept than simply visual beauty. They held that given its subjective nature, aesthetics was an invalid basis for regulation.[8]

After about 1925, and until the mid-1960s, aesthetics was given infant status by the courts. It could be used as a basis for regulation, but could not stand alone as the sole purpose for it.[9] Aesthetic purposes could only be upheld where the parental support of a traditionally accepted police power purpose was present. Coupled with traffic safety, maintaining property values, or protecting public health, aesthetics was viewed by the courts as a valid basis for exercising the police power.[10] The aesthetic purposes of a regulation were placed on the public interest side of the scale in the many cases challenging land use regulations that involved balancing the public interest in regulation against the detrimental impact on private landowners.

One can argue that during this period in the evolution of legal attitudes toward aesthetic regulation, aesthetics was a meaningless make-weight. Almost invariably, the regulation undergoing judicial scrutiny would have been upheld on the traditional basis given for it, such as traffic safety, to pick a common example, even if aesthetics had never been mentioned.[11] However, it was also during this period that aesthetics gained legitimacy. Courts became increasingly comfortable with aesthetics as a basis for regulation, as long as it was coupled with a more traditional regulatory purpose.[12]

---

[1]The remainder of the chapter is taken from a previously published article. J. Karp, "The Evolving Meaning of Aesthetics in Land Use Regulation," *Colum. J. Envtl. L.* 15 (1990): 307, 310.

[2]See E. Zeigler, Jr., "Aesthetic Controls and Derivative Human Values: The Emerging Rational Bases for Regulation," in *1986 Zoning and Planning Law Handbook*, pp. 239, 241.

[3]Costonis, J. "Law and Aesthetics: A Critique and a Reformation of the Dilemmas," 80 *Mich. L. Rev.* 355, 373 (1982).

[4]See, e.g., City of Passaic v. Patterson Bill Posting, Advertising & Sign Painting Co., 72 N.J.L. 285, 287, 62 A. 267, 268 (1905).

[5]See E. Zeigler, Jr., supra note 15, at 241.

[6]See E. Zeigler, Jr., supra note 15, at 245 (citing cases).

[7]See, e.g., City of Youngstown v. Kahn Bros. Building Co., 112 Ohio St. 654, 148 N.E. 842, 844 (Ohio 1925).

[8]See E. Zeigler, Jr., supra note 15, at 241.

[9]Id. at 242. See also N. Williams, American Land Planning Law Sections 11.07-09 (1974 & Supp. 1988).

[10]See Costonis, supra note 3.

[11]See, e.g., St. Louis Gunning Advertising Co. v. City of St. Louis, 235 Mo. 99, 137, 145 S.W. 929, 942 (Mo. 1911).

[12]See, e.g., Perlmutter v. Greene, 259 N.Y. 327, 182 N.E. 5 (N.Y. 1932).

As Chief Judge Pound stated, "[B]eauty may not be queen, but she is not an outcast beyond the pale of protection or respect."[13]

Beginning slowly in the 1960s, state courts began to develop a new approach to aesthetics regulations. Aesthetics came to be viewed as capable of standing alone as a basis for the exercise of the police power.[14] This stage in the development of judicial views on regulation for aesthetic purposes, which continues today, started in 1954 with the Supreme Court's decision in *Berman* v. *Parker.*[15]

The Supreme Court Decisions

Berman articulated a new interpretation of what could constitute regulation of the public welfare under the police power. The Supreme Court stated in *Berman* that "the concept of public welfare is broad and inclusive. The values it represents are spiritual as well as physical, aesthetic as well as monetary."[16] After *Berman,* regulations no longer had to be based solely on public health and safety. They could be based on a broader notion of public welfare encompassing the public's desires for comfort, happiness, and an enhanced cultural life.[17]

Two other landmark Supreme Court decisions further emphasized the broad scope of the public welfare basis for regulation of land use under the police power. In *Village of Belle Terre* v. *Boraas,*[18] the Court asserted that protection of "family values," the "blessings of quiet seclusion," and "clean air" are properly considered in regulation aimed at creating "a sanctuary for people."[19] In *Penn Central Transportation Co.* v. *New York City,*[20] the Court stated that a substantial body of precedent had "recognized, in a number of settings, that states and cities may enact land use restrictions or controls to enhance the quality of life by preserving the character and desirable aesthetic features of a city."[21]

State Court Decisions

Most, but not all, state courts have followed the Supreme Court's lead in treating aesthetics as a valid basis for regulation. A law review article in 1980 reported that the rule that aesthetics can stand alone as a basis for exercising the police power had become the majority rule.[22] Yet beyond the fact that the state court decisions in this area confront similar questions about the validity of aesthetics-based regulation, they appear, at least on first examination, to have little in common. Their reasons for acceptance or rejection of aesthetics-based regulation are diverse. One clear grouping of cases separates states that have constitutional provisions that authorize aesthetics-based legislation from those that do not. A second grouping is according to the type of statute or ordinance involved in the case.

State Constitutions

One of the earliest cases allowing aesthetics to stand alone was based on a state constitutional provision. In the 1967 decision *State* v. *Diamond Motors, Inc.,*[23] the Hawaii Supreme Court reviewed a conviction for violation of size and height standards on outdoor signs in an industrial zone. The court upheld the aesthetic purpose of the ordinance based on the police power in spite of the fact that many courts at that time were reaching the opposite result. The Hawaii court felt comfortable in doing so because Hawaii has a constitutional provision stating that the "State shall have the power to conserve and develop its natural beauty, objects and places of historic and cultural interest, sightliness and physical good order."[24] The court found that protection of aesthetics was not confined to the mountain and beach areas, but could include less naturally beautiful areas like the industrial zone involved in the case,[25] even though the constitutional provision was primarily

---

[13]Perlmutter v. Greene 259 N.Y. 327, 182 N.E. 5, 6 (1932).

[14]See, e.g., State v. Diamond Motors, Inc., 50 Haw. 33, 429 P.2d 825 (Haw. 1967); Cromwell v. Ferrier, 19 N.Y.2d 263, 255 N.E.2d 749, 279 N.Y.S.2d 22 (N.Y. 1967); People v. Stover, 12 N.Y.2d 462, 191 N.E.2d 272, 240 N.Y.S.2d 734 (N.Y. 1963).

[15]348 U.S. 26 (1954).

[16]Id. at 33.

[17]Westfield Motor Sales Co. v. Town of Westfield, 129 N.J. Super. 528, 324 A.2d 113 (1974).

[18]416 U.S. 1 (1974).

[19]Id. at 9.

[20]438 U.S. 104 (1978).

[21]Id. at 129.

[22](See footnote 22 on page 24.)

[23]50 Haw. 33, 429 P.2d 825 (1967).

[24]Id. at 193, 429 P.2d at 827.

[25]Id. at 194, 429 P.2d at 828.

aimed at protection of the mountains and beaches, which are central to Hawaii's tradition and economy.

There are similar constitutional provisions in several other states whose heritage and economy are less closely tied to their natural beauty. For example, Montana's Constitution declares that its citizens have an inalienable right to a "clean and healthful environment."[26] In *State* v. *Bernhard*[27] the Montana Supreme Court held that this constitutional provision authorized legislation for the purpose of preserving and enhancing the aesthetic values of its citizens. Likewise, the Pennsylvania Constitution states that the "people have a right to clean air, pure water, and to the preservation of the natural, scenic, historic and esthetic values of the environment."[28] Although state constitutional provisions framed in such general language need legislative enactments to provide adequate standards,[29] they clearly authorize aesthetics-based legislation.

Only a few states have the luxury of constitutional provisions clearly encompassing aesthetics. When such a constitutional provision exists the state's legislature can pass aesthetics-based legislation directly on the basis of the provision. This makes it easier for a court to uphold aesthetics-based regulations. In states that do not have a constitutional provision, the state legislature must act on the basis of the general police power, and the courts must inquire into whether the legislation is for a legitimate police power purpose, whether it is reasonable given its purpose, and whether it satisfies substantive due process.[30]

State Statutes

State aesthetics-based statutes have taken many forms, most prominently, environmental impact requirements, state land use planning controls, and highway beautification regulations.[31] For example,

Washington, like many other states, requires that environmental impact analysis be done prior to approving major development projects.[32] Such statutes are sometimes treated simply as minimal disclosure and consideration laws, mandating that an environmental impact statement be prepared and circulated, and that the decision-makers have and consider this environmental information. However, statutes requiring environmental impact analysis also uniformly contain language requiring attention to the aesthetic impact of the project.[33]

In *Polygon Corp.* v. *City of Seattle*[34] the Washington Supreme Court reviewed the application of the law in a case denying a building permit. While the court waffled on the issue of whether or not aesthetics can stand alone as a police power purpose, it acknowledged that the most significant impacts of the project were aesthetic.[35] It held that in addition to the procedural provisions of the law, which required disclosure and consideration, the law had substantive purposes as well, in that aesthetics, coupled with other factors, could be a basis for rejecting the proposed development. The court stated that reading the statute otherwise "would thwart the policies it establishes and would render the provision that environmental amenities and values will be given appropriate consideration in decision making a nullity."[36] In states in which courts have ruled that aesthetics can stand alone and which also have environmental impact analysis statutes, aesthetics is a relevant concern in development proposals since it may by itself afford a basis for rejecting a proposal.

Vermont is one of a small group of states in which the state has reclaimed land use powers from the localities.[37] A state board reviews development proposals according to ten criteria.[38] One criterion, number eight, asks whether the project would "have an undue adverse

---

[26]Montana Const. art. II, § 3 (1972).

[27]173 Mont. 464, 568 P.2d 136 (1977).

[28]Pa. Const. art. I, § 27 (1971).

[29]Commonwealth v. National Gettysburg Battlefield Tower, Inc., 454 Pa. 193, 205, 311 A.2d 588, 595 (1972).

[30]See, e.g., Boundary Drive Associates v. Shrewsbury Township Bd. of Supervisors, 491 A.2d 86, 90 (Pa. 1985).

[31]See, e.g., State Dept. of Transp. v. Pile, 603 P.2d 337 (Okla. 1979); Polygon Corp. v. City of Seattle, 90 Wash. 2d 59, 578 P.2d 1309 (1978); Vt. Stat. Ann. Title 10, §§ 6001–6092 (1984).

[32]Wash. Rev. Code §§ 43.21C.030–43.21C.031 (1989).

[33]See Office of Research and Development, U.S. Envtl. Protection Agency, Aesthetics in Environmental Planning 28-38 (1973).

[34]90 Wash. 2d 59, 578 P.2d 1309 (1978).

[35]Id. at 66, 578 P.2d at 1315.

[36]Id. at 63, 578 P.2d at 1312. This opinion may be more enlightened than its federal counterpart, Robertson v. Methow Valley Citizens Council, 109 S.Ct. 1835 (1989), in which the opposite conclusion was reached.

[37]Vt. Stat. Ann. Title 10, §§ 6001–6092 (1984). See also F. Bosselman & D. Collins, The Quiet Revolution in Land Use Control (1971); J. De Grove & N. Stroud, 1989 Zoning and Planning Law Handbook, 55–58.

[38]Vt. Stat. Ann. Title 10, § 6086(a)(1–10) (1984).

effect on the scenic or natural beauty of the area, aesthetics, historic sites or rare and irreplaceable natural areas."[39] The state legislature recognized that any development activity interferes with scenic preservation, but required the decision-makers to perform a substantive due process analysis examining whether the interference was undue.[40]

There are several other examples of a new breed of state environmental statutes that uniformly include aesthetic criteria. For example, Washington's Shoreline Management Act[41] has been interpreted as an expression of the state's public policy supporting protection of aesthetic values.[42] Minnesota's Wild and Scenic Rivers Act[43] asserts that its intent of preserving the "unique natural and scenic resources of the state does have an aesthetic purpose."[44] Minnesota has a highway beautification law that declares a legislative policy to "conserve the natural beauty of areas adjacent to certain highways," making it necessary to regulate advertising devices.[45] These types of statutes raise aesthetics, whatever its precise meaning, to the level of statewide importance in development issues involving certain natural resources.

Local Ordinances

Ordinances on signs and billboards are the most numerous form of regulation openly based on aesthetics. Outdoor advertising companies have not had a great deal of success recently in challenging this type of ordinance. In *John Donnelly & Sons, Inc.* v. *Outdoor Advertising Board*[46] the Massachusetts Supreme Judicial Court acknowledged that in the past sign restrictions were justified legislatively and judicially on the grounds of protecting property values and promoting highway safety. It stated that these grounds were a legal fiction designed to avoid recognizing aesthetics as the real purpose behind the law.[47] The court noted that due to changing community values, society demanded aes-

thetically pleasing cities and a visually satisfying environment.[48]

Other courts have arrived at similar conclusions. The New Mexico Supreme Court upheld a city sign ordinance because it aided in creating or preserving a desirable ambience in the community.[49] The New Jersey Supreme Court, approving a limitation on signs in a residential area, sanctioned the "development and preservation of natural resources and clean, salubrious neighborhoods [that] contribute to psychological and emotional stability and well-being as well as stimulate a sense of civic pride."[50]

Cases involving the review of junkyard regulations are the second largest category of cases in which aesthetic purposes are an issue. Even more than signs and billboards, junkyards arouse community ire. They are highly visible and often give visual notoriety to a municipality. As in the case of sign ordinances, owners of junkyards have seldom tasted victory when confronting their regulators.

The Oregon Supreme Court, in an early case examining aesthetic purposes, *Oregon City* v. *Hartke*,[51] reviewed the regulation of a junkyard. The court found that such regulations were the product of a "change in attitude, a reflection of the refinement of our tastes and the growing appreciation of cultural values in a maturing society."[52] It stated that it is "not irrational for those who live in a community . . . to plan their physical surroundings in such a way that unsightliness is minimized."[53] Similarly, the North Carolina Supreme Court, in reviewing a decision involving a junkyard ordinance, referred, inter alia, to the benefits provided to the general community by such a law stemming from the "preservation of the character and integrity of the community, and promotion of comfort, happiness, and emotional stability of area residents."[54] These benefits were placed in the due process calculation and weighed against the interests of the individual property owner to decide if the ordinance was reasonable.[55]

[39]Vt. Stat. Ann. Title 10, § 6086(a)(8) (1984).

[40]Vermont Elec. Power Co. v. Bandel, 135 Vt. 141, 148, 375 A.2d 975, 981 (1977).

[41]Wash. Rev. Code Ann. § 43.21C.010 (1983).

[42]State Dept. of Ecology v. Pacesetter Construction Co., 89 Wash. 2d 203, 212, 571 P.2d 196, 201 (1977).

[43]Minn. Stat. §§ 104.31–104.40 (1982).

[44]County of Pine v. State Dept. of Natural Resources, 280 N.W.2d 625, 629 (Minn. 1979).

[45]Minn. Stat. § 173.01 (1982).

[46]369 Mass. 206, 339 N.E.2d 709 (1975).

[47]Id. at 217, 339 N.E.2d at 716.

[48]Id. at 218, 339 N.E.2d at 717.

[49]Temple Baptist Church v. City of Albuquerque, 98 N.M. 138, 144, 646 P.2d 565, 571 (1982).

[50]State v. Miller, 83 N.J. 402, 409, 416 A.2d 821, 824 (1980).

[51]240 Or. 35, 400 P.2d 255 (1965).

[52]Id. at 47, 400 P.2d at 261.

[53]Id. at 50, 400 P.2d at 263.

[54]State v. Jones, 305 N.C. 520, 530, 290 S.E.2d 675, 681 (1982).

[55]Id.

The language abstracted here from the sign and junkyard cases has implications for areas of regulation far beyond these obvious targets. One area in which the issue of aesthetic purposes has arisen is zoning. Zoning cases have differed from sign and junkyard cases, however, in that challenges to zoning regulations have been somewhat more successful.[56] Yet aesthetic purposes have been upheld in many of these cases as well. For example, an Arizona Court of Appeals upheld zoning regulations that required development proposals to be approved by a city architectural review board. The court noted that both parties were in agreement that the great weight of precedent upheld regulations based on aesthetics and design.[57]

The Colorado Supreme Court upheld a regulation limiting the height of buildings in order to preserve the mountain view from a city park. The court found that Denver's "civic identity" was within the city's police power.[58] Similarly, the Idaho Supreme Court approved a zoning provision whose purpose was to maintain the rural character of the county and the Wood River Valley.[59]

An interesting duo of cases arose in the New Hampshire Supreme Court. In 1975, in Sibson v. State,[60] the Court reviewed the denial of a permit to fill a wetland. In 1981, in Burrows v. City of Keene,[61] the court scrutinized a dispute involving the denial of subdivision approval on land the city wanted to preserve as open space. Both cases were found to involve regulatory takings, but in Sibson the court affirmed the denial of the permit to fill a wetland and in Burrows it rejected the denial of the subdivision approval. In Sibson the court singled out wetlands as unique areas entitled to protection even if substantial private property rights are enjoined.[62] In Burrows, the court found that the Sibson decision was based on the need to prevent harm to a unique type of land, and refused to extend the decision to land lacking that characteristic of uniqueness.[63]

Beyond signs and junkyards, aesthetics is the underlying rationale for protecting certain valuable features of the landscape, like spectacular mountain views, the rural character of an area, and wetlands.[64] These features do not necessarily have to be endowed with any particular natural beauty. The wetlands involved in Sibson, for example, were considered valuable and worth preserving not for any visual attractiveness they may have had, but areas of great natural productivity.[65]

THE EVOLUTION IN THE MEANING OF AESTHETICS

The question that remains open in cases involving aesthetics-based regulation is what courts mean today when they use the term "aesthetics." Is the concept still generally confined to visual beauty, or to the prevention of nuisance-type harms? Is aesthetics a manifestation of shared human values, as posited by Professor Costonis, which envelops resources whether they are beautiful or not, harmful or not? Or, is aesthetics a concept indicating our movement beyond concern solely for human values to a broader definition of values, a definition that pertains to nonhuman values as well as human ones? There is case law supporting all four of the proposed meanings of aesthetics.

Visual Beauty

Early cases involving regulation for aesthetic purposes generally equated aesthetics with visual beauty.[66] Many modern cases do as well.[67] This definition of aesthetics has created much of the legal quicksand through which the concept has struggled.[68] Critics of aesthetics-based regulation argue that beliefs about what is visually beautiful are matters of individual taste, and that regulation based on such beliefs lacks standards necessary to guide administrators in implementation or to allow meaningful judicial review.[69]

[56]See, e.g., City of Scottsdale v. Arizona Sign Assoc., 115 Ariz. 233, 564 P.2d 922 (Ariz. 1987).

[57]Id. at 234, 564 P.2d at 923.

[58]Landmark Land Co. v. City and County of Denver, 728 P.2d 1281, 1285 (Colo. 1986), app. dismissed sub. nom. Harsh Investment Corp. v. City and County of Denver, 483 U.S. 1001 (1987).

[59]Dawson Enterprises, Inc. v. Blaine County, 98 Idaho 506, 518, 567 P.2d 1257, 1269 (1977).

[60]115 N.H. 124, 336 A.2d 239 (1975).

[61]121 N.H. 590, 432 A.2d 15 (1981).

[62]Sibson v. State, 115 N.H. 124, 126, 129, 336 A.2d 239, 240, 242–243 (1975).

[63]Burrows v. City of Keene, 121 N.H. 590, 601, 432 A.2d 15, 21 (1981).

[64]See, e.g., Landmark Land Co., Inc. v. City and County of Denver, 728 P.2d 1281 (Colo. 1986); Dawson Enterprises, Inc. v. Blaine County, 99 Idaho 506, 567 P.2d 1257 (Idaho 1977); County of Pine v. Dept. of Natural Resources, 280 N.W.2d 625 (Minn. 1979).

[65]Sibson v. State, 115 N.H. 124, 126, 336, A.2d 239, 240 (1975).

[66]See E. Zeigler, Jr., supra note 2, at 241.

[67]See, e.g., Metromedia, Inc. v. City of San Diego, 453 U.S. 490 (1981); City of Fayetteville v. McIlroy Bank and Trust Co., 278 Ark. 500, 647 S.W.2d 439 (1983).

[68]See E. Zeigler, Jr., supra note 2, at 245.

[69]See Costonis, supra note 3, at 377–379.

The United States Supreme Court rejected this line of criticism in *Metromedia, Inc.* v. *City of San Diego.*[70] The Court acknowledged that the purpose of San Diego's sign ordinance was an aesthetic one.[71] The court then equated aesthetics with visual beauty.[72] It agreed that "esthetic judgments are necessarily subjective, defying objective evaluation," but found that this did not mean that aesthetics-based regulations must be invalidated, but rather that they "must be carefully scrutinized to determine if they are only a public rationalization of an impermissible purpose."[73] Thus, the Court resolved the problem of subjectivity by requiring careful scrutiny of aesthetics-based laws and regulations.

Some state courts have adopted similar reasoning. In upholding regulations concerning highway beautification, the Maine Supreme Court in *Finks* v. *Maine State Hwy. Comm'n.*[74] stated that an adequate response to the impossibility of detailed, specific standards in aesthetic regulations is "the presence of adequate procedural safeguards to protect against an abuse of discretion by administrators."[75] The court also found that while natural scenic beauty can be an overly general, subjective concept, it connotes "a sufficiently definite concrete image" when considered in the context of highway beautification.[76]

The New Jersey Supreme Court elaborated on the latter method of controlling subjectivity in *Wes Outdoor Advertising Co.* v. *Goldberg.*[77] The court found that the statute being reviewed contemplated

a certain basic beauty in natural terrain and vegetation unspoiled by the hands of man, which it proposes to recapture or retain. Although the extent to which each individual finds a specific landscape beautiful must be determined by a subjective test, this does not denote that there is no catholic criterion for the ascertainment of whether any scenic beauty exists in a given panorama.[78]

The court recognized that there may be variations in taste as to the outside dimensions of visual beauty, but that there is a core of universal acceptance of what is beautiful in a given setting.

Some courts have been less concerned about the subjective nature of regulations intended to preserve scenic beauty. The Arkansas Supreme Court, in *City of Fayetteville* v. *McIlroy Bank and Trust Co.,*[79] contended that "If the inhabitants of a city or town want to make the surroundings in which they live and work more beautiful or more attractive or more charming, there is nothing in the constitution forbidding the adoption of reasonable measures to attain that goal."[80] The court saw no need for any special constraints on legislative or administrative action in the area of aesthetics-based regulation.

On the other hand, the equation of aesthetics with visual beauty and the resulting apparent subjectivity of aesthetics has led a number of state courts to reject aesthetics-based regulation altogether.[81] For example, the Oklahoma Supreme Court, in *State Dept. of Transp.* v. *Pile,*[82] equated aesthetics with beauty and concluded that aesthetic standards are "indeterminate, incapable of concrete definition, fluid and everchanging."[83] Likewise, in *Mayor and City Council of Baltimore* v. *Mano Swartz, Inc.*[84] the Maryland Court of Appeals found that standards provided by the city of Baltimore in its regulations regarding the prevention of gaudiness and drabness to be invalid as an expression of individual taste and lacking in objectivity.[85]

Prevention of Harm

Some cases reviewing aesthetics-based regulations describe them as attempts to prevent or eliminate nuisances. The bulk of these cases was decided in the 1960s, when exclusively aesthetics-based regulation

---

[70]453 U.S. 490 (1981).

[71]Id. at 508-512.

[72]Id.

[73]Id. at 510.

[74]328 A.2d 791 (Me. 1974).

[75]Id. at 796.

[76]Id.

[77]55 N.J. 347, 262 A.2d 199 (1970).

[78]Id. at 351, 262 A.2d at 202.

[79]278 Ark. 500, 647 S.W.2d 439 (1983).

[80]Id. at 503, 647 S.W.2d at 440.

[81]See State v. Diamond Motors, Inc., 50 Haw. 33, 429 P.2d 825 (Haw. 1967); Cromwell v. Ferrier, 19 N.Y.2d 263, 225 N.E.2d 749, 279 N.Y.S.2d 22 (N.Y. 1967); People v. Stover, 12 N.Y.2d 462, 191 N.E.2d 272, 240 N.Y.S.2d 734 (N.Y. 1963).

[82]603 P.2d 337 (Okla. 1979), cert. denied 453 U.S. 922 (1981).

[83]Id. at 342.

[84]268 Md. 79, 299 A.2d 828 (1973).

[85]Id. at 83, 299 A.2d at 833.

was first being accepted as legitimate. They do not follow the lead of *Berman* v. *Parker*[86] in replacing the traditional nuisance analysis for reviewing state land use regulations with a public welfare analysis.

In 1963, in the seminal New York case, *People* v. *Stover*,[87] an ordinance against clotheslines in the frontyard was upheld, on the ground that the law did not seek to establish an arbitrary standard of beauty, but "to proscribe conduct which is unnecessarily offensive to the visual sensibilities of the average person," just as regulations in the past legislated against offenses to the senses of hearing and smell.[88] In 1965, the Oregon Supreme Court spoke in terms of preventing or minimizing "discordant and unsightly surroundings."[89] In 1967, the Ohio Supreme Court, in approving a junkyard ordinance, indicated that the fencing requirement was based on aesthetics and was intended to prevent the "patent and gross."[90]

Not all the rationales based on harm prevention, however, are older cases. The Utah Supreme Court in *Buhler* v. *Stone*[91] reviewed an ordinance that prohibited keeping property in an unclean and unsightly manner. The court held the ordinance valid, indicating that taking reasonable measures to minimize discordant, unsightly, and offensive surroundings was legitimate within the scope of public welfare. The court went on to state that the ordinance had a positive side, equally legitimate, of preserving beauty and the usefulness of the environment.[92] The Supreme Court of Florida, in *City of Lake Wales* v. *Lamar Advertising Ass'n. of Lakeland,* stated that "cities have the authority to take steps to minimize sight pollution."[93]

Shared Human Values

These modern aesthetics cases give strong credence to Professor Costonis's position that shared human values are what actually underline many courts' perception of aesthetic regulations. In *Sun Oil Co.* v. *City of Madison Heights,*[94] the Michigan Court of Appeals noted that "a community's aesthetic well-being can contribute to urban man's psychological and emotional stability," and that "a visually satisfying city can stimulate an identity and pride which is the foundation for social responsibility and citizenship."[95] Though the case involves a sign ordinance and the court focuses its attention on the visual landscape, it speaks of what is "visually satisfying" rather than what is visually beautiful, and emphasizes the need for preserving the city's "identity and pride." These themes are consistent with the shared human values premise.

In *Metromedia, Inc.* v. *City of San Diego,*[96] the California Supreme Court validated the purpose of protecting the community's appearance in its review of a sign ordinance. The court discussed the interwoven nature of the concepts of economics, aesthetics, and quality of life. It stated that "economic and aesthetic considerations together constitute the nearly inseparable warp and woof of the fabric upon which the modern city must design its future"[97] and asserted that city planning would be virtually impossible without the power to regulate for "aesthetic purposes." Then it declared that virtually every city in the state has regulated to improve the "appearance of the urban environment and the quality of metropolitan life."[98] The court's language does not focus narrowly on visual beauty, but more broadly on the inseparable fabric of the city and the quality of urban life.

The "local" nature of these shared human values is indicated by the New Hampshire Supreme Court's reference to protection "of the atmosphere of the town,"[99] the Idaho Supreme Court's sanctioning of zoning aimed at protecting the rural character of the county,[100] the New York Court of Appeals holding that courts may look to the "setting" of the regulated community in deciding on the reasonableness of an aesthetic regu-

[86]348 U.S. 26 (1954).

[87]12 N.Y.2d 462, 240 N.Y.S.2d 734, 191 N.E.2d 272 (1963), app. dismissed, 375 U.S. 42 (1973).

[88]Id. at 468, 240 N.Y.S.2d at 739, 191 N.E.2d at 276.

[89]Oregon City v. Hartke, 240 Or. 35, 41, 400 P.2d 255, 261 (1965).

[90]State v. Buckley, 16 Ohio St. 2d 128, 132, 243 N.E.2d 66, 70 (1968), cert. denied & app. dismissed, 395 U.S. 163 (1969).

[91]533 P.2d 292 (Utah 1975).

[92]Id. at 294.

[93]414 So.2d 1030, 1032 (Fla. 1982).

[94]41 Mich. App. 47. 199 N.W.2d 525 (1972).

[95]Id. at 50, 199 N.W.2d at 529.

[96]23 Cal.3d 762, 154 Cal Rptr. 212, 592, P.2d 728 (1979) (this part of the California Court's opinion was subsequently affirmed by the U.S. Supreme Court. 453 U.S. 490, 1980)

[97]Id. at 769, 154 Cal. Rptr. 220, 592 P.2d at 735.

[98]Id. at 769, 154 Cal. Rptr. 220, 592 P.2d at 736.

[99]Piper v. Meredith, 110 N.H. 291, 296, 266 A.2d 103, 108 (1970).

[100]Dawson Enterprises v. Blaine County, 98 Idaho 506, 518, 567 P.2d 1257, 1269 (1977).

lation,[101] and the Ohio Supreme Court's approval of special regulations attempting to "promote the overall quality" of urban life.[102]

The changeable character of these shared human values seems evident. In *Cromwell* v. *Ferrier,* the court in New York stated that "[c]ircumstances, surrounding conditions, changed social attitudes, newly-acquired knowledge . . . alter our view of what is reasonable" in reviewing an aesthetic regulation.[103] The Michigan Supreme Court discussed how times had changed in *Robinson Township* v. *Knoll.*[104] It stated that mobile homes can no longer be automatically confined to mobile home parks, but rather municipal decision-makers must decide on an ad hoc basis whether mobile homes meet normal community aesthetic standards.[105]

If a community can adequately document that it is regulating to protect its historical heritage, courts generally have little trouble in upholding historic preservation statutes and ordinances. The North Carolina Supreme Court in *A-S-P Associates* v. *City of Raleigh*[106] reviewed an historic district overlay to a zoning code. The court comfortably affirmed the ordinance because the attempt to control the exterior appearance of structures had as its purpose "the preservation of the State's legacy of historically significant structures."[107] The court found that this type of preservation provides a visual medium "for understanding our historic and cultural heritage." That understanding gives a "valuable perspective on the social, cultural, and economic mores of past generations of Americans."[108]

Environmental Harmony

Recent decisions support the proposition that "aesthetics" is a term expressing the desire of decision-makers to blend development with its natural surroundings — that is, to seek environmental harmony. The Ohio Supreme Court[109] upheld an ordinance creating environmental quality districts and imposing on those districts additional restrictions, that is, overlay

zoning. It stated that the law was to assist "the development of land and structures to be compatible with the environment, and to protect the quality of the urban environment in those locations.[110] The court stated that the basis for the law was aesthetics.

The New York Court of Appeals, in reviewing a sign ordinance based on aesthetics, stated that in order to be found valid, regulation of signage must bear substantially on the economic, social, and cultural patterns of the community. The ordinance was upheld on the ground that it was intended to protect the cultural and natural resources values that derived from the village's unique setting on a narrow spit of land between a bay and the ocean. The court spoke of adapting "use to fit" the cultural and natural features of the area.[111]

The Minnesota Supreme Court upheld an ordinance, adopted pursuant to state enabling legislation, designating the Kettle River as a wild and scenic river. The court stated that "preserving the unique natural and scenic resources of this state does have an aesthetic purpose.[112] The court asserted that the ordinance presents "no radical departure from traditional zoning. It merely reflects the increasing complexity of society and the realization that property must be viewed more interdependently."[113]

The Ohio Supreme Court approved an aesthetics-based regulation because there was a right to prevent interference "with the natural aesthetics of the surrounding countryside caused by an unfenced or inadequately fenced junk yard.[114] Similarly, the Massachusetts Supreme Judicial Court has indicated that cities can adopt regulations designed to preserve and improve their physical environment.[115]

Some key phrases in these cases supporting the premise that aesthetics is akin to environmental harmony are "compatible," "use to fit," "viewed more interdependently," "natural aesthetics of the surrounding countryside," and "preserve and improve the physical environment." These phrases are excerpts of language used by courts to connote a concern for devel-

[101]People v. Goodman, 31 N.Y.2d 262, 266, 388 N.Y.S.2d 97, 101, 290 N.E.2d 139, 142 (1972).

[102]Franchise Developers, Inc. v. City of Cincinnati, 30 Ohio St.3d 28, 33, 505 N.E.2d 966, 971 (1977).

[103]19 N.Y.2d 263, 268–269, 279 N.Y.S.2d 22, 26, 225 N.E.2d 749, 752 (1967), quoting Mid-State Adv. Corp. v. Bond, 274 N.Y. 82, 87, 8 N.E.2d 286, 288 (1937) (dissent).

[104]410 Mich. 293, 302 N.W.2d 146 (1981).

[105]Id. at 298, 302 N.W.2d at 152.

[106]298 N.C. 207, 258 S.E.2d 444 (1979).

[107]Id. at 450.

[108]Id.

[109]Franchise Developers, Inc. v. City of Cincinnati, 30 Ohio St.3d 28, 505 N.E.2d 966 (1987).

[110]Id. at 968.

[111]People v. Goodman, 31 N.Y.2d 262, 266, 290 N.E.2d 139, 142 (1972).

[112]County of Pine v. State Dept. of Natural Resources, 280 N.W.2d 625, 629 (Minn. 1979).

[113]Id. at 630.

[114]State v. Buckley, 16 Ohio St.2d 128, 243 N.E.2d 66, 70 (1968).

[115]John Donnelly and Sons, Inc. v. Outdoor Advertising Board, 339 N.E.2d 709, 717 (1975).

oping land in harmony with existing natural systems, shared human values, and visual beauty. These concerns travel through law today under the rubric of aesthetics.

Modern land use decision-making incorporates a weighing of values that come close to resembling Aldo Leopold's land ethic. For example, the Pennsylvania Constitution proclaims a right to "the preservation of the natural, scenic, historic and esthetic values of the environment." What does the word "esthetic" add to this list of values? Evidently the framers did not consider aesthetic values to be properly represented by natural, scenic, or historic values, but to reflect some other essence. "Natural," "scenic," and "historic" would appear to be sufficient for the protection of the shared human values in Professor Costonis's framework. The values represented by the word "esthetic" could be something broader than shared human values: an overarching convergence of ecological, human, and visual concerns.

[22]Bufford, Beyond the Eye of the Beholder: A New Majority of Jurisdictions Authorize Aesthetic Regulations, 48 U.M.K.C. L. Rev. 125 (1980).

In the over ten years since that article was written even more states have adopted the majority rule. Based on a recent survey of state appeals court decisions, thirty-one states have either held or indicated strongly in dicta that aesthetics can stand alone. See Barber v. Municipality of Anchorage, 776 P.2d 1035 (Alaska 1989); Donrey Communications Co. v. City of Fayetteville, 280 Ark. 408, 660 S.W.2d 900 (1983); City of Fayetteville v. McIlroy Bank and Trust Co., 278 Ark. 500, 647 S.W.2d 439 (1983); Metromedia, Inc. v. City of San Diego, 26 Cal. 3d 848, 610 P.2d 407, 164 Cal. Rptr. 510 (1980); Landmark Land Co. v. City and County of Denver, 728 P.2d 1281 (Colo. 1986); Mayor and Council of New Castle v. Rollins Outdoor Advertising, Inc. 475 A.2d 355 (Del. 1984); Franklin Builders Inc. v. Alan Construction Co., 58 Del. 173, 207 A.2d 12 (1964); City of Lake Wales v. Lamar Advertising Ass'n. of Lakeland, Fla., 414 So. 2d 1030 (Fla. 1982); Merritt v. Peters, 65 So.2d 861 (Fla. 1952); Gouge v. City of Snellville, 249 Ga. 91, 287 S.E. 2d 239 (1982); State v. Diamond Motors, Inc., 50 Haw. 33, 429 P.2d 825 (1967); Dawson Enter., Inc. v. Blaine County, 98 Idaho 506, 567 P.2d 1257 (1977); Jasper v. Commonwealth, 375 S.W.2d 709 (Ky.Ct.App. 1964); Finks v. Maine State Hwy. Comm'n., 328 A.2d 791 (Me. 1974); Mayor and City Council of Baltimore v. Mano Swartz, Inc., 268 Md. 79, 299 A.2d 828 (1973); John Donnelly & Sons, Inc. v. Outdoor Advertising Bd., 369 Mass. 206, 339 N.E.2d 709 (1975); Gannett Outdoor Co. v. City of Troy, 156 Mich. App. 126 409 N.W.2d 719 (1986); National Used Cars, Inc. v. City of Kalamazoo, 61 Mich. App.520, 233 N.W.2d 64 (1975); Mississippi State Hwy. Comm'n. v. Roberts Enter., Inc. 304 So. 2d 637 (Miss. 1974); Diemeke v. State Hwy. Comm'n. 444 S.W.2d 480 (Mo. 1969); State v. Bernhard, 173 Mont. 464, 568 P.2d 136 (1977); Board of County Comm'rs. v. CMC of Nevada, Inc. 99 Nev. 739, 670 P.2d 102 (1983); State v. Miller, 83 N.J. 402, 416 A.2d 821 (1980); Westfield Motor Sales Co. v. Town of Westfield, 129 N.J. Super. 528, 324 A.2d 113 (1974); Temple Baptist Church v. City of Albuquerque, 98 N.M. 138, 646 P.2d 565 (1982); People v. Stover, 12 N.Y.2d 462, 191 N.E.2d 272 (1963); State v. Jones, 305 N.C. 520, 290 S.E.2d 675 (1982); Village of Hudson v. Albrecht, Inc. 9 Ohio St.3d 69, 458 N.E.2d 852 (1984); State v. Buckley, 16 Ohio St.2d 128, 243 N.E.2d 66 (1968); Oregon City v. Hartke, 240 Or. 35, 400 P.2d 255 (1965); Sanderson v. City of Mobridge, 317 N.W.2d 828 (S.D. 1982); State v. Smith, 618 S.W.2d 474 (Tenn. 1981); Buhler v. Stone, 533 P.2d 292 (Utah 1975); Vermont Elec. Power Co. v. Bandel, 135 Vt. 141, 375 A.2d 975 (1977); Farley v. Graney, 146 W.Va. 22, 119 S.E.2d 833 (1960); Racine County v. Plourde, 38 Wis.2d 403, 157 N.W.2d 591 (1968).

In addition, three states' appellate courts reviewed state constitutional provisions or state statutes based on aesthetics without criticizing those purposes. See Metropolitan Dev. Comm'n. v. Douglas, 180 Ind. App. 567, 390 N.E.2d 663 (1979); Lynch v. Urban Redev. Auth. of Pittsburgh, 91 Pa. Commw. 260, 496 A.2d 1331 (1985); Young v. South Carolina Dept. of Highways and Public Transp., 287 S.C. 108, 336 S.E.2d 879 (1985).

References

Bosselman, F., and Callies, D. 1971. The quiet revolution in land use control. Council on Environmental Quality, Washington, DC.

Brooks, R., and Lavigne, P. 1985. Aesthetic theory and landscape protection: the many meanings of beauty and their implications for the design, control and protection of Vermont's landscape. *Journal of Environmental Law* 4. 129.

Costonis, J. 1989. Icons and aliens: law, aesthetics and environmental change. University of Illinois Press.

Costonis, J. 1982. Law and aesthetics: a critique and a reformation of the dilemmas. *Michigan Law Review* 80. 355.

De Grove, J., and Stround, M. 1989. *Zoning and Planning Law Handbooks* 55–58.

Karp, J. 1990. The evolving meaning of aesthetics in land use regulation. *Columbia Journal of Environmental Law* 15. 307.

U. S. Environmental Protection Agency. 1973. Aesthetics in environmental planning.

Williams, N. 1974 & Supp. 1988. American land planning law sections 11.07-11.09, Callaghan.

Ziegler, Jr., E. 1986. Aesthetic controls and derivative human values: the emerging rational bases for regulation. *Zoning and Planning Law Handbook* 239.

Chapter 4

Current Status of Aesthetics, State by State

The best reflection of the current status of the validity of aesthetics regulation in each state are the most recent pronouncements of the state's appeals court. The language of these judicial opinions is used to indicate whether the courts consider aesthetics regulation to continue to need the support of other traditional health and safety reasons, whether the courts conclude that aesthetics can stand alone, or whether the status of aesthetics law is uncertain at this time.

There is no attempt in the following discussion of state court views to differentiate between the types of laws being scrutinized. Most of the cases involve either sign or junkyard control ordinances. Though the state court may be willing to accept aesthetics standing alone in a law controlling signs, it is possible that it may not be receptive to the use of aesthetics alone in another regulatory area. It is assumed, however, that once the court accepts the notion of aesthetics standing alone, it will take the same position on any reasonable, nonarbitrary law. For a summary of the results in the states, see Table 4.1.

ALABAMA

In 1980 the Alabama Supreme Court decided the case *Sigler* v. *City of Mobile.*[1] The landowner sought a resubdivision of his land and complied with all the subdivision requirements. The planning commission disapproved the proposal because "it was out of character with other lots in the area."

The court rejected the planning commission's action

because there was compliance with its own regulations. It stated that it appreciated "their desire to protect the aesthetic quality of the area," but these concerns must be directed to the zoning officials to obtain changes in the subdivision regulations. Aesthetics can be taken into account but must be done so normatively through subdivision regulations, and not in an ad hoc fashion over and above the operating rules.

The court did not say whether aesthetics can stand alone, though that is the implication drawn because the commission's decision was based solely on aesthetics. The safest conclusion, however, is that the question is open in Alabama.

ALASKA

In *Barber* v. *Municipality of Anchorage,*[2] the Alaska Supreme Court reviewed a city ordinance that prohibits several types of off-premises signs. The court stated that the ordinance was instigated by the desire to remove aesthetic blights.

The court determined that the aesthetic purpose of the ordinance was "substantial" and therefore adequate to justify the law.

Aesthetics can stand alone as a basis for regulation in Alaska.

ARIZONA

The status of regulations based on aesthetics in Arizona is uncertain. The two most recent cases are from two different departments of the intermediate appeals

---

[1]387 So.2d 813 (1980).
[2]776 P.2d 1035 (1989), *cert.den.* 493 U.S. 922 (1989).

TABLE 4.1   Summary by State of Key Cases and Aesthetics Standing

State Aesthetics Standing

State	Key Cases	Alone	No	Open
Alabama	Sigler v. City of Mobile (1980)			X
Alaska	Barber v. Anchorage (1989)	X		
Arizona	Scottsdale v. Ariz. Sign (1977)			
	Corrigan v. Scottsdale (1986)			X
Arkansas	Fayetteville v. McIlroy Bank (1983)			
	Donrey Comm. Co. v. Fayetteville	X		
California	Metromedia Inc. v. San Diego (1976)			
Colorado	Landmark Land v. Denver (1986)	X		
Connecticut	Murphy v. Westport (1944)			
	Cappalbo v. Plan. & Zon. Bd. (1988)			X
Delaware	Franklin Build. v. Alan Const. Co. (1964)			
	New Castle v. Rollins Outdoor Adv.	X		
D.C.	Berman v. Parker (1954)	X		
Florida	Merritt v. Peters (1953)			
	Lake Wales v. Lamar Adv. Asso.	X		
Georgia	Gouge v. City of Snellville (1982)			
	Brown v. Dougherty (1983)	X		
Hawaii	State v. Diamond Motors (1967)	X		
Idaho	Dawson Enterprise v. Blaine Co. (1977)	X		
Illinois	LaSalle Nat'l. Bank v. Evanston (1974)			
	Lake Co. v. Bank of Lake Forest (1980)			
	Skokie v. Walton on Dempster (1983)			X
Indiana	Gen. Outdoor Adv. v. Indianapolis (1930)			
	Metro. Devel. Com. v. Douglas (1979)		X	
Iowa	Stone McCray Sys. v. Des Moines (1956)			
	Iowa DOT v. Nebraska-Iowa Supply (1978)		X	
Kansas	R. L. Reilke Bldg. v. Overland Pk. (1983)			X
Kentucky	Jasper v. Commonwealth (1964)			
	Moore v. Ward (1964)	X		
	Diemer v. Commonwealth, 786 S.W.2d 861 (1990).			
Louisiana	Sears Roebuck v. New Orleans (1960)			
	Maher v. New Orleans (1975)			
	Will of Pomeroy v. Westlake (1978)			X
Maine	Finks v. Maine Highway Com. (1974)	X		
Maryland	Mayor & Cncl. Balt. v. Swartz (1973)			
	Coscan Wash. v. Mid-Nat. Cap. Park (1991)		X	
Mass.	Donnelly & Sons v. Out. Adv. Bd. (1975)	X		
Michigan	Nat. Used Cars v. Kalamazoo (1975)			
	Gannett Outdoor Co. v. Troy (1986)	X		
Minnesota	Pine Co. v. Dept. of Nat. Res. (1979)			
	Hubbard Broad. Inc. v. Afton (1982)			X
Miss.	Miss. HIghway Com. v. Roberts (1974)	X		
Missouri	Deimeke v. State Highway Com. (1969)			
	Nat. Adv. Co. v. Bridgeton (1985)	X		
Montana	State v. Bernhard (1985)	X		
Nebraska	Schaffer v. City of Omaha (1977)			X
Nevada	Bd. of Co. Com. v. CMC (1983)	X		
New Hamp.	Piper v. Meredith (1970)			
	Sibson v. State (1975)			
	Burrows v. City of Keene (1981)			X
New Jersey	State v. Miller (1980)			
	Westfield Motor Co. v. Westfield (1970)			
	Wes Out. Adv. v. Goldberg (1970)	X		
New Mexico	Temple Baptist v. Albuquerque (1982)	X		
New York	People v. Stover (1983)			
	Cromwell v. Ferrier (1967)			
	Sackson v. Zimmerman (1984)	X		
N. Carolina	State v. Jones (1982)	X		
N. Dakota	Newman Signs v. Hjelle (1978)			X
Ohio	State v. Buckley (1968)			
	Vil. Hudson v. Albrecht Inc. (1984)	X		
Oklahoma	State DOT v. Pile (1979)			X

(Continued)

TABLE 4.1   Summary by State of Key Cases and Aesthetics Standing (*Continued*)

	State Aesthetics Standing			
State	Key Cases	Alone	No	Open
Oregon	Oregon City v. Hartke (1965)	X		
Pennsylvania	Redevelop. Auth. v. Woodring (1982)			
	Heck v. Zoning Hearing Bd. (1979)			
	Lynch v. URA of Pittsburgh (1985)	X		
Rhode Island	Providence v. Stephens (1926)			
	Sakonnet Rodgers v. Coastal Res.			
	Mgmt. Council (1988)		X	
S. Carolina	Young v. SC DH & PT (1985)			X
S. Dakota	Sanderson v. Mobridge (1982)	X		
Tennessee	State v. Smith (1981)	X		
Texas	Houston v. J. Frank's Auto (1972)			
	Houston v. Harris Co. Out. Adv. Asso. (1987)			X
Utah	Butler v. Stone (1975)	X		
Vermont	Vt. Electric Power v. Bandel (1977)			
	Wildlife Wonderland Inc. (1975)	X		
Virginia	Bd. of Supervisors v. Rowe (1975)		X	
Washington	State DOE v. Pacesetter Cons. (1977)			
	Polygon Corp. v. Seattle (1978)			X
W. Virginia	Farley v. Graney (1960)	X		
Wisconsin	Racine Co. v. Plourde (1968)			
	State ex. re. Saveland P.H. Corp. v. Wieland (1955)			
	Kamrowski v. State (1966)	X		
Wyoming	Cheyenne Airport Bd. v. Rodgers (1985)			X

court. The older of the two cases, *City of Scottsdale* v. *Arizona Sign Assoc., Inc.*,[3] involved a challenge to the constitutionality of part of the city's zoning code requiring that site plans be submitted to the development review board. The trial court struck down three of eight standards by which the board was to review site plans because they were vague. The three stricken standards were aesthetics-based.

The appeals court noted that both parties appeared to agree that community authority to regulate aesthetic matters through the zoning power and to create architectural boards was clear. It stated that the authority was particularly strong where the ordinance is tied to the economic and general well-being of the community.

The later case, *Corrigan* v. *City of Scottsdale*,[4] questioned the validity of the city's zoning ordinance establishing the Hillside District, which limited development in the mountain areas. This court appeared less favorably inclined toward aesthetics. In a footnote it cited the *Arizona Sign Assoc.* case for the principle that aesthetics is a proper consideration in determining the validity of a zoning ordinance, especially where it is auxiliary to more traditional public interests. In the body of the opinion it stated that the public interest in aesthetics is often too vague to offset substantial injury to landowners. The evidence did not support a safety

concern or the existence of a deplorable condition and therefore the ordinance was not upheld.

It is clear that Arizona recognizes aesthetics as an appropriate consideration when coupled with a traditional police power or nuisance concern. The *Arizona Sign Assoc.* case in dicta appears to accept that an aesthetics regulation can stand alone. Even the *Corrigan* case states that aesthetics is often too vague to stand alone. Implicitly this means that there are instances where aesthetics can stand alone. It appears that currently a regulation based solely on aesthetics would be a risky venture in Arizona.

ARKANSAS

The Arkansas Supreme Court reviewed a comprehensive city ordinance regulating size, height, and setback requirements for signs in *City of Fayetteville* v. *McIlroy Bank and Trust Co.*[5] The ordinance candidly stated that its purpose was to preserve the city's natural beauty and scenic resources. It noted also that the scenic resources contributed greatly to the economic development of the city.

A majority of the court in this 1983 case upheld the validity of the ordinance. It stated that the view that aesthetics could not stand alone was disappearing, and

[3]115 Ariz. 233, 564 P.2d 922 (1977), *cert. den.* 479 U.S. 986 (1986).
[4]149 Ariz. 538, 720 P.2d 513 (1986).
[5]278 Ark. 500, 647 S.W.2d 439 (Ark. 1983), *cert. den.* 466 U.S. 959 (1984).

that "if the inhabitants of a city or town want to make the surroundings in which they live and work more beautiful or more attractive or more charming, there is nothing in the constitution forbidding the adoption of reasonable measures to attain that goal." Additionally, the court approved a seven-year amortization provision for existing signs. It averred that the principle of amortization is firmly embedded in the law. Later in 1983 the supreme court affirmed this position when it approved a four-year amortization period in *Donrey Communications Co., Inc.* v. *City of Fayetteville.*[6] The only caution to note in relying on either of those cases is that three justices dissented on constitutional grounds.

CALIFORNIA

The leading case in California is *Metromedia, Inc.* v. *City of San Diego.*[7] A city ordinance banned all off-site advertising billboards and required removal of existing billboards following an amortization period. The stated purpose of the ordinance was to promote traffic safety and to improve the appearance of the city. A prior decision, *Varney and Green* v. *Williams,*[8] held that a regulation based on aesthetics alone was unconstitutional.

The court in *Metromedia* stated that the current case was distinguishable from *Varney and Green* because the regulation currently under review was not enacted exclusively for aesthetic purposes. Arguably anything said by the court after this statement is dicta and not binding as precedent. The court made it clear, however, that it was repudiating *Varney and Green*. The prior case's holding that aesthetic regulations cannot stand on its own "is unworkable, discordant with modern thought as to the scope of the police power, and therefore compels forthright repudiation," according to the *Metromedia* case.

The court then proceeded to tie the aesthetics argument to an economic base. It noted that the state relies on its scenery to attract tourists so that aesthetics considerations assume economic value. It went on: "economic and aesthetics considerations together constitutes the nearly inseparable warp and woof of the fabric upon which the modern city must design its future."

Despite the caution caused by the argument that the repudiation of *Varney and Green* may be dicta, and by the fact that the court linked aesthetics to economic value, one can confidently assert that a regulation based on aesthetics alone will be upheld in California.

The *Metromedia* court quoted favorably several of the most prominent cases from other states espousing the aesthetics alone proposition. Finally, the court stated that it would be virtually impossible for a city to operate if it could not regulate for aesthetics, and that virtually every city in the state had done so.

The U.S. Supreme Court overruled the California court in *Metromedia* on constitutional free speech grounds, but wrote affirmatively about the portion of the opinion dealing with regulations based on aesthetics.[9]

COLORADO

A 1986 Colorado Supreme Court case, *Landmark Land Co., Inc.* v. *City and County of Denver,*[10] examined an ordinance that limited the height of buildings in order to protect the mountain view from seven public parks. The stated purpose of the ordinance was to preserve Denver's "unique environmental heritage," and it related the protection of mountain views to the promotion of aesthetics, tourism, and civic pride.

The court upheld the regulation stating that the protection of aesthetics was a well-established legislative function. This is especially true since the city's identity is associated with the mountains. The court noted that once it concluded that aesthetics alone was a reasonable basis for exercising the police power, the means of accomplishing the goal would be left up to the legislature.

The *Landmark Land* case makes it clear that Colorado has adopted the rule of permitting aesthetics alone to support a land use regulation.

CONNECTICUT

No recent case dealing directly with the subject of aesthetics was found. In a 1944 case, *Murphy* v. *Town of Westport,*[11] the Connecticut Supreme Court reviewed an ordinance banning off-site signs. The court recognized that aesthetics was a valid basis for regulation when coupled with a public health or safety purpose. Further, it noted that some writers indicated the belief that the law regarding aesthetics was not yet settled. The court upheld the ordinance.

A 1988 case, *Capalbo* v. *Planning and Zoning Board,*[12] made mention of the aesthetics issue. The ordinance limited the number of different colors that can

[6]280 Ark. 408, 660 S.W.2d 900 (Ark. 1983).

[7]26 Cal.3d 848, 164 Cal. Rptr. 510, 610 P.2d 407 (1976).

[8]155 Cal. 318, 100 P. 867 (1909).

[9]Metromedia, Inc. v. City of San Diego, 453 U.S. 490, 101 S.Ct. 2882, 69 L. Ed. 800 (1981).

[10]728 P.2d 1281 (Colo. 1986).

[11]131 Conn. 292, 40 A.2d 177 (1944).

[12]208 Conn. 480, 547 A.2d 528 (1988).

be used in an outdoor advertising sign. The court ruled that the power to regulate sign colors was not specifically granted to municipalities in the state enabling legislation and therefore was lacking. The town argued that regulation of sign colors was an aesthetics interest that had been approved by the U.S. Supreme Court in several cases dating back to *Berman* v. *Parker*. The court stated that the issue was not "the accommodation of aesthetics concerns within state and local police power but rather the division of regulatory authority under home rule." The case is of little help except to point to the validity of the conclusion that the question of aesthetics standing alone is debatable in Connecticut.

DELAWARE

Delaware has not addressed the issue of aesthetics in recent years. The leading case may be *Franklin Builders, Inc.* v. *Alan Construction Co.,*[13] decided by an intermediate court in 1964, which reviewed the denial of a permit to erect an off-premises sign. The court's opinion is a crazy-quilt of patched-together excerpts from many other cases. Among the cases extensively quoted in upholding the zoning ordinance regulation of signs is *Berman* v. *Parker*. It cited affirmatively the language in that case, acknowledging the expansion of the concept of general welfare to include regulating for aesthetics.

In a more recent case that may have some relevance, *Mayor and Council of New Castle* v. *Rollins Outdoor Advertising, Inc.* (1984),[14] the same court reviewed an ordinance mandating the elimination of nonconforming signs over a three-year amortization period. The court did not mention the legislatively established purpose behind the ordinance, nor did it mention aesthetics in upholding the validity of the amortization provision. The case's relevance lies in the fact that most courts today recognize that ordinances regulating outdoor signs are solely or predominantly based on an aesthetic purpose. The court is not sufficiently troubled by this apparent aesthetics base for the law to even mention it.

To rely on the *Franklin Builders* case for the conclusion that regulations based on aesthetics alone are valid may be risky given the age of the case, the disjointed nature of the opinion, and the fact that it is not a state supreme court case. However, it apparently asserts that aesthetics can stand alone, and that has not been repudiated or discussed by the highest state court. The *New*

Castle case may add a little support for the conclusion. An educated guess is that aesthetics can stand alone in Delaware as a basis for exercising the police power.

DISTRICT OF COLUMBIA

The impetus for the movement among the states to free aesthetics so that it can stand alone as a basis for regulation comes from the U.S. Supreme Court in *Berman* v. *Parker*.[15] This 1954 case reviewed a condemnation of land under the District of Columbia Redevelopment Act of 1945. The purpose of the law was to rid the area of slums.

Though strictly speaking it is an eminent domain case, Justice Douglas spoke at some length about the police power. He referred to the concept of public welfare as "broad and inclusive." He went on: "[T]he values it represents are spiritual as well as physical, aesthetic as well as monetary. It is within the power of the legislature to determine that a community should be beautiful as well as carefully patrolled." This often quoted language made it clear that there is no federal constitutional impediment to any reasonable regulation for the purpose of aesthetics.

Aesthetics can stand alone as a purpose in exercising the police power in the District of Columbia.

FLORIDA

Florida approved regulations based on aesthetics early. In *Merritt* v. *Peters*,[16] the court stated: "[W]e have no hesitancy in agreeing . . . that the factors of health, safety and morals are not involved in restricting the proportions of a sign board, but we disagree . . . that the restriction cannot be sustained on aesthetics grounds alone." In a more recent case, *City of Lake Wales* v. *Lamar Advertising Assoc. of Lakeland, Florida*,[17] the court reviewed an ordinance that distinguished between off-site and on-site signs, restricting the size of off-site signs only. The basis for the ordinance was solely aesthetics. The court upheld the validity of the ordinance. It stated that zoning for aesthetics alone is an idea whose time has come. It recognized that municipalities can distinguish between off-site and on-site signs on aesthetic grounds.

The Florida Supreme Court's language affirming an aesthetics alone stance seems unequivocal. An older Florida case related the validity of a sign control ordinance to the fact that the city of Sarasota was a center for culture and beauty.[18] Although Florida is one of

---

[13]207 A.2d 12 (Del. Supr. 1964).

[14]475 A.2d 355 (Del. Supr. 1984).

[15]348 U.S. 26 (1954).

[16]65 So.2d 861 (Fla 1953).

[17]414 So.2d 1030 (Fla 1982).

[18]Sunad, Inc. v. City of Sarasota, 122 So.2d 611 (Fla 1960).

those states that might legitimately link its aesthetic quality to the economic strength of its tourist industry, the court placed no such limitation on its rationale.

GEORGIA

In a recent Georgia case the constitutionality of a zoning ordinance providing that structures were permitted only in the rear yards of residential developments was challenged. The plaintiff-landowner maintained a satellite television antenna in the front yard for personal and business purposes. He sold antennas out of his home.

In the case, *Gouge* v. *City of Snellville*,[19] the Georgia Supreme Court noted that the purpose of the ordinance was the advancement of the city's aesthetics. It held that aesthetics interests are a reasonable and proper justification for exercising the police power.

The following year in *Brown* v. *Dougherty Co.*[20] the court made it clear that the aesthetic purpose must be supported by reviewable standards. It overturned the denial of a zone change request to rezone for mobile home development. The court found that the only justifiable reason for the denial was the aesthetic quality of the neighborhood. It found this aesthetic interest "too vague and weighs too lightly in the balance" to offset a substantial interest to the landowner.

Georgia's law is clearly in the column of states that permit regulation based on aesthetics alone.

HAWAII

In a leading case on aesthetics, the state adopted a comprehensive ordinance regulating outdoor signs. In the 1967 case *State* v. *Diamond Motors, Inc.,* the Hawaii Supreme Court approved the ordinance, stating:

[W]e accept beauty as a proper community objective, attainable through the use of the police power. We are mindful of the reasoning of most courts that have upheld the validity of ordinances regulating outdoor advertising and of the need felt by them to find some basis in economics, health, safety, or even morality. We do not feel so constrained.[21]

The court had the benefit of a state constitutional provision that specifically authorizes the state to conserve and develop its natural beauty. The court rejected the notion that the power was confined to preventing nuisances, like junkyards and slaughterhouses, but placed its emphasis on the broad shoulders of public welfare.

Hawaii has endorsed regulating for aesthetics alone for over twenty years. It has explicitly rejected the notion of tying its approval to an economic argument based on tourism.

IDAHO

The leading case in Idaho is *Dawson Enterprises, Inc.* v. *Blaine County,*[22] in which the plaintiff-landowner was denied a zone change. The landowner argued that the zoning ordinance's limitation of the property to agricultural and residential uses rather than commercial ones, given its location, was unreasonable. The ordinance was seeking to avoid strip development along a highway and to maintain the glen and rural character of Wood River Valley near the Sun Valley ski resort.

The court ruled in favor of the county, acknowledging that aesthetic considerations played a prominent role in the particular zoning ordinance. It stated that to the extent that the purpose of the ordinance was to maintain the rural character of the county and the Wood River Valley, it was a valid exercise of the police power under its general welfare language.

It is difficult to be certain, given some of the language cited from other cases by the court, but it appears that the Idaho court has endorsed the concept that regulations based solely on aesthetics are valid.

ILLINOIS

The status of aesthetics in Illinois is unclear. There is a line of cases from the state supreme court beginning with *LaSalle National Bank* v. *City of Evanston*[23] in 1974 through *County of Lake* v. *First National Bank of Lake Forest*[24] in 1980 that state that aesthetics is not disregarded but is often a matter of personal choice and not to be controlling. These are zoning cases and say little on the subject of aesthetics beyond the fact that a regulation must combine aesthetics with other police powers interests to withstand an attack on its validity.

The ability of aesthetics to stand alone may depend on the type of regulation involved. In *Village of Skokie* v. *Walton on Dempster, Inc.,*[25] the appellate court in 1983 held that a sign control ordinance could withstand a challenge though based on aesthetics alone. The court

[19]249 Ga. 91, 287 S.E.2d 539 (1982).

[20]250 Ga. 658, 300 S.E.2d 509 (1983).

[21]429 P.2d 825 (1967).

[22]98 Idaho 506, 567 P.2d 1257 (1977).

[23]57 Ill.2d 415, 312 N.E.2d 625 (1974).

[24]79 Ill.2d 221, 37 Ill. Dec. 589, 402 N.E.2d 591 (1980).

[25]119 Ill. App.2d 299, 74 Ill. Dec. 791, 456 N.E.2d 293 (1983).

did not mention the line of zoning cases from the supreme court, but quoted one of its own prior cases to the point that "the role of aesthetics in zoning is an element of the public health, safety and welfare" and that a sign ordinance can be upheld on the basis of aesthetics under public welfare as well as under a public safety argument.

The safest conclusion based on the state supreme court cases is that aesthetics cannot stand alone in Illinois. The appellate court case may indicate that the rule applies only to zoning cases and that regulations outside the zoning area, like sign ordinances, will be treated differently. Any logic behind such a distinction is not immediately obvious. Either aesthetics alone is or is not an adequate public welfare basis to regulate. Whether an aesthetics-alone regulation based on public welfare can withstand as strong an attack as can a public safety regulation from a seriously injured plaintiff is a separate question.

INDIANA

The leading case on aesthetics in Indiana is an old one. The 1930 case, *General Outdoor Advertising Co.* v. *City of Indianapolis,*[26] involved an ordinance restricting the location of signs near parks. The supreme court stated that "citizens must not be compelled under the police power to give up rights in property solely for the attainment of aesthetic objects." The court acknowledged that aesthetics can be an "auxiliary consideration" with other police power purposes to support a regulation.

The only more recent case found is of limited use. In *Metropolitan Development Comm'n.* v. *Douglas,*[27] the court of appeals reviewed a case concerning the location of a carport in violation of a five-foot minimum side yard setback. In affirming the decision to enforce the setback restriction, the court stated: "[A]s the distance between structures on adjoining property decreases, so does the aesthetic balance of a residential community." It went on to note that "equally important" as aesthetic reasons was the fire hazard caused by structures sited too closely together. One can reason that regulations based on fire hazards alone are unquestionably legal under the police power, and that if fire hazards and aesthetics are "equally important," then a regulation based solely on aesthetics is legitimate. Despite the appeal of such an argument, it may

make too much of a few sentences in an intermediate appeals court decision.

Though this statute arguably supports the premise, the case law in Indiana does not directly support the proposition that aesthetics can stand alone as a basis for the exercise of the police power.

The state legislature enacted an environmental impact statement statute modeled after the National Environmental Policy Act. This law mandates that the state use all practical means, to among other things, "assure for all citizens . . . esthetically and culturally pleasing surrounds."[28] The statutory language adds some credence to the proposition that aesthetics is by itself a legitimate reason for regulation in Indiana.

IOWA

In a 1956 Iowa Supreme Court case, *Stoner McCray Systems* v. *City of Des Moines,*[29] involving a law regulating billboards, the court made it clear that aesthetic considerations can be used as an "auxiliary consideration" in a zoning regulation. The position that aesthetics must be coupled with other factors to legitimate a regulation may continue to be the Iowa position.

A later decision in 1978 by the same court in *Iowa Dept. of Transp.* v. *Nebraska-Iowa Supply Co.*[30] the court upheld the Iowa Junkyard Beautification and Billboard Control Act against a challenge. Despite what appears to be a predominantly aesthetic purpose, the court approved the exercise of the police power based upon traffic safety, promotion of the comfort of those using the highways, and finally, promotion of aesthetic values.

The most recent case does not expressly reject the notion of aesthetics standing alone, but the court is careful to buffer it with a variety of other justifications. At this time in Iowa a regulation stating aesthetics alone as a purpose would be risky based on existing case precedents.

KANSAS

A recent supreme court case in Kansas suggests, but does not hold, that a regulation based on aesthetics alone is valid. In *Robert L. Reilke Building Co.* v. *City of Overland Park,*[31] the court reviewed a zoning code provision that required a special-use permit in order to use "attention-getting devices" like the high-powered

---

[26]172 N.E. 309 (1930).

[27]390 N.E. 663 (1979).

[28]Ind. Code 13-1-10-3(b)(2).

[29]78 N.W.2d 843 (Iowa 1956).

[30]272 N.W.2d 6 (Iowa 1978).

[31]232 Kan. 634, 657 P.2d 1121 (1983).

searchlights furnished by the plaintiff for advertising and promotional purposes.

The court noted that throughout the United States today billboards and other forms of advertising can be validly regulated under the police power. The three reasons offered for such regulations are promotion of traffic safety, aesthetic considerations, and preservation of property values. The court went on to point out that the current trend is to permit regulations for aesthetic reasons, citing California's *Metromedia, Inc.* case. It did not elaborate further, and upheld the ordinance based on the promotion of traffic safety and on the aesthetic appearance of the city.

Despite citing approvingly several cases from other states that hold that aesthetics can stand alone, the Kansas Supreme Court did not explicitly adopt that position. It coupled aesthetics with traffic safety. It may be safe to say that the court is leaning in the direction of the current trend.

KENTUCKY

In a case examining the validity of a statute requiring a permit to operate an automobile junkyard within 2,000 feet of a highway, the Kentucky Court of Appeals found the law valid. The court recognized that the purpose of the act was to enhance the scenic beauty of the state's roadways.

In *Jasper* v. *Commonwealth,*[32] the court relied primarily on the leading New York case *People* v. *Stover,*[33] referring the reader to the language in that case. The court expressly concluded that aesthetics considerations can stand alone as a basis for regulating under the public power. That conclusion was affirmed later in 1964 in the case of *Moore* v. *Ward,*[34] and again in 1990 by *Diemer* v. *Commonwealth.*[35]

Kentucky is an "aesthetics can stand alone" state.

LOUISIANA

In an early case, *Sears Roebuck and Company* v. *City of New Orleans* (1960),[36] the Louisiana Supreme Court reviewed an ordinance that regulated some types of signs used by gas stations. The stated legislative pur-

pose of the law was to prevent fraud in advertising and to improve aesthetic conditions. The court found no rational relationship between the purposes of the ordinance and the limitation on signs. After rejecting the fraud argument the court did say, however, that "it may be within the powers of the City, for aesthetics considerations, to pass a general ordinance applying to all business signs."

In a federal Fifth Circuit case, *Maher* v. *City of New Orleans,*[37] the court maintained that zoning ordinances can be upheld under the police power where motivated by a desire to enhance the aesthetic appeal of the community. The court thereby approved an ordinance mandating that a landowner obtain a permit prior to attempting to perform any construction or demolition in the New Orleans French Quarter. The court relied on *Berman* v. *Parker* for support, and did not mention any state cases supporting the aesthetics alone premise.

In a 1978 intermediate appeals court case, *Trustees under the Will of Pomeroy* v. *Town of Westlake,*[38] a zoning regulation based solely on aesthetics was struck down because it deprived the owner of all reasonable use of the land. This is not very revealing since no police power regulation, regardless of its purpose, is likely to justify a confiscation. The state court did cite the *Maher* case mentioned above for the proposition that an owner did not have a right to develop land to its maximum economic potential.

A definitive position on aesthetics is difficult to discover within state case law. If the federal court in *Maher* accurately states the position, aesthetics can stand alone. The state court cases are less convincing.

MAINE

The state condemned the plaintiff's land as part of a comprehensive plan to preserve and develop the natural scenic beauty along its highways. The resulting case, *Finks* v. *Maine State Highway Comm'n.,*[39] is not a regulation case but one of eminent domain. The state must show a *public use* for eminent domain, a traditionally narrower concept than the *public purpose* required in a regulation case.[40] The court found that aesthetics alone was a satisfactory basis for condemning land under the public use criterion, so that aesthetics

[32]375 S.W.2d 709 (Ky. 1964).

[33]12 N.Y.2d 462, 240 N.Y.S.2d 734, 191 N.E.2d 272 (1963).

[34]377 S.W.2d 881 (Ky. 1964).

[35]786 S.W.2d 861 (1990).

[36]238 La. 936, 117 So.2d 64 (1960).

[37]516 F.2d 1051 (1975), *cert. den.* 426 U.S. 905 (1976).

[38]357 So.2d 1299 (La. App. 1978).

[39]328 A.2d 791 (Me. 1974).

[40]The distinction between public use and public purpose has long been blurred and may have been put to rest by the U.S. Supreme Court in Hawaii Housing Authority v. Midkoff, 104 S. Ct. 2321 (1984).

can certainly stand alone under the public purpose test. The court stated that it fully agreed with a New Jersey case that had "no hesitancy in stating that restoration, preservation and enhancement of scenic beauty along public highways is a public use [sic] for the public welfare, filling a social need of our times."[41] In Maine aesthetics alone is an adequate basis for a land use regulation.

MARYLAND

The leading case in Maryland is *Mayor and City Council of Baltimore* v. *Mano Swartz, Inc.,*[42] involving a challenge to a city ordinance regulating signs in the central business district. The purpose of the ordinance was to provide aesthetic advertising structures and to relieve conditions of "gaudiness and drabness." The ordinance included a five-year amortization period for nonconforming signs.

The state court of appeals struck down the ordinance, contending that aesthetics can be an additional legislative purpose where other health and safety purposes exist, but aesthetics cannot be the sole purpose as it was under the ordinance in question. The court was concerned that standards of beauty, like gaudiness, were too subjective to constitute valid legislative standards. However, at the end of the case the court apparently agreed that aesthetics can sometimes stand alone. It stated that if the purpose of the ordinance is to preserve or protect something aesthetically pleasing, such as a work of nature or of art, from disfigurement, then a regulation would be valid. In this case the court opined that the purpose was to establish standards of community taste with no thought toward enhancing the public welfare.

The doubt seems to have been laid to rest in *Coscan Washington, Inc.* v. *Maryland–National Capital Park & Planning Commission*[43] in 1991. The court of appeals held that aesthetic reasons cannot be the sole basis for completely or partially prohibiting certain acts. Aesthetics must be coupled with some other police power purpose to be valid in Maryland.

MASSACHUSETTS

In one of the leading aesthetics cases in the country, *John Donnelly and Sons, Inc.* v. *Outdoor Advertising Board,*[44] the state's highest court gave its approval to an ordinance that banned off-premise signs in any zone in the town. The law had a five-year amortization period for nonconforming signs.

The court stated that the issue was whether an ordinance based solely on aesthetics can be upheld under the police power. It concluded that aesthetics alone can justify the exercise of the police power under the broad concept of the general welfare. It noted that we live in a changing world and the law must adapt to the demands of a modern society. One of those changes, the court observed, was that towns should be aesthetically pleasing, as a visually satisfying environment contributes to the well-being of its inhabitants. In addition, the court noted that the legislature in 1972 had ratified an amendment to the state constitution, making it state policy to protect the right to a natural, scenic, historic, and aesthetic environment.

Massachusetts has unequivocally affirmed that regulations can be based on aesthetics alone.

MICHIGAN

In *National Used Cars, Inc.* v. *City of Kalamazoo,*[45] the intermediate appeals court reviewed a junkyard control ordinance that required the yards to be shielded from view. The court stated that it found the view of more recent decisions, such as *Oregon City* v. *Hartke* (Oregon), to be persuasive. These cases held that a regulation can stand on aesthetics ground alone. It noted that aesthetics standing alone has been recognized by the Michigan State Legislature (a junkyard control law), by the U.S. Congress, and by the U.S. Supreme Court (*Berman* v. *Parker*).[46]

In a later case from the appeals court, *Gannett Outdoor Co. of Michigan* v. *City of Troy,*[47] the court reviewed the denial of a permit to erect two billboards under a sign control law. The core issue in the case pertained to a possible invasion of constitutionally protected speech. The court stated unequivocally, however, that the "city's aesthetic interests are alone sufficient to justify billboard regulation."

No cases from the state supreme court were located. Based on these two opinions of the intermediate court, it appears that in Michigan aesthetics alone can support a police power regulation.

---

[41]Wes Outdoor Advertising Co. v. Goldberg, 55 N.J. 347, 262 A.2d 199 (1970).

[42]299 A.2d 828 (Md. 1973).

[43]87 Md. App. 602, 590 A.2d 1080, 1088 (1991).

[44]339 N.E.2d 709 (Mass. 1975).

[45]61 Mich. App. 520, 233 N.W.2d 64 (1975).

[46]A more recent case citing *National Used Cars* language is People v. McKendrick, 188 Mich. App. 128, 468 N.W.2d 903 (1991).

[47]156 Mich. App. 126, 409 N.W.2d 719 (1986).

MINNESOTA

The supreme court may be in the twilight zone between perceiving aesthetics as a make-weight in the balancing process and accepting aesthetics as a factor that can stand alone. In 1979, in *County of Pine* v. *Dept. of Natural Resources,*[48] the court upheld an ordinance protecting wild and scenic views. The court held that it did not share the discomfort that the trial judge experienced in affirming a law whose dominant purpose was aesthetics. Preserving the unique natural and scenic resources of the state did have an aesthetics purpose, but that in no way diminished the ordinance's validity. The court then took pains to point out that the ordinance was supported by other traditional zoning objectives, such as prevention of a safety hazard, e.g., building too close to the bluff.

In 1982, in *Hubbard Broadcasting, Inc.* v. *City of Afton,*[49] the court reviewed an action denying a special-use permit to construct a satellite station. The court denied the permit on eight separate grounds, but generally held the station would be inconsistent with the comprehensive plan's strongly stated desire to preserve the rural character and unique scenic beauty of the city. The court opined that the denial of the permit could not be based upon environmental characteristics, like aesthetics, alone, but such concerns are factors that could be considered in the context of the comprehensive plan and the conservancy district purposes. The meaning of this language is unclear. The court may mean that so long as the aesthetics purpose is an integral part of a comprehensive plan, the purpose is legal.

The Minnesota Supreme Court seems to be moving in the direction of adopting an aesthetics alone stance. It appears at this stage, however, that the court is unwillingly to thrust aesthetics to the forefront without paying lip service to other traditional supportive criteria.

MISSISSIPPI

In *Mississippi State Highway Comm'n.* v. *Roberts Enterprises, Inc.,*[50] the supreme court upheld a state statute requiring the removal of billboards along the main highways in the state. The court concluded that the major reason for the legislation was the preservation of natural beauty.

The court concurred in the reasoning used in *Berman* v. *Parker*[51] and in the Kentucky case *Jasper* v. *Commonwealth,*[52] both of which confirmed regulation for aesthetics alone. The court stated that it was making the finding based on the police power and not on narrow public nuisance grounds.

MISSOURI

In *Deimeke* v. *State Highway Comm'n.,*[53] the Missouri Supreme Court reviewed a junkyard licensing statute. It affirmed the validity of the ordinance despite the fact that it was based predominantly on aesthetics and that earlier Missouri cases held that aesthetics could not stand alone. The court cited approvingly *Oregon City* v. *Hartke*[54] (Oregon) and *People* v. *Stover*[55] (New York), two of the leading "aesthetics alone" cases. With the *Hartke* case the Missouri court noted that the public welfare concept is constantly changing and expanding, adapting to the needs of society at any particular time. It explicitly relied on the language of the Kentucky case *Jasper* v. *Commonwealth,* which in turn relied on the *Stover* case.

The *Deimeke* opinion was written in 1969, but it appears to be a valid statement of Missouri law. Like several other leading cases cited in this chapter, the court upheld the notion of aesthetics standing alone, but to overcome its discomfort with the newness of its position threw in some more traditional bases to smooth over its new position.

In a Missouri federal district court case in 1985, *National Advertising Co.* v. *City of Bridgeton,* an ordinance prohibiting off-site commercial billboards was upheld. The purpose of the ordinance was aesthetics. The court relied on the Missouri Constitution, which enables the General Assembly to enact laws "to preserve places of historic or archaeological interest or scenic beauty."[56] This federal trial court case, applying its perception of Missouri law, provides some back-up for the conclusions of the earlier *Deimeke* case.

---

[48]280 N.W.2d 625 (Minn. 1979).

[49]323 N.W.2d 757 (Minn. 1982).

[50]304 So.2d 637 (1974).

[51]348 U.S. 26 (1954).

[52]375 S.W.2d 709 (Ky. 1964).

[53]444 S.W.2d 480 (1969).

[54]240 Or. 35, 400 P.2d 255 (1965).

[55]12 N.Y.2d 462, 240 N.Y.S.2d 734, 191 N.E.2d 272 (1963).

[56]626 F. Supp. 837 (E.D.Mo. 1985).

MONTANA

In *State* v. *Bernhard*[57] the Montana Supreme Court examined the constitutionality of a law requiring that automobile wrecking facilities have a license. The purpose of the act was aesthetics.

The court held that aesthetics is a satisfactory ground for adopting a land use regulation. It supported its conclusion by referring to other cases, such as *Oregon City* v. *Hartke*,[58] that held that aesthetics can stand alone as a public welfare regulation. In addition, the court cited the state constitution, which declared a public right to a "clean and healthful environment." This provision is a sufficient basis for legislative enactments based upon aesthetics values.

NEBRASKA

When most of the states moved from the rule requiring that aesthetics be coupled with other police power justifications to one allowing the aesthetics to stand alone, the laws involved were either sign or junkyard controls. In *Schaffer* v. *City of Omaha*[59] the Nebraska Supreme Court reviewed a case involving the regulation of advertising signs.

The court ruled that the regulation was neither unreasonable nor discriminatory when applied to mobile signs that were effectively banned. It stated that the regulations appeared justified based on "preventing traffic hazards, restrictions of view, interference with residential comfort, fire hazards and the safety of citizenry," all of which seemed reasonable to the court. There was no recognition by the court that the primary, if not sole, basis for controlling signs is aesthetics.

On the slim evidence provided by this case, it is apparent that Nebraska has not ruled that aesthetics can stand alone. Aesthetics must continue to be supported by other health and safety factors.

NEVADA

The Nevada case *Board of County Commissioners* v. *CMC of Nevada, Inc.*[60] does not directly address the issue of aesthetics standing alone as a land use regulation. The court appears by implication, however, to have approved the idea.

The case involved the refusal of the county to give an applicant architectural approval and a building permit. The applicant argued that the relevant ordinance had solely an aesthetics purpose, that the refusal was not based on aesthetics, and that therefore the refusal was arbitrary. The court spent much of its time in the case trying to find a broader purpose than aesthetics to determine if the county action could be upheld. It never flinched or indicated any difficulty with aesthetics being the sole basis for the architectural regulation. The county did not argue that the ordinance could not be sustained based on aesthetics alone.

Though not the holding of the case, it appears that the Nevada Supreme Court is completely comfortable with regulations based solely on aesthetics.

NEW HAMPSHIRE

The New Hampshire Supreme Court has not ruled in recent years on the issue of whether an aesthetics regulation can stand without the support of another public health, safety, or welfare purpose. In *Piper* v. *Meredith*,[61] the court ruled in favor of an ordinance that had aesthetics as one of its purposes. It made clear that aesthetics can be one of an array of police power purposes, but went no further.

From reading other New Hampshire cases not directly on point, it seems that if the aesthetics-based regulation did not substantially eliminate the economic value of the land or, alternatively, was being used to protect land of a unique character, it would be upheld. In *Sibson* v. *State*[62] a regulation restricting the filling of wetlands because of their ecological importance (considerably broader than aesthetics) was approved by the court, but in *Burrows* v. *City of Keene*,[63] zoning an area for open space was disapproved because it substantially reduced the economic value of the land, and because the land was not unique in nature.

The issue of whether aesthetics can stand alone is uncertain in New Hampshire.

NEW JERSEY

In *State* v. *Miller*[64] the New Jersey Supreme Court reviewed the validity of a sign ordinance based on aesthetics. It endorsed the concept of aesthetics standing

[57]568 P.2d 136 (Mont. 1977).
[58]240 Or. 35, 400 P.2d 255 (1965).
[59]197 Neb. 328, 248 N.W.2d 764 (1977).
[60]670 P.2d 102 (Nev. 1983).
[61]266 A.2d 103 (N.H. 1970).
[62]336 A.2d 239 (N.H. 1975).
[63]432 A.2d 15 (N.H. 1981).
[64]83 N.J. 402, 416 A.2d 821 (1980).

alone, relying on the *John Donnelly and Sons* case from Massachusetts and the U.S. Supreme Court's *Berman* v. *Parker* case, as well as quoting Henry David Thoreau and Ogden Nash.

The court stated that the "development and preservation of natural resources and clean, salubrious neighborhoods contribute to psychological and emotional stability and well-being as well as stimulate a sense of civic pride. We therefore hold that a zoning ordinance may accommodate aesthetics concerns." Two earlier cases are often cited by other jurisdictions for their language supportive of aesthetics regulations. They are *Westfield Motor Sales Co.* v. *Town of Westfield*[65] in 1974 and *Wes Outdoor Advertising Co.* v. *Goldberg*[66] in 1970.

New Jersey has clearly endorsed regulations based on aesthetics alone.

NEW MEXICO

The leading case in New Mexico, as it is in many states, is one reviewing the validity of a sign ordinance. In *Temple Baptist Church* v. *City of Albuquerque*,[67] citing *Berman* v. *Parker* and other cases, the court endorsed the conclusion that aesthetics considerations alone justify the exercise of police power. The court referred to the *Berman* case as representing "the emerging majority" view. It reasoned that "aesthetics is inextricably intertwined" with the general welfare in providing "comfort, happiness, and enhancement of the citizens' cultural life."

Aesthetics can stand alone as the foundation of a land use regulation in New Mexico.

NEW YORK

One of the earliest states to adopt the position that a regulation based on aesthetics alone is valid is New York. In 1963 in *People* v. *Stover*[68] the state's highest court reviewed an ordinance that prohibited clotheslines in the front yard abutting the street without a permit. The defendant maintained several clotheslines with rags on them as a protest against high taxes.

The court had doubts that the health and safety purposes offered by the city were adequate, but stated that the ordinance can be sustained on the basis of the purpose of preserving the residential appearance of the city. The validity of the ordinance should be based on whether it was an arbitrary method of achieving an attractive community, and not on whether the objective was aesthetics. The court admitted, however, that legislatures can go too far in the name of aesthetics.

The *Stover* case and a later case, *Cromwell* v. *Ferrier*,[69] a 1967 sign control case, state that aesthetics considerations must "bear substantially on the economic, social, and cultural patterns of a community or district." The eye is entitled to protection from offense as much as the other senses.

A later case,[70] similar in its facts to *Cromwell*, stated that once the law has an established police power basis, the only question to satisfying the issue of constitutionality is whether "it is reasonably related to the objective for which it was enacted."

An intermediate appeals court case, *Sackson* v. *Zimmerman*,[71] stated that where a landowner otherwise has the right to use his land in a certain fashion, a denial of the right on aesthetics grounds must be based upon a showing that the offense to the eye is substantial and that it has a material effect on the community. In short, it must be based on more than a "generalized feeling" of the neighbors as to what they would prefer in their neighborhood.

The New York courts have endorsed the concept of aesthetics standing alone and have spelled out the remainder of the analysis for determining the validity of individual aesthetics-based laws.

NORTH CAROLINA

The state supreme court reviewed the constitutionality of an ordinance requiring that junkyards be fenced. The purpose of the ordinance was aesthetics. The court concluded that the former minority rule that aesthetics can stand alone as a basis for a regulation had now become the majority rule.

The court in *State* v. *Jones*[72] expressly overruled prior North Carolina holdings that indicated that aesthetics cannot stand alone. Whether any specific regulation based on aesthetics would be upheld depended on a test balancing the public interest in regulation against the private owner's interest in being free of regulation. The court then conducted a modified "takings" and due process analysis by stating that factors to be considered were whether the regulation takes "a

[65]129 N.J. Super. 528, 324 A.2d 113 (1974).

[66]55 N.J. 347, 262 A.2d 199 (1970).

[67]98 N.M. 138, 646 P.2d 565 (1982).

[68]12 N.Y.2d 462, 191 N.E.2d 272 (1963).

[69]19 N.Y.2d 263, 225 N.E.2d 749 (1967).

[70]Suffolk Outdoor Advertising Co., Inc. v. Halse, 43 N.Y.2d 483, 402 N.Y.S.2d 368, 373 N.E.2d 263 (1977).

[71]103 A.D.2d 843, 478 N.Y.S.2d 354 (1984).

[72]290 S.E.2d 675 (1982).

substantial part of the value of the property, deprives the owner of reasonable use, has an adequate purpose, and adopts a method likely to achieve that purpose." In the reversal of traditional analysis in this area, which used aesthetics as a supplementary factor only, this court stated that an aesthetics regulation may in addition provide "corollary benefits" in the form of protecting property values, promoting tourism, protecting health and safety, preserving the character and integrity of the community, and promoting the general welfare of the local residents.

The North Carolina court expressly held that a reasonable regulation based on aesthetics alone is a valid exercise of the police power. It did caution, however, that the authority to so regulate should not be delegated to groups and organizations "not authorized to exercise the police power by the General Assembly."

NORTH DAKOTA

In a 1978 case the supreme court reviewed a state law implementing the Federal Highway Beautification Act, which regulates signs along interstate highways and other primary state roads. The purpose of the state law is the "restoring, enhancing, and preserving scenic beauty" as well as promoting safety and convenience of highway users, protecting public investment in highways, and promoting enjoyment and recreational values of state roads.

The court in *Newman Signs, Inc.* v. *Hjelle*[73] concluded that these "purposes are within the proper scope of the police power." It acknowledged that the U.S. Supreme Court in *Berman* v. *Parker* and several other state courts concluded that aesthetics can stand alone as a valid exercise of the police power. The court stated, however, that "we need not decide whether aesthetics considerations alone justify this regulation because the regulation is based upon a combination of purposes which we find to be within the police power."

The question of whether aesthetics can stand alone is open at this time in North Dakota.

OHIO

The leading case on aesthetics for some time in Ohio was the 1968 *State* v. *Buckley*.[74] The law in the case involved the regulation of junkyards solely for aesthetics reasons. The court stated that the "primary question here is whether aesthetics considerations may support such an exercise of the police power."

The supreme court confirmed the law, stating that "aesthetics considerations can support these statutes, because interference with the natural aesthetics of the countryside caused by an unfenced or inadequately fenced junk yard is generally patent and gross, and not merely a matter of taste." Note the court's emphasis on the nuisance aspect of the law and its steering clear of purely subjective aspects such as taste. Later, the court qualified its holdings by stating that the opinion is not to be read as a blanket approval of all regulations based on aesthetics. Whether the court is stating merely that aesthetics-based regulations must be reasonable, like other police power regulations, or is intending to be more restrictive is unclear. The court is clearly concerned about the legitimacy of regulating community tastes.

Later cases cast some doubt on the conclusion of *Buckley* that aesthetics can stand alone, but that doubt was put to rest in the 1984 case *Village of Hudson* v. *Albrecht, Inc.*[75] where the court affirmed the *Buckley* holding and averred that aesthetics is a legitimate government interest.

Aesthetics can stand alone in Ohio.

OKLAHOMA

In *State Dept. of Transportation* v. *Pile*[76] the Oklahoma Supreme Court reviewed a statute requiring the removal of billboards. The speech on the billboard in question was political, and the court decided that a ban on all billboards along highways cannot apply to ones used for noncommercial speech.

The state supported the billboard restriction based on aesthetics and urged the court to adopt the position of *Berman* v. *Parker*. The court agreed that the state may determine under its police power that the community should be beautiful. However, aesthetics is not strong enough to uphold a restriction on noncommercial speech. Aesthetics, the court stated in a footnote, does not constitute the compelling state interest necessary to justify a constraint on political speech. The court noted that "aesthetics standards are indeterminate, incapable of concrete definition, fluid and ever-changing, while the freedoms guaranteed by the first amendment are as absolute as the nature of the republic will allow," and therefore speech cannot be held subservient to aesthetics.

Oklahoma must go into the uncertain column on the issue of aesthetics standing alone. On the one hand, it recognizes that aesthetics can be a valid reason for ex-

---

[73]268 N.W.2d 741 (N.Dak. 1978).
[74]16 Ohio St.2d 128, 243 N.E.2d 66 (1968).
[75]9 Ohio St.3d 69, 458 N.E.2d 852, 856 (1984).
[76]603 P.2d 337 (Okla. 1979).

ercising the police power. On the other hand, it is reluctant to uphold an aesthetics purpose where law involves the regulation of billboards, the type of situation where many other states adopted their aesthetics alone posture. It should be emphasized that the court perceived the law as potentially a total ban on political speech, and not as merely a time, place, and manner restriction. The regulation of commercial signs or junkyards appears to be palatable to the court in Oklahoma.

OREGON

Oregon was one of the earliest states to adopt the aesthetics alone position in its leading case, *Oregon City* v. *Hartke*.[77] The defendant in the case was charged with violating the zoning ordinance by extending his legal nonconforming use as a wrecking yard to additional land without permission.

The Oregon court endorsed the position of the courts in *Berman* v. *Parker* (U.S. Supreme Court) and *People* v. *Stover* (New York) in holding that under the rubric of the general welfare, aesthetic considerations alone may warrant an exercise of the police power. The court stated that the change of attitude toward aesthetics-based regulations is "a reflection of the refinement of our tastes and the growing appreciation of cultural values in a maturing society."

Oregon unequivocally authorizes regulation based on aesthetics alone.

PENNSYLVANIA

Several Commonwealth court cases from Pennsylvania reviewed the aesthetics issue. In *Redevelopment Authority of Oil City* v. *Woodring*[78] the court stated that "it is axiomatic that any exercise of the police power must be rationally related to the general health, safety and welfare and such an exercise may not be grounded solely on considerations of aesthetics." The redevelopment authority required utility lines to be placed underground for aesthetics reasons. The court held that this was an exercise of eminent domain and not of the police power.

In *Heck* v. *Zoning Hearing Board*[79] the court used similar language to reject the board's denial of a special exception to the zoning code based solely on aesthetics. This case presented the argument that the construct-

ing of a vertical addition to a building would interfere with the scenic beauty of the lake. The court conceded that a consideration of aesthetics in zoning matters under the general welfare concept was legitimate, but aesthetics alone cannot be a basis for denying a special exception to the zoning code.

A discordant note is found in the dicta of a later case by the same court. In *Lynch* v. *Urban Redevelopment Authority of Pittsburgh*,[80] the court upheld the authority's denial of permission to a landowner to lease part of the land for the erection of a billboard. The permission was sought under a contractual arrangement between the parties that the landowner needed prior approval before making a major change in the utilization of the property. The court agreed that a 72-foot-high billboard was a major change. In responding to the landowner's argument that the denial created a First Amendment speech problem, the court paraphrased language from the U.S. Supreme Court's *Metromedia*[81] case to the effect that "the Supreme Court recognized a municipality's legitimate interest in protecting esthetics and specifically recognized that billboards, by their very nature, wherever located or however constructed, can be perceived as an 'esthetic harm.'" In addition, it quoted a federal district court case that cited aesthetics as the sole reason for an authority's denial of an approval. Finally, the Pennsylvania court concluded that the authority's denial based on the fact that the billboard did not aesthetically fit in did not deny the landowners their constitutional speech rights.

There is no mention of the fact that prior cases held that aesthetic reasons cannot stand alone, nor is there an attempt to distinguish the contractually based aesthetic restriction in this case from aesthetics-based regulations applicable to the public at large. The judge who wrote the opinion in the *Woodring* and *Heck* cases was part of the unanimous opinion in *Lynch*.

It is clear, however, that if the state legislature adopts enabling legislation based on aesthetics, it is valid. In 1971, the citizens of the state amended the Constitution, Article 1, Section 27, agreeing that the "people have a right to clean air, pure water, and to the preservation of the natural, scenic, historic and esthetic values of the environment."[82] Though this constitutional language has been held not to be self-executing, it provides a foundation for aesthetic legislation whenever the legislature sees fit to adopt it.

---

[77]400 P.2d 255 (Ore. 1965).

[78]430 A.2d 1243 (Pa. 1981), affd. 445 A.2d 724 (1982).

[79]397 A.2d 15 (Pa. 1979).

[80]496 A.2d 1331 (Pa. Comwlth 1985).

[81]Commonwealth v. Nat'l. Gettysburg Battlefield Tower, Inc., 311 A.2d 588 (Pa. 1973).

[82]Art. I, §27 1971 Pa. Const.

It appears that aesthetics can stand alone in Pennsylvania.

RHODE ISLAND

No modern case was found for Rhode Island, though a 1926 case, *City of Providence* v. *Stephens*,[83] indicates that aesthetics cannot by itself be the basis for a regulation.

Of limited value is a more recent case, *Sakonnet Rogers, Inc.* v. *Coastal Resources Management Council*.[84] The case reviewed a decision by the council denying an application to move a structure into an area designated as a "coastal natural area." Under the law the council was to review applications to determine the proposed activities impact on nine environmental criteria. The fourth criterion is "aesthetics and/or recreational value." It appears that the council can reject an application on any one of the nine criteria, including aesthetics. Some of the testimony received at the hearing on the application opposed it solely on aesthetic grounds. The court made no objection to the aesthetics criterion or the testimony regarding aesthetics, but neither was aesthetics involved in the court's holding. The court held that the council had not based its denial on any of the nine relevant criteria, but on irrelevant ones.

The safest conclusion to reach is that Rhode Island has not yet concluded that aesthetics can stand alone.

SOUTH CAROLINA

No appeals court case was located indicating a position on aesthetics as a basis for land use regulation. There is a state statute allowing for the regulation of outdoor signs based on the need "to prevent the unreasonable distraction of operators of motor vehicles . . . and to preserve and enhance the natural scenic beauty or aesthetic features of the highways and adjacent areas."[85] Given the illusory nature of the first purpose, it appears the legislature felt compelled to couple the aesthetics reason with a safety purpose. A recent court of appeals case, *Young* v. *So. Carolina Dept. of Hwys. and Public Transp.*,[86] reviewed the statute but did not comment on its foundation in aesthetics.

The law regarding aesthetics standing alone is uncertain in South Carolina.

SOUTH DAKOTA

In *Sanderson* v. *Mobridge*,[87] the Supreme Court of South Dakota reviewed a decision by the city of Mobridge to deny plaintiffs a permit to move their house over city streets to another site. The city's reasons for denying the permit focused "on the destruction of the aesthetic value of the area occasioned by the removal or disfigurement of trees along the moving route."

The court held that the grounds for the city's refusal "are reasonable and reflect a real and commendable concern for the aesthetic preservation of Mobridge." No reasons other than aesthetics are cited by the court.

South Dakota accepts the concept of aesthetics standing alone as a valid reason for exercising the police power.

TENNESSEE

The leading case in Tennessee is *State* v. *Smith*,[88] in which the validity of a junkyard regulation was called into question. The purposes of the statute were stated in broad terms, with preserving and enhancing the scenic beauty of lands along public highways among them.

The court held that aesthetics was not the only basis for the statute. It went on, however, to reject its prior rule and to conclude that "in modern society aesthetics considerations may well constitute a legitimate basis for the exercise of the police power, depending upon the facts and circumstances."

Although it may be categorized as dicta, the unanimous Tennessee Supreme Court, quoting from many of the important cases in other states and federal courts, clearly affirms that aesthetics can stand alone.

TEXAS

In *City of Houston* v. *Johnny Frank's Auto Parts Co.*,[89] the state intermediate appeals court reviewed an ordinance that regulated the operation of automobile wrecking and salvage yards. The purpose of the ordinance was stated in broad public health, safety, and welfare terms.

The court acknowledged that one of the reasons for the ordinance was aesthetics, but took pains to link the law to other health and safety factors. Having decided

[83]133 A.614 (1926).
[84]536 A.2d 893 (1988).
[85]Section 57-25-130, 1976 Code of Laws of S. Carolina.
[86]336 S.E.2d 879 (S.C. App. 1985).
[87]317 N.W.2d 828 (1982).
[88]618 S.W.2d 474 (Tenn. 1981).
[89]480 S.W.2d 774 (Tex. 1972).

that the ordinance was not based on aesthetics alone, it did not have to address the question of whether aesthetics can stand alone.

In a later case, *City of Houston* v. *Harris County Outdoor Advertising Association*,[90] the same court reviewed the city's sign control ordinance to determine, inter alia, whether the law's provision for amortizing nonconforming signs was valid. The court upheld the ordinance and its amortization provisions. Although the court did not discuss the issue of aesthetics standing alone, the ordinance is clearly based on aesthetics grounds.

Under the current state of the case law, it is unclear as to whether aesthetics can stand alone. It is obvious that wrecking yard ordinances and sign control ordinances are predominantly aimed at aesthetic goals, and the recitation of other goals is at best of the makeweight variety. Yet, the Texas court has not felt the need to explicitly approve the principle that aesthetics can stand alone.

UTAH

The leading case in Utah is *Buhler* v. *Stone*,[91] involving the examination of an ordinance prohibiting the accumulation of junk, scrap, and metal, inter alia, if the items became unsightly. The defendant-landowner had collected 250 old cars on his 40 acres of land. The purpose of the ordinance, stated to be unsightliness, is clearly aesthetics.

The majority of the Utah Supreme Court approved the validity of the ordinance. In doing so the court stated that "surely among the factors which may be considered in the general welfare is the taking of reasonable measures to minimize discordant, unsightly and offensive surroundings; and to preserve the beauty as well as the usefulness of the environment." The court cited several leading "aesthetics alone" cases from other states as support for this statement.

Utah has adopted the premise that aesthetics can stand by itself as a purpose for the exercise of the police power.

VERMONT

Vermont has several statutes that are either based solely on aesthetics, or have criteria that can stand alone and are based solely on aesthetics. The Scenic Highway Act,[92] a statute governing power-line location,[93] and, especially, Act 250[94] have criteria based on aesthetics and to date the Vermont court has not uttered a whimper of protest.

In *Vermont Electric Power Co., Inc.* v. *Bandel*,[95] the supreme court reviewed a decision involving the location of a 115 KV power line noting the statutory language that condemnation of land must "not unduly interfere with . . . scenic preservation." The court discussed the fact that interference with scenic beauty by development was usually inevitable and that the key word was "unduly." It did not consider whether aesthetics can stand alone, but went immediately to the question of balancing the scenic preservation interest against the public interest in the utility line under the "unduly interfere" language.

Vermont's Act 250 regulates development on a statewide basis. Review of development proposals is carried out under ten statutory criteria. The eighth of these criteria pertains to development not having "an undue adverse effect on the scenic and natural beauty of the area, aesthetics, historic sites or rare irreplaceable natural areas." The criterion based solely on aesthetics has been reviewed several times by the supreme court, which has exhibited no concern over the legitimacy of the aesthetic basis. One should look to *Wildlife Wonderland, Inc.*,[96] *In re Patch*,[97] and to the latter portions of an article in the *Journal of Environmental Law*[98] for further support for this position.

Aesthetics can stand alone in Vermont.

VIRGINIA

In *Board of Supervisors* v. *Rowe*,[99] the Virginia Supreme Court examined the strictures within a zoning ordinance that, among other things, required that all plans for development in the business-tourist zone be sub-

---

[90]732 S.W.2d 42 (1987).

[91]533 P.2d 292 (Utah 1975).

[92]Vt. Stat. Ann. Title 10, § 425.

[93]Vt. Stat. Ann. Title 30, § 112.

[94]Vt. Stat. Ann. Title 10, § 6086 (a)(8).

[95]375 A.2d 975 (1977).

[96]346 A.2d 645 (1975).

[97]437 A.2d 121 (1981).

[98]Brooks, R., & Lavigne, P. "Aesthetic Theory and Landscape Protection: The Many Meanings of Beauty and Their Implications for the Design, Control and Protection of Vermont's Landscape," 4 *J. of Env. L.* 129 (1985).

[99]216 Va. 128, 216 S.E.2d 199 (1975).

mitted to the Architectural Design Review Board. The board was to review the plans solely for purposes of architectural design.

The court pointedly stated that the county cannot restrict the use of private property under the guise of the police power and justify it solely on aesthetics. While the entry of aesthetics considerations as a reason for passing the ordinance will not invalidate it, the law must be supported by other elements within the domain of the police power.

Virginia clearly holds that aesthetics cannot stand alone as a basis for exercising the police power.

WASHINGTON

Two cases decided in the late seventies raised the issue of the appropriateness of regulating based on aesthetics, but the conclusions seem inconsistent. In 1977 in *State Dept. of Ecology* v. *Pacesetter Construction Co.*[100] the court reviewed a proposed development under the state's Shoreline Management Act (SMA). The dispute initially arose between the defendant developer and other landowners in the area. The state intervened under the authority of the SMA. The main thrust of the problem was that the defendant's development would obstruct the existing residents' view of Lake Washington.

The court noted that the legislature had expressed a public policy in the SMA protecting aesthetic values, and implied that regulations based on aesthetics alone were satisfactory. It went on to tie the decision to the notion that the aesthetic protection also protected property values. Justice Hicks in a brief concurring opinion noted that he disagreed with the part of the majority opinion "indicating that the police power of the state may be used to regulate property solely for aesthetics reasons."

In 1978 in *Polygon Corp.* v. *City of Seattle*,[101] the plaintiff was denied a building permit because its proposed building would adversely impact the environment. The most significant environmental impact was aesthetic in nature. Justice Hicks, writing for the majority this time, cited the *Pacesetter* case for the proposition that aesthetics alone will not support an exercise of the police power. His conclusion in this case seems at variance with his conclusion the year before in a concurring opinion.

Whether Washington will uphold a law based solely on aesthetics is unclear at this time.

WEST VIRGINIA

In the 1960 case of *Farley* v. *Graney*[102] the West Virginia Supreme Court reviewed a junkyard operation and maintenance statute based solely on aesthetics. The court observed that the great weight of opinion at that time held that aesthetics could not stand alone as a basis for regulation. It went on to note that there was a current marked tendency to give aesthetics greater weight, and that courts frequently went to great pains to find other grounds upon which to base the law's validity when clearly the predominant purpose was aesthetics. The court concluded by deferring to the legislative judgment, and that judgment approves regulating for aesthetics alone.

A long dissenting opinion was written by Justice Haymond in which he disagreed with the majority opinion to the extent that it upheld the junkyard law based solely on aesthetics.

It appears from the *Farley* case that West Virginia affirms that aesthetics alone can provide a valid foundation for the exercise of the police power.

WISCONSIN

In *Racine County* v. *Plourde*,[103] the court reviewed a county action attempting to compel an automobile salvage yard operator to bring his business into compliance with an ordinance regulating that type of facility. The dominant objective of the law was to prevent the creation of an unsightly condition.

The supreme court stated that it was "cognizant that aesthetics considerations alone may now be sufficient to justify a prohibited use in a zoning ordinance." It noted this position was initially adopted by the court in *State ex. re. Saveland P.H. Corp.* v. *Wieland*[104] in 1955 and was affirmed by *Kamrowski* v. *State*[105] in 1966.

Aesthetics can stand alone as a purpose for exercising the police power in Wisconsin.

WYOMING

No cases directly deciding the legitimacy of aesthetics in land use regulation in Wyoming were found. In a 1985 case, *Cheyenne Airport Board* v. *Rogers*,[106] the su-

---

[100]89 Wash.2d 203, 571 P.2d 196 (1977).
[101]90 Wash.2d 59, 578 P.2d 1309 (1978).
[102]119 S.E.2d 833 (1960).
[103]38 Wis.2d 403, 157 N.W.2d 591 (1968).
[104]269 Wis. 262, 69 N.W.2d 217 (1955).
[105]31 Wis.2d 256, 142 N.W.2d 793 (1966).
[106]707 P.2d 717 (Wyo. 1985).

preme court reviewed a case brought by landowners attacking a municipal airport zoning ordinance limiting the height of obstructions on residential property. The plaintiffs had a tree that exceeded those limitations.

In affirming the ordinance's height limitations, the court relied on the U.S. Supreme Court's *Penn Central*[107] case, which sustained height limitations imposed to protect historic and aesthetic landmarks. The usefulness of that reliance is very limited because the *Penn Central* regulation is based on protecting aesthetics under public welfare, while the purpose of the ordinance in the *Cheyenne Airport* case is the protection of public safety.

The state does have a statute, called the Industrial Development Information and Siting Act,[108] that requires the issuance of a construction permit for certain types of development. One of the relevant criteria under the statute's § 114 is aesthetics.

Whether aesthetics can stand alone in Wyoming is an open question.

References

Bufford. 1990. Beyond the eye of the beholder: a new majority of jurisdictions authorize aesthetic regulations, 48. *U.M.K.C. Law Review* 125.

Granger, R. 1992. In Re Quechee Lakes Corporation: mitigating aesthetic environmental damage or an eyesore on Act 250 Land Use Protections? 16 *Vermont Law Review* 541.

---

[107]Penn Central Transp. Co. v. City of New York, 438 U.S. 104 (1978).
[108]§ 35-12-101 et. seq., W. S. 1977.

II
Constraints Applied to Community Issues

Chapter 5

Zoning and Land Use Control

The first section of this chapter traces the historical evolution of land use zoning from its foundations under common law to the development of present-day discretionary techniques. The second section of this chapter describes the movement toward aesthetically defensible zoning. The third section discusses reasonable tests; and the final section is a case study involving aesthetic analysis and its integration with other resource values for land use planning and management (see Fig. 5.1).

TRADITIONAL METHODS OF LAND USE CONTROL

Common Law

Land use zoning in the United States has its foundation in English common law. These zoning laws placed restrictions on a person's use of land for the benefit of surrounding landowners. The two concepts closely related to land use zoning are *trespass* and *nuisance*. Trespass is defined as "wrongful, physical invasion of the property of another." The act of entering or remaining upon the land in possession of another without authority to do so from the occupant (Gibson, Karp, and Klyman 1992, p. 434). Nuisance is an unreasonable interference by one party with another's enjoyment of his or her land (Gibson, Karp, and Klyman 1992, p. 433). Nuisance does not require a physical invasion of the complainant's land. Noise, dust, vibration, and odors are among the many items covered under this law.

These zoning laws gave a private owner some control over an adjoining owner's land. However, land use con-

trol by this method had to be dealt with on a case-by-case basis. In most states, an injunction was granted only after balancing the equities between the parties and determining if the benefit of the injunction outweighs the ensuing detriment to the perpetrator. As a result of the balancing process, injunctions are not readily available to small landholders plagued by nuisances from larger landholders, such as polluting industries and noisy manufacturing facilities (Gibson, Karp, and Klyman 1983, p. 237).

Property Rights and Responsibilities

Almost from the beginning of U.S. history inception, landowners owed no duty to anyone; they had only to refrain from acts on the property that would significantly hinder the use of other landowners. Once the property was purchased, the buyer owed no additional duty to the seller or any other party (Gibson, Karp, and Klyman 1992, pp. 433–34). At the turn of the twentieth century, the traditional concept of unrestricted use of one's own land came under severe challenge due to the deplorable conditions developing in many cities. Serious health and safety problems began to arise because of unrestricted land development in urban areas. In the first half of the nineteenth century, almost no government action had been taken to combat these horrible housing and living conditions, either through control or redirection of private development. Court injunctions were occasionally issued against specific establishments; however, these were few and far between. Around the turn of the century, the combined mass migration to this country along with weak municipal au-

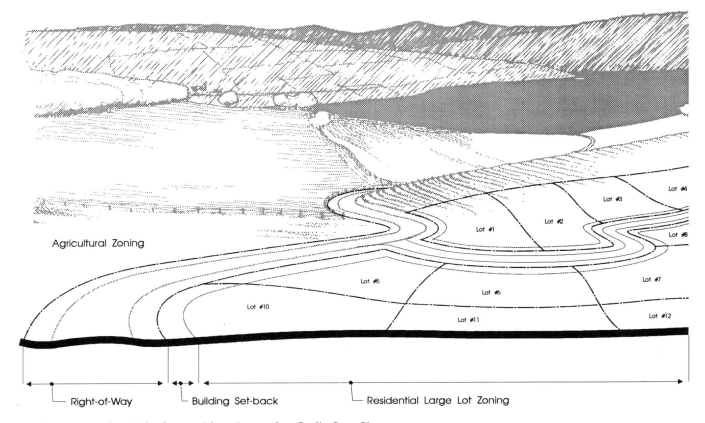

Agricultural Zoning

Lot #4
Lot #3
Lot #2
Lot #1
Lot #5
Lot #5
Lot #6
Lot #7
Lot #10
Lot #11
Lot #12

Right-of-Way   Building Set-back   Residential Large Lot Zoning

FIGURE 5.1   Generic landscape with zoning overlay. *Credit: Scott Shannon*

thorities of new state-centered political systems, and an antiurban bias of an agrarian society, caused American cities to become congested, polluted centers of disease and decay (Arnold 1979, p. 27).

City planners became increasingly aware that public restraint on land development was necessary since common law solutions were inadequate to meet the rapid growth and the problems of American cities (Anderson 1984, p. 14). The first step toward municipal prevention under controlled growth came with the idea of planning for community development. City planning, although hardly a new concept, had been virtually disregarded in U.S. cities after the Founding Fathers had laid out the original patterns of development.

Planning Boards

The first official, local, and permanent town planning board in the United States was created in 1907 by the Connecticut legislature, called the Hartford Commission. Similar boards were created in Milwaukee in 1908 and in Chicago, Detroit, and Baltimore in 1909 (Arnold 1979, p. 32). The early planning boards usually consisted of municipal officials, citizen appointees, businesspeople, bankers, and a large contingent of architects and landscape architects. These boards had little funding, minimal authority, and no clear understanding as to their purpose or direction (Arnold 1979, p. 33). However, they started a trend toward city planning, and by the early 1920s nearly all municipalities engaged in some form of planning for future development (Anderson 1984, p. 13).

Planning could range from a study of the parking needs of a community to an analysis of proposed school sites. However, the most important type of planning came with the concept of the comprehensive or master land use plan.[1] This type of planning laid the foundation for support of land use zoning in the United

---

[1]A comprehensive plan is a document or a series of documents prepared by a planning commission or department setting forth policies for the future of a community. It is normally the result of considerable study and analysis of existing physical, economic, and social conditions, and a projection of future conditions (Meshenberg, 1976 PAS Report no. 322, p.10).

States.[2] The development of the community plan in and of itself did little to correct the conditions of American cities. In fact, the comprehensive plan often conflicted with the self-interest of local landholders. This being the case, it was unrealistic to expect such owners to refrain from developing land use inconsistent with the plan, if such conduct were not prohibited by law.

As stated previously, the concept of nuisance in common law offered little help in restricting overall land use development. Control over development was strictly dependent on private initiative. Restrictions imposed were scattered and unrelated. Consequently, resolutions to land use conflicts often came after the fact through litigation between two adjacent landowners. This form of regulation did little to enforce and direct growth prior to construction, which is best based on a community's comprehensive plan.

Other techniques for control over land development were also explored. Eminent domain[2] failed as an important control technique because it was time-consuming, expensive, and presented the difficulty of determining fair-market value. Official maps[3] gained some popularity for fixing the location of streets, parks, public buildings, and other essential community facilities. Most municipalities also adopted building codes and subdivision regulations,[4] based on state standards, to protect the community from ill-designed and poorly serviced subdivisions and other large-scale developments. None of these techniques seemed adequate, however, for controlling all land use development in a community. The solution seemed to be in a broader use of the police power.

THE POLICE POWER

The police power was employed successfully to exclude noxious uses from certain neighborhoods with positive results. These results seemed to indicate that a broader use of this power could be made to achieve the goals of an entire development plan for a community (Anderson 1984, p. 15). The use of the police power proved less expensive than eminent domain. The landowner absorbed the loss (caused by restrictions placed upon that particular parcel of land) in the same manner that all persons are required to absorb losses caused by limitations imposed by proper police regulations.

Early ordinances usually dealt with issues that could be directly linked to health and safety. Building codes are examples of health and safety regulations within the purview of the police power. Fire laws imposed minimum restrictions favoring fire-resistant materials as well as requirements for ingress and egress. In many of the cases upholding these restrictions, the cost to the landowner was high enough to destroy the "highest and best use" interest of the owner (Anderson 1984, p. 16). (This should not be confused with the taking of all possible land uses; see "highest and best use" and "taking" below.[5])

Early ordinances that excluded certain uses from designated residential or commercial areas were not as

---

[2]Eminent domain is the legal right of the government to acquire or "take" private property for public use or public purpose upon paying just compensation to the owner. While originally used only when land was to be kept in public ownership, that is, for highways, public buildings, or parks, property has been condemned under eminent domain powers for private use in the public interest, such as for urban renewal (Meshenberg, 1976 PAS Report no. 322, p. 14).

[3]Official maps are legal documents, adopted by the governing body of a community, that pinpoint the location of future streets and sites for other anticipated public facilities. It allows land to be reserved for a limited time, giving the community a chance to acquire the land before it becomes developed. State enabling legislation typically prohibits further private development in areas currently undeveloped but designated on an official map for future use.

[4]Subdivision regulations are local ordinances that regulate the conversion of raw land into building lots for residential or other purposes. The regulations establish requirements for streets, utilities, site design, and procedures for dedicating land for open space or other public purposes to the local government, or fees in lieu of dedication, and prescribe procedures for plan review and payment of fees (Meshenberg, 1976 PAS Report no. 322, p. 33).

[5]"Highest and best use" is the use of a property that will bring its owner the greatest profit if offered for sale. In theory, the economics of the real estate market establishes a maximum value for each parcel of land at any given time. Except in developed areas or along transportation corridors where there is pressure to develop, this "highest and best use" is likely to be residential or agricultural. Zoning, by placing each property in a particular district, may interfere with market operations and raise or lower the property value.

"Taking" is the appropriation by government of private land for which compensation must be paid. Under the U.S. Constitution, property cannot be condemned through eminent domain for public use or purpose without just compensation. The "taking" issue concerns use of the police power to regulate land through zoning controls. When zoning controls diminish the value of property considerably, then a form of inverse condemnation occurs and a fine line is drawn between regulation and illegal "taking without just compensation." From Meshenberg 1976 19, pp. 18, 34.

obviously tied to the police power but were still demonstrably within its power. Cases that involved exclusion of land uses within previously established residential or commercial districts were upheld if it could be shown that a land use restriction was reasonably related to public health or safety. These examples indicate that the police power was used as a basis for supporting legislative restrictions of land use before comprehensive zoning came on the scene.

From Police Power in General to Comprehensive Zoning

The most significant contribution of this period toward developing land use controls were the legal precedents set for the use of municipal zoning regulations. Land use zoning developed in West Coast communities, with the first codes legislatively enacted in the 1910s in San Francisco, and also in New York City. However, zoning districts according to land use classifications were seldom used for implementing a community's entire comprehensive plan because it was not clear where the courts would stand on the degree of restriction involved. Some piecemeal zoning was attempted prior to the first comprehensive zoning regulations; however, these ordinances were often disapproved by the courts due to their discriminatory nature (Anderson 1984, p. 59). The codes restricted some lands; therefore, those owners were unfairly discriminated against relative to all other unregulated landowners within a municipality. This is a violation of the Fourteenth Amendment's Equal Protection Clause.

These issues began to be resolved in 1915 when zoning met its first test in a case of municipal control over private land in the Supreme Court case *Hadacheck* v. *Sebastian*.[6] Up to this time only a few communities had enacted land use control ordinances due to the uncertainty of the law. The greatest obstacle was the fear that the courts might find restrictions on more profitable uses to be an unconstitutional taking of property without just compensation (Anderson 1984, p. 12). In deciding this case, the Court agreed with the California Supreme Court that "regulation was not precluded by the fact . . . the value of investments made . . . prior to any legislative action will be greatly diminished" (Arnold 1979, p. 35).

Municipalities began to prepare land use control programs based on the premise that the decision in *Hadachek* v. *Sebastian* meant the U.S. Supreme Court had given approval to land use zoning. Prior to the *Hadachek* case, a New York City commission had created a scheme for the effective control of future urban development of the city (1913). This commission came up with the concept of a comprehensive zoning code to control all types of land use in the city. This code contained land use controls, controls on building heights, and controls of building setbacks and yards in an integrated ordinance.[7] By this time all three of these elements had constitutional approval, explicitly or implied, of the Supreme Court (height control in *Welch* v. *Swasey;* building setback control in *Eubank* v. *City of Richmond;* and land use control in *Hadacheck* v. *Sebastian*) (Arnold 1979, p. 36). Assuming the Supreme Court would present no hurdle, replicas of the New York City ordinance were rapidly adopted in many other large municipalities across the nation.

During the early 1920s the U.S. Department of Commerce encouraged the spread of this new comprehensive zoning[8] by publishing a model state enabling act. By 1926, when the first zoning ordinance encouraged by the enabling act reached the U.S. Supreme Court, zoning was to be found not only in large cities but also in many small communities (Anderson 1984, p. 36). The New York City zoning code was far from a good model to follow for the development of a zoning code. First, the code tended to freeze current land uses rather than provide for beneficial change. Also, the code was not related to any comprehensive plan for community development. In fact, the code was substituted for the plan causing further confusion over the terms "comprehensive plan" and "comprehensive zoning ordinance." The code was generally protective of current land interests and was unrelated to any reasonable forecast or projections of future land use demand (Arnold 1979, p. 36). The code was generally a list of allowable land uses keyed to a zoning map whereas a plan included the rationale of why specific uses were allowed or not allowed for specific land areas/zones.

Comprehensive land use zoning was tested in the 1926 case *Euclid* v. *Ambler Realty Company*.[9] In this case the U.S. Supreme Court held that "a municipal ordinance which divided the whole territory of the municipality into districts and imposed land use restrictions

---

[6]239 U.S. 394 (1915).

[7]Arnold 1979, p. 36. It should be noted that this first ordinance was established by entrepreneurial factions in the city with the intent of removing the garment district business from the Fifth Avenue district where rich shoppers did not like having to mingle with swarms of garment workers during lunch hours. (See Fitch, Robert, 1977, in Rodger Alcaly and David Mermelstein, eds., *The Fiscal Crisis of American Cities*, Vintage, pp. 246–284.)

[8]The present-day definition of comprehensive zoning is far removed from this early unrestricted and undefined interpretation of what constituted such an ordinance.

[9]272 U.S. 365 (1926).

on the basis of district classifications was within the police power of the municipal corporation."[10] The Supreme Court based its decision on the police power's public health, safety, and welfare language, stating that the regulations would improve fire protection, reduce street congestion, decrease noise, which produces or intensifies nervous disorders, and preserve a more favorable environment for raising children (Anderson 1984, p. 64).

The *Euclid* case established the constitutionality of comprehensive zoning. It determined that the following features were within the police power:

1. The community could be divided into districts.
2. Restrictions upon the use of private land in such districts were acceptable provided such use was consistent for all similarly designated districts.
3. Exclusion of certain industrial, commercial, and nonresidential uses from certain residential districts was within this authority.

Therefore, this case established the basic components of an orthodox zoning ordinance and more importantly swayed judicial support nationally in favor of this kind of land use control. Ultimately, the courts of all the states approved comprehensive zoning (Anderson 1984, p. 64).

In deciding the *Euclid* case, the Supreme Court stated that its holding was confined to the case at hand. The Court specifically acknowledged that an ordinance might be valid on its face but unconstitutional in its specific application to a parcel of land (Anderson 1984, p. 65). The *Euclid* decision therefore set the stage for the case-by-case system of resolving zoning litigation. Constitutional litigation in the field of zoning law since *Euclid* has consisted mainly of two kinds of cases: (1) those that closely examine the ordinance for constitutional defects, and (2) those that challenge the constitutionality of an ordinance as it applies to a particular piece of property (Anderson 1984, p. 65). The *Euclid* case established that zoning is based on local *legislative* authority and is thus a legislative act, presumed to be constitutional and valid. This presumption places upon anyone challenging a zoning ordinance the burden of proving that the ordinance is unreasonable or arbitrary (Anderson 1984, p. 70).

Comprehensive Zoning and Comprehensive Planning

Establishing the constitutionality of zoning ordinances was a major step in the evolution of land use controls. However, it was not until the 1970s that a clearer understanding of the distinction between comprehensive zoning and comprehensive planning and the relationship between the two evolved into a usable form. Since the 1920s courts have rendered opinions on zoning matters without requiring that a city have a plan or that zoning be consistent with a plan, should there be one. This is not totally surprising given the rather static nature of early Euclidian zoning.[11]

Even though the standard state zoning enabling act, which most municipalities copied in setting up zoning legislation, specifically states that zoning "shall be in accordance with a comprehensive plan," few mandated such plans (Arnold 1979, p. 170). In the early days of zoning it was assumed that a city would prepare a zoning map that would identify the basic zoning areas, such as residential, commercial, and industrial. Property owners needed only to look at the map and the zoning text to determine what they could and could not do with their property. The zoning map and text became the plan, thus creating the confusion between a comprehensive land use plan and a comprehensive zoning ordinance. This issue was further complicated by the courts. The zoning map and text became the plan and the courts looked no further.

With the advent of flexible zoning techniques[12] and growth management programs, the courts have increasingly turned away from accepting the zoning ordinance as evidence of a community's needs without first referring to the city's comprehensive plan (Arnold 1979, p. 170).

Flexible zoning codes were established when cities recognized that it was nearly impossible to predict future land use needs. No matter how carefully a zoning ordinance was prepared, something unanticipated would happen to make the code obsolete. Flexible techniques also increased a community's negotiating power, which often led to the exclusion of land uses unwanted by the community. This system suited the community's desire to control its own destiny. However, the courts began to question the fundamental fairness of the system. New flexibility in zoning changed its traditional you-can-do-anything-you-want with your

---

[10]Id.

[11]"Euclidian zoning" is a division of the territory of a municipality into districts and an assignment of particular uses to each district. The term was derived from the zoning ordinance of the Village of Euclid, Ohio, which was reviewed and approved by the U.S. Supreme Court in Euclid v. Ambler Realty Co., 272 U.S. 365 (1926).

[12]Flexible zoning means new techniques such as planned unit development, performance standards, and overlay zoning.

property image to one of indicating a procedure one had to follow to find out what might be done on one's property. This system could be highly abused by local communities, and in fact was (Arnold 1979, p. 170).

Growth management programs added a new twist to traditional zoning, that of timing. Growth has its negative consequences and some cities adopted no-growth policies. Again the courts questioned these techniques and required additional planning backup documentation to support local zoning ordinances. The courts indicated that if a city wanted to control the rate of growth, it would have to show some evidence of a coordinated approach in order to avoid charges of arbitrary and capricious enforcement. This indicates that the courts wish to see some form of comprehensive land use plan (Arnold 1979, p. 170).

AESTHETICS, ZONING, AND LAND USE CONTROL HISTORY

The earliest problem facing the courts with respect to aesthetic considerations in zoning was whether the benefit to the public, traditionally thought of in terms of need but never luxury, outweighed the damages to individual use of property. A historical view of some of the zoning cases follows (a more encompassing and current overview is found in Chapter 3).

Early Period: Traditional Disregard

The prevailing judicial attitude toward aesthetic considerations in zoning from 1900 to 1930 was basically twofold:

1. The courts refused to uphold zoning ordinances that were either solely, primarily, or even partially motivated by aesthetic considerations.
2. Even when aesthetics was a reasonably obvious and legitimate factor in creating the ordinance, the court—while simply alluding to or completely ignoring the aesthetic viewpoint—would not necessarily invalidate the regulation so long as there was some other independent grounds to warrant employment of the police power (Pearlstein 1972).

Guberman (1976) illustrates the court's strong resistance to ordinances motivated largely by aesthetic considerations. The New Jersey Supreme Court, in 1905, suggested that a man may not be deprived of his property because his tastes are not those of his neighbors. The court also stated: "Aesthetic considerations are a matter of luxury and indulgence rather than necessity, and it is necessity alone which justifies the exercise of the police power to take property without compensation" (Guberman 1976).

The primary obstacles to aesthetics considerations in early zoning cases were:

1. Aesthetic issues were considered a luxury to please a few rather than a necessity that alone justifies the exercise of the police power.
2. Aesthetics was also considered subjective in nature, having no intelligent or consistent standard and therefore no standing as a factor under the general welfare (Masotti and Selfon 1969).
3. The potential discriminatory application of aesthetics-based ordinance (based on the above) was considered reason for dismissal by the courts. Because of vagueness, luxury, and inconsistent standards, it was feared by the courts and regulators to lead to widespread abuse (Wilcox 1970).

Aesthetics was therefore recognized as such a personal and controversial value as to be unlegislatable. The view was that it would be impossible to draw up a statute to reflect the desires of everyone. Primarily for these reasons, early case law reacted negatively to zoning restrictions based on aesthetics, or even to the mere inclusion of aesthetics in the reasoning.

A New Trend Toward Valid Consideration

A new trend in judicial attitudes toward aesthetic considerations in zoning developed at a time when the United States was starting to experience the growth of vast urban communities, with their attendant economic and social repercussions. Because of the lack of aesthetic consideration given in early 1900s zoning, various kinds of developments were intermixed, including retail stores and gasoline stations in residential areas. Ordinances that tried to prevent such inharmonious uses within such districts were considered to satisfy the subjective desires of those individuals affected by the aesthetically offensive use. The resulting depreciation of property value was viewed merely as a consequence of a lawful use of one's property.

Increased growth also brought increased earnings and spending, and values changed correspondingly from a demand for necessities to a demand for luxuries. Persons affected by zoning soon realized the value of not having a factory next door or their view of a lake blocked by a ten-story building. Communities developed pride in aesthetic qualities and wished to preserve their integrity from unsightly development. In the case of aesthetic zoning, as the public pressure built, the courts were forced to review approaches addressing individual interests (Masotti and Selfon 1969). Though the courts realized the need to reshape land use controls, they also felt the need to move slowly when limiting the common law rights inherent in private property (Rose and Yim 1962).

Aesthetics as "Auxiliary" Consideration

As judicial attitudes began to change, aesthetic consideration began to take on an auxiliary position in zoning ordinances. As an auxiliary factor, aesthetics had to rely on some other dominant consideration with which it could form a partnership to enhance the "general welfare" term of the police power. Aesthetics, in most cases, was best suited for association with property value (Pearlstein 1972).

In *Welch* v. *Swasney*, a case concerning height limitations on buildings to be erected in Boston (Figure 5.2), the court stated:

The inhabitants of a city or town cannot be compelled to give up rights in property, or to pay taxes for purely aesthetic objects; but if the primary and substantive purpose of the legislation is such as justifies the act, considerations of taste and beauty may enter in, as auxiliary.[13]

This case gave aesthetics the initial push that helped to generate aesthetic objectives in zoning regulation.

Another case at the time in which aesthetics was delegated a minor supportive position involved setback lines. In 1920, the Connecticut Supreme Court acknowledged the importance of aesthetics as an auxiliary factor. In addition to upholding traditional aims of promoting public health and safety, courts also commented that streets of reasonable width add to the value of land and beauty of the neighborhood (Pearlstein 1972).

In 1923, the Louisiana Supreme Court in *Civello* v. *New Orleans* (see Figure 5.3) expanded the auxiliary theory by broadening the term "general welfare" to include aesthetic considerations.

If the term "aesthetic considerations" is meant a regard merely for outward appearances, for good taste in the matter of beauty of the neighborhood itself we do not observe any substantial reason for saying such a consideration is not a matter of general welfare. The beauty of a fashionable residence neighborhood in a city is for the comfort and happiness in the neighborhood. It is therefore as much a matter of general welfare as in any other condition that fosters comfort or happiness and consequent values generally of the property in the neighborhood.[14]

The court also went on to include offensive sights within the more universally recognized nuisances of smell and noise.[15]

The court, in these cases, reasoned in contrast to

FIGURE 5.2   Downtown Boston Faniuel Hall area before redevelopment. *Photo credit: R. C. Smardon*

earlier cases in which aesthetics was considered personal and inapplicable to a "general or public" interest, but rather the visual character of a neighborhood was a value to be protected and fostered. The courts found it necessary to link aesthetics and property value, because property value was more definitely associated with general welfare (Masotti and Selfon 1969). Agee (1965) suggests as a concept, it is less radical and more easily understood than aesthetics, and has the virtue of more accurate measurement by everyday standards of dollars and cents, not like the irrational value of an eyesore.

As a result of such decisions, as well as the *Euclid* decision of 1926, the next quarter of a century provided aesthetics as at least a relevant supporting factor status in zoning legislation.

Aesthetics as Economic Well-Being

Aesthetics has received acknowledgement beyond the auxilliary level when, as a proponent of the "general welfare," it is linked with economic well-being (Pearlstein 1972). The argument is that an area of a city or state needs to be aesthetically pleasing for mainte-

---

[13]214 U.S. 91 (1908).

[14]154 La. 283, 97 So. 440 (1923).

[15]Id.

FIGURE 5.3 a, b   New Orleans historic district. *Photo credit: M. Potteiger*

nance of economic well-being, since it is an extension of the concept of promoting the general welfare (Minano 1971). Aesthetics in this regard have played an important part in preserving historic sites and fostering tourism in certain states such as Florida, Louisiana, and New York (Masotti and Delfon 1969). The Florida courts have said that certain portions of the state have a particular monetary dependency on its tourist trade. Since tourist trade is enriched by aesthetic appeal (see Figure 5.3), such ordinances can be upheld (Masotti and Selfon 1969).

In one such Florida case, *City of Miami Beach* v. *Ocean & Inland Company,* the court sustained a zoning law that permitted only hotel apartment sites on an approach to Miami Beach:

In view of the nature of Miami Beach, it is not important to consider here in indispensability of the restrictions to the health, the safety, the morals of the community but only their necessity to the general welfare. . . . The limitation of the use by the plaintiff of his property seem a fair, just and responsible contribution to the economic

good, the prosperity, the welfare of the whole community and not so burdensome that it contravenes the organic inhibition against deprivation without due process.[16]

Thus the court sustained a zoning law based primarily upon aesthetics because it promoted the general prosperity of the community (Swietlik 1955). Most courts in these jurisdictions, while reluctant to uphold aesthetics solely as a basis for police power employment, did assert that aesthetics, when coupled with aspects of economic prosperity, consequently affect the "general welfare" of the community (Pearlstein 1972).

Aesthetics Within the Term "General Welfare"

In 1954, the Supreme Court case of *Berman* v. *Parker*[17] helped give aesthetics a more legitimate consideration in legislative actions. The District of Columbia Redevelopment Act, ruled to be constitutional, provided for condemnation of private property to allow for the construction of better quality housing. The Court ruled

---

[16]City of Miami Beach v. Ocean & Inland Co., 141 Fla. 480, 3 So.2d. 364 (1941).
[17]348 U.S. 26 (1954).

that an exercise of eminent domain by the police power did not violate the Fifth Amendment prohibition against the taking of private property for public use without compensation. The Court said the taking was done in order to promote a more attractive community (Wilcox 1970).

The concept of the public welfare is broad and inclusive. . . . The values it represents are spiritual as well as physical, aesthetic as well as monetary. It is within the power of the legislature to determine that the community should be beautiful as well as clean. . . . If those who govern the District of Columbia decide that the Nation's Capitol should be beautiful as well as sanitary, there is nothing in the Fifth Amendment that stands in the way.[18]

The effect of this case was significant with regard to expanding the scope of what is meant by the term "general welfare." This case was also considered a strong argument for the value of aesthetics in zoning by specifically including aesthetic consideration in the much broadened concept of general welfare suggested by the court.

Still, state courts were hesitant to place more weight on aesthetics considerations and generally referred back to economic impacts of aesthetics as a detriment to property value rather than aesthetics as an idealistic goal of the community. For example, in *Saveland Park Holding Corporation* v. *Wieland,*[19] the Wisconsin Supreme Court based their ruling on both aesthetics and a depreciation of property values, but admitted the two are inseparable and even identical. The courts concluded that under the public welfare concept, the consideration of aesthetics as an auxiliary standard was constitutional (Masotti and Selfon 1969).

This case was soon followed by others which clearly stated that aesthetics was a proper element of the general welfare. For example, in *Best* v. *Zoning Board,*[20] the issue involved the validity of an ordinance restricting development to only single family housing. The court stated: "Not only is the preservation of an attractive character of the community a proper element in the general welfare, but also the preservation of property value is a legitimate consideration."[21]

Such cases helped settle the theory that aesthetics was within the meaning of the term "general welfare." However, only a few decisions followed this lead, and it

was not until a number of years later that the courts begin to omit the economic factor attached to an aesthetics standard and recognize the latter on its own merit (Minano 1971).

Aesthetics (Alone) Warrants Exercise of the Police Power

It was not until 1963 that the New York Supreme Court supported a theory that zoning for aesthetic considerations is a valid exercise of the police power. The case of *People* v. *Stover*[22] involved a general ordinance prohibiting clotheslines in the front and side yards abutting a street, with a provision that in the case of unnecessary hardship, a permit could be applied for to circumvent the ordinance (Pearlstein 1972). The plaintiffs protesting the city's high taxes began to hang old clothes and rags in their front yard. When they applied for a permit to maintain the lines, it was denied. The plaintiffs appealed, alleging the ordinance was unconstitutionally depriving them of their property without due process.

The court first addressed the allegation by arguing that the ordinance had the assigned purpose of providing clear visibility at streetcorners to reduce accidents, thereby promoting the public safety. It went on to further hold that

the ordinance may be sustained as an attempt to preserve the residential appearance of the city and its property value by banning, insofar as practical, unsightly clotheslines from yards abutting a public street. In other words, the statute, though based on what may be termed aesthetic considerations, proscribes conduct which offends sensibilities and tends to debase the community and reduce real estate value.[23]

The court went further than any previous one and analyzed the problem by restricting the use of land for aesthetics purposes (Pearlstein 1972). After reviewing the trends in aesthetic zoning up to that time, the court held that once aesthetics was considered a valid subject of legislative concern, it was justifiable that reasonable legislation designed to promote an aesthetics purpose was a valid exercise of the police power (Minano 1971). (See Chapter 4 for an up-to-date state-by-state review of the trend to accept aesthetics alone as a valid basis for land use control through zoning.)

[18]Id. at 33.
[19]69 N.W.2d 217 (269 Wis. 262) cert. den. 350 U.S. 841 (1955).
[20]Best v. Zoning Board of Adjustment 393 Pa.106, 141 A.2d 606 (1958).
[21]141 A.2d at 612.
[22]12 N.Y.2d 462, 191 N.E.2d 272, 240 N.Y.S.2d 734, appeal dismissed, 375 U.S. 42 (1963).
[23]Id. at 738, 191 N.E.2d at 277.

The environmental or community planner can utilize his or her knowledge of the aesthetic contextual situation, flexibility of means, and planning sophistication to preserve neighborhood character and minimize exclusionary practices of zoning. To illustrate this planning approach, we will describe how a scenic resource inventory was incorporated into the land use planning of Dennis, Massachusetts. However, before presenting this case study, let us review some key concepts from Chapter 2.

AESTHETIC OR SCENIC INVENTORIES AND ANALYSIS

An inventory of scenic resources can be an important component of an overall environmental inventory. The results of a scenic inventory can be used in developing comprehensive plans, land use ordinances, and design guidelines; determining the potential visual impact of a proposed development; educating community residents; deciding what properties to acquire or protect through easements; and determining locations of new developments, roads, trails, or utility lines. In this case, we are particularly interested in the application of the scenic inventory to the development of comprehensive plans and local land use control ordinances.

The scenic analysis approach chosen should depend largely on how the information will be used. If a zoning ordinance is going to be based in part on a survey of citizens' preferences, for example, a statistically sound system of sampling public opinion is necessary. An inventory of scenic features should not be limited to what is "beautiful." Scraggly hedgerows and a dilapidated store, while not scenic, may be prominent visual features that serve as major points to identify a community and should be preserved because of their cultural and social significance (Lynch 1960).

A good way to introduce the issue of visual quality in a community is to show photographs (both scenic and less so) to residents and ask them to discuss their impressions of the views, their opinions on what constitutes good design, and their feelings about what resources are important to protect (see Wilmott, Smardon, and McNeil 1983).

CITIZEN PREFERENCE SURVEYS

Appraisals using the opinions of citizens have the obvious advantage of reflecting a community's values and attitudes. However, professional assistance is advisable, particularly if results of the survey will be used as the basis for an ordinance. Community volunteers can undertake much of the work. Discussion of the scenic qualities they appreciate in their community's landscape gives citizens an opportunity to increase their environmental awareness.

There are many ways to solicit citizens' opinions (see Smardon, Palmer, and Felleman 1986; Palmer 1983b). One method is for surveyors to take photographs of typical scenes throughout the community and ask citizens to rate the beauty of each scene on, say, a five-point scale or to rank the photographs in order of scenic preference. The results can be mapped. To ensure optimum objectivity, those conducting the survey should attempt to obtain photographs as uniform in quality and lighting conditions as possible. Obviously, how a picture is taken can have a major bearing on how a viewer ranks the quality of the scene it depicts.

Case Study: Dennis, Massachusetts, Visual Survey for Comprehensive Planning[24]

Introduction

Local citizens are left feeling helpless in the wake of unchecked growth. This sense of helplessness is particularly acute when they are trying to protect the visual resources to which they have intense emotional associations yet find difficult to describe systematically. This case study illustrates how a group of citizens from the town of Dennis on Cape Cod sought to inventory and evaluate their local visual resources. This effort was part of a larger resource analysis conducted by citizens of Dennis with technical assistance from the Massachusetts Natural Resource Planning Program administered by the Soil Conservation Service (Chandler 1976).[25]

---

[24]This case study was previously published as J. F. Palmer, 1983, *Assessment of Coastal Wetlands in Dennis, Massachusetts* in R. C. Smardon, ed., *The Future of Wetlands; Assessing Visual-Cultural Values,* Allenheld-Osmun, Totowa, NJ. Reproduced with the permission of the author.

[25]The data used in this case study were collected by members of the Dennis Comprehensive Planning Committee with technical assistance from Geoffrey Chandler as part of the Massachusetts Natural Resource Planning Program. This planning program of the Soil Conservation Service offers the methods and technical assistance for communities systematically to collect, evaluate, and utilize information concerning their natural resources.

The objectives of the visual resource survey were:

1. Involve a large number of people in the planning process and increase their awareness of the community's visual resources.
2. Find the community's special image of its land and preserve this image for future residents.
3. Determine which local landscapes are preferred by local citizens.
4. Provide communities with useful information on landscape quality for practical planning purposes (USDA SCS 1977).

To meet these objectives, two types of information concerning local perceptions of the Dennis landscape were collected. The first type is used to classify landscape views based on their perceived similarity; the second provides a rating of the scenic value of these same landscape views.

Procedure

Preparation for the visual resource inventory began in the spring of 1976 with a committee of concerned citizens. In order to develop a sample of landscape views, each member of the committee indicated, on a local street map, views that he or she considered representative of the range of views in Dennis. Each of these views was photographed in color using a 35-millimeter wide-angle lens. The 5-by-7-inch prints of these scenes were borderless with a matte finish and were mounted on thin cardboard. The committee then selected the 56 photographs that it felt most accurately portrayed the range of landscapes in Dennis.

The cooperation of a random sample of registered voters was then sought to evaluate the visual quality of these 56 landscape views. A total of 96 citizens contributed judgments of landscape quality by sorting the photographs according to one of the different sets of instructions. In the first set the participants were told:

Each of these photographs represents a landscape view found in Dennis. For the purposes of this study, the "landscape" may be thought of as all the various elements that you see in the photograph.
Please sort these photographs into piles containing other landscapes which you feel are similar. We request that each pile you form has three or more landscapes each. You may make as many piles as you like.

In addition, for each pile the participants were asked to "describe in a few words or phrases those characteristics that best represent the similarities of the landscapes in the group."

The second set of instructions asked the participants to

sort the 56 photographs into 7 piles according to the scenic value of the landscape in the photos. In pile #1, place 3 landscapes which you think have the highest scenic value. In pile #7, place 3 landscapes which you think have the lowest scenic value. From

the remaining 50 landscapes place the 7 with the highest scenic value in pile #2, and 7 with the lowest scenic value in pile #6. From the remaining 36 landscapes, place the 11 with the highest scenic value in pile #3, and 11 with the lowest scenic value in pile #5. Place the remaining 14 landscapes in pile #4.

Each respondent was then randomly selected to answer one or two additional sets of questions investigating the different factors that contribute to the scenic value of the landscape. In one case they were instructed to:

describe in either a few words or phrases those factors which add the most to the scenic value of pile #1. . . . Identify those factors which detract the most from the scenic value of pile #7. . . . Describe those factors which make the scenic value of pile #4 mediocre.

In the other case respondents were provided with a checklist of 56 factors that were thought to influence scenic value. The respondents were asked to

identify three landscape factors that add to the scenic value of each of the three photographs in pile #1. . . . Next identify three landscape factors that detract from the scenic value of each of the three landscapes you placed in pile #7. . . . Now take the first six photographs from pile #4 and for each of these landscapes identify three factors which add and detract from the scenic value of these landscapes.

The participants' recorded responses were later analyzed by a local citizens' committee and a technical assistant.

Results

While the citizens who participated in the visual resource survey were selected randomly from the current list of registered voters, it is not possible to test their representativeness of the total population of Dennis. The town has grown so fast in the last decade that local census data are outdated and current population characteristics are unknown. However, the participants do represent a full range of ages, occupations, sex, residential neighborhoods, and lengths of residence. In addition, there are no significant differences among the groups of participants who performed the three sorting tasks. Possibly the most important test of representativeness is that the townfolk seem to accept the validity of the results and are comfortable with its representation of their point of view.

Conceptual Classification of Landscapes

A total of 27 citizens sorted the landscape views according to their similarity. Using a clustering procedure developed by

Palmer and Zube (1976), the judgments of landscape similarity made by these citizens are aggregated into a conceptual classification of the different landscape types in Dennis. Six distinct types are identified: (1) marsh and wooded landscapes; (2) beach and water landscapes; (3) suburban development; (4) developed open land; (5) commercial and municipal landscapes; and (6) high-density residential landscapes. A diagrammatic summary of perceived similarity among these types is shown in Figure 5.4. A description of the essential characteristics of each landscape type is obtained through a systematic content analysis of the words and phrases that the participants used to characterize their piles of similar landscapes.

Marsh and Wooded Landscapes

These are perceived to be the most "natural" scenes in Dennis. "They are the open spaces we want to protect and keep for birds and men alike." Evoking a sense of "peacefulness" and "beauty," this type is closely identified with the "Cape Cod landscape." As illustrated in Figure 5.5, a wide variety of wetland types is represented, ranging from coastal marshes to shrub swamp. The identifying characteristic as perceived by the participants is the comparatively lush vegetation pattern, which varies from low-lying "marshland" to higher "woodlands." Those wooded areas in the landscape sample are included in this type.

It is interesting to speculate that the more wooded scenes might have been placed in a class of their own if suitable photographic representations had been available. However, given the Cape's gently undulating topography, it is nearly impossible to photograph the woods because of the trees in the way.

Beach and Water Landscapes

The interface between "beaches and sand dunes" and "saltwater" is the dominant conceptual characteristic of this type, as exemplified by Figure 5.6. Therefore, a tidal salt marsh is perceived as part of this class when the tide is in and as a marsh landscape when the tide is out.

These scenes are generally "unspoiled" and "void of

FIGURE 5.5 a, b　Marsh and wooded landscapes of high and low scenic value

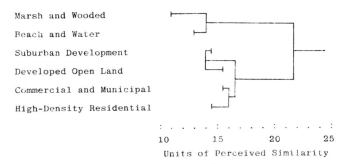

FIGURE 5.4　Perceived similarity among the landscape types in Dennis, Massachusetts

human habitation": Appropriate human presence is manifested through such recreational attractions as "swimming and fishing." The participants in this survey are sensitive to the use of certain areas in this landscape type by "tourists," while others are "for the year-round resident who wants to get away from the tourists." These scenes are "attractive" in their more natural state but are beset by the pressures of "capitalistic endeavor," which invariably creates a sense "that it is not very appealing to the eye." This degradation through private exploitation becomes more significant because of the important role this landscape type plays in the local perception of the Cape's regional identity.

Suburban Development

In describing suburban development, the roles played by the natural elements, the presence of water, or aspects of landform are rarely mentioned. These are "low-density residen-

FIGURE 5.6 a, b   Beach and water landscapes of high and low scenic value

FIGURE 5.7 a, b   Suburban developments of high and low scenic value

tial areas" and "quiet country lanes" that pass "through the countryside without houses directly on the roads." This is the "hometown Cape" in which the "locals" live. Participants frequently distinguish the more traditional, older developments from the newer, more modern forms within this type. For instance, in grouping photos one participant separates "single-family dwellings in developments" from "quiet country roads with vintage houses." Figure 5.7 illustrates a residence and a highway that are both from this landscape type.

Developed Open Land

Developed open land is illustrated in a small group of scenes depicting open land associated with some form of development (Figure 5.8). Included with this group are a cemetery, a

power-line right-of-way, a golf course, and a churchyard. Their distinguishing characteristic is that they are perceived as "developed areas that exhibit compatibility with the environment." Participants commonly associate them with one of the other developed landscape types — sometimes with suburban development because they are "historic" and conceptually part of the "hometown Cape," and other times with the commercial and municipal landscapes because of their "public service" character.

Commercial and Municipal Landscapes

Different types of nonresidential developed areas are gathered together in this conceptual class, which is illustrated in

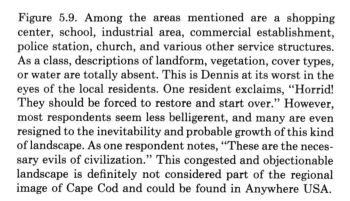

FIGURE 5.8 a, b   Developed open land of high and low scenic value

FIGURE 5.9 a, b   Commercial and municipal landscapes of high and low scenic value

Figure 5.9. Among the areas mentioned are a shopping center, school, industrial area, commercial establishment, police station, church, and various other service structures. As a class, descriptions of landform, vegetation, cover types, or water are totally absent. This is Dennis at its worst in the eyes of the local residents. One resident exclaims, "Horrid! They should be forced to restore and start over." However, most respondents seem less belligerent, and many are even resigned to the inevitability and probable growth of this kind of landscape. As one respondent notes, "These are the necessary evils of civilization." This congested and objectionable landscape is definitely not considered part of the regional image of Cape Cod and could be found in Anywhere USA.

High-Density Residential Landscapes

High-density residential landscapes, exemplified in Figure 5.10, are perceived as the places where the "off-Cape" population stays. Interestingly, they are not called "homes" but "rental units," a type of commercial venture. Termed "claptraps" and "schlock residential" areas, they are a scenic

blight in the eyes of the local residents. There is some resignation that they are "necessary," but there is also substantial concern that they are rapidly encroaching upon the most valuable areas of the Cape. One respondent observes acutely: "Here's some near epitome of the gross overpopulation of an area. Everyone wants a piece of beauty and bit by bit the beauty is removed." In this case, the beauty comes from the beach and water landscapes, which have special qualities that are conspicuously absent from the suburban landscapes where the respondents live.

Judgments of Scenic Value

Two groups of citizens, which were part of 95 local citizens, were asked to sort the landscape views according to scenic value: 37 were asked to use their own words or phrases to describe the qualities that added or detracted from the scenes; 32 were given a landscape-factor checklist as a means of providing similar information. The scenic resource value for a particular landscape view is the mean rating it received from the respondents. The scenic resource values for all landscape

FIGURE 5.10 a, b   High-density residential landscapes of high and low scenic value

views as judged by both groups are compared using t-tests. In only two instances are the judgments significantly different ($p < .05$). Therefore, the scenic resource values used below are calculated from the ratings by all 69 respondents.

A clear pattern emerges from the content analysis of the words and phrases respondents used to describe the factors that contribute to the landscape's scenic value. The most scenic landscapes are overwhelmingly perceived as "natural" and even "wild" by some. The presence of water and the dominance of "green" vegetation are mentioned only in connection with these highly valued scenes. Respondents seem to favor a pastoral notion of what is scenic, characterizing it as "well kept" and "spacious" with "distant prospects," the way Cape Cod "should look." There are no "gross manmade additions," and where buildings appear in the scene they are "distant" and "fit in on the Cape." There also seems to be a compositional value seen in the "interplay of land and water, colors and shapes."

The least scenic landscapes are perceived as "cluttered" and "unimaginative" views dominated by features that do not fit, such as "signs," "overhead wires," "broken asphalt," "supermarkets," "concrete mixing plant." These are "lifeless" and "artificial" scenes "without trees and bushes."

Those scenes that are given moderate ratings are primarily characterized as being "ordinary" and "anywhere" — not unique to Cape Cod. "Misfit" features also characterize this group, but they are less dominant than in the least scenic landscapes.

The Scenic Value of Landscape Types

The usefulness of the visual resource survey in Dennis becomes more apparent when the scenic value for each landscape type is compared with the other types. An analysis of variance ($F = 642.4$, $df = 5, 3789, 3794$, $p < .001$) indicates more significant differences in scenic value among rather than within landscape types. The differences in scenic value between landscape types are investigated further using t-tests, shown in Table 5.1. In most cases, significant differ-

TABLE 5.1   *T*-tests Comparing Mean Scenic Value for Each Landscape Type

Landscape Type	n[b]	$\bar{x}$	T-value[a]				
			Beach	Marsh	Suburban	Open Land	Commercial
Beach and Water	759	2.99					
Marsh and Wooded	552	2.91	1.10n.s.				
Suburban Development	759	3.47	−8.04*	−8.80*			
Developed Open Land	276	3.52	−5.85*	−6.50*	−.54n.s.		
Commercial and Municipal	828	5.32	−39.78*	−38.92*	−33.36*	−20.62*	
High-Density Residential	621	5.27	−37.78*	−37.09*	−31.38*	−19.74*	.98n.s

Notes. [a]The t-values reported here are for independent groups with unequal variances; therefore, the values are an approximation.

[b]This value is the total number of ratings made by 69 respondents of all the scenes within a landscape type.

Significance: n.s. $p \geq .05$* $p < .001$

ences were found. However, no significance is found between those pairs of landscape types that are shown in Figure 5.4 as being conceptually most similar. For instance, the marsh and wooded landscapes and the beach and water landscapes are perceived as being very similar and thus do not have significantly different scenic values. However, they are both perceived as quite dissimilar from the high-density residential landscapes, which have significantly poorer scenic value.

The results of the landscape-factor checklist, which are summarized in Tables 5.2 and 5.3 according to landscape type, give some indication of what factors influence scenic value for each type. The pattern that emerges from these tables corroborates the prior content analysis of what contributes to scenic value. A romantic notion of the most scenic prevails, while misfit characteristics dominate the least scenic landscapes. This pattern can also be seen by comparing the examples in Figures 5.5 through 5.10 of high and low scenic value for each landscape type.

A more careful examination of Tables 5.2 and 5.3 provides several additional insights. For instance, both beach and water and marsh and wooded landscapes are valued for their "naturalness." However, the marshes are primarily valued for their emotional association—their serenity, vastness, and uniqueness. In contrast, those aspects of a beach that contribute to its quality are physical—the water, sand, and shoreline.

Another interesting implication of these tables is that vegetation and natural materials play an important role in the scenic value of the less densely developed areas. Where roads, overhead lines, and the like are not effectively screened, scenic value drops. In contrast, building characteristics such as materials, design, color, and setback become important in more densely developed landscape types. In these situations the buildings are so concentrated or massive that they cannot be completely screened. All one expects is the mitigation of a barren appearance through appropriate landscaping.

Summary and Implementation

Sometimes it is awkward to be a landscape planner committed to the development of systematic methods for considera-tion of the landscape as a visual resource. The public often responds with skepticism. It is a measure of success that the results of this visual survey seem so obvious. Yet few critics would ever give prior support to the possibility that there is substantial agreement regarding the landscape types perceived in an area as well as what contributes to their scenic value.

In Dennis there seems to be a reasonable acceptance of the results of the visual resource survey, probably because of the large degree of local control and participation throughout the entire process. This survey is one of the reasons why Dennis was named All-American City for 1978. When bestowing the award, the National Municipal League of Cities and Towns stated that it was particularly impressed by the example Dennis provided other towns for (1) citizen participation, (2) comprehensive planning, and (3) conservation acquisition and historic preservation. The visual resource survey contributed to each of these areas.

One important ramification of the visual resource survey is its utility as a powerful tool for education. It has brought "visual quality" out of the closet and made it a respectable topic in local planning. It is now clearer to the local decision-makers that there are ways to describe landscape appearances systematically. Even more important, there is much more substantial agreement among town residents than anyone had expected. In addition to being used in town meetings, photographs are being shown to students in the public schools to make them more aware of their local visual resource.

The second ramification of the survey is its influence on the new zoning bylaws for the town of Dennis. While all the changes are founded on some aspect of the Comprehensive Natural Resource Planning Program survey, they also have a visual basis that is recognized by the local citizens. For instance, the study's results suggest that if the presence of any structure in the foreground of a beach and water or marsh and wooded landscape becomes so dominant, then the pastoral image is destroyed. The possibility of this visual incompatibility is given some credence by one landscape view that did not belong to any landscape type—a scene viewed across a salt marsh toward a densely developed residential area. Other

TABLE 5.2   Landscape Factors That Add to the Scenic Value of Each Landscape Type

	Landscape Types					
Rank[a]	Beach and Water	Marsh and Wooded	Suburban Development	Developed Open Land	Commercial and Municipal	High-Density Residential
Highest:						
1.	Naturalness	Serenity	Serenity	Serenity		
2.	Water	Vastness	Local character			
3.	Shoreline	Naturalness				
Moderate:						
1.	Water	Naturalness	Vegetation	Serenity	Building color	Building design
2.	Depth of view	Natural color	Natural color	Naturalness	Building design	Walls and fences
3.	Natural color		Naturalness		Natural color	
4.			Depth of view			

Notes.   The landscape factor checklist was completed by 28 respondents.
[a]Landscapes with the highest scenic value were in pile #1, and those with moderate scenic value were in pile #4.

TABLE 5.3 Landscape Factors that Detract from the Scenic Value of Each Landscape Type

Rank[a]	Beach and Water	Marsh and Wooded	Suburban Development	Developed Open Land	Commercial and Municipal	High-Density Residential
Lowest:						
1.					Overhead wire	Bare earth
2.					Barrenness	Barrenness
3.					Cars and trucks	Building design
4.						Overhead wire
5.						Building material
6.						Building setback
Moderate:						
1.	Horizon line	Horizon line	Roads	Overhead wire	Overhead wire	Building color
2.	Building design	Barrenness	Pavement	Roads	Cars and trucks	Building material
3.	Overhead wire	Natural color	Cars and trucks			Straight line
4.	Flatness					

Notes: The landscape factor checklist was completed by 28 respondents.

[a]Landscapes with the lowest scenic value were in pile #7, and those with moderate scenic value were in pile #4.

areas where beach cottages composed the foreground were obviously judged high-density residential landscapes. Therefore, future commercial and high-density residential developments will be concentrated in those areas already identified with these landscape types. Through zoning, a serious attempt is being made to halt the sprawl of these landscapes and encourage infilling. An attempt is also being made to protect the integrity of undeveloped natural areas. Those areas near coastal beaches and marshes are rezoned from a minimum lot size of 20,000 square feet to a minimum of 60,000 square feet. These areas have the highest scenic value and are least able to absorb development. The remaining natural landscapes are rezoned to a minimum lot size of 40,000 square feet. All areas that are already considered suburban development remain at the previous minimum lot size of 20,000 square feet.

The third ramification of the survey is the town's commitment to make a public acquisition of those areas that are visually most valuable. In 1979 the citizens of Dennis purchased 25 acres of prime marshland and 200 acres of beachfront. More has been acquired since. These areas are added to the town's already extensive public conservation and recreation areas.

The key phrase here is "shared perceptions." A well-done survey of visual perceptions of a community could be used, as in Dennis, to legislate local ordinances for protecting aesthetic resources. By doing their homework, communities will find that such ordinances will be very defensible from both legal and scientific perspectives.

References

Agee, J. 1965. Aesthetic zoning; A current evaluation of the law. *University of Florida Law Review,* 18: 430–439.

Anderson, R. M. 1984. *New York zoning law and practice.* Lawyers Cooperative Publishing.

Arnold, D. S., ed. 1979. *The practice of local government planning.* International City Management Association, Washington, D.C.

Brace, P. 1980. Urban aesthetics and the courts. *Environmental Comment* July (1980) 16–19.

Carlin, P. N. 1960. The aesthetic as a factor considered in zoning. *Wyoming Law Journal,* 15(1): 77–85.

Chandler, G. B. 1976. *Natural and visual resources, Dennis, Massachusetts.* Dennis Conservation Commission and Planning Board, Dennis, MA.

Dukerminier, J. J., Jr. 1955. Zoning for aesthetic objectives: A reappraisal. *Law and Contemporary Problems,* 20: 218–237.

Gibson, F., J. Karp, and E. Klyman. 1992. *Real estate law.* Dearborn.

Guberman, T. 1976. Aesthetic zoning. *Urban Law Annual,* 2: 295–307.

King, J. B., Jr. 1970. Zoning for aesthetics substantially reducing property values. *Washington and Lee Law Review,* 27: 303–311.

Leighty, L. L. 1971. Aesthetics as a legal basis for environmental control. *Wayne Law Review,* 17: 1347–1396.

Lorensen, W. D. 1957. Municipal corporations: Aesthetic zoning under the police power. *Nebraska Law Review,* 35: 143–146.

Lynch, K. 1960. *Image of a city.* MIT Press.

Masotti, L. H., and Selfon, B. D. 1969. Aesthetic zoning under the police power. *Journal of Urban Law,* 46: 773–787.

Meshenberg, M. J. *The Language of zoning.* Planning Advisory Report No. 322, American Planning Association.

Miller, D. J. 1967. Aesthetic zoning: An answer to billboard blight. *Syracuse Law Review.* 19(1): 87–94.

Minano, D. R. 1971. Aesthetic zoning: The creation of a new standard. *Journal of Urban Law,* 48: 740–754.

Newsom, M. D. 1969. Zoning for beauty. *New England Law Review,* 5(1): 1–16.

Norton, T. M. 1967. Police power, planning and aesthetics. *Santa Clara Lawyer,* 7(2): 171–187.

Note 1964. Zoning, aesthetics and the First Amendment. *Columbia Law Review,* 64: 81–108.

O'Neil, V. R. 1967. Aesthetic zoning: The chameleon of zoning. *Tulsa Law Journal,* 4(1): 48–68.

Palmer, J. F. 1983a. Assessment of coastal wetlands in Dennis, Massachusetts. In *The future of wetlands: Assessing visual-cultural values,* R. C. Smardon, ed., Allenheld-Osmun, pp. 65–80.

———. 1983b. Visual quality and visual assessment. In *Social impact assessment methods,* K. Finsterbusch, L. G. Llewellyn, and C. P. Wolf, ed., Sage. pp. 263–283.

Palmer, J. F and E. H. Zube. 1976. Numerical and perceptual landscape classification. In E. H. Zube, ed., *Studies in Landscape Perception.* Institute for Man and Environment, University of Massachusetts, Amherst.

Pearlstein, R. S. 1972. The aesthetic factor in zoning. *Duquesne Law Review,* 11: 204–241.

Rodda, C. 1954. The accomplishment of aesthetic purposes under the police power. *Southern California Law Review,* 27: 149–179.

Rose, M., and G. Yim. 1962. Aesthetics as a zoning consideration. *The Hastings Law Journal,* 13(3): 374–381.

Sager, L. G. 1969. Tight little islands: Exclusionary zoning, equal protection, and the indigent. *Stanford Law Review,* 21(4): 767–800.

Smardon, R. C., Palmer, J. F., and Felleman, J. P., eds. 1986. *Foundations for visual project analysis.* John Wiley.

Stokes, S., and Watson, E. 1989. *Saving the countryside.* Johns Hopkins University Press, Baltimore.

Swietlik, J. 1955. Aesthetics under the zoning power. *Marquette Law Review,* 39(1): 135–145.

Univ. of Southern Maine. 1990. *The hidden design in land use ordinances.* University of Southern Maine Design Arts Project, Portland.

USDA Soil Conservation Service. 1977. *A natural resources planning program handbook* (draft).

Wilcox, C. J. 1970. Aesthetic considerations in land use planning. *Albany Law Review,* 35(1): 126–147.

Wilmott, G., Smardon, R. C., and McNeil, R. 1983. Waterfront revitalization in Clayton, New York. *Small Town,* 14(3): 12–19.

Chapter 6

Architectural Regulation, Preservation, and Design Review

INTRODUCTION

This chapter addresses issues related to architectural regulation, preservation, and design review. Architectural control, as opposed to traditional zoning and land use control, has to do with the preservation or changes related to individual structures or groups of structures in terms of the structures' height, mass, design, materials, color, and other physical architectural attributes (Figure 6.1).

As America became more urban, and as new architectural and building techniques allowed the construction of ever more massive structures, cities and towns increasingly showed concern about retaining their character. Drawing on European precedents, particularly from Germany, local governments began experimenting with zoning and architectural controls. Some of the pioneer cases involved height restrictions. As early as 1888, a New York court approved an 80-foot height limitation on residential structures. In 1904, the city of Baltimore adopted a 70-foot maximum-height regulation to maintain the character of its neighborhoods and commercial areas. The same year, the city of Boston, which had grown sensitive to the need for preservation due to the destruction of many historic build-

ings in the 1800s, enacted similar legislation that prescribed a lower height for buildings constructed in residential areas than for those in commercial districts. So communities started early with architectural regulation and preservation.

Preservation of historic values is very much bound up with aesthetics values. In a dissent by Judge Jason in a New York Court of Appeals case *Lutheran Church in America* v. *City of New York,* he states:

[W]hile economics is perhaps inextricably intertwined with such legislation, in the main the purposes sought to be achieved are aesthetic. Historic preservation promotes aesthetic values by adding to the variety, the beauty and the quality of life.[1]

To preserve the aesthetic character of "quaint" and delightful villages in the face of urban growth, the federal government,[2] all states, and over 2,000 municipalities[3] have enacted historic preservation laws. Federal preservation activities include the Historic American Buildings and Sites Surveys of the 1930s,[4] the consolidation of control over historic property in the National Park Service in 1933,[5] and the Historic Sites Act of 1935,[6] which declared the preservation of historic prop-

---

[1]Lutheran Church in America v. City of N.Y. 316 N.E.2d 305, 314 n. 14 (1974).

[2]Historic Sites Act, 19 U.S.C. ss. 461–67 (1988).

[3]See Duerkson, 1983, A handbook of Historic Preservation Law, The Conservation Foundation, Wash., D.C.

[4]R. Lee, United States: Historical and Archeological Monuments. National Historic Trust Team Memo 11 (1951) at 14.

[5]Id. at 16.

[6]16 U.S.C. ss. 461–67 (1988).

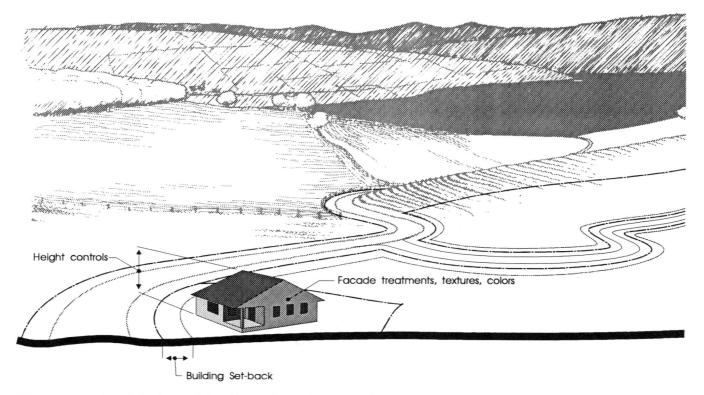

Height controls

Facade treatments, textures, colors

Building Set-back

FIGURE 6.1   Generic landscape with architectural control measures. *Credit: Scott Shannon*

erty a national policy of the United States.[7] State preservation activities (Wilson and Winkler 1971) have centered on the creation of historic parks and museums and the encouragement of quasi-official state historical societies. The National Trust for Historic Preservation was created to succeed the National Council for Historic Sites and Buildings in 1949.[8] It is a nationwide organization that coordinates the activities of the diverse state and local preservation organizations.

A key piece of federal legislation regarding the protection of historical aesthetic values is the National Historic Preservation Act of 1966.[9] Section 106[10] of the act requires the consideration, prior to the expenditure of federal funds, of the effect of any federal, federally assisted, or federally licensed undertaking on any district, site, building, structure, or object that is listed on the National Register of Historic Places. This provision, in conjunction with the National Environmental Policy Act,[11] has created problems for urban development and especially federally funded highway projects proposed for historically "rich" urban areas. Section 106 requires a detailed analysis of impacts on historic structures and properties as part of the environmental analysis of such projects, thus causing delays and sometimes even stopping a project.

The National Register of Historic Places lists districts, sites, buildings, structures, or objects that are significant to the history, architecture, archeology, and culture of the United States. Published procedures[12] set forth the policy of the Advisory Council on Historic Preservation regarding compliance with Section 106 of the National Historic Preservation Act of 1966.[13]

Other federal acts affecting historical resources include Public Law 92-6362, which allows donation of federally owned historical properties to state or local governments, and the Open Space Act,[14] which pro-

[7]Id.

[8]16 U.S.C. ss. 468–68c (1988).

[9]16 U.S.C. 470 et seq. (1988).

[10]Id.

[11]42 U.S.C. 4321 et seq. (1988).

[12]See FR 37, Volume 220 (Nov. 14, 1972). Advisory Council on Historic Preservation, "National Register of Historic Places — Protection of Properties; Procedures for Compliance."

[13]16 U.S.C. 470 et seq. (1988).

[14]42 U.S.C. s. 1500 a-1.

vides grants for historic preservation administered by the Secretary of Housing and Urban Development.

Much of the action though, in terms of litigation[15] and development of useful tools[16] for historical preservation, has been at the local level and in a predominantly urban context (see Rose 1981; Crumpler 1974; McMillan 1971; Costonis 1985; Poole 1987; Anderson 1960; Loflin 1971; Rankin 1971; and Goldstone 1971). By looking at some of the early roots of legislation for historic preservation one can see basic rationales or themes for preservation.

THEMES FOR PRESERVATION

Rose (1981) suggests three themes, or rationales, for community building preservation: (1) preservation as inspiration, (2) preservation for architectural merit, and (3) preservation for community.

Preservation as "Inspiration" (see Figure 6.2)

The inspirational view of preservation was developed in the nineteenth century via inspiration and the no-

[15]See City of New Orleans v. Levy, 223 La. 14, 64 So. 2d. 798 (1953) (upholding the New Orleans ordinance to preserve the Vieux Carré section); Reynolds Metals Co. v. Martin, 269 Ky. 378, 107 S.W.2d. 251 (1937) (Use of property tax exemption to encourage private expenditures for restoration purposes); U.S. v. Gettysburg Elec. R. Co., 160 U.S. 668 (1896) (eminent domain power upheld in acquiring historic property); and Vieux Carré Property Owners v. City of New Orleans, 246 La. 788, 167 So.2d.367 (1964) (ordinance which exempts part of the Vieux Carré section of the preservation regulations is unconstitutional).

[16]See Jacob Morrison, 1965, Historic Preservation Law, National Trust for Historic Preservation, Wash, D.C. (2d. edition); Supplement, April 5, 1972, self-published, 315 Carondelet Building, New Orleans, Louisiana; National Trust for Historic Preservation, 1972, Legal Techniques in Historic Preservation, National Trust for Historic Preservation, Wash., D.C.

FIGURE 6.2 a, b, c   Preservation as inspiration — Gettysburg National Battlefield and Sachetts Harbor, N.Y. *Photo credit: James F. Palmer*

tion that civic education was intended to have important political ramifications (Rose 1981). This was true of both public and private preservation efforts. Embodied in private activities was the idea that reminders of the past can link us together in a national community. One of the inspirational view preservation cases of that era, *United States* v. *Gettysburg Electric Railway Company,*[17] is illustrative (see Figure 6.2). The United States condemned property for the creation of a national battlefield memorial at Gettysburg, and the question arose whether condemnation was for a "public use." Justice Peck's opinion in this decision states two key elements of continuing and critical importance:

1. the idea that preservation can in fact have a political purpose of fostering a sense of community;
2. the understanding that a place can convey this sense of community, or more generally, that visual surroundings work a political effect on our consciousness (Rose 1981).

Preservation for Architectural Merit

According to Rose (1981), with the shift in interest to architectural merit, public involvement took the form of architectural controls designed to protect a few well-known old districts, such as Charleston, South Carolina, and New Orleans (see Figure 6.3). Challenges to these architectural controls gave courts an opportunity for reasoned articulation of the purpose of preservation. According to some legal commentators, although judicial opinions have generally upheld architectural controls in such application contexts, analysis (1) has not included anything more than the validity (or invalidity) of aesthetics regulation, and (2) has not distinguished historic preservation from aesthetics. Paramount to some legal critics (see Rose 1981; Costonis 1985; Poole 1987; Crumpler 1974; and McMillan 1971) is the need to build considerations of how and when communities may participate in the basic rationale for, and decisions affecting, historic preservation for architectural merit. Thus, who sets the standards and who are the tastemakers?

Preservation for Community

The third phase of historic preservation builds on elements of the past by expanding the substantive considerations implicit in *Gettysburg*. It increases the attention paid to procedure and focuses on the contribution of the physical environment to the maintenance of community—not the national community as in *Get-*

FIGURE 6.3   Preservation for architectural merit—historic building in San Antonio. *Photo credit: R. C. Smardon*

tysburg, but the smaller community of the city or neighborhood (Figure 6.4).

If community building is the central direction of recent preservation activity, then several consequences must flow according to Rose (1981). First, the age and fame of a structure are only two among several elements, including scale, distinctiveness of design, and location, that should be considered in assessing a building's importance to the community. Second, because a community exists over time, the present community members' perception of building value should be considered. However important it may be to conserve the indicators of the past, some latitude must remain for the contribution of the present. Third, a community-building rationale should place preservation, and the

---

[17]160 U.S. 668 (1896).

FIGURE 6.4   Preservation for community character—in Brooklyn Heights streetscape. *Photo credit: George W. Curry*

physical surroundings generally, in a larger perspective of community needs. Finally, it should be recognized that physical surroundings play a critical role in the community. Those surroundings cannot be viewed as the preserve of the aesthetics buffs but must become an issue for a broader constituency.

Thus the motivation for architectural preservation and control has evolved from national historic inspirational preservation, to preservation for architectural merit, to community-motivated preservation.

APPLICATION CONTEXTS FOR ARCHITECTURAL CONTROL

It is instructive to look at how architectural review ordinances have been created and at their intended application. Poole (1987), in a review of architectural appearance regulations, provides a very useful list of application contexts:

1. To prevent the construction of buildings that are excessively different from nearby buildings (Figure 6.5). This is what Costonis (1989) terms protection from "aliens." It is probably the most common form of appearance review ordinance. As revealed by case law and by the nature of communities adopting such ordinances, this form is principally suburban. It is frequently used to protect existing mid- and upper-level income, single-family neighborhoods from the intrusion of radically different architectural designs. However, many communities exclude single-family homes from their review. An example would be the Lake Forest, Illinois, ordinance.
2. To prevent the construction of buildings that are excessively similar, or an anti-lookalike ordinance (Figure 6.6). This form of architectural control is also a suburban concern, originating from the ex-

FIGURE 6.5   Architectural "Alien" in Louisville, Kentucky. *Photo credit: R. C. Smardon*

plosive growth of tract housing (such as Levittowns) in the 1950s. The ordinance is aimed principally at preventing the monotony of the same or similar home design in large subdivisions. An example, again, would be the Lake Forest, Illinois, ordinance.

FIGURE 6.6   Excessively similar architecture in Washington, D.C. *Photo credit: George W. Curry*

FIGURE 6.7   Historic district preservation in Back Bay, Boston. *Photo credit: George W. Curry*

FIGURE 6.9   Common architectural style in San Francisco. *Photo credit: George W. Curry*

3. To preserve the architectural style and integrity of a historic district (Figure 6.7). This is the type of ordinance enacted to preserve the French Quarter in New Orleans. It is probably the second most common type of architectural appearance review program. Its purpose is to prevent the destruction of

FIGURE 6.8   Architectural Landmark in Massachusetts. *Photo credit: R. C. Smardon*

historic buildings within a district and to require that new construction therein conform to the district's historic style. This is generally an urban application, inasmuch as districts imply a concentration of structures.

4. To preserve architectural features of a particular building designated as a landmark (Figure 6.8). The most prominent example of this form of review is the preservation of Grand Central Terminal in New York City. This landmark designation is for a structure in contrast to a historic district. Those programs may occur in urban, suburban, or rural settings, although the most controversial and noted cases are in urban settings. Costonis (1989) calls it protection of "icons." Whole books have been written about the legal and administrative issues of landmarks preservation programs (Costonis 1974 and 1989).

5. To create an architectural style within a district, such as an alpine village in Colorado. This use of architectural review generally requires an agreement at the earliest stages of community development. It may be both a suburban or central city residential (Figure 6.9) and a central business district concept in application. One of the earliest and most well known is the Coral Gables, Florida, program.

6. To create urban spaces, such as mini-parks and plazas that attract (desirable) users (Figure 6.10). Recent studies have shown that with proper architectural design, urban plazas and mini-parks can be made much more inviting to city residents as lunching, meeting, and recreation places. This "people activity" in turn makes an urban area more interesting and safe. The urban open-space program in New York City, which utilizes bonus points in negotiations with developers, is an example of such a program. Most programs are urban.

7. To create entrance districts along transportation

FIGURE 6.10   Create urban spaces — Paley Park, New York.
Photo credit: Mathew Potteiger

corridors. This type of appearance review program recognizes that people share familiar visual experiences in approaching cities and seeks to create a favorable impression. In a 1917 ordinance[18] Philadelphia provided for an art jury review of all works of art and all buildings within 200 feet of the Benjamin Franklin Parkway, a 1.25-mile drive into the city center. This last application will be treated in the following chapter, which focuses on outdoor advertising and visual corridor management.

Two applications, historic districts and historic landmarks, are of a historic preservation nature, but the rest of the architectural control programs are not and address different values or purposes. As we might expect, there have been court challenges to the legal defensibility of such architectural control ordinances, both historic preservation–based and others.

LEGAL ISSUES AND ARCHITECTURAL CONTROL

There have been two major constitutional issues related to implementation of architectural review programs and ordinances. These are the conflicts with the Fifth Amendment in terms of the due process and takings clauses, and with the First Amendment guarantee of freedom of expression, specifically, whether architecture is to be protected as a First Amendment right.

One of the most sensitive issues is the use of the police power regulation to restrict uses of a historic property or building without providing compensation.

The U.S. Supreme Court decided[19] that New York City did not violate the Penn Central Transportation Company's Fifth Amendment property rights when it designated Grand Central Terminal as a historic landmark, thus blocking the company's proposal for an office tower above the facility.

In a major decision that has sparked preservation efforts in other cities, the Court recognized that regulations for historic preservation, like zoning and other conventional land use controls, are valid exercises of the police power. During the last 50 years, the Court noted, over 500 cities and states have adopted landmark protection laws "to encourage or require the preservation of buildings and areas with historic or aesthetic importance."[20]

As stated in Justice William Brennan's opinion, the Court rejected Penn Central's argument that the landmark designation constituted a "taking" of property for which "just compensation" is required under the Fifth Amendment. The restrictions posed on the terminal site, Brennan said, "are substantially related to the promotion of the general welfare" and "permit reasonable beneficial use of the landmark site,"[21] namely, the terminal itself.

In a detailed review of the *Penn Central* case, Marcus (1979) suggests that the Supreme Court used three criteria for assessing whether there was an unconstitutional taking:

1) A government restriction on real property "not reasonably necessary to the effectuation of a substantial public purpose" may constitute a "taking" (i. e., arbitrariness).
2) A government restriction may have such "an unduly harsh impact on the owner's use of the property" or may so frustrate distinct investment-backed expectations as to amount to a "taking" (i. e., harshness).
3) Government actions that may be characterized as acquisitions of resources to permit or facilitate uniquely public functions have often been held to constitute "taking" (i. e., appropriation).

This case provided a blanket of protection for communities concerned about the taking issue and about individual landmark regulation because of the potentially expensive inverse condemnation consequences. Inverse condemnation in this context happens when a historic preservation ordinance prevents all alternative uses/reuses of a property and the property owner then sues the city for a condemnation award. In finding New York City's legislative judgment contained in its zoning

---

[18]Architectural Control, Am. Soc. of Planning Officials Information Report no. 6 (1949) at page 5.
[19]Penn Central Transp. Co. v. New York City, 438 U.S. 104, 129 (1978).
[20]Id.
[21]Id.

and landmark laws consistent with Fifth and Fourteenth Amendment requirements, the Supreme Court signaled to communities across the nation that they may consider awarding transferable development rights to property owners. These land owners are singled out to bear special burdens for public purpose land use reasons, as a valid means to cushion otherwise harsh regulatory impacts and restore an additional measure of real estate investment expectations.

Some interesting possibilities are suggested by the decision. While it emphasizes "historic" preservation, Justice William Brennan's opinion also stresses the need to protect areas of "aesthetic importance." That phrase is sufficiently vague to protect communities seeking to block development proposals on specific sites that have no real "historic" significance. Several legal commentators have taken up this issue since they feel this part of the *Penn Central* case opened the door to communities misusing historic or aesthetics rationales to stop development proposals (see Costonis 1985 and 1989). For further commentary addressing the Fifth Amendment and this case, please see Loflin (1971), Rankin (1971), and Costonis (1985).

There is also the issue of due process. In 1980 a federal district court[22] invalidated the federal National Historic Landmarks program because the program failed to provide due process protections to property owners when it declared a 14,000-acre site as the Green Springs National Historic District and enrolled the district in the National Register of Historic Places. The court held that the designation violated the due process rights of landowners within the district. The court also found that the two government actions, National Historic Landmark designation and National Register of Historic Places enrollment, constituted separate and concurrent interferences with property interests of area landowners. Such interests included targeting property for acquisition via eminent domain, federal restrictions through Section 106 of the National Historic Preservation Act, delay or denial of federal assistance because of Section 106 ties, and the tax status of property owners. Edmundson (1982) outlines these procedural concerns and suggests ways of protecting

the due process rights of property owners through development of appropriate notice, hearings, and standards.

Much of the case law related to architectural control ordinances focuses on First Amendment issues, including the often cited cases of *Schad*,[23] *Young*,[24] *Stoyanoff*,[25] *Metromedia*,[26] and *Vincent*.[27] One of the key issues throughout these cases is the regulation of protected expression (architecture) based on content (whatever is expressed by the architecture or signage). According to Poole (1987), government regulation of protected expression based on content is prohibited when the sole purpose of the regulation is to take a non-neutral (favorable or unfavorable) position. The example given is that Detroit's anti–skid row ordinance that regulates adult theaters was upheld not because of the city's disapproval of content but because centralization of such theaters in one location causes blight or further deterioration of neighborhoods. This is called the sole purpose/viewpoint neutral threshold inquiry and can be applied to all ordinances that propose to control architecture.

A four-part test used by the courts evolved from the *O'Brien*[28] case. It states that government regulation is sufficiently justified:

1. If it is within the constitutional power of government.
2. If it furthers an important or substantial government interest.
3. If the government interest is unrelated to the suppression of free expression.
4. If the incidental restriction on alleged First Amendment freedoms is no greater than is essential to the furtherance of that interest.

Costonis, on the other hand, rejects the *O'Brien* test and advocates the two-part test from *Schad:*

[w]hen a zoning law infringes upon a protected liberty it
(1) must be narrowly drawn, and
(2) must further a sufficiently substantial government interest.[29]

---

[22]Historic Green Springs, Inc. v. Bergland, 497 F. Supp. 839 (E.D. Va. 1980).

[23]Schad v. Borough of Mt. Ephraim, 482 U.S. 601 (1981) (invalidated ordinance preventing live nude dancing).

[24]Young v. American Mini Theaters Inc. 427 U.S. 50, *rch'g. denied* 429 U.S. 873 (1976). (Detroit ordinance requiring dispersal of adult theaters—upheld).

[25]State ex rel. Stoyanoff v. Berkeley 458 S.W.2d 305 (Mo. 1970) (rejection of a pyramid shaped home by citizens of Ladue, Missouri—local ordinance upheld).

[26]Metromedia Inc. v. City of San Diego 453 U.S. 490 (1981) (invalidated ordinance that curtailed billboards).

[27]City Council of Los Angeles v. Taxpayers for Vincent 466 U.S. 789. 804 (1984) (land use regulation impacting on protected expression—prohibiting signs on public property).

[28]United States v. O'Brien, 391 U.S. 367 (1968).

[29]Schad v. Borough of Mt. Ephraim, 482 U.S. 601 (1981).

Poole (1987) doesn't like either the four-part or the two-part test and proposed a set of four questions that can be used to look at First Amendment issues and architectural control ordinances:

1. What is the purpose of the government regulation? This includes balancing the state's interest in regulation against individual liberty; in other words, there should be a good reason for such regulation.
2. What is the impact of regulation on protected expression? How much does the regulation limit potential expression? Are there reasonable alternative locations, means, and levels of scrutiny?
3. What is the nature of the protected expression? There can be a hierarchy of expression from obscenity to political or religious freedom, or possibly noncommercial speech could be considered more important than commercial speech.
4. Balancing of public and private interests may include (a) the strength of the community reason and clarity of the relationship, and (b) the impact of the regulation on protected expression.

If we were to apply Poole's questions to "no excessive difference" architectural control ordinances, we might find, first, that "no excessive difference" regulations curtail diversity, which is a fundamental content distinction, meaning they would fail Poole's non-neutral inquiry test mentioned earlier. Second, in terms of interest balancing we have the validity of the review criteria or the standing of the review board or commission versus the architect/owner; this often results in a draw. Third, in terms of the impact on protected expression, there are often no alternatives for an architect/owner to express a particular architectural message, and an alternative location may be problematic or impractical. Fourth, in terms of the nature of protected expression, architecture is valued as such under the First Amendment. Fifth, balancing public versus private interests may yield the finding that we don't like the appearance of that structure in this neighborhood; this may not constitute a community-wide appearance issue. As we can see, there are multiple problems with "excessive difference" regulations unless these legal issues can be resolved.

Landmarks preservation ordinances, on the other hand, first, promote or enhance community diversity, passing the non-neutral inquiry test. Second, historic/heritage/economic and identity reasons for landmark preservation do well on the interest-balancing test. Third, in terms of protected expression with landmarks, there is the issue of who the historic architect was. Fourth, in terms of protected expression, landmarks are often highly visible and well used, although some are not accessible to the public. Fifth, with regard to the balancing of public and private interests, the Supreme Court had no problem in *Penn Central* with the substantive interest by communities throughout the United States in the New York City landmarks program. Thus, landmark preservation programs do rather well under Poole's tests.

A First Amendment challenge of "no excessive similarity" regulations making structures look the same is likely to fail, according to Poole (1987), because architectural repetition is not protected expression. Excluding unacceptable architecture from historic districts is likely to be upheld. The question of reasonable alternative locations is difficult, but there is widespread acceptance of historic preservation districts by the courts.

In the example of the Coral Gables, Florida, ordinance that creates a "certain community style," there is a clear relationship between regulation and purpose. There is discrimination based on the content of the architecture similar to the Cleveland Heights, Ohio, and Lake Forest, Illinois, ordinances. However, overall content of the comprehensive-style plan minimizes the likelihood of problems. The balancing of public and private interests is very difficult and rests on the definition of community and whether these are values shared by the whole community.

In summary, with regard to First Amendment and architectural control: (1) architecture is a form of protected expression; (2) architectural appearance ordinances for most program purposes are burdensome regulations on protected expression; but (3) only "no excessive difference" and "no excessive similarity" regulations are unconstitutional intrusions on protected expression, making the latter type of appearance review difficult to defend from a legal perspective. For further discussion of First Amendment issues, see McMillan (1971), Rose (1981), Poole (1987), and Crumpler (1974).

DESIGN REVIEW

Some 2,000 communities in the United States have enacted local preservation ordinances, many of which place strong controls on new construction in historic areas. Increasing numbers of cities and towns are also imposing government design review on new buildings in their environs in nonhistoric and suburban settings, not just landmark and historic district protection. Thus, there is a need for careful crafting of review standards and administration of these architectural control programs if we are to avoid some of the legal challenges that were previously reviewed. Duerksen (1986) has done an excellent job of outlining design review considerations for both historic and nonhistoric areas, and much of the following material follows his work closely.

Design Review in Historic Areas

Preservation controls raise many legal issues, as we have just seen, but one of the most important involves the standards an agency uses to review an application for new construction in a historic district. Generally, the failure of an agency to establish in advance coherent written standards and regulations to be applied in all cases amounts to a denial of due process. Costonis (1989) discusses in detail the complexities and subjective nature of such standards; they must be articulated to pass legal muster and give permit applicants advance notice of what is required. Courts have shown great deference to local review bodies, as witnessed by the language of the U.S. Supreme Court in *Penn Central.*[30]

Demolition, Alteration, and New Construction

The most controversial power exercised by preservation commissions is reviewing applications for demolition or alteration of a landmark or new construction in a historic area, often referred to collectively as applications for "certificates of appropriateness." The key, according to Duerksen (1986), in addressing demolition or alteration proposals (Figure 6.11) is to encourage upgrading and continued maintenance of existing landmarks, and to guide the process of change so it is sympathetic to the existing character of the historic area. Thus, the process of setting standards that reflect this character as well as providing sound administrative procedures is critical.

Setting Review Standards

Preservationists, traditionally, have been concerned that a demolition "not have an adverse effect on the fabric of the district," or that new construction not be "incongruous," but that it should be "in harmony" with the "character," "significant features," or "atmosphere" of the area. (See Williams 1975; Weming Lu 1980; and Duerksen 1986.) These criteria are very subjective if not defined or augmented with guidance documents (see Figure 6.12). Some legal professionals have provided physically based review standards, such as those provided by Professor Williams:

- Mass—the height of a building, its bulk, and the nature of its roofline;
- The proportions between the height of a building and its width;
- The nature of the open space around buildings, including the extent of setbacks, the existence of any yards and their size, and the continuity of such spaces along the street;

FIGURE 6.11   Demolition of historic structure in Boston. *Photo credit: George W. Curry*

- The existence of trees and other landscaping, and the extent of paving;
- The nature of the openings in the facade, primarily doors and windows—their location, size, and proportion;
- The type of roof—flat, gabled, hip, gambrel, mansard, etc.
- The nature of projections from the buildings, particularly porches;
- The nature of the architectural details—and in a broader sense, the predominant architectural style;
- The nature of the materials;
- Color;
- Texture;
- The details of ornamentation;
- Signs.[31]

---

[30]Penn Central Transp. Co. v. New York City, 438 U.S. 104, 129 (1978).

[31]N. Williams, 1975, American Planning Law 3.31 Sec. A. 07; also see Weming Lu "Preservation Criteria: Defining and Protection Design Relationships," In *Old and New Architecture Design Relationships* (Wash., D.C., Preservation Press 1980), p. 180.

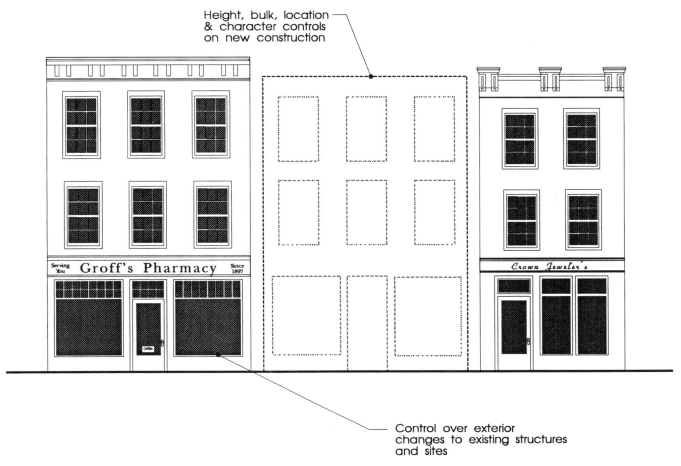

Height, bulk, location
& character controls
on new construction

Serving You   Groff's Pharmacy   Since 1897

Crown Jeweler's

OPEN

Control over exterior
changes to existing structures
and sites

FIGURE 6.12   Design Review Standards — generic urban scene with overlay. *Graphic credit: Scott Shannon*

These physically based criteria can be used to narrow and provide definitions for more broadly based review standards. As noted by Duerksen (1986), promulgating adequate review standards is much less difficult in historic areas because they have distinctive style and character. Thus, in a number of challenges to preservation restrictions, judges have had little trouble upholding the action of the local review body because of the district's distinctive style.

The application of permit review standards to landmarks or districts that do not exhibit a single, distinctive style has been more troublesome to many legal scholars (Costonis 1985; Poole 1987; Rose 1981) and has been fodder for whole books on the subject (Costonis 1986). In instances in which the ordinance contains relatively vague review standards, the courts have attached great importance to other criteria in the local law or regulations that narrow commission discretion. In other cases, the courts have looked to background studies and surveys that were incorporated by reference. Courts also have relied on procedural protections to uphold broad standards. In still other instances, courts have held that appointing people with special

expertise to a commission helps limit what might otherwise have been excessive discretion.

Narrowing Broad Review Standards

A typical preservation ordinance sets forth broad review standards for demolition or development permits, but relates these broad standards to specific criteria. Courts have uniformly approved the broad review standards in such cases. A case from the historic small town of Georgetown, Colorado, is a good example.

In this case, the plaintiff developer alleged that the standard the local commission was to apply in reviewing an application to construct new townhouses was unconstitutionally vague. The six criteria included in this ordinance were:

1. The effect of the proposed change on the general historic and/or architectural character of the structures in the area;
2. The architectural style, arrangement, texture, and materials used on existing and proposed structures, and their relation to other structures in the area;

3. The effects of the proposed work in creating, changing, destroying, or affecting otherwise the exterior architectural features of the structure upon which the work is to be done;
4. The effects of the proposed work upon the protection, enhancement, perpetuation, and use of the structure or area;
5. The use to which the structure or area will be put;
6. The condition of existing improvements and whether or not they are a hazard to public health or safety (Duerksen, 1986).

The Colorado Supreme Court noted that the phrase "historical and/or architectural significance" was defined in the ordinance, and more importantly, the ordinance set forth "six specific criteria that focus the attention of the commission and of potential applicants for certificates of appropriateness on objective and discernible factors,"[32] consequently, it rejected the plaintiff's contention of vagueness.

If a local ordinance does not contain such narrowing criteria, the preservation commission would do well to adopt them by way of regulation or informal review guidelines.

Standards Found in Background Documents

Background documents such as old city plans, historical documents, photographs, and contemporary writings or studies may provide enough substance for approval of a local action, even though these criteria appear in documents outside the preservation ordinance. Such was the case with *Mahr* v. *City of New Orleans*.[33] In this case, the court upheld the New Orleans preservation ordinance, even though the city admitted it had not articulated any review standard.

Procedural Safeguards

The application of standards by a uniquely qualified body to avoid the possibility of arbitrary action or abuse is also an important consideration for architectural review boards. Such procedural considerations combined with the existence of comprehensive background studies and the obvious character of most historic areas helps to explain why courts look so favorably on historic preservation controls but are somewhat suspicious of other design controls.

Administering Design Review

There are a number of important steps that can be taken to improve the efficiency of the design process. The following steps are suggested by Duerksen (1986):

1. **Preparation of a succinct summary sheet of local preservation requirements.** This can be distributed to applicants by building officials.
2. **Holding preapplication meetings.** Misunderstandings can be avoided if the project proponent is given a chance to meet informally with staff and commission members prior to submitting a formal application.
3. **Imposition of time limits.** An increasing number of local governments are placing limits on the time a local commission has to consider a project once a completed application is submitted. These time limits usually range from 30 to 60 days.
4. **Keeping records.** Now that local ordinances have real "teeth," local commissions must improve their record-keeping, particularly minutes and transcripts from hearings dealing with projects that are controversial and may end up in litigation.

Other steps also suggested by Duerksen (1986) that can improve the substance of design review include:

5. **Generic approvals of preapproved sign designs.** Some commissions have published booklets that contain five or six preapproved sign designs for a historic area. If the applicant adopts a preapproved design, the normal review process can be waived.
6. **Using visual design guides.** More and more communities are going beyond relying on written design review standards and are adopting visual design guides that graphically depict, for example, what constitutes a compatible design.
7. **Avoiding nit-picking.** Commissions and preservationists are slowly learning the importance of concentrating their efforts and attention on major cases and avoiding extended review of other items, such as spacing of pickets in a fence, design of wrought-iron gates, and similar considerations.

Design Review Beyond Historic Areas

Increasing dissatisfaction with the appearance of new buildings and their relationship to surrounding structures and neighborhoods has been manifested in the growing number of design review ordinances applied beyond historic districts. No longer content to regulate traditional zoning aspects of development such as bulk and setbacks, communities throughout the United States are specifying height, architectural styles, building orientation, and other aesthetic aspects of new projects.

Initially, this concern over design was most preva-

---

[32] 580 P.2d 807, 810 (Colo. 1978).
[33] 516 F.2d 1051, 1063 (5th Cir. 1975).

lent in exclusive suburban communities like Santa Barbara, California, and Fox Point, Wisconsin, which capture a distinctive architectural style or atmosphere. One of the earliest ordinances was passed by West Palm Beach, Florida, in the mid-1940s, followed by a similar ordinance in Santa Barbara in 1949.

By the 1970s many communities that had a variety of architectural styles and character adopted appearance codes. Recently, design review went downtown in places like San Francisco, Seattle, and Boston, where architectural height, style, and view preservation are major issues (see Figures 6.13 and 6.14).

Design review outside historic areas poses many of the same legal and practical challenges that protecting historic structures do. Experience has demonstrated that careful planning and legal draftsmanship, coupled with strong commitment to common-sense implementation and consistent administration, help make design review work.

FIGURE 6.14   Boston skyline. *Photo credit: Mathew Potteiger*

Special Legal Issues for Nonhistoric Design Review

The troublesome aspects of First and Fifth Amendment conflicts mentioned earlier in this chapter hold for these ordinances, especially anti-lookalike and no excessive difference ordinances. In addition, vagueness of review standards is the other major issue that is the focus of court cases[34] in which similarity or anti-lookalike ordinances were challenged.

Developments

In response to growing citizen concern plus favorable court review, more communities are enacting design review ordinances. Some of the most far-reaching ordinances can be found in major cities. San Francisco and Seattle offer a sample of recent developments:

San Francisco is still attempting to address impacts from a building boom that has altered its downtown skyline, blocking views of the bay. Stiff public opposition in the 1960s and 1970s led the city to reduce height and bulk limits and to issue an urban design plan (see O'Hern 1973 and Vettel 1985). Results were disappointing, and in 1979 a citizens' initiative almost succeeded in placing a growth cap on downtown, which spurred further action. After much debate and politicking, the city council enacted a series of design-related ordinances. Among other things, the new ordinances require that:

a. The upper portion of any tall building be tapered and treated in a manner to create a visually distinctive roof or other termination of the building facade,

FIGURE 6.13   San Francisco skyline. *Photo credit: R. C. Smardon*

---

[34]See Old Farm Road, Inc. v. Town of New Castle, 259 N.E. 920 (N.Y. 1970); Gates ex. rel. Saveland Park Holding Co. v. Wieland, 69 N.W.2d. 217 (Wisc.) *cert. den.* 350 U.S. 841 (1955); Village of Hudson v. Albrecht, Inc. 458 N.E.2d 852 (Ohio, 1984); Novi v. City of Pacifica, Cal. Rpt. 439 (Cal. App. 1985); Reid v. Architectural Rev. Bd., 192 N.E.2d. 74 (Ohio 1963); State ex. rel. Stoyanoff v. Berkeley 458 S.W.2d. 305 (Mo. 1970).

thereby avoiding boxy high-rise buildings and a "benching" effect of the skyline;

b. New or expanded structures abutting certain streets avoid penetration of a sun-access plane so that shadows are not cast at certain times of day on sidewalks and city parks and plazas;

c. Buildings be designed so the development will not cause excessive ground-level wind currents in areas of substantial pedestrian use or public seating;

d. The city consider the historical and aesthetic characteristic of the area along with the impact on tourism when issuing a building permit;

e. Building heights downtown be reduced from 700 to 550 feet (from about 56 to 44 stories) (Duerksen, 1986, Id.).

Seattle has enacted a range of similar, although less detailed restrictions on high-rise construction in its downtown. The requirements limit building heights, establish setbacks to maintain light and air, and ensure designs that reduce wind tunneling and retain views of Elliot Bay. The new laws eliminate density bonuses for projects that displace landmarks; they also provide for glare protection for pedestrians and motorists through restricting use of glare-producing materials and finishes on the lower stories of structures (Erickson 1980).

Implementing Design Review

Past experience with design review procedures and administration in historic areas offers some general guidelines that communities should keep in mind when drafting and implementing design review regulations. It should also be noted that Hamid Shirvani (1981) has written a useful book, *Urban Design Review: A Guide for Planners.* The following guidelines from Duerksen (1986) can also improve the design review process:

1. Successful design review efforts are products of community-based efforts to identify what is special, unique, or worthy of conserving in an area.
2. If detailed design review in an area is to take place, it should be administered by a well-qualified board supported by adequate staff and resources.
3. Written design standards should be supplemented with visual aids and guidelines to make clear what the community desires, thus reducing uncertainty for prospective developers.
4. Design guidelines should not concentrate solely or even primarily on detailed design review.
5. Design review should be carefully integrated with other planning goals for the area.

Case Study: Visual Architectural Review in San Francisco

First, let's review some history of San Francisco's early planning efforts. In 1966 the Department of City Planning completed a comprehensive set of zoning studies that set out aesthetic and urban design goals. These studies ultimately became the basis for the zoning ordinances enacted in 1968. Beyond the density restrictions and the retail district's ground-level retail-frontage requirement, however, the zoning ordinances did not require compliance with any of the urban design goals, and as a result, have had limited success in promoting transferable development rights. The TDR provision of the 1968 zoning ordinance was so restrictive that in many cases there was a disincentive for developers to use it. Since a developer could transfer only half of the unused development rights of a small building to an adjacent lot, it often made economic sense to simply demolish the small building. Many architecturally significant buildings that did not fully use the allowable density are now gone for this reason.

Height and Bulk Controls

Although height controls had been imposed on a few scattered areas of San Francisco since the 1920s, before 1972 there was no citywide height control system. In that year, following adoption of an urban design plan, the board of supervisors approved a citywide height and bulk ordinance.

Height Controls

The ordinances for controlling height limits on downtown development contemplated an artificial hill form, though consonant with the city's topography. A seven-block area at the center of the financial district was zoned at 700 feet, with a gradual lowering of heights at the office district's edge. Height limits in the retail district varied from 140 feet, surrounding Union Square, to 400 feet along a one-block stretch of Market Street. Buildings along the waterfront were limited to 84 feet. Existing public space was zoned as open space to preclude future development on those sites.

Bulk Controls

In each height district, a set of bulk controls was also imposed. The bulk controls were measured across three dimensions: (1) the height above which maximum dimensions applied, (2) the maximum facade width, and (3) the maximum diagonal dimension (corner to opposite diagonal corner). The bulk ordinance provided for some flexibility in administration. The planning commission was authorized to grant conditional permits for buildings exceeding the bulk limits.

Critical Analysis

The height and bulk controls have had their greatest urban design impact in residential neighborhoods. New development, although not necessarily compatible stylistically, has at least respected the generally small scale of San Francisco's residential pattern. The height and bulk controls, according to Vettel (1985), have been fairly effective in channeling the construction of major commercial projects to the central downtown area, thus minimizing the disruptive impact such buildings would have if they were adjacent to residential neighborhoods or along the waterfront.

The height and bulk limits have not adequately protected the central office district environment. Although no building as completely out of scale as the federal building has been constructed since 1972, structures too large to be integrated successfully into the city's fiber have been approved under the ordinance. In addition, while channeling development to the downtown area, the height controls inevitably have contributed to the demolition of many structures of historic value.

The height limits in the retail district also invited disaster because the heights were much greater than those of existing buildings. The many box-shaped buildings that rise to about forty floors, uninterrupted by setbacks or other architectural embellishments that might lessen their apparent size, detract severely from the skyline's diversity, human scale, and interest.

Landmarks Ordinance

In 1967 the city enacted a cautious landmarks ordinance. It set up a Landmarks Preservation Advisory Board, which, together with the planning commission, is empowered to recommend the designation of historic districts and landmarks. Designations must receive the approval of the board of supervisors.

Once a landmark has been designated, its demolition or alteration requires a certificate of appropriateness from the planning commission. While the planning commission may refuse to approve alteration of a landmark, it may not prohibit its demolition. Instead, the commission may only delay approval of the certificate of appropriateness for up to 360 days while seeking voluntary public or private means to preserve the landmark.

The alteration or demolition of structures within a historic district also requires a certificate of appropriateness from the planning commission. As with landmarks, the commission is authorized to deny petitions to make alterations to such structures, but it is powerless to prevent demolition. Again, where demolition is sought, the commission may only delay the issuance of a certificate of appropriateness.

The ordinance also authorizes the planning commission to "recognize" structures of historical, architectural, or aesthetic "merit" which are not officially designated landmarks. Following surveys by the Department of City Planning and a private group, the Foundation for San Francisco's Architectural Heritage (Heritage Foundation), the planning commission in 1980 designated 236 downtown buildings as having "merit."

Critical Analysis

The 1967 landmarks ordinance, for a number of reasons, has proved to be too weak to guarantee that San Francisco's valuable historic resources will remain intact. First, because the planning commission has no power to prevent the demolition of historic or meritorious structures, the authority that it does have to regulate extensive alterations is markedly circumscribed. A second difficulty with the 1967 ordinance has been the politicizing of the designation process. Landmark

designation requires legislative action and is accordingly subject to the traditional political pitfalls of compromise, fiscal pressure, and minimal judicial review. Third, the ordinance also has failed to protect adequately the character of many downtown areas containing groups of early-twentieth-century buildings that give a distinctive flavor but are not individual landmarks. Only Jackson Square was designated as a historic district. Despite the apparent weakness of the landmarks ordinance, many buildings have survived because private owners, hotels, and corporations have voluntarily preserved their buildings and have constructed towers on adjoining lots.

Environmental Review

California Environmental Quality Act

San Francisco gained a significant means of influencing design of private development when the California legislature enacted the California Environmental Quality Act (CEQA)[35] in 1970. Although the act was initially designed to augment existing planning and review procedures, its effect has been to turn environmental review into a critical step in San Francisco's project approval process. Developers must refer their proposals to the Department of City Planning's Office of Environmental Review (OER) for initial assessment. Following the initial review, OER determines whether any of the project's environmental effects may be "significant." CEQA defines a significant effect as a "substantial, or potentially substantial adverse change in the environment."

Critical Analysis

By requiring a standardized inquiry into potential environmental effects, CEQA provides an objective means of evaluating proposed development. However, CEQA does not address many urban design issues. First, its "significant" effects cause changes in physical conditions, but in practice, subjective design decisions rarely change physical conditions. Second, OER requires an assessment of visual impacts only if a proposal will have a "substantial, demonstrable negative aesthetic effect," using as a standard the principles of San Francisco's master plan, including its urban design element. To date, only clearly discernible impacts such as destruction of significant historic structures and the casting of shadows on public parks have been certified as significant effects.

Another shortcoming of the CEQA-mandated environmental review process has been the Department of City Planning's failure to adequately stress the need to evaluate the cumulative impact of the proposed development when combined with other development in the area. An all-downtown EIR (environmental impact report) published in 1984 analyzed the impacts of continued growth in San Francisco and provided some guidance for assessing cumulative impacts. Despite CEQA's weaknesses, the environmental review process has perceptibly increased the planning commission's power to require improvements in the design of new development (Vettel 1985).

Discretionary Review

San Francisco's downtown use, density, height, and bulk controls fail to address the more subtle impacts of urban development, such as the effects a building design might have

---

[35]Cal. Pub. Res. Code ss. 21,000-21,176 (West 1977 E Supp. 1984).

on streetscape character, the harmony of adjoining facades, and the city's skyline. These subtle aspects, however, may well determine a city's character. Rather than leave urban design decisions to private developers and their architects, city planners in San Francisco have tried to fill the regulatory gap by creating a discretionary permitting system, which has three urban design components: (1) an urban design plan, (2) informal Department of City Planning design consultation, and (3) the planning commission's discretionary review power.

Urban Design Plan

San Francisco's urban design plan adopted by the planning commission in 1971 was the first of its kind in the nation. Rather than projecting an image of what the city should look like in twenty or thirty years, the plan defines essential needs in an urban environment, proposes public and private objectives to attain those needs, articulates fundamental urban design principles, and sets forth a series of general design policies to guide the discretionary approval process. The four sections of the plan address: (1) preservation and creation of city patterns, (2) conservation of historic and other resources, (3) moderation of new development, and (4) protection of neighborhood environment.

The urban design plan established a set of general policy objectives to guide not only future planning and zoning regulation, but also individual project review. It has worked well for the former, but as a concrete set of policies to guide individual downtown project review, it has been demonstrably inadequate.

Informal Design Consultation

In 1967 the Department of City Planning instituted a voluntary design review procedure to encourage developers to consult with city planners at each stage in the planning of new development. Developers and their architects are advised to inform the department at the outset of their plans and development goals rather than wait until design plans are finalized to seek approval. For its part, the department informs developers of specific public goals, such as the design criteria peculiar to the proposed site, that should be considered in addition to the objective zoning requirements. Ideally, as design plans progress, developers and planners meet often, review plans, negotiate conditions, and eventually agree upon a mutually acceptable design.

The success of informal design consultation, like the success of most negotiation processes, depends ultimately on the political strengths of the negotiating parties. At times, departmental review has been exacting, and the threat of a negative staff recommendation is a powerful inducement for developers to achieve a project design acceptable to the department.

Discretionary Review Power

The planning commission possesses a broad power to review all permits, variances, and conditional-use authorizations, even if the applicant has satisfied every zoning restriction. When used aggressively this "discretionary review" power gives teeth to the urban design plan and the department's informal design review process.

Perhaps, surprisingly, no challenge to the commission's exercise of discretionary review has reached an appellate court in recent years. Rather, most developers have accepted the conditions imposed by the commission during discretionary review. Even outright disapproval of a proposal will not necessarily prevent the ultimate development of the project. The commission typically informs the developer of the conditions it will require before granting approval. To date, such conditions, particularly those involving project design, have been economically feasible, and it has been advantageous for developers to redesign projects rather than suffer the delay of a court challenge to discretionary review.

Summary: 1967–1972 Plans and Processes

Downtown regulation has been piecemeal, often inconsistent, and generally inadequate according to authorities in the know (Vettel 1985). In the later years, environmental and discretionary review were used aggressively to promote more sensitive building designs and to exact measures to mitigate development impacts. But often the changes and mitigation measures the city required were only marginally effective. Further, efforts to reshape individual projects failed to address cumulative growth effects in a realistic or meaningful way.

The Role of the U.C.-Berkeley Environmental Simulation Laboratory

The Environmental Simulation Laboratory at the University of California at Berkeley has pioneered environmental simulation techniques and applied them to urban design problems and architectural control analysis. (Bosselman 1983a and 1983b). The laboratory has also been used extensively as a testing and communication tool. For the last fifteen years it has illustrated alternatives for downtown growth in San Francisco. Realistic skyline and street-level views of future development have been created that have enriched the discussion on the policies shaping zoning regulations and urban design guidelines (see Figure 6.15).

FIGURE 6.15   Use of an environmental simulator to test alternatives and conditions. *Photo Credit: Peter Bosselman, U.C. Berkeley Environmental Simulation Laboratory*

Skyline Views

In 1972 Donald Appleyard used a scale model of the city of San Francisco housed in the laboratory to make a film that showed from an eye-level perspective how the skyline of San Francisco had changed in the last forty years. In 1979, during the high-rise controversy, the laboratory produced a second film that showed the effects of a general height limit of 260 feet. This limit, proposed by an alliance of groups under the leadership of San Franciscans for Reasonable Growth, represented an actual reduction of existing heights. The film was shown prior to the city election of 1979 on public television and was followed by a debate between the opponents and proponents of the measure. The referendum failed, as had the two previous ones. Forty-five percent of the votes were in favor — a narrow margin, but the signal was clear: San Franciscans were concerned about the appearance and quality of their downtown.

The Environmental Simulation Laboratory at U.C.-Berkeley has been asked frequently to test the visual impacts of proposed changes to San Francisco's downtown zoning ordinance. An urban design plan in 1971 envisioned a downtown well contained within a small area without spreading into the neighborhoods. This basic and widely acclaimed policy was complemented by height zones that give downtown the shape of a hill, compatible with surrounding natural hills. In 1972 the "downtown hill" policy was developed in response to the construction of two high-rise office buildings, built in the late 1960s on the periphery of the financial district — the Bank of America building, with its 792-foot-high dark tower, and the 845-foot-high pyramid building housing the Transamerica Corporation. However, even with the hill policy in place, existing developmental controls have failed to produce the designed hill shape. The highest buildings continued to flank the edges of the financial district, giving the city the shape of an abruptly rising plateau. The sweeping views from a 30-to-40-story office building at the edge of downtown over hills, bay, and bridges are economically valuable. However, the view of downtown from neighborhoods and surrounding communities across the bay, though experienced by more people, cannot compete with this economic incentive.

Years after the urban design plan, it appears that the notion of the downtown hill form is likely to remain a concept. Only a few vanishing points allow an inside view of the downtown hill. Changes to the height zones have tried to force future development to fill in at least the south slope of the hill.

Street-Level Views

In the 1980s discussion of urban design issues focused not on the skyline but on street-level concerns. Like midtown Manhattan, with its new zoning ordinance, San Francisco adopted a downtown plan that includes, among other items, an ordinance that will produce tiered high-rise towers similar to those built in the 1920s and 1930s. Future building may once again bring more light and air into streets.

The model stage at the environmental simulation laboratory was again used to simulate the visual impacts of future high-rise buildings. Models and photography are used to measure the openness of downtown streets to light and sun. As a result, guidelines based on sun-access criteria, which are closely related to street scale and bulk considerations, have been developed and tested. A more detailed presentation of this work can be seen in Bosselman (1987).

The Downtown Plan of 1984–1985

In May 1981 and again in July 1982 the Department of City Planning published preliminary rezoning proposals. Then in May 1983, the downtown EIR consultant's report was released. Finally in August 1983 the Department published its proposed downtown plan for citizen and commission review. The board of supervisors imposed a moratorium on all downtown development proposals while public hearings and environmental assessment of the plan proceeded. A draft downtown EIR analyzing the plan was published by the department in March 1984, and the final EIR was certified on October 18, 1984. On November 29, 1984, after additional hearings, the downtown plan as amended was adopted by the city planning commission. The key features were incorporated into proposed amendments to the planning code, which had to be approved by the board of supervisors for the plan to become law in 1985.

Under the downtown plan, building designs are subject to demanding objective requirements as described previously. Principal features of the plan affecting urban design include: a reduction in allowable density, redirection of office development south of Market Street, lower height limits, "post-modern" bulk controls (requiring slender, sculpted towers), preservation of architecturally significant buildings, mandatory incorporation of open space and public art, retail or public service ground-level uses, and preservation of direct sunlight to sidewalks and open spaces. The downtown plan of 1984 leaves far less room for discretionary decision-making and provides detailed standards for any discretion remaining. Detailed preliminary evaluation and description of the plan's effects are offered by Vettel (1985) but it has not been completely evaluated since 1985.

The images produced at the U.C.-Berkeley Environmental Simulation Laboratory over the last fifteen years have enriched the public discussion over the existing as well as future visual resources of San Francisco. So far, however, the economic forces that have given downtown its shape have proven to be stronger than the rationale developed in visual assessment studies. However, there is reason to be optimistic that the ideas and information generated in the laboratory have helped to establish a constituency in San Francisco that will continue to speak out for quality-of-life issues such as preservation of views, sunlight, and the openness of downtown streets to the sky.

References

Anderson, R. M. 1960. Architectural controls. *Syracuse Law Review,* 12: 26–49.

Bosselman, P. 1983a. Visual impact at Berkeley. *Urban Design International,* 4(3): 34–37.

———. 1983b. Simulating the visual impacts of urban development. *Garten & Landschaft,* August: 636–640.

———. 1987. Experiencing downtown streets in San Francisco. In Anne Vernez Moudon, ed, *Public streets for public use.* Van Nostrand Reinhold, New York: 203–220.

Bross, J. L. 1979. Taking design review beyond the beauty part: Aesthetics in perspective. *Environmental Law,* 9: 211–240.

Costonis, J. J. 1974. *Space adrift: Landmark preservation and the marketplace.* University of Illinois Press.

———. 1982. Law and aesthetics: A critique and a reformulation of the dilemmas. *Michigan Law Review,* 80: 355–461.

———. 1985. The Chicago plan: Incentive zoning and the preservation of urban landmarks. *Harvard Law Review,* 85: 574–634.

———. 1989. *Icons and aliens: law, aesthetics and environmental change.* University of Illinois Press.

Crumplar, T. 1974. Architectural controls: Aesthetic regulation of the urban environment. *The Urban Lawyer* 6(3): 622–644.

Duerksen, C. J. 1983. *A handbook of historic preservation law.* Conservation Foundation.

———. 1986. *Aesthetics and land use controls: Beyond ecology and economics.* PAS Report 399. American Planning Association.

Edmundson, P. W. 1981. Historic preservation regulation and procedural due process. *Ecology Law Quarterly,* 9: 743–775.

Erickson, D. K. 1980. Seattle — coping with visual impact: evaluation of light and glare. *Environmental Comment,* July 1980: 8–15.

Glasford, 1983. *Appearance codes for small communities.* PAS Report 379, American Planning Association.

Goldstone, H. H. 1971. Aesthetics in historic districts. *Law and Contemporary Problems,* 36(3): 379–431.

Gray, O. S. 1971. The response of federal legislation to historic preservation. *Law and Contemporary Problems,* 36(3): 314–328.

Lee, R. 1951. United States: Historical and archeological monuments 11. Office of History and Historic Architecture, National Park Service U.S. Dept. of Interior, Wash., D.C.

Loflin, J. J. 1971. Historic preservation in the American city: A new case study. *Law and Contemporary Problems,* 36(3): 362–367.

Lu, W. 1980. Preservation criteria: Defining and protecting design relationships. In *Old and new architecture: design relationships.* Preservation Press.

Marcus, N. 1978. The grand slam Grand Central Terminal decision: A Euclid for landmarks, favorable notice for TDR and a resolution of regulatory/taking impasse. *Ecology Law Quarterly,* 7: 731–752.

McMillan, R. R. 1971. Community-wide architectural controls in Missouri. *Missouri Law Review,* 38(3): 423–430.

Morrison, J. 1965. *Historic preservation law.* National Trust for Historic Preservation.

O'Hern, P. J. 1973. Reclaiming the urban environment: The San Francisco urban design plan. *Ecology Law Quarterly,* 3: 535–595.

Poole, S. E., III. 1987. Architectural appearance review regulations and the First Amendment: The good, the bad, and the consensus ugly. *The Urban Lawyer,* 19(2): 287–344.

Rankin, J. L. 1971. Operation and interpretation of the New York City landmarks preservation law. *Law and Contemporary Problems,* 36(3): 366–372.

Rathkopf, A. 1975. *The law of zoning and planning,* 4th ed. Clark Boardman.

Roddewig, R. 1983. *Preparing a historic preservation ordinance.* PAS Report 374, American Planning Association.

Rose, C. M. 1981. Preservation and community: New directions in the law of historic preservation. *Stanford Law Review,* 33(4/3): 473–534.

Shirvani, H. 1981. *Urban design review: A guide for planners.* American Planning Association.

Vettel, S. L. 1985. San Francisco's downtown plan: Environmental and urban design values in central business district regulation. *Ecology Law Quarterly,* 12: 511–566.

Williams, N., Jr. 1975. *American planning law: Land use and the police power,* vol. 5. Callaghan. 3.31S A.07.

Wilson, P. E., and Winkler, J., II. 1971. The response of state legislation to historic preservation. *Law and contemporary problems,* 36(3): 329–399.

Chapter 7

Outdoor Advertising and Sign Control

INTRODUCTION

This chapter addresses outdoor advertising and sign control within the visual corridor (Figure 7.1). The issue of "billboard" or sign control has and continues to be a problematic visual landscape issue at the national, state, and local levels of government — from both a regulatory and a visual impact perspective. This is probably why "Scenic America" (a national visual quality advocacy group) spends much of its efforts trying to address legislative and communication issues regarding outdoor advertising.

Unlike Chapters 5 and 6, which focused on aesthetic zoning affecting land use and architectural controls affecting structures and districts, respectively, this chapter focuses on signs and billboards — structures that deliver messages. Signs are not standing alone — but are along the visual corridor generally created by a highway or road. There is something about this relationship — Is it public or private visual occupancy? Negative or positive visual quality? It is definitely problematic.

According to a recent handbook, *Visual Pollution and Sign Control* (McNett 1987, pp. 1–2), signs or billboards (see Figure 7.2):

1. Are a form of visual pollution, intruding and distracting from the surrounding environment.
2. Are the most intrusive form of advertising.
3. Provide few if any compensating benefits.
4. Devalue the public's intensive investment in highway beautification.

What is it about this billion-dollar-a-year business that seems to have a political hold on major legislators through the well-funded billboard lobby? We look briefly to the turn of the century as billboards or outdoor advertising were involved in legal litigation.

EARLY HISTORY OF SIGN REGULATION

Originally, aesthetics was "masked" by other issues dealing with public morals, health, or safety. This tendency is exceedingly well illustrated in the Missouri Supreme Court case of *St. Louis Gunning Advertising Company* v. *St. Louis*[1] where the court was looking for some handle to deal with billboard control. This case provided the doctrinal shift by taking the position that the police power might be exercised to protect community, health, safety, and morals. It found that billboards

endanger the public health, promote immorality, constitute hiding places and retreats for criminals and all classes of miscreants. They are also inartistic and unsightly. In cases of fire they often cause their spread and constitute barriers against their extinction; and in cases of high wind, their temporary character, frail structure and broad surface, render them liable to be blown down and to fall upon and injure those who happen to be in the vicinity. The evidence shows and common observation teaches us that the ground in the rear thereof is being constantly used as privie and dumping ground for all kinds of waste and deleterious matters, and thereby creating public nuisances and jeopardizing public health; the evidence also shows that

---

[1]253 Mo. 99, 137 S.W. 929 (1911), appeal dismissed, 231 U.S. 761 (1913).

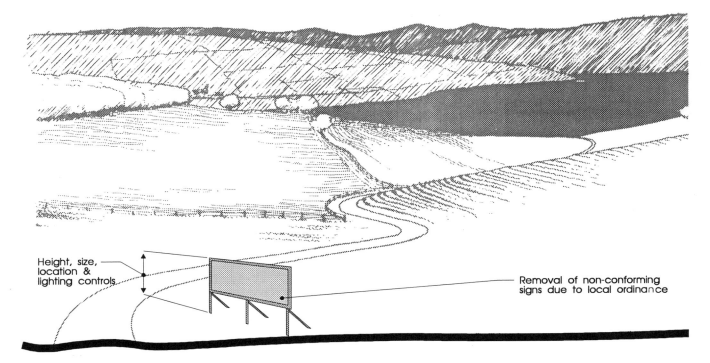

FIGURE 7.1   Generic landscape with billboard in place. *Graphic credit: Scott Shannon*

behind these obstructions the lowest forms of prostitution and other acts of immorality are frequently carried on, almost under the public gaze; they offer shelter and concealment for the criminal while lying in wait for his victim; and last but not least, they obstruct light, sunshine, and air, which are so conducive to health and comfort.[2]

Thus, the contemporary doctrine derived from *St. Louis Gunning* as phrased by Dukeminer (1955, p. 220) was:

a.) the police power may not be used to attain objectives primarily aesthetic, but

b.) the police power may be used to attain objectives primarily related to health, safety or morals; based upon the following proposition of fact;

c.) billboards and signs are primarily deleterious to health, safety and morals.

Other cases of this period held that signs may fall on pedestrians in heavy winds and become fire hazards.[3] It has only been fairly recently that control of signs for aesthetic purposes has been upheld in the courts.[4]

In 1931 Proffit characterized existing billboard regulation as falling into several groups:

1. California forbade the placing or displaying of any advertisement on public property without consent, and declared that anyone violating the statute is guilty of a misdemeanor. Similar legislation was also adopted in Colorado, Connecticut, Illinois, Iowa, Louisiana, Maine, Maryland, Michigan, Minnesota, New Jersey, North Carolina, North Dakota, Pennsylvania, and Utah.

2. A North Carolina statute provided that anyone placing advertising matter on private property without first obtaining the written consent of the owner is guilty of a misdemeanor and subject to fine or imprisonment. Legislation of similar nature had been adopted in California, Colorado, Connecticut, Illinois, Indiana, Louisiana, Maryland, New Jersey, New York, Pennsylvania, Rhode Island, and Utah.

3. New York permits anyone to remove from public highways advertising matter that had been placed there without permission from the proper government authority. New Jersey and Rhode Island adopted similar legislation.

4. In New Jersey, by statute, a presumption is raised that the person whose goods are advertised autho-

---

[2]Id. at 242.

[3]St. Louis Poster Advertising Co. v. City of St. Louis 249 U.S. 269 (1914).

[4]Major Media of the Southeast v. City of Raleigh 792 F.2d 1269 (4th Cir. 1986), cert. den., 107 S. Ct. 1334 (1987).

FIGURE 7.2 a, b, c   Mosaic of signscapes. *Photo credit: R. C. Smardon*

rized the unlawful placing of the advertisement. Similar provisions appeared in New York and Colorado laws.

5. Vermont exacts a license from anyone engaging in the business of outdoor advertising within the state. Statutes requiring licenses for anyone engaged in the business of outdoor advertising or statutes taxing billboards were also adopted in Connecticut, Florida, Michigan, Mississippi, and New Jersey.

6. A statute was adopted in Colorado prohibiting the erection of billboards along any highway outside city limits within 300 feet of intersecting corners or sharp curves if such structure would interfere with the view of an approaching vehicle. Legislation of similar nature was enacted in Iowa, Kansas, Maine, Michigan, Nebraska, North Dakota, South Dakota, Vermont, Washington, and Wisconsin.

7. Arkansas enacted legislation prohibiting the erection of any billboard within 100 yards of a state highway and along any public road to any town, etc. in the state unless the person erecting such a billboard first obtains permission of the state highway commission.

Billboards were springing up at this time, and local jurisdictions were trying to deal with them. Vermont's 1925 legislation was an early comprehensive program. It included size parameters for commercial outdoor advertising, licensing requirements, allowable proximity to dangerous curves and public parks, as well as provisions for the removal of billboards. Little legal problem was encountered with these statutes. Statutes that received the most attention from the billboard interests were those like Nevada's, which prohibited billboards that "destroy the natural beauty of the scenery." Such statutes were apparently quite frequently challenged as being too subjective.

England dealt with the billboard problem in the Advertisements Regulation Acts of 1907 and 1925 which, read together, authorize the prescribed local authorities to make bylaws for regulating, restricting, or preventing within their district the exhibition of advertisements in such places and in such a manner as to negatively affect:

a.) the amenities of a public park or pleasure promenade; or
b.) the natural beauties of a landscape; or

c.) the view of rural scenery from a highway or railroad or from any public place or water; or

d.) the amenities of any village within the district of a rural district council; or

e.) any amenities of any historic building or monument of any places frequented by the public solely or generally on account of its beauty or historic interest (Proffit 1931; p. 175).

Legislation for the control and restriction of billboard advertising was also adopted in Bermuda in 1923; Newfoundland in 1916; Ontario in 1926 and 1927; New Zealand in 1903 and 1906; New South Wales in 1906, 1908, and 1920; Hong Kong in 1912, 1913, and 1924; Palestine in 1926; Queensland in 1902 and 1911; South Australia in 1916; Victoria in 1914; and Western Australia in 1906. Thus, regulation of outdoor advertising was underway in the first quarter of this century in the United States, England, Canada, and Australia, with obviously a clearer legal mandate in the British Commonwealth than in the United States.

In 1936 there was a critical case in the Massachusetts Supreme Court[5] that started the doctrinal shift to substantiating regulation of billboards solely on aesthetics-based considerations (Gardner 1936) — a battle that continues state-by-state to the present day (see Chapter 4; also see articles by Aronovsky 1981, Lucking 1977, and Peters 1978 for more on the history of billboards and sign control).

THE HIGHWAY BEAUTIFICATION ACT: THE FEDERAL EFFORT

Billboards, or outdoor advertising, are regulated by federal, state, and local laws, and this complex interrelationship needs to be understood before we move on to other legal issues and implementation. The structure and evolution of the Federal Highway Beautification Act and specific programs and related problems with the act as implemented are discussed here.

The federal highway system includes about 300,000 miles of federally financed roads — the 40,000-mile interstate system and 260,000 miles of primary roads (Figure 7.3). Signs and sign regulation started in the 1920s, as we have seen, but as the highway system grew in the 1950s and 1960s, and as more people owned cars, so, too, proliferated outdoor advertising. Congress began considering ways to control this.

The first effort at regulating billboards along federal highways was the Bonus Program of the Federal Aid Highway Act of 1958. Under this program, states that complied with federal outdoor advertising regulations

FIGURE 7.3   Typical Interstate highway scene. *Photo credit: R. C. Smardon*

received a bonus payment of 0.5 percent of the federal highway funds otherwise allocated to that state. The Bonus Program was not widely accepted; only half the states took advantage of it before eligibility to participate expired in 1965 (Gould 1986).

The failure of the Bonus Program to adequately and comprehensively address the billboard problem increased the pressure to develop alternate remedies. The federal government's next attempt at billboard control was the Highway Beautification Act of 1965, supported by President and Lady Bird Johnson. Unlike the Bonus Program, which used a "carrot" to induce states to control billboards along federal roads, the 1965 act imposed penalties for failure to meet federal standards. States that do not comply with federal regulations risk losing 10 percent of their federal highway funds.

According to many commentors and experts (Floyd 1982; Lam and Yasinow 1968; Cunningham 1973), the Highway Beautification Act has been a failure. It was supposed to result in the removal of existing billboards from rural roads and the prohibition of new signs; instead, it has subsidized the industry it was meant to regulate and has shielded billboard companies from state and local government attempts to control billboard blight (Floyd 1982).

The Legal Requirements of the Act

The Highway Beautification Act calls for each state to require "effective control" over billboards along its federal-aid highways or risk losing 10 percent of its appropriation.[6] The statute defines "effective control" as the prohibition of the following types of new signs visible from the highway:

[5]General Outdoor Advertising Co. v. Department of Public Works 289 Mass. 149 (1936) 193 N.E. 799, *app'ls. dismissed* 56 U.S. 495–96 (1936).
[6]23 U.S.C. 131 (b) (1988).

1. Directional and official signs
2. On-site "for sale" and lease signs
3. Signs identifying and advertising on-site businesses
4. Landmark signs of historical or artistic significance
5. "Free coffee" signs for travelers[7]

A significant exception to the act, however, is the provision that permits the construction of billboards in zoned and unzoned commercial and industrial areas.[8] An agreement between the states and the secretary of transportation determines the definition of an unzoned commercial and industrial area, and the definition may vary from state to state. This provision also calls for the agreement between the federal government and the states to establish size, spacing, and lighting consistent with "customary use."

The law also provides for the removal of all nonconforming signs after a five-year period and for payment of cash compensation to the owners for such removal.[9] Other sections of the act provide for travel information signs at interchanges (logo system) and rest area information centers.[10] Regulations enacted by the Federal Highway Administration (FHWA) further define the terms of the act.[11]

There are several problems with the act, some of which affect local communities and sign control. These issues are cash compensation to sign owners for removal of signs, impacts on local laws, use and misuse of commercial and industrial zones, sign size and spacing standards, and tree cutting to keep signs visible.

Cash Compensation to Sign Owners

The most counterproductive provision of the Highway Beautification Act is the requirement that sign owners be paid "just compensation" for nonconforming signs that are removed, even when the removal occurs after the five-year grace period provided by the act. Failure to pay cash compensation for sign removal also subjects the state to the risk of losing 10 percent of its federal highway funds. This provision was included through the efforts of the outdoor advertising lobby. Payment of just compensation is not constitutionally mandated if a reasonable amortization period is included in the local or state zoning statute.

Paying the industry to take down billboards has not necessarily meant a reduction in the number of signs.

When a billboard is still in good physical condition, a company may simply move it to a new location and thereby retain its use at the same time it collects compensation. If the government later wants to remove the billboard from its new site, it will have to compensate the owner a second time. Alternately, sign companies can use their compensation money to put up new signs. According to a 1985 report by the U.S. General Accounting Office (1985), 13,875 signs were removed under the Highway Beautification Act in 1983, but 13,522 new ones were erected in commercial and industrial areas.

The compensation provision originally applied only to signs that were removed because of the requirements of the federal act. A 1978 amendment, however, extended the requirement to sign removals accomplished under any law, including state and local land use control and zoning laws.[12] States and communities are deprived of their traditional right to remove nonconforming signs from federal highways under the police power. Ordinances that required the removal of such signs, after an amortization period and without paying compensation, become invalid. Some state laws, influenced by representatives of the billboard industry, even extended the cash compensation requirement to all state roads.

In summary, because states may not want to risk losing 10 percent of their highway funding, it is probable that no signs will be removed from federal interstate and primary aid (federally funded) highways unless cash compensation is paid. However, since no federal money is available, no removal is taking place.

Methods to Force Compliance with Local Laws

To prevent the proliferation of new signs a locality can pass a comprehensive ordinance forbidding new construction even on a federal highway. In addition, communities may also require existing billboards on federal roads to meet stricter size and height restrictions. According to a 1987 FHWA memorandum, signs that are not brought into compliance with such local restrictions may be removed without compensation.[13] Such a question arose in connection with a Denver ordinance and was upheld by the local FHWA office. This administrative opinion gives local communities and state gov-

---

[7]23 U.S.C. 131 (c) (1988).
[8]23 U.S.C. 131 (d) (1988).
[9]23 U.S.C. 131 (e)(g) (1988).
[10]23 U.S.C. 131 (f)(i) (1988).
[11]23 C.F.R. § 750, pt. G (1991).
[12]23 U.S.C. 131 (g) (1988).
[13]Memorandum of Federal Highway Administration, dated May 13, 1987, re Colorado Outdoor Advertising Control Denver Sign Ordinance and 23 U.S.C. 131(g) (1988).

ernments a tool for affecting signs on federal highways utilizing their own police powers.

Commercial and Industrial Zones

Although the Highway Beautification Act generally prohibited new billboards, it exempted all zoned and unzoned industrial and commercial areas. This exemption has allowed hundreds of thousands of new billboards to be erected under the act. Some rural communities have used this exemption to circumvent the law by zoning strips of land along rural highways as commercial and industrial areas simply to allow billboards to be erected. This practice of "phony zoning" is not legal under the act and its regulations. However, documented cases have occurred in many states, including Nevada, South Dakota, New Mexico, South Carolina, and North Carolina (Floyd 1982).

Because of the FHWA's interpretation of this section of the act, rural areas that are zoned commercial and industrial, but that are currently undeveloped, may become sites for numerous billboards. The most straightforward solution to this problem is passage of a strong local ordinance prohibiting new billboards. This will stop sign proliferation on local sections of the federal highway regardless of a community's land use decisions.

The other problem is unzoned areas actually used for commercial and industrial purposes. Sign companies exploit this loophole by using small, obscure businesses, which may not even be visible from the highway, to qualify a rural site for the erection of several billboards.

Size and Spacing Standards

The Highway Beautification Act does not include any specific limitations on the size, lighting, or spacing of billboards (Figure 7.4). Rather, it requires federal and state highway officials to agree on restrictions based on customary use. At the time the act was passed billboards were generally limited to 300 square feet (Miller 1985). Under a model agreement developed by the Federal Highway Administration (FHWA) in conjunction with Outdoor Advertising Association of America, the maximum sign size suggested was 1,200 square feet — four times the old limit — with no regulation in height. Such "size restrictions" plus improved sign technology have led to the erection of monopoles, large signs supported by a single metal pole. Such billboards can be up to fifteen stories high, are visible over long distances, and frequently break the natural skyline or horizon.

Spacing requirements recommended by the FHWA are similarly lax. Billboard sites must be 500 feet apart on interstate highways and 100 feet apart on primary roads. If both sides of the road are used, there can be twenty-one signs per mile on interstates and many more on primary roads. The most effective way to regulate sign size on federal highways may be to pass local

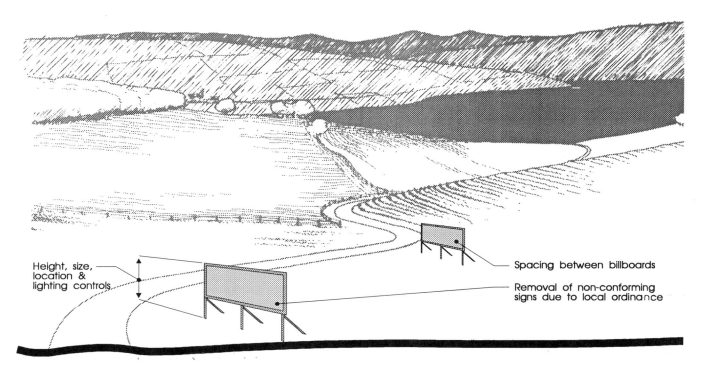

FIGURE 7.4   Size and spacing standards. *Graphic credit: Scott Shannon*

ordinances that prohibit new signs, or that limit size and height and prohibit doubledecking of signs.

Tree Cutting

Major public outcry has resulted from the destruction of trees and vegetation on public rights-of-way to make signs more visible. Thousands of permits are issued each year for such work. Ironically, many of the trees cut were planted under federally funded landscape programs.

The FHWA grants the states the discretion to remove trees from federal roadsides. Some states, like Tennessee, allow tree cutting by statute, while others, like North Carolina, have promulagated regulations permitting "vegetation control." According to the Coalition for Scenic Beauty, twenty-nine states, including Iowa, New York, and Massachusetts, prohibit the practice of cutting vegetation to make signs more visible.

STATE EFFORTS AND BILLBOARD CONTROL

In response to the Highway Beautification Act and its amendments, each state eventually passed legislation establishing "effective control of billboards." For review of such efforts before 1973 the reader is referred to Cunningham's (1973) comprehensive review of state programs. For the most part, these laws were enacted simply to avoid the 10 percent reduction in federal highway funding. Although the Highway Beautification Act permits states to pass stricter legislation, most state laws go no further than the federal act requires, and control is generally limited to interstate and primary roads. Some state laws, however, also include specified state roads such as turnpikes, secondary roads, and designated scenic highways. All the state laws require that compensation be paid for any legal, nonconforming billboard removed from areas adjacent to interstate and primary roads as mandated by the federal act.

As a result of lobbying pressure from the billboard companies, some states also require payments for the removal of signs from nonfederal roads. Georgia, for example, requires that compensation be paid for the removal of all lawfully erected signs that fail to conform to "any lawful ordinance, regulation or resolution."[14]

Other states, such as Florida,[15] specifically allow cities and counties to enact legislation that is stricter than state law, as long as compensation is paid for sign removal along federal roads. Although billboard control is usually a local rather than a state issue, several states have tackled the problem at the state level. Vermont,[16] Maine,[17] Alaska,[18] and Hawaii have banned billboards entirely and have removed any existing billboards. Oregon[19] and Washington[20] also have strong sign control laws.

RECENT TRENDS IN LOCAL SIGN REGULATION

In the wake of favorable federal and state court decisions, there has been a flurry of new sign ordinances enacted at the local level. A number of cities and towns are going beyond traditional sign regulation to ensure that billboards and other outdoor advertising media are compatible with their surroundings. The following cities have enacted some of the more interesting and innovative ordinances. (See Zeigler 1985 and Duerksen 1986 for a more detailed review.)

Lake Charles, Louisiana, has enacted a sign control ordinance representing a judicious attempt to balance sign control with the needs of merchants and the public. Its notable features include:

1. A flexible size provision based on location, height, and setback.
2. A bonus arrangement based on the amount of landscaping, materials, color, and compatibility.
3. Spacing of off-premise signs.
4. Minimum landscaping and architectural treatment for off-premise signs.

In Chula Vista, California, the local zoning code authorizes planned sign districts for commercial and industrial projects larger than two acres. These provisions, which may be chosen by the developer as an alternative to regular sign regulations, allow more latitude regarding number and size of signs if the project proponent advances a coordinated program for style, materials, and placement.

As part of its recently adopted downtown plan, San Francisco has created several special sign districts for historic areas, redevelopment zones, and pedestrian-oriented commercial areas. Regulations vary from dis-

---

[14]Ga. Code Sec. 32-6-83 (1985).
[15]Fla. Stat. Ann. Sec. 479.155, 479.24 (1986).
[16]10 Vt. Stat. Ann. Sec. 481-505 (1985).
[17]23 Me. Rev. Stat. Ann. Sec. 1901-1925 (1986).
[18]Alaska Stat. Sec. 19.25.090 (1986).
[19]Or. Stat. Sec. 372.700–377.840, 377.992 (1983).
[20]Wash. Rev. Code Ann. Sec. 47.42 (1986).

trict to district depending on the character of the area. Particular attention is paid to signs that might obscure or damage public amenities such as street trees. (For a good step-by-step overview of development and implementation of a local sign ordinance see Chapter 5 in McNett 1987.)

CONSTITUTIONAL AND OTHER LEGAL ISSUES INVOLVED WITH SIGN CONTROL

Billboard companies and sometimes local businesses have challenged sign control ordinances in court on the constitutional grounds that they violate the First Amendment right of free speech and the Fifth Amendment prohibition against government's taking of private property without compensation. (See Aronovsky 1981; Lucking 1977; and Peters 1978 for a more detailed discussion.)

The First Amendment: Freedom of Speech

The U.S. Supreme Court, in recent decisions involving sign ordinances attacked as unconstitutional infringements on free speech (Figure 7.5), has held that an aesthetic interest is a valid basis for a sign regulation. In the case *Taxpayers for Vincent*,[21] the Court ruled that political, or noncommercial, speech is entitled to a higher degree of protection than commercial speech. If a sign ordinance has a significant impact on a form or method of political expression, in order to be valid it must:

1. Be content neutral.
2. Promote a substantial government interest, unrelated to the suppression of speech.
3. Restrict the speech only to the extent necessary to accomplish the substantial government interest.

In this case, the Court upheld a total ban on all posted signs, political or otherwise, because aesthetics and traffic safety were substantial government interests and adequate alternative channels for political communication existed in the community. It would appear, conversely, that if adequate alternative channels to transmit the political message were lacking, the sign law would fail constitutionally.

Several other conclusions may be inferred from *Taxpayers for Vincent* and other recent cases. It appears that if a regulation gives more favorable treatment to commercial signs than to political signs, it would be

FIGURE 7.5   Using signs for Freedom of Speech. *Photo credit: R. C. Smardon*

held unconstitutional. This seems consistent with the Court's expressed intent of giving political speech a higher degree of protection than commercial speech. The Court has not otherwise made clear the precise nature of favored position of political speech. In addition, a "time, place, and manner" restriction on signs, for example, regarding height, setback, and size limits, is likely to pass constitutional muster.

In 1981, in the *Metromedia*[22] case the U.S. Supreme Court held that a content neutral regulation on commercial signs would be upheld, if it

1. Seeks to promote a substantial government interest.
2. Directly advances that interest.
3. Is no broader than necessary to accomplish the government interest.

The Court made clear that regulators may differentiate between on-site and off-site signs. A ban on off-site signs only will be valid because businesses and the public have a greater interest in the service provided by on-site signs of identifying the business and its wares.

In 1986 the Fourth Circuit Court of Appeals applied the *Metromedia* decision to a Raleigh, North Carolina, sign ordinance in *Major Media of the Southeast, Inc.* v. *City of Raleigh*.[23] The ordinance sharply restricted the size and location of the off-site signs. Applying the *Metromedia* opinion to the ordinance, the court concluded "that a City may justifiably prohibit all off-premise signs or billboards."[24] The Raleigh ordinance used lan-

[21]Members of the City Council of Los Angeles v. Taxpayers for Vincent 466 U.S. 789 (1984).

[22]Metromedia Inc. v. City of San Diego 453 U.S. 490, 501 (1981).

[23]792 F.2d 1269 (4th Cir. 1986), cert. denied, 107 S. Ct. 1334 (1987).

[24]Id. at 1272.

guage to permit noncommercial messages whenever signs are permitted, thus avoiding the constitutional problem identified in *Taxpayers for Vincent* and *Metromedia*.

First Amendment Guidelines

The U.S. Supreme Court has developed several tests that it uses to judge whether regulations impermissibly infringe on First Amendment rights. The *Metromedia* and the *Taxpayers for Vincent* opinions applied several different constitutional tests, but each focused on the same basic issues.

1. An ordinance must be content neutral and impartially administered. It cannot:

    (a) Be aimed at the suppression of free expression.

    (b) Be biased to any particular point of view.

    (c) Attempt to choose permissible subjects for public debate.

One of the reasons why the Supreme Court found San Diego's ordinance unconstitutional in *Metromedia* was that it distinguished between types of noncommercial speech. Even if an ordinance does not distinguish among topics, it could be found invalid if it gives officials the discretion to grant or refuse permits. Such arbitrary discretion, which could become a means of suppressing a particular point of view, has been deemed unconstitutional.[25] To avoid possible arbitrariness, it is important to define commercial and noncommercial speech in the ordinance.

2. An ordinance must directly advance a substantial government interest. Both aesthetics and traffic safety are generally accepted as substantial government interest.

3. An ordinance must be narrowly tailored so that it reaches no further than is necessary to achieve the substantial government interest.

4. An ordinance may be unconstitutional if it does not leave open ample alternative means of communication.

To prevent First Amendment problems in local sign ordinances, communities should not exempt certain types of political signs from their on-site sign regulations but instead should incorporate a section that exempts all noncommercial speech.

Fifth Amendment Issues

The Fifth Amendment of the United States Constitution prohibits the taking of private property without just compensation. Ordinances requiring the removal of billboards over time do not result in such takings. Although sign companies may argue that they are entitled to compensation under the Fifth Amendment, their claim is contrary to judicial rulings. Unlike eminent domain takings, billboard control does not result in government confiscation of private property. It is an exercise of the police power rather than the use of eminent domain; it only restricts the manner in which property can be used. (For the general legal background see the previous chapters.)

Because the burden of sign controls amortized over a reasonable time is limited and the public benefits are significant and widespread, courts have generally concluded that a regulation requiring the removal of billboards is a legitimate use of the police power that does not require compensation.[26]

Since billboard regulation is not a taking of private property, there is no constitutional requirement to pay compensation for sign removal. The Highway Beautification Act requires the payment of just compensation but does not define or specify a method of calculation. Regulations under the act require the states to develop appraisals or formulas to simplify valuation, but explicitly state that these formulas do not purport to calculate just compensation in terms of eminent domain.[27] Most state governments have worked out elaborate compensation formulas in conjunction with the FHWA.

Localities unable to use amortization programs may wish to take down billboards by using their power of eminent domain and paying compensation. Several different methods (Pollard 1987; Floyd 1983) are commonly used to establish fair-market value of condemned property in eminent domain proceedings, but only one of these is suitable for billboards. This is the "cost approach," which calculates the cost of repairing the billboards minus any depreciation for physical condition.[28]

The following set of guidelines is offered by Duerksen (1986, p. 33) for guidance to local communities that are drafting sign ordinances that need to pass muster on the previously mentioned legal issues.

a. First Amendment restrictions must be observed.
   Restrictions on speech are valid only if the regulation

---

[25]See Heffron v. International Society for Krishna Consciousness, Inc. 452 U.S. 640 (1981), and cases cited therein.

[26]See Art Neon Co. v. City and County of Denver 488 F.2d 118 (10th Cir. 1973).

[27]23 C.F.R. 750.304 (c) (i) (1991).

[28]See 73 A.L.R.3d 1129 (1976) for appropriate cases.

seeks to implement a substantial government interest, directly advances that interest, and reaches no further than necessary to accomplish the given objective;

b. Size, design, and placement restrictions are generally valid;

c. While promotion of aesthetic objectives alone is sufficient to regulate signs, the ordinance should clearly state the purposes for which it is being adopted. To the extent that sign control is part of a broader program of preservation districting, designating scenic roadways, or street tree planting, so much the better;

d. A distinction can be made between on-premise and off-premise signs, and the latter may be banned entirely, but care should be taken in carving out exceptions within those two categories. Unexplained differences in treatment of different kinds of noncommercial signs have been particularly troublesome;

e. All signs can be prohibited in special areas in a community such as historic districts, but great care should be taken in doing so, particularly in commercial zones and with respect to ideological signs;

f. A total communitywide ban on political and ideological signs is unconstitutional;

g. Post-campaign and post-event removal requirements are permissible, as are inspection and removal fees, if reasonable and related to administrative cost;

h. "Problem" signs, such as portable signs, can be regulated strictly, but those restrictions must bear a direct relationship to the public welfare grounds involved by the ordinance.

Regulation of an Easement of View

An interesting legal argument first developed by Wilson (1942) and endorsed by other legal scholars (Williams 1968; Martin et al. 1958) is that sign regulation is not so much an aesthetic restriction on private property as it is a regulation of an easement of view, imposed upon the public highway as a servient tenement. According to Wilson (1942, pp. 738–739):

An easement appurtenant (such as visibility from the highway) exists only for the benefit of the dominant estate, and the extent of its rightful use cannot exceed the needs of that estate.

The owner of the dominant estate cannot sever the easement from the land to which it is appurtenant — cannot sell it or reserve it apart from the land.

What is more important, he cannot use it, or authorize others to use it, for the benefit of other property, or for merely personal profit in ways that do not benefit the land to which the easement belongs and of which it is legally part.

The right of visibility is one of the rights that the law gives in order to promote the development and improvement of land bordering on public ways. It is a right appurtenant to such land, apart from which it cannot be owned and for the benefit of which it alone can be lawfully exercised. According to Wilson (1942), this means that while the owner whose property abuts the highway has the right to the advantage of visibility so far as it can further the beneficial use and occupation of the land, the owner cannot (as against the public authority owning and controlling the highway) sell or lease his right to be seen from the highway without selling or leasing the land. Also he cannot use, or authorize others to use, this privilege for the benefit of business conducted elsewhere. Legislation restricting roadside advertising encounters no legal problem except as it affects the advertising incident to the use and enjoyment of the land bordering the roads. To hold otherwise, according to Wilson, would be to ignore the *appurtenant* character of the easement of visibility as well as the public policy in which this right has its origin. The practice of making the visibility of the land a source of profit while the land is unused is in direct conflict with these principles.

This so-called "Vermont doctrine" has been upheld in court cases in Vermont,[29] New York,[30] and New Hampshire.[31] Although it has a somewhat awkward legal structure, it does go straight to the issue. What are the visibility rights of the landholder? The public regulatory agency? The viewer? This principle states that the landholder has the right of visibility, but it is tied to the bundle of property rights, and there are certain legal principles that restrict use and selling of those rights, especially uses that have nothing to do with the property.

We have already seen the regulatory structure and legal roles of federal, state, and local agencies with regard to sign control and outdoor advertising. Chapter 8 will address legal principles of visibility along major corridors in regard to the viewing public.

ALTERNATIVES TO TRADITIONAL SIGNAGE

There are alternative ways of communicating information other than billboards and traditional signage. Environmental and information design may offer compromise solutions. Some recent developments are described below.

---

[29]Kelbor v. Myrick, 113 Vt. 64, 30 A.2d 527 (1943).

[30]Perlmutter v. Greene, 259 N.Y. 327, 182 N.E. 5 (1932); New York State Thruway v. Ashley Motor Co. 10 N.Y.2d 151 176 N.E.2d 566, 218 N.Y.S.2d 240 (1961).

[31]Opinion of the Justices, 103 N.H. 268, 169 762 (1961).

FIGURE 7.6 a, b   State-designated directional signs—
Vermont. *Photo credit: Phil Smardon*

Logos: "Specific Information Signs"

The Highway Beautification Act of 1965 called for the
development of "specific information signs" along federal-aid highways to provide directional information to
the traveling public.[32] These signs came to be known as
"logo signs" since their blue backgrounds feature the
business logos of gas, food, lodging, and camping facilities. In 1972 Virginia became one of the first states to
use logos throughout its interstate network. Several
other states have used logo systems as an incentive to
get needed billboard and sign control—for instance,
Georgia and Florida.

State-Designated Directional Signs

Rather than adopting the federal logo system, some
states have designed their own motorist information

signs. Vermont's directional sign system (see Figure
7.6), for example, is one of the major reasons for the
state's success in banning billboards. It provides tourists with information they require but does so in a uniform and unobtrusive way.

Sign Plazas

On approaches to cities and in other congested areas, it
is sometimes impossible to include all available services
on logo boards or individual directional signs. One solution to this problem is to create "sign plazas" at roadside rest areas. These plazas are collections of small advertisements, usually arranged on a bulletin board that
is erected and maintained by the state transportation
agency (see Figure 7.7).

---

[32]23 U.S.C. 131 (f) (1988).

FIGURE 7.7   Sign plazas — Seaway Trail. *Photo credit: Seaway Trail Inc.*

Tourist Information Centers

A number of states have established tourist information centers at major entrances to the state and in areas off particular historical or scenic interest. Such centers are staffed by state employees or private concessionaires who provide information, answer questions, and distribute maps, guidebooks, brochures, and other advertising materials. The FHWA, in conjunction with state highway departments, is promoting research and development of such facilities.

LOCAL SIGN CONTROL ALTERNATIVES

Resources for sign control (see Glasford, undated; McNett 1987) include guides and model ordinances for local communities. Also available are the book and movie *Street Graphics* (Ewald and Mandelker 1987), which provide a performance-oriented sign ordinance system. This system is based on the bits of information a person can process when looking at a sign from a moving car. Thus the size, number of letters and images, orientation, and height of signage are determined by the rate of motion and the motorist's ability to distinguish and comprehend information. Although complicated initially to administer, such a system may be the model for future signage and regulation.

Case Study: Visual Analysis and Application: North Syracuse Signage Study

One of the keys to effective sign control (see the guidelines earlier in this chapter) is to carefully determine sign control needs based on local community characteristics. Such an approach was developed as part of a study of the village of North Syracuse's (New York) Main Street (Smardon 1985; Smardon and Goukas 1984). This study is exemplary in terms of the approach used, although several other studies addressing urban strip development could easily have been reviewed as well (Williams et al. 1982; Wickens and Nelheibel 1986).

North Syracuse's Main Street is a mix of village center, transitional land use, and full commercial strip. The basic issues were how to preserve what was left of the village center, and how to distinguish between the village center and the strip, or ribbon, development that was taking over the rest of Main Street. Signage was only one element, but it was a dominant one in terms of visual quality.

The approach used in the North Syracuse study was to assess village merchants' perceptions of the Main Street corridor image; to independently collect physical data such as existing parking, land use, and views from vehicular and pedestrian traffic; to analyze the existing village sign ordinance and conduct a review of other municipal sign ordinances and implementation processes. A detailed step-by-step methodology flow chart is shown in Figure 7.8. Unusual aspects of the approach included a door-to-door merchants' survey to enable their concerns about such matters as available parking and visibility for their signage to surface; and videotaping Main Street from both directions to capture landscape character or problems plus visibility of existing signage. The inventory was used to generate character zones for proposed sign control (Figure 7.9). A scale model of Main Street was created to simulate landscaping and sign control alternatives. A photo-questionnaire was printed in the local paper to gauge public response to proposed landscape treatment, removal of overhead utilities, and sign control (Figure 7.10a,b).

Final recommendations included a local sign ordinance

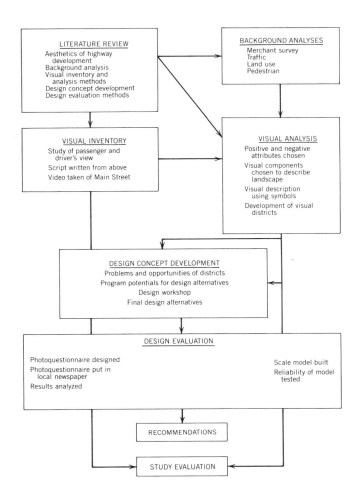

FIGURE 7.8   Flow chart of North Syracuse study. *Source: John Wiley and Sons*

keyed to the five different districts depicted in Figure 7.9. Rather than force one set of standards on all areas, which varied from village center to transitional land use to "full neon strip," it made sense to develop standards for each zone. The key is the process of looking at the local situation, then doing sufficient analysis to generate sign ordinances and control mechanisms sensitive to both the local context and the general legal requirements as reviewed earlier in this chapter.

Following the conclusion of the formal study, a North Syracuse Study Committee was established. This committee, under the leadership of one of the co-authors of the study, looked at a number of sign ordinances, then drafted a revised sign ordinance based on the original North Syracuse Study and Ewald and Mandelker (1987). The ordinance has since been adopted by the village of North Syracuse.

FIGURE 7.9   Visual character zones. *Source: John Wiley and Sons*

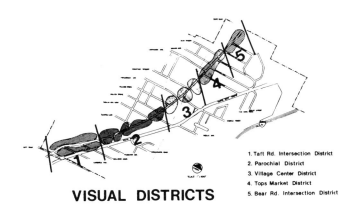

1. Taft Rd. Intersection District
2. Parochial District
3. Village Center District
4. Tops Market District
5. Bear Rd. Intersection District

VISUAL DISTRICTS

How does Main Street look to you?

How would you rate the visual appearance of Main St., North Syracuse? Are the new building facades on the buildings in the village center enough? What about the commercial signage you read while traveling this route day after day? And the landscaping; should there be more? less?

The North Syracuse Village Board consulted with Dr. Richard Smardon, from the School of Landscape Architecture, College of Environmental Science and Forestry, to try to get answers to the questions above. Two students from the masters program in the School of Landscape Architecture conducted a study to analyze the visual quality (how well does it really look) of Main St., from Bear Rd. to Taft Rd. The study inventoried and assess-

ed what Main St. had visually become and then suggested alternative solutions for changing the street's present image.

The study began in February, 1983, with a survey of thirty merchants located on Main St. as to their image of their environment. They were asked to rate such things as landscaping, commercial signage, on street parking, building facades, utility poles and lines, etc.

Next, a videotape was taken of the route from the driver's view. A video camera was mounted on a tripod and placed between the two front seats of a van. The videotape was used by the researchers to inventory and analyze Main St. block by block as to: what kind and how much vegetation is present; whether a roadside

edge exists or not; what type of open space is present; whether the signage is readible or cluttered; how noticeable the utilities are; and the building structures - their height, alignment and type. Once this information was compiled and the merchants survey was analyzed, areas exhibiting a similar character were chosen. The map to the right shows the imposed boundaries of these character areas.

Overall designs were worked out on paper by a team of landscape architects for each character area. The above-mentioned information was used as a basis for the designs. (As shown on pages 2 and 3). Photographs were taken of a representative section of each character area, ex-

cept for character areas four and five. The character of five is very similar to area one and the character of four is similar to area two. Therefore the designs would be duplicated. The design alternatives are explained next to each photograph which visually expresses the changes.

Before the study is finished, we would like your input. Please choose the alternative you prefer.

See pages two and three

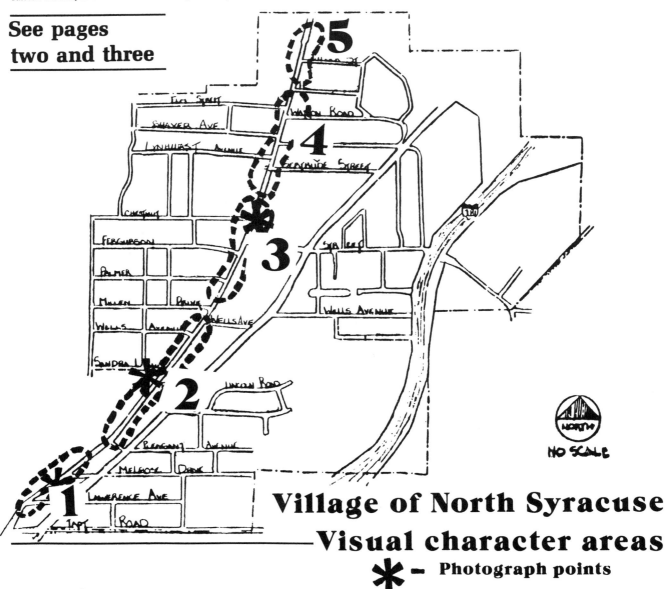

Village of North Syracuse

Visual character areas

✳ — Photograph points

FIGURE 7.10 a   Photoquestionnaire for streetscape survey. *Photo credit: Mary Burgoon*

Main Street... From Page 1

Taft Rd. intersection
Area 1

Proposed Alternative One
• No change

Proposed Alternative Two

1. Small, cluttered, signs would be removed, consolidated or put on building fronts. Large, easy to read signs would remain.
2. Gravel parking area in front of buildings would be paved.
3. Roadside edge would be added.
4. Shrubs would be planted around buildings.

Proposed Alternative Three

1. Small, cluttered, signs would be removed, consolidated or put on building fronts. Large, easy to read signs would remain.
2. Gravel parking area in front of buildings would be paved.
3. Curbs would be added.
4. Shrubs would be planted around buildings.
5. Entrances to buildings would be better defined.
6. Trees and planters would be planted along roadside edge.

Parochial
Area 2

Proposed Alternative One
• No change

Proposed Alternative Two

1. Signage would be simplified and put on the building fronts.
2. The road's edge would be grass-seeded and a curb added.
3. Some vegetation would be planted.
4. Business entrances better defined.

Proposed Alternative Three

1. Signage would be simplified and put on the building fronts.
2. Sidewalks would be added throughout area.
3. Roadside edge cleaned up.
4. Area treed heavily.
5. Utility poles and lines eliminated.

FIGURE 7.10 b   Photoquestionnaire for streetscape survey.

References

Aronovsky, R. G. 1981. *Metromedia, Inc.* v. *City of San Diego:* Aesthetics, the First Amendment, and the realities of billboard control. *Ecology Law Quarterly,* 9: 295–339.

Bufford, S. 1973. Beyond the eye of the beholder: Aesthetics and objectivity. *Michigan Law Review,* 71(6): 1438–1463.

Comptroller General, Report to the Chairman, Committee on Environment and Public Works, U.S. Senate, 1985. *The outdoor advertising control program needs to be assessed.* GAO. Accounting Office, Wash., D.C.

Cunningham, R. A. 1973. Billboard control under the Highway Beautification Act of 1965. *Michigan Law Review,* 71(7): 1296–1372.

Duerkson, C. J. 1986. Aesthetics and land use controls: beyond ecology and economics. *PAS Report 399.* American Planning Association.

Dukeminer, J. J., Jr. 1955. Zoning for aesthetic objectives: A reappraisal. Law and Contemporary Problems 20: 218–237.

Ewald, W. R., Jr., and Mandelker, D. R. 1987. *Street graphics,* 2nd ed. Landscape Architecture Foundation.

Floyd, C. F. 1982. Requiem for the Highway Beautification Act. *APA Journal* (Autumn): 441–453.

Floyd, C. F. 1983. Issues in the appraisal of outdoor advertising signs. *Appraisal Journal,* 51(10): 422–434.

Fonoroff, A. 1968. Proposed legislation for highway corridor protection. *Urban Law Annual,* 1: 128–150.

Gardner, G. K. 1936. The Massachusetts billboard decision. *Harvard Law Review,* 49(6): 869–902.

Glasford, P. *Appearance Codes for small communities.* PAS Report 379. American Planning Association.

Gould, L. L. 1986. First lady as catalyst: Lady Bird Johnson and highway beautification in the 1960's. *Environmental Review,* 10(2): 79.

Laggs, S. P. 1966. The role of aesthetics in the exercise of police power and its application to South Dakota's highway beautification statute. *South Dakota Law Review,* 11(1): 157–171.

Lam, R. D., and Yasinow, S. K. 1968. The Highway Beautification Act of 1965; A case study in legislative frustration. *Denver Law Journal,* 46: 437–452.

Lucking, J. T. 1977. The regulation of outdoor advertising: Past, present and future. *Environmental Affairs,* 6: 179–200.

McNett, K. S. 1987. *Visual pollution and sign control: A legal handbook on billboard reform.* Southern Environmental Law Center, Charlottesville. VA.

Martin, W. J., et al. 1958. Comment: Outdoor advertising control along the interstate highway system, *California Law Review,* 46(5): 796–827.

Miller, J. N. 1985. The great billboard double-cross. *Readers Digest,* June.

Moore, M. M. 1964. Regulation of outdoor advertising for aesthetic purposes. *St. Louis University Law Journal,* 8(2): 191–204.

Peters, S. 1978. The truth about beauty: The changing role of aesthetics in billboard legislation. *Environmental Law,* 9: 113–147.

Pollard, O. A., III. 1987. Billboard removal: What amount of compensation is just? *Virginia Journal of Natural Resources Law,* 6(2): 323–374.

Powers, L. 1959. Control of outdoor advertising, state implementation of federal law and standards. *Nebraska Law Review,* 38(2): 541–551.

Proffit, H. W. 1931. Public esthetics and the billboards. *Cornell Law Quarterly,* 41(2): 151–179.

Smardon, R. C. 1985. A visual approach to redesigning the commercial strip. *Transportation research record 1016.* TRB, National Research Council, pp. 1–6.

Smardon, R. C., and Goukas, M. M. 1984. *Village of North Syracuse, Main Street study.* School of Landscape Architecture Occasional Paper ESF 84-010. State University of New York, College of Environmental Science and Forestry.

Wickens, M. J., and Nelheibel, V. R. 1986. *Am image renaissance: Detroit I-94-US10 entrance corridor.* Prepared for Michigan Department of Transportation.

Williams, Hatfield and Stoner, Inc. and the Townscape Institute. 1982. *University Drive Workshop Workbook.* Townscape Institute.

Williams, N., Jr. 1968. Legal techniques to protect and to promote aesthetics along transportation corridors. *Buffalo Law Review,* 17: 701–716.

Wilson, R. I. 1942. Billboards and the right to be seen from the highway. *Georgetown Law Journal,* 30(7): 723–750.

Ziegler, E. H. 1985. Local control of signs and billboards; An analysis of recent regulatory efforts. *Zoning and Planning Law Report,* 8(10): 161–167.

Chapter 8

Scenic View Protection

INTRODUCTION

This chapter addresses the notion of view protection or preservation — that is, of particular views from particular points looking at specific visual landscape features and along transportation corridors (Figure 8.1). Corridor-specific issues include (1) visual accessibility to scenic aspects of the roadside landscape or specific landscape features such as rivers, and (2) upgrading the whole visual experience of entering a city or park. Chapters 5, 6, and 7 addressed aspects of zoning and land use control, architectural control of structures, and control of signage. This chapter is an "overlay" on them. It includes some of the previously mentioned control mechanisms but focuses on preserving visual access or quality of specific views; it thus encompasses or spills over into issues of land use, architecture, and signage (Figure 8.1).

HISTORY OF VIEW PROTECTION

Scenic view protection dates back to the late 1800s. In one early case, an ordinance was challenged whose objective was the protection of views of the Massachusetts state capitol building in Boston.[1] Boston was a leader in its attempt to protect Copley Square from being overshadowed by surrounding buildings. Boston's efforts were upheld by the Massachusetts high court and the U.S. Supreme Court.[2] The former held that the creation of high buildings might exclude sun-shine, light, and air to the detriment of the public health. Washington, D.C., had an early height-restriction ordinance based on the height of the U.S. capitol building, and several state capitals followed suit (see Figure 8.2).

In the 1930s a scenic roadway movement caught on, starting with the Winchester County parkways in New York State; the same designer was involved in the creation of the Blue Ridge Parkway in Virginia (Figure 8.3) and North Carolina, which was followed by the Natchez Trace Parkway and Skyline Drive. Many of these parkways are administered today by the National Park Service and the respective state agencies.

When the Blue Ridge and Natchez Trace parkways were planned, it was decided to use scenic easements for portions of the right of way to keep costs down (Cunningham 1968). The actual formula was 100 acres in fee simple and 50 acres subject to scenic easements per mile of parkway. Scenic easements were also acquired by the states and later transferred to the National Park Service. Eventually, the scenic easements acquired along the Blue Ridge Parkway covered nearly 1,500 acres and those along the Natchez Trace Parkway more than 4,500 acres.

Unfortunately, the experience with scenic easements along the two parkways has not been a happy one. Difficulties in negotiating and implementing scenic easements arose from (1) landowners who wanted to harvest timber and (2) owners who wanted to subdivide and develop their land for resort or residential use

---

[1]Parker v. Commonwealth 59 N.E. 634 (Mass. 1896).
[2]Welch v. Swasey 193 Mass. 364, 79 N.E. 745 (1907) *aff'd.* 214 U.S. 91 (1909).

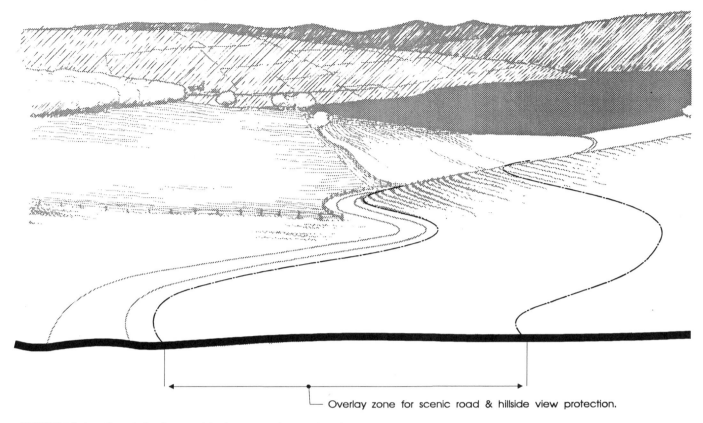

Overlay zone for scenic road & hillside view protection.

FIGURE 8.1   Generic landscape with view protection overlay. *Credit: Scott Shannon*

(Cunningham 1968). There were also problems with use of eminent domain along the Blue Ridge Parkway to acquire land in fee simple and easements. Local landowners felt that their land was being taken without due process or adequate compensation. In addition, there was much conflict with and resentment in general toward the federal government.

The other major road project that the National Park Service was historically involved in was the Great River Road, a scenic highway on both sides of the Mississippi River from New Orleans to the Lake of the Woods in Canada. It was originally conceived in the 1930s as the Mississippi River Parkway. The ten states involved were to acquire easements and rights-of-way.[3] World War II and other events intervened, but planning money became available, and the states of Wisconsin and Minnesota have made progress on acquiring scenic easements for the Great River Road.

The National Park Service has used scenic easements for special problem cases such as Cumberland Gap National Historical Park, Manassas National Battlefield Park, Piscataway Park near the Potomac River, and the Merrywood Estate adjacent to the

George Washington Memorial Parkway in Virginia. Many states have authorized legislation for scenic easement acquisition along highways. Wisconsin and California have had the most experience followed by

FIGURE 8.2   Capitol view protection zone — Montpelier, Vermont. *Photo credit: R. C. Smardon*

---

[3]All of the Mississippi River states have enabling legislation sufficient for scenic easement acquisition.

FIGURE 8.3   View from the Blue Ridge Parkway. *Photo credit: Bill Hammitt*

FIGURE 8.4   View of Rocky Mountains from Denver area. *Photo credit: Mathew Potteiger*

Iowa, Michigan, Minnesota, Illinois, Maryland, New York, Montana, and Oregon. (A good summary of past experience with scenic easements can be found in Cunningham's 1968 article.)

As Williams (1975) has stated, in few instances were special regulations imposed in order to protect scenic views of unique importance or distinction. Such regulations may apply either to the area included in the view itself, or at one or more viewpoints, or both. Such regulations may require land to be left open, or may simply impose strict height limits.

From 1968 to 1971 Denver initiated a series of ordinances collectively called the Mountain View Ordinance.[4] The Front Range of the Rocky Mountains in Colorado rises steeply for about 10,000 feet at the western edge of the Great Plains (see Figure 8.4) and is one of the most spectacular scenes in the United States. The city of Denver is about ten miles away, and superb views of the range are available from several large open spaces in Denver, especially in the city's parks. Since these views comprise Denver's most distinctive scenic experience, the city has acted to protect them by a special series of ordinances. These ordinances establish restrictions on the height of buildings in order to preserve the panoramic views of the Front Range. Specifically, a

reference point is established at the farthest (eastern) edge of each park; and buildings are not permitted to penetrate an inclined plane that extends west from that point at the rate of one foot vertical for each 100 feet horizontal.[5]

A similar principle underlies a proposed zoning amendment in Honolulu that would map a "historic-cultural-scenic overlay zone"[6] at several critical areas in the city, to protect the famous view (see Figure 8.5) of Diamond Head.[7] These proposed regulations would apply both along the lower edge of the sight to be viewed (in this case, Diamond Head) and also at a number of viewpoints. New construction would be limited to a height varying from 25 to 40 feet in the area on the lower slopes of Diamond Head and nearby, as part of a rather elaborate long-term municipal program to remove the military installations on Diamond Head (primarily hidden in the crater) and also to minimize the effects of the high-rise apartment buildings that had been permitted in the area between Diamond Head and the point to the south. In addition, the proposed regulations would prohibit any further construction at all as seen from a few critical viewpoints, particularly in Kapiolani Park (near the base of the slope) and at nearby Ala Kai golf course.

---

[4]Ordinance no. 60, Series of 1968, from Cramer Park; Ordinance no. 260 Series of 1968, from Cheesman Park, Ordinance no. 452 Series of 1969, from Ruby Hill Park; Ordinance no. 132, Series of 1971, from the Denver Civic Center.

[5]Or 1.7 feet per 100 feet in the later ordinances.

[6]This is one of the regular zoning districts in Honolulu (s. 21-380 of the zoning law) and has been used for various purposes.

[7]See "Scenic Zoning for Diamond Head," in *Oahu Development Conference,* Planning Issues Vol. IV no. 1 (Winter 1971).

FIGURE 8.5 a, b   View to and from Diamond Head, Honolulu. *Photo credit: R. C. Smardon*

VIEW PROTECTION MECHANISMS

Today capital cities, including Austin, Denver, Lincoln, Sacramento, Tallahassee, and Washington, D.C., preserve views of their capitols and surrounding environs with various setback provisions. Some city ordinances protect views of cultural amenities, such as Eastman Theater in Rochester, New York; Pittsburgh preserves river views; Denver, Colorado, Burlington, Vermont, and Portland, Oregon, protect their mountain vistas; and Seattle mandates a series of setbacks within view corridors of the Elliott Bay, West Seattle, and the Olympic Mountains. Cincinnati's hillside protection ordinance preserves prominent hillsides with views of major streams or valleys. Likewise, Austin, Texas, has designated five hill-country corridors to protect scenic views and encourage orderly and environmentally sensitive development in the city's watersheds.

View protection mechanisms are many and draw upon much of the material already presented in Chapters 5, 6, and 7. Height limits and mandatory setbacks established through special districts and overlay zones or view protection corridors build on the material presented in Chapter 5. Site plan and planned development review as well as massing and bulk requirements draw from material presented in Chapter 6. The use of environmental regulations will be covered in more detail in Chapters 10 and 11. These mechanisms typically are implemented through zoning, but they need not be. Denver's Mountain View Ordinance, for example, is part of the city's building code.

Special Districts and Zoning

The simplest technique is a mandatory cap on building height. To preserve views of the nation's capitol dome, Congress passed the Building Height Limitation Act of 1910, which established a citywide building height cap at 110 feet, with some exemptions on Pennsylvania Avenue.

Austin uses two mechanisms to protect capitol views. Its Capitol Domain Zoning District is an overlay that limits heights within one-quarter mile of the capitol building to 653 feet above sea level and permits proportional increases depending on the structure's distance from the capitol. A second method, incorporating twenty-eight Capital View Corridor Zones, is based on a comprehensive formula of trigonometric projections. This more complex method grew out of an exhaustive study that initially identified sixty significant corridors and analyzed the anticipated economic impact of protecting each. Less complicated formulas, used in Lincoln, Nebraska, and Tallahassee, Florida, work by projecting angles from the capitol dome to various sites.

Architectural Review

Other techniques for enhancing views are site plan and planned development (reviewed in Chapter 6). For instance, the zoning ordinance for downtown Rochester, New York, states: "Site plan review of all new development . . . is intended to protect significant views of the Eastman Theatre." Likewise, in Burlington, Vermont, any structure over thirty-five feet must undergo design and site plan review; one of the design criteria is the preservation of views of Lake Champlain (Figure 8.6) and the Adirondack Mountains to the west. Protecting scenic vistas is also one of the review standards for approving new development in the Wilmington, Delaware, waterfront district.

Massing and bulk controls are used to enhance views through architectural control ordinances (covered in Chapter 6). San Francisco and Pittsburgh have enacted bulk requirements that effectively slim down and

FIGURE 8.6   Waterfront view from Burlington, Vermont.
Photo credit: R. C. Smardon

"taper" buildings. San Francisco allows some exemptions from its height restrictions, of up to 10 percent, for undertaking additional bulk reduction in upper towers to create a "more slender profile and sculptured building termination." In two areas flanking Pittsburgh's Monongahela River, floor areas above 300 feet shrink according to a city-mandated formula. Also, building heights are staggered according to their proximity to the river. All or most of the aforementioned approaches are under the traditional police powers of zoning and architectural review of municipalities.

Environmental Project Review

Another approach to view protection is through environmental regulation in state and local jurisdictions. Examples include Washington's Shoreline Management Act of 1971, which sets stringent height limits on waterfront development; New York's Adirondack Park, which has detailed criteria for aesthetics concerns and for preserving scenic areas (Note 1975); and Vermont's Act 250, which reviews all development above certain size thresholds and also uses aesthetics criteria (Fonoroff 1968) as part of project review. (Environmental project review will be dealt with in more detail in Chapters 10 and 11.)

Scenic Easements

Scenic easements, a tool for preserving views, are not defined precisely very often. A 1939 Arkansas statute that created the Mississippi River Parkway defines a scenic easement as:

"Scenic, landscape, sighting or safety easement" shall mean a servitude devised to permit land to remain in private use consistent with parkway purposes determined by the secretary (U.S. Secretary of the Interior) and at the same time placing a control over the future use of the area to maintain its scenic, landscape, sightly or safety values of the parkway in the state.[8]

Cunningham (1968) notes that there is nothing in the nature of a "scenic easement" that requires it to be appurtenant, as we discussed in Chapter 7, although "scenic easements" designed to preserve scenic and historical value along highways will, normally, be appurtenant to the highway, with the highway constituting the dominant estate.

From the point of view of the servient landowner, a scenic easement is primarily a restriction upon the uses that she might otherwise lawfully make of her land. From the point of view of the persons entitled to the benefit of the easement — for instance, the traveling public on a highway to which a scenic easement is appurtenant — the scenic easement is essentially an easement of view. As such, according to Cunningham (1968, p. 171), it may provide a benefit in at least three ways:

1. Something attractive to look at within the easement area.
2. An open area to look through in order to see something attractive beyond the easement itself.
3. A screen to block out an unsightly view beyond the easement area.

Since the advantage of scenic easement is its flexibility, there are no standard forms or format. According to Cunningham (1968, p. 168), however, scenic easements usually include the following:

1. A restriction of new building construction or major alteration of existing structures to farms and residential buildings only, with an express prohibition of new commercial structures and a saving clause permitting the continuance of existing uses and structures;
2. An authorization for necessary public utility lines and roads;
3. A prohibition against cutting "mature trees and shrubs," but with a provision authorizing normal maintenance;
4. A prohibition against dumping; and
5. A prohibition against outdoor advertising, except for advertising of activities located on the premises.

---

[8]Ark. Stat. Ann. ss. 76-1801 to 1811 (1957).

In addition to the above restrictions, or negative rights, a scenic easement may include one or more affirmative privileges, such as right of entry for the state highway agency to remove structures or plantings in violation of the restrictions, to repair damage done to plantings or other vegetation in violation of the restrictions, to cut and prune brush and trees in order to keep a scenic view, or to engage in landscaping operations.

A substantial body of U.S. case law recognizes a common law negative easement of prospect or view. It has been recognized in California,[9] Massachusetts,[10] Rhode Island,[11] New York,[12] Vermont,[13] and Wisconsin.[14] The Wisconsin case is specific to scenic easements (see legal issues, below).

In general, U.S. case law supports the view that an easement of view or prospect is a recognized "legal" interest in land (Cunningham 1968). However, scenic easements are not without administrative problems in terms of valuation: How much do you pay for them? And enforcement: How do you ensure that the restrictions are observed by the present property owner or the subsequent one?

SCENIC BYWAY PROGRAMS

The Scenic Byways 88 Conference (USDOT FHWA 1988), held in Washington, D.C., showed that there were many states involved in grass roots activity to protect and manage scenic roads. These roads are the two-lane roads that William Least Heat Moon termed "Blue Highways"; they stretch over 3 million miles across the United States (Figure 8.7). Almost every state has taken some type of action to recognize them. Twenty-three states have established programs to designate them as "scenic," and three more states are considering doing so. Fifteen states, without formal programs, have an official list of historic and scenic roads. Several of the remaining states have no program or list because it is generally believed that since so many of their roads are scenic, it would be difficult to choose among them (FHWA 1988). Once such byways are designated, the most difficult aspect is managing the right-of-way and surrounding land use to keep the views open and the existing visual quality intact.

URBAN ENTRYWAYS

The final development in view preservation might be called view reclamation, as many cities are trying to

FIGURE 8.7   A scenic byway. *Photo credit: R. C. Smardon*

preserve or re-create positive visual experiences along major entryways to the community. In May 1984, New Orleans adopted new zoning provisions to prevent further unsightly commercial strip development along its major roads. The purpose of the new provisions is to provide a "superior environment and positive design image" for this historic city.

The city established an overlay district with special sign and landscaping requirements that applied to other uses as well. Some permitted uses, such as fast food restaurants and developments of one acre or more, are made conditional uses and subject to special site plan review.

Sign regulations are also tightened. The size of any sign is linked to the amount of building frontage; the maximum area is limited to 70 feet and the height to 25 feet or the building height, whichever is lower. No flashing signs are allowed, and rate signs must be integrated into the one detached sign allowed on site. Nonconforming signs are subject to a three-year amortization period. Finally, special site design requirements are imposed, including perimeter and interior landscaping, landscaped setbacks, screened loading areas, and lighting restrictions.

Austin has created special controls on land located within 200 feet of designated "scenic" and "principal" roadways. It has also enacted special protective regulations for land within 1,000 feet of Route 360, known as the Capital of Texas Highway. The following restrictions apply:

1. **Scenic Roadways.** No off-premise signs are allowed within a 200-foot zone on either side of the road.

---

[9]Peterson v. Friedman, 162 Cal. App.2d 245, 328 P.2d 264 (1958).

[10]Ladd v. Boston, 24 N.E. 858 (1890) Attorney General v. Williams, 174 Mass. 476, 55 N.E. 77 (1899).

[11]Caldwalader v. Bailey, 17 R.I. 495, 23 A. 20 (1891).

[12]Latimer v. Livermore, 72 N.Y. 174 (1878).

[13]Fuller v. Arms 45 Vt. 400 (1873); Hopkins the Florist Inc. V. Fleming 112 Vt. 389, 26 A.2d 96 (1942).

[14]Kamrowski v. State, 31 Wisc.2d 256, 142 N.W.2d 793 (1966).

On-premise signs are restricted to one small monument-style sign integrated into the landscaping plan. Special size and height limits apply as does a prohibition on flashing signs.

2. **Principal Roadways.** Only one freestanding commercial sign is permitted on each parcel; a 1,000-foot spacing requirement exists for off-premise signs.

3. **Capital of Texas Highway.** Only monument-style signs with maximum of two colors are allowed. Signs must be of natural color, and materials must be compatible with surrounding environment. No flashing or neon signs or internal lighting is permitted (Duerksen 1986, pp. 21-22).

The city of Albuquerque has enacted similar comprehensive guidelines for development along Coors Boulevard, a principal traffic artery, to protect views of the Sandia Mountains and Rio Grande River Valley and to ensure quality developments. The plan defines view planes and then prohibits buildings from penetrating them. Landscaping must also be designed so as not to intrude into the view planes. Other special guidelines relating to architectural design, signs, landscaping, and other site plan elements are also set forth. The plan is currently being revised due to some difficulties in applying the design guidelines, which have not been followed by all developers.

The Albuquerque situation illustrates the difficulty of such view protection that necessarily incorporates many elements, including zoning, architectural, and sign control, as well as trying to control new development while making old development conform to new standards.

There is no tougher operating environment for visual landscape management than the urban strip. The author has done several studies (see Figure 8.8) for urban strip reclamation in New York State (Lambe and Smardon 1986; Smardon 1985; Smardon and Goukas 1984). However, when a city such as Detroit actually studies visual upgrading the entryway from the airport to downtown Detroit, then there is hope (Wilkens 1986).

VIEW PROTECTION: THE CONTROVERSIES

Sometimes scenic view protection conflicts directly with land use and economic development. Illustrative situations and their related controversies abound.

Washington, D.C., with the traditional building height cap and the Potomac Riverbelt Greenway, is a case in point. A 52-story Port America high-rise building was proposed for Prince Georges County, Maryland, to be designed by architects Philip Johnson and John Burgee. The project has strong backing of the local government, which foresees this massive developing as putting their county "on the map." Arrayed against the development is an impressive group of pres-

ervation organizations, national capital planning entities, and federal agencies such as the National Park Service, which fear that this massive building will not only intrude on the low-rise skyline of the capital, but will set a precedent for a ring of gigantic structures around Washington, D.C. (Stuart 1980).

Similar disputes are being played out in Austin, Denver, Houston, and many other cities and towns. In Philadelphia, a proposal to build two office towers that would dwarf the William Penn statue atop city hall (long held to be the unofficial height limit for the community) has kicked off a bitter struggle and led to the mayor calling for a complete revamping of the city's downtown comprehensive plan. The buildings were not built. Similar issues have driven view access disputes in San Francisco and Seattle, as we saw in Chapter 6.

Entryways to national parks and monuments have suffered from rampant strip development leading right up to the park entrance, as well as creating views that are incompatible with the historic character of parks and monuments. Such issues have become major management problems for the National Park Service (see Sax 1980; Sax and Keiter 1987) in areas like Gettysburg National Battlefield Monument.

Control of rural ribbon development, such as in scenic portions of Vermont and in the St. Lawrence River–Thousand Island area, has its own forms of controversy. What controls are possible or defensible in order to keep views open in rural areas with little or no existing planning and land use control? This brings us to legal issues related to view protection that usually arise out of such controversies.

LEGAL ISSUES AND VIEW PROTECTION

There have been only a few challenges to scenic view ordinances, and they have generally met with little success. Typically, the primary issue involved is whether the regulations are so stringent as to deny all reasonable use and are thereby in effect a taking.

A challenge to Denver's Mountain View Ordinance, enacted in 1968, was rejected on grounds that there was no taking and that such an ordinance was supportable on aesthetic grounds.[15] The Mountain View Ordinance allowed buildings near Southmoor Park to be only 42 feet high, with two additional feet allowed for each 100 feet the building was erected away from the reference point in the park. The plaintiffs wanted to construct a 21-story office building, which the current zoning would have allowed notwithstanding the limits of the Mountain View Ordinance. Neighbors of the proposed building opposed the project and, in 1982, persuaded the city council to apply the challenged restrictions over objections of the plaintiffs and the planning board. Despite a finding that the restrictions caused a sub-

---

[15]Landmark Land Co. v. City and County of Denver 728 P.2d 1281 (Colo. 1986).

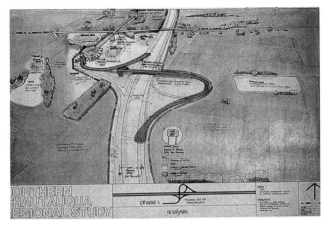

a.

b.

d.

c.

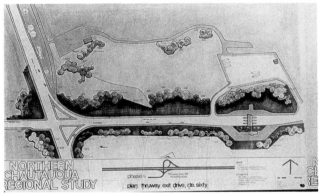

e.

FIGURE 8.8 a, b, c, d, e   Urban entryway—Fredonia study.
*Photo credit: SUNY Faculty of Landscape Architecture, Syracuse,
New York*

stantial diminution in economic value, the court held there was no taking because the properties still had real estate value. The trial court judge actually visited several parks protected by the law and rejected out-of-hand the contention that the ordinance did not serve a valid police power objective (Duerkson 1986).

In December 1986, the Colorado Supreme Court[16] upheld the Mountain View Ordinance. One of the developers' arguments was that the portion of the ordinance covering Southmoor Park was a subterfuge for the real animating initiative—growth management. The 1982 amendment to the ordinance, which extended mountain view protection to Southmoor Park,

apparently had been instigated by neighbors abutting the previously mentioned-21 story landmark project, who also had attempted to downzone the area.

The Colorado court refused to question legislative motives, stating that mountains were a fundamental part of Denver's "unique environmental heritage." The court held that protecting the right to see the distant scenery was a legitimate exercise of the city's police power, notwithstanding the fact that Landmark Land Company might be deprived of the maximum return for its property (Lassar 1987).

The Colorado Supreme Court also dismissed arguments that the city action was quasi-judicial (not fully

---

[16]Id.

legal or addressing special due process requirements) or special legislation. Citing *Berman* v. *Parker*,[17] the court stated: "It has been well established that protection of aesthetics is a legitimate function of legislation. . . . [E]specially in the context of Denver—a city whose civic identity is associated with its connection with the mountains."[18] Finally, and most significantly, the Colorado Supreme Court reiterated its high threshold for a successful claim that a land use regulation constitutes an unconstitutional "taking.":

It is well-settled rule in Colorado that in order to establish that an ordinance which restricts the use of land is unconstitutional it must be shown that the ordinance precludes the use of (the) property for *any* reasonable purpose (due process and just compensation clauses of Federal and State Constitutions do not require that a landowner be allowed to make the most profitable use of his property).[19]

Generally, scenic protection measures will not be so onerous as to deny all reasonable use of a property. However, a case from Arizona demonstrates that in extreme situations they may be so strict as to effect a taking.[20] Scottsdale had enacted a hillside protection ordinance that severely restricted development in the McDowell Mountains, a unique geographic area of hilly and mountainous terrain. The hillside ordinance established two areas: a conservation zone within which land was set aside solely for open space and had development limitations due to steep slopes, rockfalls or landslides, and soil erosion; and a development area in which land could be developed subject to certain limits. Development rights for building structures could be transferred from the conservation zone to the development area to alleviate potential hardship. Under the ordinance, 80 percent of the plaintiff's land was in a conservation area.

Finding that Scottsdale was actually attempting to establish a public mountain preserve without paying for it, the Arizona Court of Appeals struck down the ordinance as a taking and also held that only money, not density credits could amount to "just compensation." Moreover, the court held that, under Arizona law,

public interest in aesthetics, standing alone, is often too vague to offset substantial injury to landowners in a rezoning case. . . . The evidence does not support nor did the trial judge find that a deplorable condition exists or would exist without the hillside ordinance.[21]

This decision was upheld on appeal to the Arizona Supreme Court, which also ruled that damages were payable for a temporary taking while the offending regulations were in place. While the *Corrigan* decision is limited in application to Arizona and has come under severe criticism, it stands as a warning to local governments to proceed carefully in the area of protecting scenic views when restrictions effectively prohibit development on significant tracks of land.

SCENIC EASEMENTS AND EMINENT DOMAIN

Two important cases on the public use requirements related to scenic easements in eminent domain cases are *Berman* v. *Parker*[22] and *Kamrowski* v. *State*.[23] In *Berman* the U.S. Supreme Court sustained a congressional act authorizing urban redevelopment in the District of Columbia against constitutional attack, even though the statute authorized the taking by eminent domain of private property and the sale or lease thereof to other private persons for private rather than public uses (Cunningham 1968).

Although the Supreme Court in *Berman* used the term "police power" in its broadest sense, as constituting the totality of legislative power—including the power of eminent domain—rather than simply the power to regulate, many state courts have relied on the *Berman* dictum on aesthetic values in sustaining aesthetic zoning under the police power, as in the Denver Mountain View Ordinance case. Whether the *Berman* holding really supports "aesthetic regulation" or not, it seems clear that it does support the use of the eminent domain power to condemn land for aesthetic purposes. Since *Hawaii Housing Authority* v. *Midkiff*[24] in 1984 the distinction between a public use under eminent domain and a public purpose under the police power is academic. In *Midkiff*, the Court held that the concepts are "coterminus" (also see Lewis 1985).

The *Berman* case did not, and could not, decide that

[17]348 U.S. 26 (1954).

[18]Landmark Land Co. v. City and County of Denver 728 P.2d 1281, 1285 (Colo. 1986).

[19]Id.

[20]Corrigan v. City of Scottsdale, 720 P.2d 528 (Ariz. App. 1986) *aff'd. in part, rev'd. in part* 720 P.2d 513 (Ariz. 1986).

[21]Id.

[22]348 U.S. 26 (1954).

[23]31 Wisc.2d 256, 142 N.W.2d 793 (1966).

[24]467 U.S. 229 (1984).

the Fourteenth Amendment permits the exercise of state eminent domain powers for purposes that do not involve any "use by the public" in the narrow sense, or primarily for aesthetic purposes. The case did decide that the Fifth Amendment permits this when the Supreme Court applies different standards in dealing with an attack on state scenic easement enabling legislation based on the Fourteenth Amendment. It thus seems clear the Supreme Court will sustain state scenic easement-enabling legislation against Fourteenth Amendment attack based on the arguments that land made subject to scenic easement restrictions will not be available for use by the public, and that aesthetic purposes are not public purposes. The *Berman* opinion is viewed as a persuasive precedent by state courts in dealing with attacks on scenic easement enabling legislation grounded upon state constitutional provisions.

The Wisconsin Supreme Court in *Kamrowski* v. *State* specifically upheld the acquisition of scenic easements under the power of eminent domain. This case dealt with a legislative program in Wisconsin for the condemnation of scenic easements along the Mississippi River to preserve natural, undeveloped views for passing motorists. The condemned area would continue to be used for agricultural production but could not be used for more intensive purposes such as residential or commercial. The scenic easement program was challenged on the basis that "public enjoyment of the scenic beauty of certain land is not a public use of such land."[25] The court held that aesthetics may provide the dominant objective for a condemnation proceeding, using support from an earlier case[26] that had declared that "enjoyment of scenic beauty is a legal right."[27] What is even more interesting is the court's definition of public use in a purely aesthetic vein:

The learned trial judge succinctly answered plaintiff's claim that occupancy by the public is essential in order to have public use by saying in the instant case, 'the occupancy is visual.' The enjoyment of the scenic beauty by the public which passes along the highway seems to be a direct use by the public of the rights in land which have been taken in the form of a scenic easement.[28]

There are two possible lines of attack on the public use issue. First, following the Wisconsin court in *Kamrowski,* the courts could simply hold that the "enjoyment of the scenic beauty by the public which passes along the highway" is a direct use by the public of the rights in land that have been taken in the form of a scenic easement. Second, the state courts might rely on cases holding "public use" to mean simply public purpose, as the U.S. Supreme Court did in the *Hawaii Housing Authority* case.

Whatever the line of defense used, the authors are more interested in the clear logic in "public visual occupancy," which defines the public use related to the purpose of scenic easements and also nicely defines the public use question raised in Chapter 7. Also, public occupancy can be analytically determined by visibility analysis techniques that will be illustrated in the case study below.

Case Study: St. Lawrence River Scenic Access Study

The concept of "visual occupancy" prompted the author to study public enjoyment of views of the St. Lawrence River from the Seaway Trail (Figure 8.9) beginning in 1983 (see Smardon 1987 or Smardon et al. 1984). In New York State, Section 247 of the municipal law allows local jurisdictions to acquire scenic easements to preserve views and visual access. We wanted to know what views needed to be protected for the towns through which the Seaway Trail passed.

We used two basic evaluative criteria: the general quality of the view, and the amount of visual access to the river. These criteria were arranged within a management matrix, with the views with the highest quality and degree of visual access demanding the highest priority for protection. Since almost all views in this study extended over private land (key views from riverside access points extend from public lands), our ultimate concern was initiating appropriate management techniques. The towns involved in the study were concerned that we would find a lot of land in need of acquisition via scenic easements.

Documenting Visual Occupancy

Black-and-white photographs documented all views from the Seaway Trail to the St. Lawrence River for a 50-mile stretch of highway. Through detailed field notes, highway tenth-mile markers, compass, and standard angle of view (22.5 or 30 degrees) progressing from left to right, view beginnings and endings were precisely located, as well as width of angle and direction on 1-inch-equals-800-feet scale maps (See Figure 8.10). The photographs were enlarged to 5-by-7 inches and spliced together to create panoramas. Photographs were taken in late summer and mid-fall to show views from the same position on the roadside with and without leaves on the trees.

---

[25]Kamrowski v. State, 31 Wisc.2d 256, 261, 142 N.W.2d 793, 795 (1966).
[26]Muench v. Public Serv. Comm'n. 261 Wisc. 492, 53 N.W.2d 514 (1952).
[27]Id. at 511–12, 53 N.W.2d at 522.
[28]Kamrowski v. State 31 Wisc.2d 256, 142 N.W.2d 793 (1966).

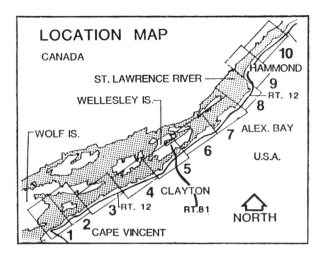

LOCATION MAP

CANADA

ST. LAWRENCE RIVER

WELLESLEY IS.

WOLF IS.

10

HAMMOND

9

RT. 12

8

7   ALEX. BAY

6

U.S.A.

5

4   CLAYTON

3   RT. 12   RT. 81

2   CAPE VINCENT

1

NORTH

FIGURE 8.9   Location map for the St. Lawrence Study

Detailed notes, field measurements, photographs, and ac-etate jig allowed transposition of view locations to base maps, using either direct compass reading or compass-bearing method. By this method one could see the land area over which each view of the river extended (see Figure 8.11). After transferring this information to paper-copy maps delineating year-round and seasonal view sheds, a clear display method was developed that facilitated making copies of the base maps (see Figure 8.12).

Determining View Quality

The second step in the process was determining the relative quality of the 125 views along the Seaway Trail. This was done via visual preference testing. Two groups of respondents, local residents and students, were asked to rate 20 black-and-white panoramas that were representative of the 125 views compiled. Once the 1 (low) to 10 (high) ratings were compiled for all 20 scenes for the two rating groups, scenes fell out into high, medium, and low visual quality categories.

The question then was why scenes were so rated. Another group was asked to determine specific negative and positive attributes of the original 20 rated scenes (Figure 8.13). The visual cues (Figure 8.14) used from this exercise plus the original quantitative ratings were used as guidance to rank the rest of the 125 views either high, medium, or low visual quality. These rankings were then applied to the mapped views already obtained from the visual documentation process. Thus, all views now had both visual access and visual quality mapped in documented form.

Results

After identifying the intersecting point of town boundaries and the Seaway Trail, the total length of road associated with each view was measured and noted for each town. These measurements were converted into equivalent miles to determine each town's mileage total; the percentage of each town's low-, moderate-, and high-ranked views; each town's total miles of visual access; and the percentage relationships for each town.

Of the 43.8 miles of Seaway Trail in the first study area, 37.5 percent, or 16 miles of the highway, have visual access to the river. Of this portion, 8.3 percent (3.6 miles) were rated

high; 21.5 percent (9.4 miles) were moderate; and 7.7 percent (3.4 miles) were low. Of the visually accessible road areas, the ratio of low-, moderate-, and high-quality views is approximately 1 : 3 : 1, respectively. We did not, but easily could have, calculated the land area for which scenic easements would need to be acquired. There was a lot less land area involved than some towns had feared, but two towns that had more visual access to the river did need more area protected.

Recommendations

Future planning and management decisions will have the greatest potential impact on moderate-quality views. These views may be enhanced in order to create high-quality views by changing land use character, removing certain distracting features, or managing vegetative growth. On the other hand, certain views could easily be degraded further. Detailed recommendations included:

- Use of scenic easements by the St. Lawrence–Eastern Ontario Commission (for whom we did the study) and local governments to ensure protection of high quality views in danger of imminent land use changes.
- Use of the New York State Environmental Quality Review Act and designation of high-quality views as scenic areas of statewide significance under Coastal Policy 24 to ensure protection by state and local government action.
- Development of an educational/interpretive program stressing the importance of scenic resources and the need for local governments to develop appropriate policy and legal tools to control adverse development.
- Development of overlay zoning and site review mechanisms to restrict encroachment from private development on high-quality view areas. Design guidelines could be developed for problematic land uses, such as trailer parks, vacation homes, and commercial development.

Since the study was completed in 1984 there has been some limited use of scenic easements, especially to protect island shoreline. We have studied another 50-mile segment of Seaway Trail—this time documenting the view from the water to the land via video—to help make recommendations for a green-line park within the St. Lawrence–Thousand Island area (Shannon et al. 1990).

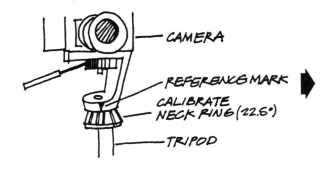

CAMERA

REFERENCE MARK

CALIBRATE
NECK RING (22.5°)

TRIPOD

Tripod Pan Head

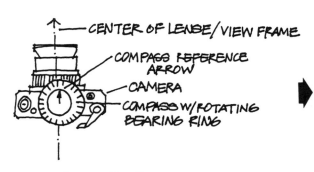

CENTER OF LENSE/VIEW FRAME

COMPASS REFERENCE ARROW

CAMERA

COMPASS W/ ROTATING BEARING RING

Compass Mounting

PLUMB BOB

SHUTTER RELEASE

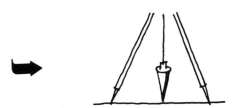

Camera Height Adjustment

ALIGN CAMERA TO DIRECT COMPASS HEADING

Compass Direction

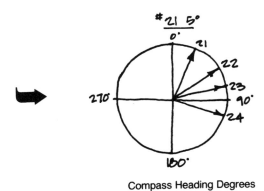

Compass Heading Degrees

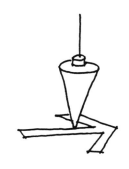

View Point Marking

FIGURE 8.10   Photo documentation process

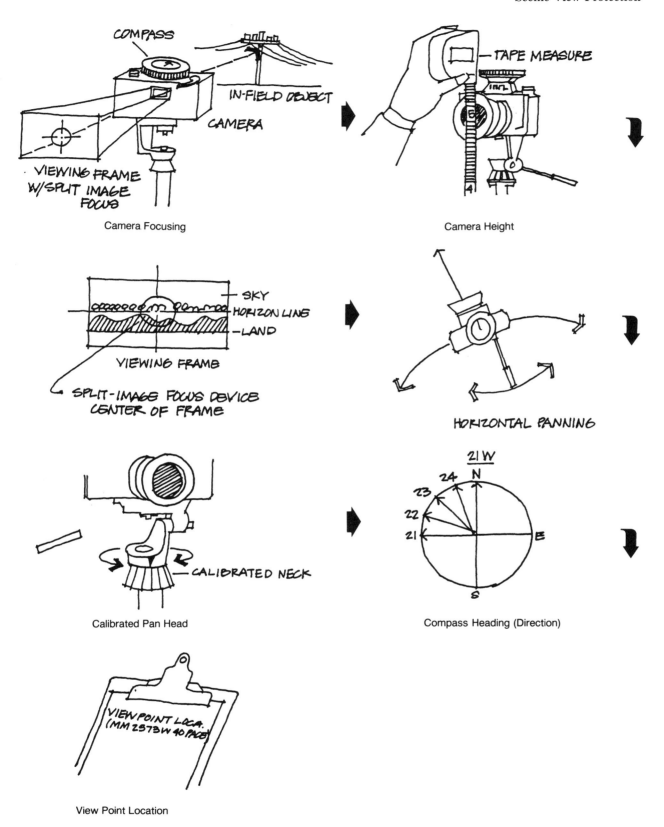

Camera Focusing

Camera Height

Viewing Frame

Horizontal Panning

Calibrated Pan Head

Compass Heading (Direction)

View Point Location

FIGURE 8.10   (*Continued*) Photo documentation process

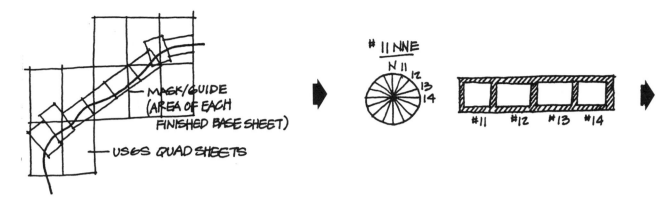

Base Map Production

Data Sheet Information

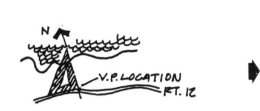

Locate North on Base Map

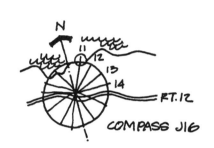

Compass Jig

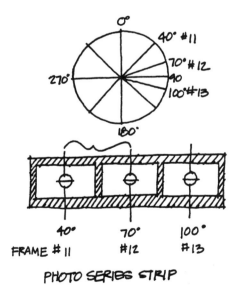

Compass Bearing

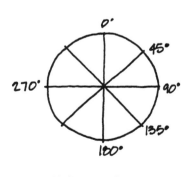

360 Compass Jig

FIGURE 8.11   Map transfer process

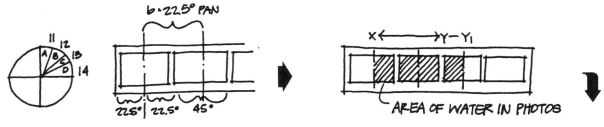

b = AREA OF OVERLAP

Direct Compass Reading

Amount of Water in Photos

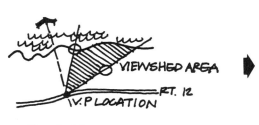

Viewshed Area

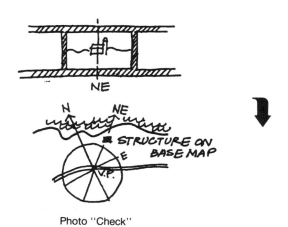

Photo "Check"

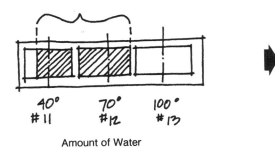

Amount of Water

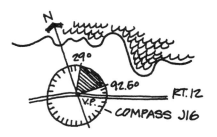

Mapping Viewshed

FIGURE 8.11   (*Continued*) Map transfer process

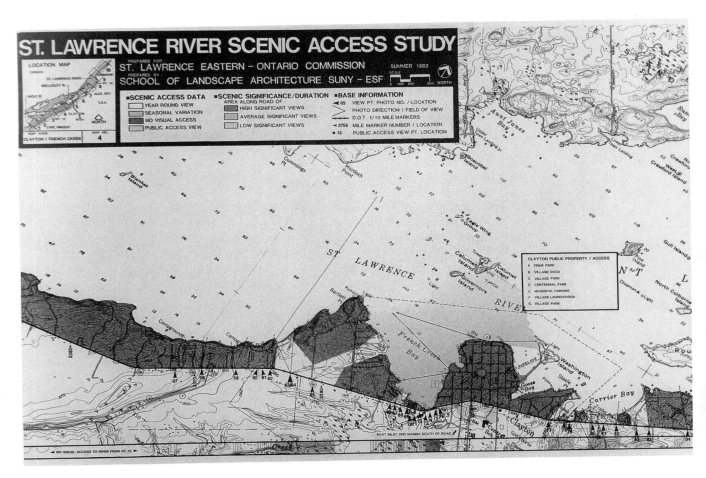

FIGURE 8.12   Sample base maps

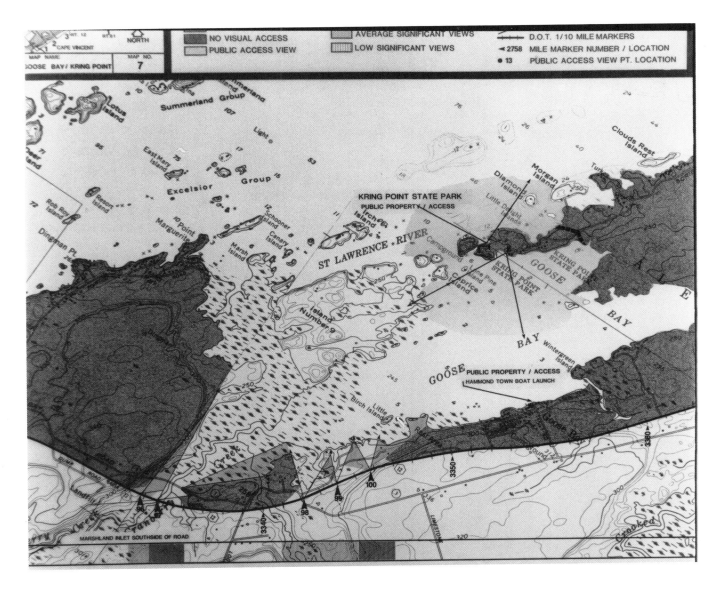

FIGURE 8.12   (*Continued*) Sample base maps

FIGURE 8.13   Sample scenes for visual preference ratings

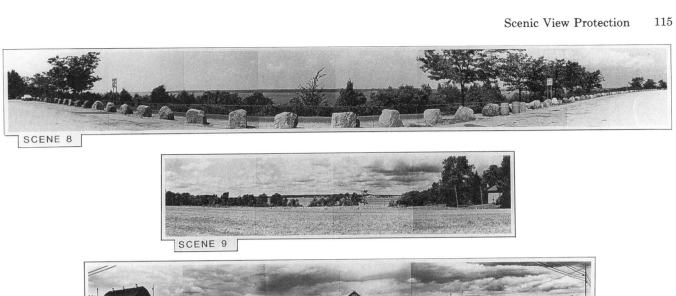

FIGURE 8.13   (*Continued*) Sample scenes for visual preference ratings

LAND USE CHARACTER

DOMINANT OR SALIENT VISUAL APPEARANCE FOR WHICH LANDSCAPE IS BEING USED OR EXISTS NATURALLY, AND WHICH EFFECTS THE VIEW OF THE RIVER.

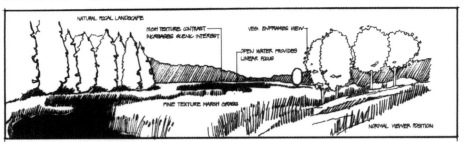

NATURAL MARSHLAND

(INCLUDES SWAMPS AND WETLANDS)

WITH MARSH VEGETATION AND THE PRESENCE OF OPEN WATER, ADJACENT TO THE RIVER. USUALLY A LINEAR TRIBUTARY OF STANDING WATER WHICH PROVIDES VISUAL AND PHYSICAL ACCESS TO THE RIVER. THE PRESENCE OF MANMADE ELEMENTS IS MINIMAL. VISUAL ACCESS TO THE RIVER MAY OR MAY NOT BE PRESENT FROM THE VIEWER POSITION.

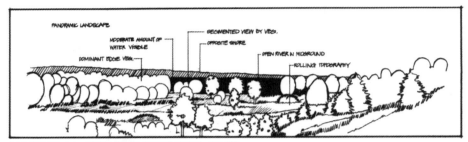

NATURAL BRUSH/WOODLAND

INCLUDES A MIXTURE OF CONIFEROUS AND DECIDUOUS VEGETATION TYPES FROM GRASSES AND LOW BUSHES TO TALL TREES. THE PRESENCE OF MANMADE ELEMENTS AND MAINTAINED OPEN SPACE IS MINIMAL. SIGNIFICANT NATURAL FEATURES MAY ALSO BE ASSOCIATED, SUCH AS UNDULATING TOPOGRAPHY AND ROCK OUTCROPS.

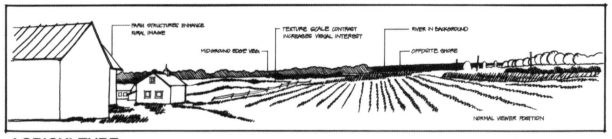

AGRICULTURE

CHARACTERISTIC VISUAL APPEARANCE ASSOCIATED WITH ACTIVELY CULTIVATED FARMING, GRAZED PASTURES OR INACTIVE FARM LAND REVERTING TO BRUSHLAND OR MAINTAINED OPEN SPACE. THE PRESENCE OF SUPPORT STRUCTURES SUCH AS BARNS, CYLOS, FARM HOUSES AND FARM EQUIPMENT MIGHT ENHANCE RURAL IMAGE AND SCENIC QUALITY.

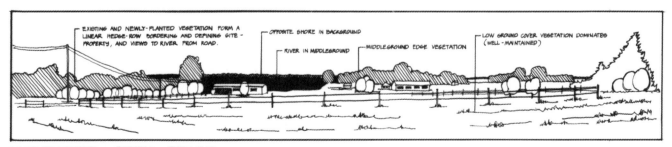

MAINTAINED OPEN SPACE

USUALLY ASSOCIATED WITH RESIDENTIAL AND RECREATION-TYPE LAND USES. THE VISUAL LANDSCAPE APPEARANCE IS DOMINATED BY A LOW GROUND COVER (MAINTAINED) AND A FEW SMALL TREES. EXISTING NATURAL VEGETATION AND NEW HEDGE-ROW TYPE PLANTING ARRANGEMENTS BORDER AND DEFINE PROPERTIES, AS WELL AS SCREEN AND DEFINE VIEWS OF THE RIVER FROM THE SCENIC HIGHWAY.

FIGURE 8.14 (pages 116–120) Visual cues for diagnosis of land use character, edge character, amount of water visible, distance to water, viewer position, water feature characteristics, and length of view

LAND USE CHARACTER

DOMINANT OR SALIENT VISUAL APPEARANCE FOR WHICH THE LANDSCAPE IS BEING USED OR EXISTS NATURALLY, AND WHICH EFFECTS THE VIEW OF THE RIVER.

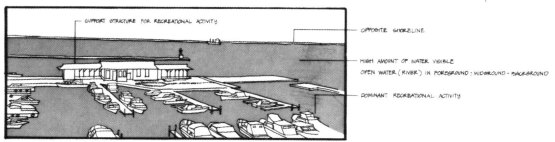

RECREATIONAL
(WATER-RELATED RECREATION USES)

MAY INCLUDE PUBLIC OR PRIVATE DOCKING FACILITIES, BOAT RAMPS, FISHING PIERS, BEACHES AND PARKS. ASSOCIATED ELEMENTS MAY INCLUDE BOAT SALES AND SERVICE, GAS DOCK, RESTROOM AND FOOD SERVICE FACILITIES.

RECREATIONAL
(SEASONAL AND SHORT-TERM RECREATION-RELATED ACCOMODATIONS)

INCLUDES PUBLIC AND PRIVATE CAMPING, TRAILER PARKS AND RECREATION VEHICLE FACILITIES. ASSOCIATE ELEMENTS MAY INCLUDE PARK OFFICE, PICNIC AREAS AND RESTROOM FACILITIES. SCENIC QUALITY IS INFLUENCED, AND MAY VARY WITH THE SEASONAL USAGE, CHACATERISTIC OF THIS LAND USE. SIGNIFICANT AREAS OF MAINTAINED OPEN SPACE ARE GENERALLY ASSOCIATE WITH LAND USE.

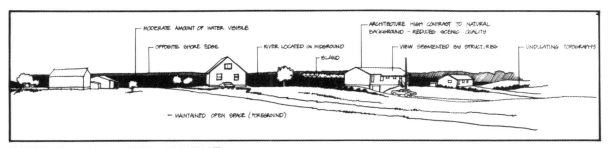

RESIDENTIAL PERMANENT
YEAR ROUND RESIDENTIAL DEVELOPMENT, INCLUDES TYPICAL SINGLE FAMILY DETACHED-TYPE STRUCTURES AND ASSOCIATED ELEMENTS. SIGNIFICANT AREAS OF MAINTAINED OPEN SPACE ARE ASSOCIATED WITH THIS LAND USE. MOST DEVELOPMENTS OF THIS TYPE TAKE ADVANTAGE OF RIVER VIEWS BY ORIENTING STRUCTURES IN A LINEAR ARRANGEMENT, PARALLEL TO THE RIVER AND THE SCENIC HIGHWAY.

RESIDENTIAL SEASONAL
SECOND HOME TYPE DEVELOPMENT INCLUDING COTTAGES, CABINS AND MOBILE HOME PARK COMMUNITIES. SIGNIFICANT AREAS OF MAINTAINED OPEN SPACE ASSOCIATED WITH THIS LAND USE. MOST DEVELOPMENT OF THIS TYPE ALSO TAKES ADVANTAGES OF RIVER VIEWS BY ORIENTING STRUCTURES IN A LINEAR ARRANGEMENT, PARALLEL TO THE RIVER AND THE SCENIC HIGHWAY.

EDGE CHARACTER

PERTAINS TO THE ORGANIZATION OF LANDSCAPE ELEMENTS ALONG THE LAND-RIVER EDGE (BETWEEN VIEWER AND THE RIVER) WHICH EFFECT THE QUALITY AND DEFINE THE VIEW OF THE RIVER. THE PRIMARY ELEMENTS INCLUDE NATURAL VEGETATION, LANDFORM, AND MANMADE STRUCTURES.

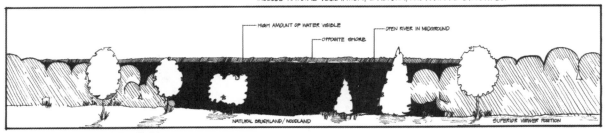

ENFRAMED NATURAL

"ENFRAMED" VIEWS ARE CREATED WHEN AN ELEMENT OR COMBINATION OF LAND ELEMENTS ARE ARRANGED TO PROVIDE A DEFINED, ENCLOSED OR FOCUSED VIEW OF THE RIVER.

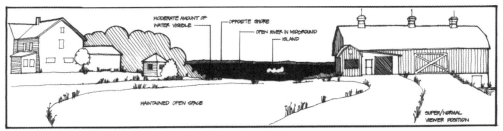

ENFRAMED MIXED

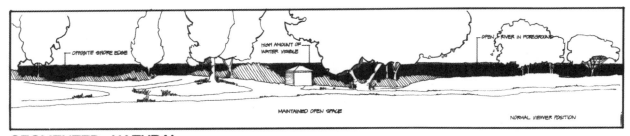

SEGMENTED NATURAL

"SEGMENTED" VIEWS INVOLVE A MORE RANDOM ORGANIZATION OR DISTRIBUTION OF LANDSCAPE ELEMENTS CREATING A LESS DEFINED, MORE RANDOM VIEWS OF THE RIVER, AS SEEN BY THE OBSERVER.

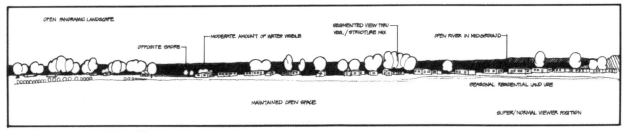

SEGMENTED MIXED

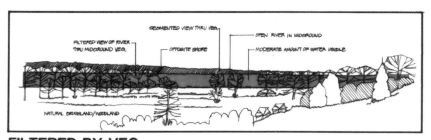

FILTERED BY VEG. [SEASONAL CONDITION]

DIFFERENCES IN SCENIC QUALITY FOR THE SAME LANDSCAPE CAN VARY DUE TO SEASONAL VARIATION IN LANDSCAPE VEGETATION, PRIMARILY DECIDUOUS-TYPE VEGETATION ALONG THE LAND-RIVER EDGE. THIS CONDITION CAN INCREASE THE "AMOUNT OF WATER VISIBLE" IN THE SCENE AS WELL AS CREATE NEW RIVER VIEWS IN ADDITIONAL LOCATIONS FROM LATE FALL TO EARLY SPRING. LIKEWISE, NEGATIVE STRUCTURAL ELEMENTS, SCREENED FROM VIEW IN THE SUMMER (LEAF-OUT) SEASON CAN BE MUCH MORE OBVIOUS THROUGH THE BARE TREE BRANCHES DURING THE "LEAF-IN" CONDITION WHICH CAN NEGATIVELY EFFECT SCENIC QUALITY.

AMOUNT OF WATER VISIBLE

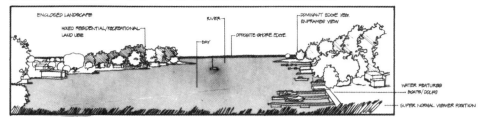

HIGH

MODERATE

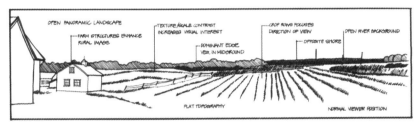

LOW

DISTANCE TO WATER

DESCRIBES THE PHYSICAL PROXIMITY OF THE VIEWER RELATIVE TO THE RIVER. THIS CAN BE DESCRIBED BY DIVIDING A LANDSCAPE SCENE (VIEW) INTO A SERIES OF 3 PLANES OR DISTANCE ZONES - FOREGROUND, MIDDLEGROUND, BACKGROUND.

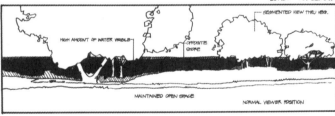

FOREGROUND

THE FOREGROUND ZONE REPRESENTS THE AREA CLOSEST TO THE OBSERVER. THE BASIC FOREGROUND CHARACTERISTICS INCLUDE:
■ FINE DETAIL OF SURFACE PATTERN, TEXTURE, COLORS AND EDGES.
■ PROVIDES SENSE OF RELATIONSHIP BETWEEN VIEWER AND LANDSCAPE

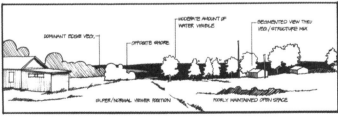

MIDGROUND

THE MOST CRITICAL LANDSCAPE ZONE WHICH TENDS TO DOMINATE THE VIEW. THE LINKAGE BETWEEN ELEMENTS OF THE LANDSCAPE MAY BE SEEN. IN THIS ZONE THE JOINING OF THE ELEMENTS CAN BE SEEN. ALSO, SHAPES AND PATTERNS ARE OBVIOUS.

BACKGROUND

THE DISTANT LANDSCAPE REDUCES FORM TO SIMPLE OUTLINE SHAPES AND HAS LITTLE SENSE OF SURFACE TEXTURE OR DETAIL. ONLY GROSS PATTERNS STAND OUT.

PLAN VIEW

MIDGROUND

FOREGROUND

BACKGROUND

BACKGROUND
beyond 1/2 mile

MIDGROUND
400' - 1/2 mile

FOREGROUND
0 - 400 feet

viewer position

NOT TO SCALE

VIEWER POSITION

DESCRIBES THE LOCATION OF THE VIEWER RELATIVE TO THE RIVER, PARTICULARLY WITH REGARD TO BEING AT EQUAL LEVEL WITH, HIGH ABOVE, OR AT SOME INTERMEDIATE POSITION ABOVE THE RIVER.

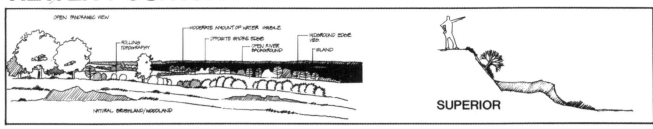

SUPERIOR THE VIEWER SUPERIOR POSITION ORIENTS VIEWS DOWN UPON AND OVER THE RIVER AND LANDSCAPE. IT PROVIDES MINIMAL VIEW BLOCKAGE AND MAXIMUM OPPORTUNITIES TO OBSERVE DISTANT VIEWS AND THE LANDSCAPE CONTEXT. IT MIGHT ALSO CREATE A SENSE OF OPENNESS AND EXPANSE COMMON TO PANORAMIC LANDSCAPE VIEWS.

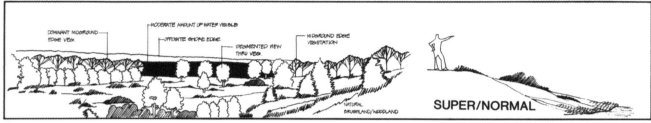

SUPER/NORMAL THIS INTERMEDIATE POSITION REPRESENTS THE VIEWER POSITION BETWEEN SUPERIOR AND NORMAL - EYE LEVEL POSITION RELATIVE TO THE RIVER.

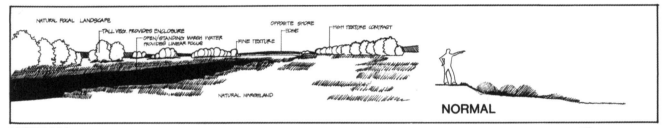

NORMAL THE VIEWER NORMAL POSITION PROVIDES A LEVEL LINE-OF-SIGHT WITH RESPECT TO THE RIVER OR ANY ASSOCIATED WATER BODIES. LANDSCAPE ELEMENTS MIGHT EFFECTIVELY ENCLOSE, DIRECT, OR SCREEN VIEWS OF THE RIVER AT THIS LEVEL.

WATER FEATURE CHARACTERISTICS

WATER FEATURE CHARACTERISTICS INCLUDE THOSE ELEMENTS COMMONLY ASSOCIATED WITH THE NATURAL FORMATION, FUNCTIONAL USAGE, RECREATIONAL ACTIVITIES OF THE RIVER. CHARACTERISTICS INCLUDE:

- ISLAND FORMATIONS
- BAYS, INLETS
- MARSHLANDS, SWAMPS
- RIVERFRONT SHORELINE
- BRIDGES
- MARINAS/DOCKING FACILITIES

LENGTH OF VIEW

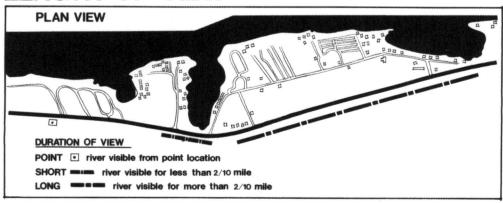

PLAN VIEW

DURATION OF VIEW

POINT ⊡ river visible from point location

SHORT ▰▬ river visible for less than 2/10 mile

LONG ▬ ▬ ▬ river visible for more than 2/10 mile

References

Bozing, L. J., and Randall, M. 1987. Land uses planning and zoning in 1987: A national survey. *The Urban Lawyer,* 19(4): 899–939.

Cunningham, R. A. 1968. Scenic easements in the highway beautification program. *Denver Law Journal,* 45: 168–264.

Duerksen, C. 1986. *Aesthetics and land-use controls: Beyond ecology and economics.* PAS Report 399. American Planning Association.

Fonoroff, A. 1968. Proposed legislation for highway corridor protection. *Urban Law Annual,* 1968: 128–149.

Lambe, R. A., and Smardon, R. C. 1986. Commercial highway landscape reclamation: A participatory approach. *Landscape Planning,* 12(1986): 353–385.

Lasser, T. J. 1987. View protection: A capital idea. *Urban Land,* 46(6): 36–37.

Lewis, G. 1985. *Hawaii Housing Authority v. Midkiff:* The public use requirement in eminent domain. *Environmental Law,* 15: 565–591.

Note 1975. Preserving scenic areas: The Adirondack land use program. *Yale Law Journal,* 84: 1705–1721.

Olson, J. A. 1965. Progress and problems in Wisconsin's scenic and conservation easement program. *Wisconsin Law Review,* 1956(2): 352–373.

Sax, J. L. 1980. Buying scenery: Land acquisitions for the National Park Service. *Duke Law Journal,* 1980(4): 709–740.

Sax, J. L., and Keiter, R. B. 1987. Glacier National Park and its neighbors: A study of federal interagency relations. *Ecology Law Quarterly,* Vol. 14: 207–263.

Shanahan, D. M., and Smardon, R. C. 1989. Participatory process for managing roadside vegetation. *Transportation Research Record 1224.* TRB, National Research Council, pp. 6–14.

Shannon, S. S., et al. 1990. *St. Lawrence River scenic quality study.* Faculty of Landscape Architecture, State University of New York, College of Environmental Science and Forestry. Prepared for New York Power Authority.

Smardon, R. C. 1985. A visual approach to redesigning the commercial strip. *Transportation Research Record 1016.* TRB, National Research Council, pp. 1–6.

———. 1987. Visual access to the 1,000 Islands. *Landscape Architecture,* 77(3): 86–91.

Smardon, R. C., and Goukas, M. M. 1984. *Village of North Syracuse, Main Street study.* School of Landscape Architecture Occasional Paper ESF 84-010. State University of New York, College of Environmental Science and Forestry.

Smardon, R. C., Price, W., and Volpe, M. R. 1984. *St. Lawrence River scenic access study.* School of Landscape Architecture Occasional Paper ESF 84-004. State University of New York, College of Environmental Science and Forestry.

Stuart, N. H. 1980. Rosslyn: A monumental intrusion. *Environmental Comment,* July: 4–7.

U.S. DOT, Federal Highway Administration. 1988. *Scenic byways.* Publication FHWA-DF-88-002.

Wilkens, M. J. 1986. *An image renaissance, Detroit I-94 US-10 entrance corridor.* Prepared for Michigan Department of Transportation, East Lansing Michigan.

Williams, N., Jr. 1968. Legal techniques to protect and to promote aesthetics along transportation corridors. *Buffalo Law Review,* 17: 701–716.

———. 1975. *American planning law: land use and the police power,* vol. 5. Callaghan.

III
Federal and State Aesthetic Regulation

OVERVIEW

Chapters 9 through 14 will address specific aspects of aesthetics and legal issues: from a wilderness preservation context; a sensitive land management context; an aesthetic project review context; and a context of specialized concerns such as land-disturbing activities like mining, timber harvesting, and energy production. Parts I and II of this book have laid the foundation in terms of key legal concepts and aesthetic control from a community perspective. Part III has a more federal and state perspective and ties together key regulatory programs, litigation, and aesthetic control issues.

Chapter 9

Wilderness and Natural Area Preservation

INTRODUCTION

Much of the impact for aesthetic control and management of landscape comes from early preservation efforts in the United States, so some historical review is in order. Much of the rationale for preservation of the wilderness and protection of wild and scenic rivers and national trails is aesthetic, so some examination of key programs and implementation issues is pertinent. Also, significant litigation over some of these programs (such as wilderness designation) has raised such critical legal issues as which individuals or groups have "standing" to stop or review specifications and their impact on the landscape.

Preservation became conservation for all intents and purposes in 1864, when George Perkins Marsh published *Man and Nature.* "Conservation" is a Utilitarian concept and antithetical to the Romantic view. As Gifford Pinchot put it at the turn of the century in connection with the conservation of forests, "the greatest good for the greatest number for the longest time."

Natural landscape appreciation can also be seen in the works of the geographers of the nineteenth and early twentieth century. Many of our early American geomorphologists were keen perceivers of landscape attributes.[1] Cornish (1934) wrote on the aesthetic quality of landscapes in England and developed the phrase "scenic amenity." It was a long time before it became popular and was accepted as common jargon. In the United States, concern for landscape preservation, or "aesthetic conservation," can be traced to the development of the state and national park systems, starting with Yosemite Valley (Figure 9.1) in 1864 (Zube 1973) and the preservation of Niagara Falls (Figure 9.2) in 1862 (Runte 1972). The cession of Yosemite Valley to the state of California by the Congress in 1864 for use as a state park is one of the earliest recognitions of scenery as a natural resource. Yosemite was also the first individual land area to be managed through the promulgation of public policy and enactment of federal legislation.[2] Shortly thereafter (1872) Yellowstone was recognized as a scenic natural resource by the creation of Yellowstone National Park.[3]

The development of American aesthetic conservation involved people such as Muir, Mather, and Udall (Strong 1970). These men, along with certain events, help to explain the strong "naturalness" and "wilderness" concepts that developed into a unique American landscape preservation aesthetic (McCloskey 1966).

---

[1]See W. Powell, 1957, The Exploration of the Colorado River, abridged, University of Chicago Press, Chicago, Illinois. and Dutton, 1880, Geology of the High Plateaus of Utah with Atlas, Dept. of the Interior, U.S.G.S. of the Rocky Mountain Region Monograph, U.S.G.P.O. Wash., D.C. and 1882 Tertiary History of the Grand Canyon District, U.S.G.S. Monograph, U.S.G.P.O.

[2]U.S. Senate Bill 203, 38th Congress, 1st Session, Cong. Rec. March 28, 1864, 1310; May 17, 1864, 2300 Stat. 17.

[3]U.S. Senate Bill 392, House of Representatives Bill 464, 42nd Congress, 2nd Session, Stat. 17.

FIGURE 9.1   Yosemite half-dome. *Photo credit: Mathew Potteiger*

FIGURE 9.3   Boundary Waters Canoe Area. *Photo credit: Chad Dawson*

WILDERNESS AND NATURAL AREAS

The first landscape architect hired by the U.S. Forest Service, Arthur Carhart, was instrumental in the move to preserve "roadless areas." During his time of service (1919–1923), he argued that the best development plan for the Trappers Lake, Colorado, area in the Rocky Mountains was one that protected the natural beauty of the shoreline, although he did allow for some summer home and camping facilities development (which never occurred), set well back from the lake. Trappers Lake is now part of the Flat Tops Wilderness Area. Carhart's feelings were similar with respect to recreational development of the U.S.-Canada border lakes area now known as the Boundary Waters Canoe Area in Minne-

FIGURE 9.2   Niagara Falls. *Photo credit: Peter Black*

sota (Figure 9.3). His 1921 recreation plan for the area called for its preservation as a "watertrail wilderness." Later, in 1926, Carhart (then a private citizen) and other conservationists were successful in helping to get the area administratively designated by the Forest Service as the Superior Area, with the express written support of the Secretary of Agriculture William Lurdine.[4]

In a memorandum written in 1919, Carhart listed types of areas that should be free of summer home development. They were: "the superlative area, the unsuited high ridge of a mountain range, the area that should be for the group rather than the individual, such as lakeshore, stream bank, and the area of greatest use for preservation owned by the federal government" (Frome 1974, p. 119). It is not clear, however, that he had in mind the vast expanses we now think of as wilderness areas.

Aldo Leopold, a Forest Service colleague of Carhart's, developed his own wilderness philosophy. He proposed a new guide for the preparation of management plans for the national forests. The richest and most accessible forest regions, capable of high-quality timber production, would be reserved for logging, while the remaining regions would be kept for recreation, game management, and wilderness uses. He developed a concept of wild areas for the Southwest based on four objectives: "(1) prevent annihilation of rare plants and animals, like the grizzly; (2) guard against biotic disruption of areas still wild; (3) secure recognition, as wilderness, of low-altitude desert generally regarded as valueless for recreation because it offered no pines, lakes, or other conventional scenery; and (4) induce

[4]September 17, 1926. Copy in Regional Archives and Records Center, Chicago, Illinois. It recognized wilderness designation as part of national recreation policy by the U.S. Forest Service. Reference: Frome, *Battle of the Wilderness* (New York: Praeger, 1974) p. 119.

Mexico to cooperate in wilderness protection." (Frome 1974, p. 120). Leopold specifically sought to establish a wild area within the Gila National Forest in New Mexico. The designation was approved in 1924 by the district forester (now called regional forester).

Chief of the Forest Service in the mid-1920s, William B. Greely, cautious at first and mindful of timber demands, later became a proponent of the Gila designation and encouraged other district foresters to do the same with comparable areas, especially to safeguard potential "wilderness" areas.[5]

Undoubtedly, one of the most controversial pieces of natural resource legislation of national stature dealing with aesthetic values in the natural environment is the so-called "Wilderness Act"[6] of 1964. Although there have been relatively few court cases[7] testing the merits of the Wilderness Act, there continue to be battles between commodity- (to take resources from the landscape, e.g. timber and mining) and noncommodity-oriented (to take experiences only) interest groups over each study and designation of proposed wilderness areas.

This section discusses briefly the legal and aesthetic issues related to the Wilderness Act, the Eastern Wilderness Act,[8] and various "natural area" programs and legislation implemented by federal and state agencies.

Section 2(c) of the Wilderness Act defines the wilderness resource as follows:

A Wilderness, in contrast with those areas where man and his works dominate the landscape, is hereby recognized as an area where the earth and its community of life are untrammeled by man, where man himself is a visitor who does not remain. An area of Wilderness is further defined to mean in this act an area of undeveloped Federal land retaining its primeval character and influence, without permanent improvements or human habitation, which is protected and managed so as to preserve its natural conditions and which (1) generally appears to have been affected primarily by the forces of nature, with the imprint of man's work substantially unnoticeable; (2) has outstanding opportunities for solitude or a primitive and unconfined type of recreation; (3) has at least five thousand acres of land or is of sufficient size as to make practicable its preservation and use in an unimpaired condition; and (4) may also contain ecological, geological, or other features of scientific, educational, scenic or historical value.[9]

The lands included (Figure 9.4) in the National Wilderness Preservation System are to be managed in such a manner as to leave them unimpaired for future use and enjoyment as wilderness. They are to be devoted to the public purposes of recreational, scenic, scientific, educational, conservation, and historical use.

Protection is ensured by the specific provision of the act that states:

Except as otherwise provided in this Act, each agency administering any area designated as wilderness shall be responsible for preserving the wilderness character of the area and shall so administer such area for such other purposes for which it may have been established as also to preserve its wilderness character. Except as otherwise provided in this Act, wilderness areas shall be devoted to the public purposes of recreational, *scenic*, scientific, education, conservation and historical use.[10] (Emphasis provided.)

What values were enhanced in the creation of an act calling for preservation of wilderness? McCloskey (1966) in his authoritative article on the act lists eleven (two more are added by other writers) different values associated with wilderness, both early and contemporary. Early valuations are:

1. *Wilderness*, as a challenging historical setting for triumphing over adversity and self-discovery.
2. As an aid to religion and as a setting for religious experience.
3. As a setting of political reform.
4. As a refuge or sanctuary.
5. As a need to protect wild country from threats to nature.

Contemporary valuations are:

6. *Wilderness*, as a cultural heritage and a setting for an aesthetic experience.
7. As a setting for scientific research in the biological sciences.
8. Maintenance of, as an ethical obligation for a "land ethic" or biocentric view.
9. As an opportunity for an educational experience.
10. As a setting for therapeutic experiences to relieve urban stress.

---

[5]Memo to each of the western District Foresters, December 30, 1926.

[6]16 U.S.C. 1131 et seq. (1988).

[7]See Isaak Walton League of America v. St. Clair, 313 F. Supp. 1312 (D. Minn. 1970); and at 353 F. Supp. 698 (D. Minn. 1973); Parker v. U.S., 307 F. Supp. 685 (D. Colo. 1969), and at 309 F. Sierra Club v. Lyng, Supp. 593 (D. Colo. 1970); and at 662 F. Supp. 40 (D.D.C. 1987) [Lyng I]; Sierra Club v. Lyng, 663 F. Supp. 566 (D.D.C. 1987) [Lyng II].

[8]16 U.S.C. s. 1132 (1988).

[9]16 U.S.C. s. 1131(c) (1988).

[10]16 U.S.C. s. 1133(b) (1988).

FIGURE 9.4 a, b, c   Wilderness mosaic of three scenes. *Photo credit: R. C. Smardon*

11. As an optimum setting for many highly individualized and stylized sport forms which require low-impact equipment and a self-restraining code of technique.
12. A setting for allowing freedom of individual development (Sax, 1977).
13. As a setting conducive to fostering self-actualization and the occurrence of peak outdoor experiences (Scott, 1974).

An interesting observation is made by the book's authors as to what characterizes "ideal" wilderness. The literature of key people instrumental in the beginnings of the wilderness movement[11] as well as the visual concept reinforced by the major agency[12] involved in wilderness management decisions thus far maintain that a pristine alpine or subalpine mountainous wilderness is "ideal." We hear relatively little about other physical landscape typologies of wilderness. In an interesting

paper (see Watson and Smith 1971), it has been argued that caves constitute an underground wilderness of sorts. It is also held that "real" wilderness can only be found in the Western states (McCabe 1971), and that highest regarded wilderness areas in the U.S. would probably be in Alaska. It is interesting how such stereotypes and preconceptions have limited the dimensionality of the wilderness concept. Perhaps we should re-examine what constitutes wilderness as perceived through our regional and cultural biases.

Some key definitions in relation to terms often used in relation to the Wilderness Act are given by Haight (1974, p. 276):

1) wilderness (without capitalization or quotation marks) is used as the equivalent of what conservationists refer to as de facto wilderness; i.e., the kind of area the ordinary person would think of if he were asked to

---

[11]Such as Aldo Leopold, John Muir, and others.

[12]The U.S. Forest Service was the most active agency in wilderness studies, and most of its lands are upland forest areas.

describe wilderness — an area naturally wild, pretty much unaffected by man or man's works.

2) "wilderness"; certain naturally wild areas designated by executive agencies prior to passage of the Wilderness Act, regulated and managed with preservation of their wild character as the primary objective. It is therefore an administrative, as opposed to statutory, designation. "Wild area" is a similar official but administrative designation, having the same meaning as "wilderness" but applied to areas smaller in size than "wilderness" areas.

3) Wilderness, or Wilderness Area; an area designated by Congress under the terms of the Wilderness Act as a component of the National Wilderness Preservation System (NWPS).

4) "roadless area" is another administrative designation pretty much equivalent to "wilderness." The most important difference between the two is simply that "wilderness" is administered by the Forest Service of the Agriculture Department, while "roadless areas" are administered by components of the Interior Department.

The federal agencies presently involved with administering wilderness areas, and which also administered "wilderness areas" in the past, are the Forest Service of the Department of Agriculture, and the National Park Service and Fish and Wildlife Service of the Interior Department. The Bureau of Land Management is now involved with wilderness surveys under the jurisdiction of their new "Organic Act" within the U.S. Department of Interior.[13]

McCloskey (1966) has written extensively on the history and meaning of the Wilderness Act and Haight (1974) wrote an evaluation of the status of the act ten years after its passage. There have been other commentators (Foote 1973; Foster 1976; Wolcott 1973; Sokol 1976; Henning 1971; and McCabe 1971) who have described and criticized implementation on the Act by specific agencies.

McCloskey and Haight describe three major problem areas in relation to the interpretation and implementation of the act. These areas are: (1) the apparent exclusiveness of rules of entrance to the system, (2) the so-called "Purist's Controversy" about what constitutes a wilderness for entrance purposes, and (3) the "compatibility of use" question regarding what is allowed after an area becomes wilderness.

Exclusiveness

Conservationists got a congressionally created National Wilderness Preservation System (NWPS), safeguarded from potential erosion by administrative

agencies and with specified prohibited activities. However, an area can only be added to or removed from the NWPS by congressional act and not by administrative action. Furthermore, the act appeared to restrict the mechanism so as to exclude de facto wilderness consideration (see definition, p. 128). If narrowly construed, Section 3 of the act,[14] pertaining to study and review procedure, was applicable only to (1) the Forest Service areas already designated as primitive, and (2) the "roadless areas" of 5,000 contiguous acres or more in the National Park System (under the National Park Service) and wildlife refuges and game ranges (administered by the Fish and Wildlife Service). There was no mention of the Bureau of Land Management lands or other large federal land-holding agencies such as the Department of Defense. Section 7 of the act[15] provided that the Agriculture and Interior secretaries could make recommendations when they submitted their annual reports on implementation of the act to Congress.

The upshot, as reported by Haight (1974, p. 286), is that Congress does make the final determination on entrance to the NWPS. However, Congress has also decided that it can make its own determination to create a Wilderness area as its own initiative (the so-called "short-cut" method). It should be noted that congressionally initiated wilderness area legislation "may be lengthy and intricate, and may involve legislative purposes not directly achievable within the structured procedures of the Wilderness Act" (Haight 1974, p. 280). This is in contrast to congressional reaction to an administrative recommendation which is usually a brief, almost identical piece of legislation differing only in the name of the area.

The difference in the author's mind is extremely significant because the legislation, custom made when Congress initiates a wilderness area designation, gives the area much more protection. First, it describes in more detail the unique or contextual qualities of the area that may be utilized at a later point for instance, to determine whether to classify an area as Class I for nondegradation air quality standards (See Chapter 10 Air Quality, p. 163). Second, it provides more protection than the Wilderness Act can from incompatible uses. Third, it provides a truer preference of congressional management policy through the political process.

The act creating the Sawtooth Wilderness Area in Idaho[16] is a good case in point. The legislation for the area provides limited condemnation authority[17] to the Secretary of Agriculture, and withdrawal of private

[13]The Federal Land Policy and Management Act of 1976, 43 U.S.C. 1701 et seq. (1988).

[14]16 U.S.C. s. 1131(C) (1988).

[15]Id., s. 1132(d) (1988).

[16]U.S.C.a. s. 460aa (1988).

[17]Id. ss. 460aa-2(c), (e), (f), (h) (1988).

needs acquired from mineral rights and development.[18] It was intended to be a multiple-purpose act (1) to establish a wilderness area with even stricter preservation features than those found in the Wilderness Act; (2) to establish a general-purpose national recreation area surrounding the wilderness area; and (3) to require the Interior Department to study the recreation area for the possible creation of a national park. Quick action was needed to protect the area from increasingly rapid commercial and residential development. Congress also recognized the need to regulate already existing molybdenum mining activity to "assure that this activity will not impair the visual grandeur of the area, adversely affect fish and wildlife resources, and cause pollution of downstream waters."[19]

A second development in relation to the "exclusiveness issue" is administrative in nature. Only the Department of Interior was required to review its "roadless areas" under the Wilderness Act. The Forest Service was not required to review its roadless areas under the Wilderness Act but opted to under its Roadless Area Review and Evaluation (RARE) Program. This program has been criticized both by conservationists (Haight 1974, p. 287) and by those critical of the review criteria and methodology used (see Burke and Twiss 1976). The Forest Service did not consider itself legally confined with the procedures of the act any more than Congress does. However, it is ironic that the Forest Service should suffer bad press while the National Park Service falls ever behind the schedule laid down by the act because specific wilderness studies have been subordinated to its master planning program, which is contended by some to be unconstitutional (see Williams 1975).

The third development in relation to the exclusiveness issue comes from the case *Sierra Club* v. *Hardins*.[20] The plaintiffs used the Wilderness Act as partial grounds for its suit regarding an area in the Tongass National Forest in Alaska. The court rejected outright the plaintiff's claim that the act imposed study and recommendation requirements, as there were no designated "primitive" areas in the whole state of Alaska. There could then obviously be no duty to conduct wilderness studies of such areas contiguous to them. Thus, a blatant loophole in the act was the failure to require, rather than merely permit, studies to be done on de facto wilderness areas.

The Purist's Controversy

The first Roadless Area Review and Evaluation (RARE I) brought out into the open the dispute be-

tween the Forest Service philosophy and that of conservationists (see Costley 1972; Foote 1973) as to exactly what constitutes wilderness. More exactly, the issue is whether an area can qualify for wilderness status if it had been seriously affected by human activity in the past but is now restored or is restorable to a natural-appearing condition. The Forest Service stresses such words as "untrammeled" and "retaining its primeval character" to construe the statutory definition narrowly and restrict potential wilderness status to areas that have never been significantly affected by human activity. Certain members of Congress and wilderness advocates interpret the act more loosely in this regard. The dispute has not been resolved.

The "purists controversy," which was initiated with the Forest Service, has caused problems for incorporation of certain Bureau of Land Management (BLM) visual resource management concepts into their wilderness review (Curran 1978). Conservationists objected to the use of the term "intrusion," which was defined by the BLM as a feature or change influenced or made by people, land, water, vegetation, or structure, which is in contrast with the natural characteristics of the existing landscape. Conservationists would like the BLM to stay with the original language of the act, which specified that an area suitable for wilderness "generally appears to have been affected primarily by the forces of nature, with the imprint of man substantially unnoticeable." Conservationists are also urging the BLM to abandon the "sights and sounds" doctrine, under which potential wilderness areas have been disqualified in the past because they possess a view of a nearby city or disturbed area. Thus, the tactical maneuvers of wilderness advocates are to discourage inventive techniques that would surface any problems with a potential de facto wilderness area so as to sustain the overall strategy of preservation of the area under the conditions of the Wilderness Act.

The Compatibility Issue

The act hedges in its prohibition of incompatible activities in several ways. Prohibition is subject to exceptions for existing rights and practices (see the discussion of mining, Chapter 12). Thus Congress avoided the issue of giving priority to wilderness use versus extractive uses that are incompatible with wilderness use. A second part of the issue is the degree of incompatibility with wilderness values that would be acceptable in the nonwilderness activities allowed by the act.

Two court cases affecting use of the Boundary Waters Canoe Area (BWCA) in northeastern Minne-

---

[18]Id., s. 460aa-2(e) and s. 460aa-9 (1988).
[19]U.S. Code Cong. and Adm. News, 92nd Congress, 2nd Session at 3045.
[20]325 F. Supp. 99 (D. Alas. 1971).

sota deal directly with the issue of compatibility of use of wilderness areas. The first case, *Izaak Walton League* v. *St. Clair*,[21] (Butz I) deals with mineral prospecting on lands in which the mineral rights were privately acquired within the BWCA. The second case, *Minnesota Public Interest Research Group* v. *Butz*,[22] (Butz II) was a suit brought by environmental interests to stop logging that had gone on for many years. In both cases the judges found that the contemplated activities were in fact incompatible with wilderness use of the BWCA. Haight (1974, p. 299) argues that the reasoning in the two cases hold true for all wilderness areas, although he admits that mineral claim-staking was prohibited on federal lands in Minnesota,[23] and that mining laws enacted after 1873[24] that proclaim the awareness of public domain lands to mineral exploration have never been applied to Minnesota or a fortiori to the BWCA. Thus, any extension of the *Issac Walton League* decision beyond BWCA would indeed be risky.

Extension of these decisions beyond BWCA, as Haight 1974, p. 300) points out, raises another problem. Strict interpretations regarding compatibility of certain uses on existing wilderness areas may pose problems for admission of future wilderness areas if we use the same standard. Thus, a contextual interpretation of what is suitable for admission and management of wilderness is needed. This avoids some of the problem we have just covered.

Another critical court case affecting wilderness decision-making was *Parker* v. *U.S.*,[25] which determined the extent of the Forest Service's discretion in drawing boundaries between areas to be preserved and areas to be open to commercial exploitation. The case emphasized that certain decisions regarding classification and boundary delineation "must remain open through the Presidential level" and that "contiguous lands which seem to have significant wilderness resources will be studied."[26]

Another controversy involved legal challenges to Forest Service measures to control Southern pine beetle infestations in wilderness areas in the Southeast. The Southern pine beetle controversy involved a dispute over tree cutting within wilderness boundaries. Plaintiffs in *Sierra Club* v. *Black*[27] and *Sierra Club* v. *Lyng*[28] challenged an extensive Forest Service tree-cutting program aimed at halting the spread of Southern pine beetle infestations in four federal wilderness areas in Arkansas, Louisiana, and Mississippi. The courts interpreted Section 4(d) (1), of the wilderness act which does not refer to "minimum tool" management in the control of fire, insects, and diseases. The *Lyng* court essentially adopted similar reasoning to that used in the *Butz II* decision in the BWCA: When the Wilderness Act authorized managers to take action within wilderness areas "necessary" to accomplish the purposes of the Wilderness Act, but inconsistent with the preservation of wilderness character, managers may employ only those methods that have the least adverse affect on wilderness character.

If special uses threaten wilderness character, those uses should be limited by the "minimum tool" approach embodied in Section 4(c) of the Wilderness Act.[29] The "minimum tool" approach permits actions that adversely affect wilderness character only when those actions are specifically authorized in the Wilderness Act and are the least intrusive means necessary to accomplish the task. Rohlf and Honnold (1988) argue that future controversy and litigation will revolve around such management questions. (Other significant issues affecting wilderness management and environmental quality, such as air quality and the amount of free-flowing water rights, will be covered in Chapter 10.)

Thus, we have reviewed some of the most controversial issues in relation to the implementation of the Wilderness Act. The act includes aesthetic values in its definition section, and many of the critical issues discussed relate to the aesthetic attributes of what wilderness is and how it should be maintained. Much research has been done on wilderness users and their preferences, and some of it includes their aesthetic preferences. Much work needs to be done on aesthetic judgments of land use compatibility in wilderness areas and on aesthetic appraisals of nonalpine wilderness envi-

---

[21]313 F. Supp. 1312 (D. Minn. 1970); 353 F. Supp. 698 (D. Minn. 1973).

[22]358 F. Supp. 584 (D. Minn. 1973).

[23]30 U.S.C. s. 48 (1988).

[24]16 U.S.C. ss. 478 and 482 (1988).

[25]307 F. Supp. 685 (D. Colo. 1969), 309 F. Supp. 593 (D. Colo. 1970); aff'd. 448 F.2d. 793 (10th Cir. 1971); *cert. den.* 405 U.S. 989 (1971).

[26]309 F. Supp. at 599.

[27]614 F. Supp. 488 (D.D.C. 1985).

[28]662 F. Supp. 40 (D.D.C. 1987) [Lyng I]; Sierra Club v. Lyng, 663 F. Supp. 566 (D.D.C. 1987) [Lyng II].

[29]16 U.S.C. s. 1133(c) (1988).

ronments, which may include deserts, arctic areas, underwater areas, and underground wilderness.

Other Federal and State Programs

Other natural area preservation programs of federal and state agencies will be briefly reviewed here. Many seem to be closely related to the National Wilderness Preservation System and have been instrumental in protecting scenic natural wonders.

At the federal level the 1906 Antiquities Act[30] authorizes the president to declare historic landmarks, historic or prehistoric structures, and other objects of historic or scientific interest to be national monuments, provided such monuments are on lands that are federally owned or controlled. Examples of areas designated national monuments by presidential proclamation are: the Grand Canyon (1908), Dinosaur National Monument (1915), and the Katmai National Monument (1918). Congress may respond to these actions by later altering and redefining the areas proclaimed.

The National Park Service Organic Act of 1916[31] provides management protection of these lands and resources in the act's purpose, which "is to conserve the scenery and the natural historic objects and the wildlife therein and to provide for the enjoyment of the same in such manner and by such means as will leave them unimpaired for the enjoyment of future generations."[32]

This statement has been attributed to landscape architect Frederick Olmstead, Jr., in William C. Everharts, *The National Park Service* (1972, p. 21).

The National Natural Landmarks Program was created by administrative approval of the Secretary of Interior on May 18, 1962. This is an interagency administrative program operated by the National Park Service through cooperative memoranda with the Fish and Wildlife Service, Bureau of Land Management, and the Forest Service. A national natural landmark is an area considered to have national significance; possessing exceptional value or quality in illustrating or interpreting the natural heritage of the nation; and presenting a true, accurate, and essentially unspoiled example of natural history. These areas can be disestablished by an administrative process, and thus receive no additional protection beyond that afforded by their designation. However, they must be taken into account in environmental impact statements required by NEPA before any plan by federal agencies to manipulate land or water is carried out.

A similar program was proposed by President Carter in his environmental protection message to Congress on May 23, 1977, where he took special note of the need to "preserve those places of natural, historic, cultural, and scientific value that give this nation continuity." In response, a new National Heritage Program was proposed in order to pull together and expand existing federal cultural and natural heritage preservation efforts. Part of the National Heritage Program effort shepherded by the Heritage Conservation and Recreation Service (HCRS, formerly Bureau of Outdoor Recreation) was to develop a different classification and identification system for natural heritage resources that could be used at the national and state levels. One of the classification panels was the Scenic Heritage Classification System Panel, whose report was submitted to HCRS by Chairman E. H. Zube on April 5, 1978.

The Bureau of Land Management administers a program of Outstanding Natural Areas, which are established to "preserve scenic values and areas of natural wonder. The preservation of these resources in their natural condition is the primary management objective. Access roads, parking areas and public use facilities are normally located at the periphery of the area. The public is encouraged to walk into the area for recreation purposes whenever feasible."[33]

The Forest Service administratively recognizes various areas of scenic, historical, geological, botanical, zoological, paleontological, and other values worthy of special classification. These are collectively called special-interest areas. There are currently 136 such areas in 29 states, totaling 989,744 acres. The authority for special-interest areas is the Organic Administration Act of June 4, 1897, which authorizes the Secretary of Agriculture to regulate occupancy and use of the national forests. Classification of special-interest areas that should be managed for recreation use substantially in their natural condition is authorized under 36 CFR 294.1a. Areas that are of a nature or significance to justify or require more intensive management, protection interpretation, or use are authorized under 36 CFR 294.1b.[34]

The objectives of the administratively classified special-interest areas are:

To protect and, where appropriate, foster public use and enjoyment of areas with *scenic*, historical, geological, botanical, zoological, paleontological, or other special characteristics. To classify areas that possess unusual

---

[30]16 U.S.C. s. 431 et seq. (1988).
[31]16 U.S.C. s. 1 (1988).
[32]Id.
[33]43 C.F.R., Ch.2, s. 6225.0-5(b).
[34]Forest Service Manual 2360.01.

recreation and scientific values so that these special values are available for public study, use, or enjoyment.[35] (Emphasis added.)

Definition for a type of scenic special-interest area is as follows:

Scenic Areas. Scenic areas are places of outstanding or matchless beauty which require special management to preserve these qualities. They may be established under 36 CFR 294.1 whenever lands possessing outstanding or unique natural beauty warrant this classification.[36]

The Forest Service Manual has a specific section on the protection of national natural landmarks:

Protection. Continuing integrity is essential to National Landmark values. Natural Landmarks should be managed in such a way as to pose no threat to the perpetuation of the feature or species designated. Other uses of the site or area which do not interfere with the purpose of the landmark designation or the integrity of the natural values represented are acceptable." (Forest Service Manual 2362.41).

The Natural Landmarks Program does not have the protection features of Section 106 of the National Historic Preservation Act of 1966. Thus, designation of a national natural landmark presently constitutes only an agreement with the owner to preserve, insofar as possible, the significant natural values of the site or area. Administration and preservation of national natural landmarks is solely the owner's responsibility. The agreement may be terminated by either party upon notification of the other.

It is expected that in the future Congress will provide additional protection for natural landmarks. In the meantime, regional foresters will follow the general protective features of Section 106 of the National Historic Preservation Act in managing national natural landmarks. They must determine in advance, through the preparation of environmental impact statements and consultation with professionals, whether any contemplated action involving a natural landmark will

have adverse effect. If so, they must "(1) Seek alternative actions to alleviate the effect or if this is not practical or possible; (2) Plan to minimize the effect and delay action until a request in writing for the National Park Service to remove the site or area from the Registry has been acted upon."[37]

Besides these federal acts and programs, which are designed to preserve qualities of natural areas, there are a number of state programs that are well worth mentioning. Most of the state natural area preservation programs are meant to preserve areas primarily on ecological grounds (Juday 1975; Vogelman 1969), but some natural area programs have specific provisions for protection of scenic areas via easements as the Tennessee[38] and Arkansas[39] programs do in their state legislation. Other states have provisions for state or local preservation of critical areas, including aesthetic wilderness values.[40]

WILD AND SCENIC RIVERS

Beside preserving scenic highways, preserving wild and scenic rivers has been one of the areas of greatest activity regarding management of visual resources in the country. The National Wild and Scenic Rivers Act (NW&SRA)[41] provides for acquisition and management of wild, scenic, and recreation portions of rivers (Figure 9.5) at different levels of intensity, use, and access.[42] The key agencies involved are the National Park Service, which sometimes performs the initial surveys for proposed wild and scenic rivers, the Forest Service, the Bureau of Land Management, and the Fish and Wildlife Service, all of which manage portions of wild and scenic rivers in their jurisdictions. The declaration of policy in the act states:

It is hereby declared to be the policy of the United States that certain selected rivers of the Nation, which in their immediate environments, possess outstanding remarkable *scenic, recreational,* geologic, fish and wildlife, historic, cultural, or other similar value, shall be preserved in free-flowing condition, and that they and their immediate environments shall be protected for the benefit and enjoyment of present and future generations.[43] (Emphasis added.)

---

[35]Id., F.S.M. 2360.2.

[36]Id., F.S.M. 2362.41.

[37]Id., F.S.M. 2363.37.

[38]See Tenn. Code Ann. Sec. 11-1701 thru 11-1715 (1971).

[39]See Arkansas Environmental Quality Act of 1973, Ark. Stat. Ann. Vol. 2, Title 9, Ch.14, s. 1410 (Supp. 1973).

[40]See also Minnesota Critical Areas Act., Minn. Stat. Ann. Ch. 116G s. 116G.02; and Virginia Critical Environmental Areas, Va. Codes. 10-187c.

[41]16 U.S.C. ss. 1271-1287 (1988).

[42]See U.S. Dept. of Interior and U.S. Forest Service, Guidelines for Evaluating Wild, Scenic and Recreational River Areas Proposed for inclusion in the National Wild and Scenic Rivers System under section 2, Public Law 90-542, Feb. 1970.

[43]16 U.S.C. s. 1271 (1988).

FIGURE 9.5 a, b, c   Wild and Scenic Rivers. *Photo credit: Peter Black*

Similar statements of policy can be found in any number of state acts whose purpose it is to preserve or protect wild and scenic rivers (Turner 1974).

There has been some legal commentary on wild and scenic river activity at the international level (Compton 1975) level, federal level (Tarlock 1967; Tarlock and Tippy 1976; Utter and Schultz 1976; Turner 1974 and USDIBOR), and state level (Turner 1974; Coggins and Phillips 1977). This section will include a short review of activity under the National Wild and Scenic

Rivers Act (NW & SRA) with some mention of state activity.

Even more important than the stated purpose of the act is the original impetus for its enactment in 1968. The act itself states:

The Congress declares that the established national policy of dam and other construction at appropriate sections of the rivers of the United States needs to be complemented by a policy that would preserve other selected rivers or sections thereof in their free-flowing condition.[44]

This legislation was in reaction in part to the controversy created by water development agencies such as the Army Corps of Engineers, the Federal Power Commission, and the Bureau of Reclamation (Tippy 1968; Poland, 1969). The conflict between preservationists and river development advocates led to many court cases where the aesthetic free-flowing values of rivers were primary. These cases include *High Mountain Sheep*,[45] *Namekagon Hydro Corp.* v. *FPC*,[46] and *Scenic Hudson Preservation Conference* v. *FPC*,[47] all with the Federal Power Commission, and *Friends of the Earth* v. *Armstrong*,[48] with the Bureau of Reclamation. Section 1278(a) of the NW&SRA prohibits federal licensing of the construction of any "dam, water conduit, reservoir, powerhouse, transmission line, or other project works under the Federal Power Act" on or directly affecting any protected river.[49] This section also prohibits federal assistance, "by loan, grant, license, or otherwise," of any water project that affects a protected river's values directly and adversely.[50]

The Ozark National Scenic Riverway[51] was created in 1964 in reaction to some unpopular Corps of Engineers dam proposals. The earliest congressional recognition of the aesthetic free flow of rivers was the Act of 1906,[52] which gave the Secretary of the Army the power to issue revocable permits for the diversion of water from the Niagara River as long as it did not interfere with the navigability of the river or with the scenic grandeur of Nigara Falls.

After many years of conflict over river basin development, the National Wild and Scenic Rivers Act protects the free-flowing aesthetic attributes of rivers. The act of 1968 does three things to protect the natural environment of rivers:

First, it protects both the water and area adjacent to the river by creating an elongated corridor, a quarter of a mile wide (on the average), and extending the length of the selected segment. As part of this first mode of protection, certain types of water resource projects, mining activities, and forestry practices are restricted from designated wild and scenic rivers or those under study. These restrictions, however, are subject to certain procedural requirements and provisions; that is, projects already existing are allowed and those in planning stages are subject to the National Environmental Policy Act,[53] which calls for consideration of aesthetic factors when evaluating the impacts and alternatives of major federal projects and actions.

Second, the Wild and Scenic Rivers Act creates a classification system for these areas, designed to limit incompatible development and use of the land, and to limit recreational use in a manner that will prevent the deterioration of the natural qualities of the area surrounding the river. The classification system, designed to restrict the degree and intensity of shoreline development, divides wild and scenic rivers into *wild* river areas, *scenic* river areas, and *recreational* river areas. The allowable intensity of development is determined by the classification of the river stretch. For example, almost no construction is allowed in a wild river area, and mining activity is prohibited.

Third, the act outlines broad, general guides for the benefit of agencies, and spells out allowable levels of development within wild, scenic, and recreational river areas. The act suggests that shorelines remain "largely undeveloped" in scenic river areas and "somewhat developed" in recreational river areas. This, of course, leaves wide latitude for the managing agency— whether the Forest Service, Bureau of Land Management, National Park Service, or Fish and Wildlife Service.

Recreational use is also limited by the classification of the river stretch. Recreational use in a wild river area is limited to hiking, boat floating, and hunting and fishing, with limitations placed on the number of users. Increased levels of recreational use and types of use are allowed in scenic and recreational river areas consistent with the goal of maintaining present environmental quality.

More detailed management guidelines have been issued by the Department of Interior and by the Forest Service as well as by specific management plans for each designated wild and scenic river. For instance, in 1988 Congress passed the Omnibus Oregon Wild and Scenic Rivers Act,[54] which added 1,429 miles to those

[44]Id.

[45]Pacific Northwest Power Co. 31 F.P.C. 247 (1964).

[46]216 F.2d 509 (7th Cir. 1954).

[47]354 F.2d 608 (2d Cir. 1965).

[48]485 F.2d 1 (10th Cir. 1973).

[49]16 U.S.C. s. 1278(a) (1988).

[50]Id.

[51]16 U.S.C. ss. 460 mm-7 (1988).

[52]Act of June 29, 1906, Ch. 3621, s. 2, 34 Stat. 626.

[53]42 U.S.C. 4321 et seq. (1988).

[54]S. 2148, 100th Cong. 2nd. Sess. 134 Cong. Rec. 1-10, 109 (Oct. 12, 1988).

sections already protected by the Oregon Wild and Scenic Rivers Act.

Legal Issues

The National Wild and Scenic Rivers Act has survived at least one takings challenge. Under the NW&SRA, private land may be included within the system, and activities on it that "substantially interfere with public use and enjoyment" of the values protected in the act may be prohibited. In *Schultz* v. *United States*[55] the U.S. court of claims rejected a landowner's takings challenge to federal agency conduct pursuant to the NW&SRA, but other cases suggest takings potential in the future.[56]

Generally, state laws include similar types of measures to protect their own designated wild or scenic river systems. State programs and acts vary tremendously in the amount of protection afforded to their wild and scenic rivers, whether it is the amount of control over land use or water quality, or on many other aspects. (Turner 1974). The states of California, Georgia, Iowa, Louisiana, Maine, Maryland, Massachusetts, Michigan, New York, North Carolina, Ohio, Oregon, Pennsylvania, South Carolina, Tennessee, Virginia, and West Virginia all have wild and/or scenic river acts.[57] According to Kusler (1980), there are twenty-four states with legislation for the protection of wild, recreational, and scenic rivers.

Rivers classified under the NW&SRA have two levels of protection against incompatible development: (1) federal prohibitions against water resource projects; and (2) federal acquisition authority over lands within the river corridor. There is also the issue of whether state scenic river programs provide equivalent protection or act as a deterrent to federal water resource projects. In *California* v. *United States,*[58] the California Water Resource Control Board approved a federally funded project, the New Melans Dam, with twenty-five conditions attached. The United States sought a declaratory judgment to permit it to ignore the state-imposed conditions. The Court held that Section 8 of the Reclamation Act[59] permits a state to impose conditions on "control, appropriation, use and distribution of water" as long as the conditions are not inconsistent with congressional directives respecting the project. This is termed "cooperative Federalism" (Reynolds 1989). As Reynolds points out, the Federal Power Act now functions in a legal matrix that includes the National Environmental Policy Act, the Northwest Power Act, the Fish and Wildlife Coordination Act, and the Federal Power Act amendments — the Energy Security Act of 1980 and the Electrical Consumer Protection Act of 1986.[60]

There is a wealth of research work dealing with aesthetic attributes of scenic rivers. Most applicable work done to date attempts to assess the visual attributes of riverscapes and waterscapes. The work can be categorized into four types, including: (1) work involving waterscape/water recreation perception studies; (2) work involving biological-physical models for evaluating riverscape quality; (3) economic methods for measuring aesthetic values of waterscapes; and (4) work involving professional judgment techniques for describing, rating, and ranking water-related landscapes (LSU 1977; USDA, FS 1977). (Much of the previously cited work overlaps with that being done to assess the recreational quality and psychological-social carrying capacities (crowding) of riverscapes.) There also have been two major proceedings (LSU 1977; USDA, FS 1977a) dealing with wild and scenic river management.

Despite this large volume of work, little has been done on assessing the perceived compatibility or suitability of types and intensities of development on wild, scenic, and recreational river areas. Comparatively more has been done on perceived assessment of crowding relating to river recreation experiences. The author has proposed a research strategy for dealing with visual impact on wild and scenic rivers (Smardon, 1977).

Some of the most sophisticated work applied to management of wild and scenic rivers has begun to address the question of cumulative visual impact on sce-

---

[55]740 F.2d 932 (Fed. Cir. 1984).

[56]Kentucky v. Stearns Coal & Lumber Co. 678 S.W.2d 378, 381 (Ky. 1981).

[57]See Calif. Resources Code Ch. 1259 (1972), Georgia Code Ann. s. 17-905 et seq. (1969), Iowa Code Ann. ss. 106A-108A (1970), 56 La. Rev. Stat. ss. 1841–49 (1971), 12 Maine Rev. Stat. Ann. ss. 661–680 (1966), Mass. Gen. Laws Ch. 21 s. 17B, Ann. Code of Maryland ss. 759 to 765 (1971), Mich. Stat. Ann. ss. 11.501–11.516 (1973), Laws of N.Y. Ch. 869 s. 429 (1972), N.C. Gen Stat. ss. 113A-31 to 113A-43 (1971), Ohio Rev. Code Ann. ss. 1501-16 to 1501.19 (Supp. 1968), Ore. Rev. Stat. ss. 390.805–390.925 (1973), Penn. Stat. Ann. ss. 821.1–821.8 (1972), S.C. Code Ann. s. 70.25–70.46.16 (Comm. Supp. 1974), Tenn. Stat. Ann. ss. 11-1401 to 11-1417 (1973), Va. Code s. 10-171 et seq. (1970), and W.Va. Code s. 20-5B-1 et seq. (1969).

[58]438 U.S. 645 (1978).

[59]43 U.S.C. s. 372 (1988).

[60]16 U.S.C. s. 797, 803(a) (1988).

nic rivers. Steinitz et al. (1978) developed fairly sophisticated models for simulating visual impacts from alternative policies used to preserve the North River under the Massachusetts Scenic and Recreational Rivers Act.[61] Another sophisticated study was done by EDAW (1978) for the Forest Service for the Hells Canyon National Recreation Area.[62] Part of this study dealt with the visual absorption capacity of the area to degrees of visual impact. These types of studies are on the "cutting edge" of visual analysis, which is also tied closely to legal mandates that serve to protect the visual quality of specific areas.

SCENIC TRAILS

The National Trails System Act,[63] like the wilderness and scenic rivers acts, establishes a national precedent for establishing and maintaining a linear-preserved visual corridor, and it encourages states to establish their own programs. The National Trails System Act of October 2, 1968 (16 U.S.C. 1241–1249) sets the following policy for a national system of trails:

In order to provide for the ever-increasing outdoor recreation needs of an expanding population and in order to promote public access to, travel within, and enjoyment and appreciation of the open-air, outdoor areas of the Nation, trails should be established (1) primarily near the urban areas of the Nation, and (ii) secondarily, within established scenic areas more remotely located. The purpose of this Act is to provide the means for attaining these objectives by instituting a national system for recreation and scenic trails, by designating the Appalachian Trail and the Pacific Crest Trail as the initial components of that system, and by prescribing the methods by which and standards according to which, additional components may be added to the system.[64]

The National Trails System Act (NTSA) created three types of trails: national recreation trails; national scenic trails; and connecting, or side, trails. National recreation trails provide for a variety of outdoor recreation uses in or near urban areas. They may be designated by the Secretary of the Interior or by the Secretary of Agriculture where lands administered by that department are involved. National scenic trails are long-distance trails that provide for maximum outdoor recreation potential, and for the conservation and enjoyment of nationally significant scenic, historic, natural, or cultural qualities of the area. They may be so des-

ignated only by Congress. Connecting, or side, trails provide access to or connect national recreation or scenic trails and may become part of the trails to which they are joined (USDI, BOR 1973).

The National Trails System Act directed the Interior and Agriculture secretaries to encourage states and local governments, as well as private interests, to establish national recreation trails on lands in or near urban areas; and the Secretary of Housing and Urban Development to encourage the planning of recreation trails on lands in or near urban areas, and in connection with urban recreation and transportation.

Where lands included in the right-of-way of a trail are not federally held, such land or interests in such land may be acquired by written cooperative agreement, donation, purchase with donated or appropriate funds, or exchange, provided that not more than twenty-five acres in any one mile is acquired by condemnation. According to National Trail System Act guidelines (USDI, BOR and USDA, FS 1975)

(a) The Secretary of the Interior, or the Secretary of Agriculture where lands administered by him are involved, may establish and designate national recreation trails, with the consent of the Federal agency, State, or political subdivision having jurisdiction over the lands involved, upon finding that—
  (i) such trails are reasonably accessible to urban areas, and, or
  (ii) such trails meet the criteria established in this chapter and such supplementary criterias he may prescribe.

(b) As provided in this section, trails within park, forest, and other recreation areas administered by the Secretary of the Interior or the Secretary of Agriculture or other federally administered areas may be established and designated as "National Recreation Trails" by the appropriate Secretary and, when no Federal land acquisition is involved—
  (i) trails in or reasonably accessible to urban areas may be designated as "National Recreation Trails" by the Secretary of the Interior with the consent of the States, their political subdivision, other appropriate administering agencies, and
  (ii) trails within park, forest, and other recreation areas owned or administered by States may be designated as "National Recreation Trails" by the Secretary of the Interior with the consent of the State.

    National scenic trails are authorized and designated only by acts of Congress. These trails

---

[61]Mass. G.L. Ch. 21, s. 17B.

[62]16 U.S.C. s. 460gg (1988).

[63]16 U.S.C. ss. 1241–1249 (1988).

[64]U.S.D.I., B.O.R., 1973, "National Recreation Trails: Information and Application Procedure,"
p. 1.

FIGURE 9.6 a, b, c   Scenic trails — Adirondack Trail. *Photo credit: James F. Palmer*

by their very nature must be worthy of such designation. Their scenic, historical, natural, or cultural qualities must be superior to those of other trails in the country. Because of their special characteristics, national scenic trails should be capable of promoting interest and attracting visitors from throughout the United States.

Half the states have passed comprehensive trails system legislation, and federal agencies have designated hundreds of national recreation trails. Congress has established eight national scenic and five national historic trails.[65] Most important the National Park Service has nearly succeeded in aquiring a permanent right-of-way for the Appalachian National Scenic Trail (Figure 9.6), the patriarch of American hiking trails, a 2,100-mile footpath stretching from Maine to Georgia.[66] As Davis (1986) points out though, trail mileage has decreased by about one-third since 1945, and private development threatens to destroy the scenic, cul-

tural, and biological qualities of the areas through which national trails pass.

During its first decade, from 1968 to 1978, the NTSA was not very effective or in active implementation because:

1. The legislation relied on state governments to acquire land for national scenic trails.
2. The act limited the extent of federal condemnation authority to twenty-five acres in any one mile of trail;
3. There were problems in interpretation of the act's trail-width provision due to limiting the amount of land that could be acquired to twenty-five acres per mile.

In 1976 Congress started addressing these problems and in 1978 enacted amendments to the NTSA, increasing federal amendments to the NTSA, increasing federal condemnation authority from 25 to an average

[65]16 U.S.C. s. 1244(a) (1988).
[66]Id., s. 1244 (a) (1) (1988).

of 125 acres per mile of trail, and authorizing an additional $90 million over three years for acquisition of Appalachian Trail land.[67]

President Carter became an outspoken advocate of the National Trails System and between 1978 and 1980, nearly 19,000 miles of recreation, scenic, and historic trails were added to the system, a fourfold increase. Congress amended the NTSA four times in 1979 and 1980 and gave it an extensive overhaul in 1983. Aside from the Appalachian Trail, most of the remaining eight scenic trails will be incomplete for many years because Congress has refused to fund aquisitions of trail land outside the boundaries of federally administered areas.

Section 1246(1) of NTSA permits trail protection regulation. First, the act envisions scenic trails in part as means of conserving the natural qualities of the areas through which they pass. Scenic trails are not solely recreational facilities; they are intended to preserve valuable environmental resources. Second, the act encourages multiple uses of trails and adjacent land. Third, NTSA favors alternatives to property acquisition, especially by condemnation, for trail creation and protection. While the power of condemnation is strictly circumscribed, the potential use of other forms of acquisition, such as zoning and cooperative agreements, is possible. Fourth, the act endorses the right of federal agencies to regulate the conduct of private landowners on adjacent land. Fifth, the act implicitly approves the use of zoning to protect trails.

National scenic trails are designed for hiking and other compatible uses. The National Trails System Act prohibits the use of motorized equipment on these trails. (For other aspects of management and legal aspects of the National Trails System Act, see the Nature Conservancy 1976.)

Legal Issues

The Fifth Amendment presents potentially the most formidable legal obstacle to trail protection regulations since such regulations would significantly diminish the rights of some private landowners adjacent to trails. Determining whether a particular regulatory scheme as applied to a specific parcel of property is a "taking" requiring just compensation is difficult and unpredictable. "Open space" zoning techniques, like those employed in trail protection regulations, are particularly vulnerable to takings challenges because that may reduce land values far more than conventional zoning (as we saw in Chapter 8). This issue is very similar to that of the Wild and Scenic Rivers Act.

State Legislation and Scenic Trails

It was the original intent that the NTSA would encourage enactment of state trails legislation. A 1976 survey found that seventeen states had enacted trails legislation, twenty-five operated trails, fifteen reported local government trails, and eighteen had created state trail councils. As of 1986 twenty-five states had comprehensive trails system statutes, including: Alaska,[68] Arkansas,[69] California,[70] Colorado,[71] Connecticut,[72] Florida,[73] Georgia,[74] Idaho,[75] Kentucky,[76] Maine,[77] Massachusetts,[78] Michigan,[79] Minnesota,[80] New Hampshire,[81] New Jersey,[82] New Mexico,[83] New York,[84] North Carolina,[85] Ohio,[86] Oklahoma,[87] Oregon,[88] Tennessee,[89] Texas,[90] and Washington.[91]

---

[67]16 U.S.C. 1244 (1988).

[68]Alas. Stat. ss. 41.21.850-.872 (1983 & Supp. 1984).

[69]Ark. Stat. Ann. ss. 9-601 to 609 (1985).

[70]Cal. Pub. Res. ss. 5070–5077.7 (West 1984).

[71]Colo. Rev. Stat. ss. 33-11-101 to 112 (1984).

[72]Conn. Gen. Stat. Ann. s. 23-10a (West Supp. 1984).

[73]Fla. Stat. Ann. ss. 260-011 to 018 (West Supp. 1985).

[74]Ga. Code ss. 12-3-110 to 117 (1982).

[75]Idaho Code ss. 67-4232 to 4236 (1980).

[76]Ky. Rev. Stat. ss. 148.610-.991 (1980 & Supp. 1984–85).

[77]Me. Rev. Stat. Ann. Title 12 s.602(15) (1981 & Supp. 1984).

[78]Mass. Ann. Laws. Ch. 132A ss. 38–40 (Michie/Law Co-op 1981).

[79]Mich. Comp. Laws Ann. ss. 318.231-233 (West 1984).

[80]Minn. Stat. Ann. ss. 85.015-.021, 86A.05 sub 1.4 (West 1977 & Supp. 1985).

[81]N.H. Rev. Stat. Ann. ss. 216-f:1 to 5 (1977 & Supp. 1983).

[82]N.J. Stat. Ann. ss 13:8-30 to -44 (West 1979).

[83]N.M. Stat. Ann. ss. 16-3-1 to -9 (1978).

[84]N.Y. Parks & Rec. Law s. 3.09 (7-a) (McKinney 1984).

[85]N.C. Gen. Stat. ss 113A-83 to 94 (1983).

[86]Ohio Rev. Code Ann. ss 1519.01-.99 (Page 1978).

[87]Okla Stat. Title 74 ss. 3451-3458 (1981).

[88]Or. Rev. Stat. ss. 390.950 to .990 (1983).

[89]Tenn. Code Ann. ss. 11-11-101 to 120 (1980 & Supp 1984).

[90]Tex Parks & Wild Code Ann. ss. 25.001 to .005 (Vernon Supp. 1984).

[91]Wash. Rev. Code ss. 67.32.010 to .140 (1983).

Most state acts are far weaker than the NTSA. In some states, trail officials have no authority to acquire land or interests in land for new trails. In others, trail officials may acquire land, but not through the use of eminent domain. In three of the few states that do permit the use of eminent domain for trails, acquisitions are limited to twenty-five acres per mile, the equivalent of a trail corridor 200 feet wide.

There has been some behavioral research work done on recreational trail users, but little research (Palmer 1978) assesses how people usually use and evaluate scenic trails. There has also been one national symposium of note on trails (Open Lands Project 1971).

SPECIFIC LAND AREAS

Specific land areas managed by the Forest Service, Bureau of Land Management, the National Park Service, and the Fish and Wildlife Service often have specific statutes that contain language relating to aesthetic considerations.

Some specific federally owned land areas such as the Whiskeytown-Shasta-Trinty National Recreation Areas[92] and the King Range National Conservation Area in California[93] and the Spruce Knob–Seneca Rocks National Recreation Area[94] in West Virginia have specific language pertaining to aesthetics in the statutes that created and guide administration of these areas. The same is true for many of the national parks and wilderness areas.

The Bureau of Land Management's Organic Act[95] even has specific provisions that call for study, identification, and protection of visual resources of a specific area, the California Desert Conservation Area (Figure 9.7), in the following passages:

Sec. 601. (a) The Congress finds that—

(1) the California desert contains historical, scenic, archeological, environmental, biological, cultural, scientific, educational, recreational, and economic resources that are uniquely located adjacent to an area of large population;
(2) the California desert environment is a total ecosystem that is extremely fragile, easily scarred, and slowly healed;
(3) the California desert environment and its resources, including certain rare and endangered species of wildlife, plants, and fishes, and numerous archeological land historic sites, are seriously threatened by air pollution, inadequate Federal

FIGURE 9.7   Mojave Desert—California Desert Conservation Area. *Photo credit: R. C. Smardon*

management authority, and pressures of increased use, particularly recreational use, which are certain to intensify because of the rapidly growing population of southern California;
(4) the use of all California desert resources can and should be provided for in a multiple use and sustained yield management plan to conserve these resources for future generations, and to provide present and future use and enjoyment, particularly outdoor recreation uses, including the use, where appropriate, of off-road recreational vehicles;
(5) the Secretary has initiated a comprehensive planning process and established an interim management program for the public lands in the California desert; and
(6) to insure further study of the relationship of man and the California desert environment, preserve the unique and irreplaceable resources, including archeological values, and conserve the use of the economic resources of the California desert, the public must be provided more opportunity to participate in such planning and management, and additional management authority must be provided to the Secretary to facilitate effective implementation of such planning and management.

. . .

(f) Subject to valid existing rights, nothing in this Act shall affect the applicability of the United States mining laws on the public lands within the California Desert Conservation Area, except that all mining claims located on public lands within the California Desert Conservation Area shall be subject to such reasonable regulations as the Secretary may prescribe to effectuate the purposes

---

[92]16 U.S.C. s. 460q-3 (1988).
[93]16 U.S.C. s. 460r-Y (1988).
[94]16 U.S.C. s. 460y-P (1988).
[95]43 U.S.C. s. 1701 et seq. (1988).

of this section. Any patent issued on any such mining claim shall recite this limitation and continue to be subject to such regulations. Such regulations shall provide for such measures as may be reasonable to protect the *scenic, scientific* and *environmental values* of the public lands of the California Desert Conservation Area against undue impairment, and to assure against pollution of the streams and waters within the California Desert Conservation Area.[96] (Emphasis added.)

As mentioned in previous sections, that specific statutes such as these identify and provide direct consideration of, or protection of, visual resources within these specific areas is the best legal protection available. It should leave no doubt in any court's mind about the intent of Congress concerning these areas, and that the intent constitutes a social norm or obligation of protection.

Bi-State and Regional Scenic Areas

Conservationists believed a precedent had been set when a regional commission was unable to manage a complex, bi-state natural area; Lake Tahoe. Remarkably similar to the Columbia Gorge, Lake Tahoe forms the boundary between California and Nevada. The two states have disagreed over how or whether to protect the lake. Lake Tahoe also contains scenic, natural, cultural, and recreational values of national significance.

The commission created to manage Lake Tahoe, the Tahoe Regional Planning Agency (TRPA), achieved national recognition as a failure. In the ten years from its creation in 1969, TRPA approved 96 percent of all development proposals put before it, resulting in the swift and steady deterioration of the lake's scenic and natural values. On June 15, 1984, U.S. District Judge Edward Garcia delivered a legal opinion of TRPA's effectiveness when he enjoined it from approving any development project in the Lake Tahoe Basin until the states adopted a management plan that did not violate the federal California-Nevada Bi-state compact.[97]

In contrast, the 1987 Columbia River Gorge National Scenic Area Act[98] is one of the most comprehensive acts for management of a special scenic area including parts of two states. For a detailed account of the legislative history of the act and a detailed critique of its many provisions, see the article by Blair (1987). The purposes of the act are:

(1) to establish a national scenic area to protect and provide for the enhancement of the scenic, cultural, recreational, and natural resources of the Columbia River Gorge; and
(2) to protect and support the economy of the Columbia River Gorge area by encouraging growth to occur in existing urban areas and by allowing future economic development in a manner that is consistent with paragraph (1).[99]

Although the act's basic purpose is clear, its implementation mechanisms are complex. The Gorge Scenic Area is divided into three separate land classifications: Special Management Areas (SMA's), General Management Areas (GMA's) and Urban Areas (UA's). Each area is administered by a different management entity and is subject to disparate land use standards. The boundaries for these designated areas are set on maps incorporated into the act and can be altered only in a limited fashion subject to strict criteria.

The composition of the Columbia Scenic Gorge Commission is similar to that of the 1969 Lake Tahoe Bi-State Compact (particularly that a majority, eight of twelve, of the commissioners must reside within the local counties), but the differences are more pronounced. The primary distinctions between the Gorge Commission and the TRPA are (1) that an equal number of appointments are made by authorities outside the Gorge scenic area as those made by authorities within, and (2) that elected and appointed officials — those who, theoretically, would be more likely to sacrifice long-term protection for short-term economic development — are barred from serving on the commission. The Gorge Act also differs from the Tahoe Compact, by greatly restricting commission authority through complex voting procedures, and by incorporating mandatory and specific land use standards into the act itself.

Thirteen cities and towns, or 10 percent of the scenic area, are exempt from the act's purview, and the rest of the land use activities within the Gorge scenic area must be consistent with the act's comprehensive management plan. The act also places rigorous standards upon certain land use activities. The strictest standard is an outright prohibition on "major development actions" within the SMA's. The act also prohibits commercial (except certain recreational facilities), industrial, and multi-family residential development within the SMA's as well as mining exploration, development, and production, with two limited exceptions.

---

[96]Id., s. 1781.
[97]California v. Tahoe Regional Planning Agency, 664 F. Supp. 1373 (1985).
[98]16 U.S.C.A. s. 544-544p (1988).
[99]Id.

All residential development within the Gorge scenic area (excluding the designated UA) — and even development on SMA parcels larger than 40 acres — is prohibited if it would "adversely affect" the scenic, cultural, recreational, and natural resources of the area. "Adversely affect" is defined in the act as:

A reasonable likelihood of more than moderate adverse consequences for the scenic, cultural, recreation or natural resources of the Scenic Area, the determination of which is based on

(1) the context of a proposed action;
(2) the intensity of a proposed action; including the magnitude and duration of an impact and the likelihood of its occurrence;
(3) the relationship between a proposed action and other similar actions which are individually insignificant but which may have cumulatively significant impacts; and
(4) proven mitigation measures which the proponent of the action will implement as part of the proposed action to reduce otherwise significant affects to an insignificant level.[100]

The Gorge Act also contains strong standards for industrial and commercial development, and production of mineral resources. Three years after the commission has been created by law, it must adopt a management plan for the scenic area. Note the Gorge Scenic Act is a Federal law, but there are provisions to create state laws to replace or take over Federal functions with state activity.

Private property regulation by the Forest Service and other federal agencies within federally designated areas certainly is not a novel approach. Two prominent examples, the Sawtooth National Recreation Area and Hells Canyon National Recreation Area, are in the Northwest. Both use a regulatory method derived from the Cape Cod National Seashore, popularized as the "Cape Cod formula." The Cape Cod formula, as used in the Gorge Act, requires local governments to enact zoning ordinances (and variances) that are consistent with standards promulgated and subject to approval by the Secretary of the Interior. The secretary is authorized to enforce the interim guidelines through injunctive and condemnation authority until the commission has approved zoning ordinances for the GMA's and the secretary has concurred with SMA ordinances.

The scenic area's major tributaries are protected through state-designated wild, scenic, or recreation

FIGURE 9.8   Adirondack Park view. *Photo credit: Chad Dawson*

river standards or under the National Wild and Scenic Rivers Act. The act also authorizes appropriations for preparing a program for restoring and reconstructing Oregon's scenic highway adjacent to the Columbia River Gorge.

It is too early to judge how successful the approach taken by the Gorge Act will be, but the structure of the commission is an improvement over the Tahoe Compacts. Standards for development — such as a forty-acre minimum lot size for the scenic area's most significant lands, and a requirement throughout the area that new residential development not "adversely affect" the gorge's scenic, natural, cultural, and recreational values — ensure a minimum level of protection.

The Adirondack Park Agency Act[101] is an example of a state statute aimed at the "threat of unregulated development" within a six-million-acre landscape (Figure 9.8) in northern New York State that includes private and state lands (Note 1975; Davis 1976; Booth 1975). The statute is unusual in its degree of specificity of review criteria for proposed land uses that fall within the park agency's authority.

The first criterion is that the proposed use "be compatible with the character description and purposes, policies and objectives of the land use wherein it is proposed to be located."[102] The aim of this first criterion, which applies to 87 percent of the park's private land area, is "to prevent strip development along major travel corridors in order to enhance the aesthetic and economic benefit derived from a park atmosphere along these corridors."[103]

---

[100]Id.

[101]Adirondack Park Agency Act, N.Y. Exec. Laws ss. 800 et seq. (McKinney 1972).

[102]Id., s. 809.10b.

[103]Id., ss. 805.3.f(z), 805.3g(x).

The second criterion is that the proposed use "be consistent with the overall intensity guideline for the land use area included."[104] The intent of these guidelines for six different types of zone areas" appears to be to control vacation home development by channeling it into areas where it would least detract from those scenic and environmental qualities the vacation home buyers are themselves seeking." (Note 1975)

The third criterion is that the proposed use must "comply with the shoreline restrictions if applicable."[105] These restrictions regulate shoreline building densities, building setback, and the maintenance of vegetation along the shores of all lakes and ponds and certain rivers and streams.[106]

The fourth criterion is that the proposed use "not have an undue adverse impact upon the natural, scenic, aesthetic, ecological, wildlife, historic, recreational or open space resource of the (Adirondack) park or upon the ability of the public to provide supporting facilities and services made necessary."[107] This last criterion gives the park agency a good deal of discretionary control, but its function is to prevent the park's "unique scenic, aesthetic and recreational resources"[108] from becoming victims of their own attractiveness.

Case Study: Alpine Lakes Wilderness Appraisal[109]

Introduction

The impetus for the research presented in this case study was a congressional act, the Alpine Lakes Management Act (ALMA) of July 12, 1976, that mandated the establishment of the Alpine Lakes Wilderness Area.[110] ALMA specified that all private lands within the designated wilderness boundaries would be purchased at fair-market value. At the time of the act, the Pack River Management Company (PRMC) owned more than 22,000 acreas of land within the boundary. The Forest Service offered PRMC $13 million for the property based on its timber value. While the value of the timber was not in dispute, an offering price based on timber value seemed inconsistent with the physical setting (Figure 9.9) of the land.[111]

At this juncture an interdisciplinary team of scientists from the University of Wisconsin (Madison) was engaged to appraise the property. The team was headed by the late Professor James A. Graaskamp of the University of Wisconsin, who had developed an approach to valuation based on contemporary real estate appraisal theory. Other members included Bill Gates (a computer scientist), Ralph Kiefer (a remote-sensing expert), Mike Robbins, and a landscape architecture team of Bernard Niemann and Richard Chenoweth. The marriage of contemporary real estate appraisal theory with wilderness assessment, in the context of a spatial data base utilizing remotely sensed data, formed the basis of the appraisal.

Real Estate Valuation Methodology

Establishing the most probable use of the subject property is a pivotal step in the contemporary valuation process. In this process (Figure 9.10), the analysis moves inductively from what is known about the property to be appraised toward identification of alternative uses. The alternatives uses are

FIGURE 9.9   Scene of Alpine Lakes Wilderness Area. *Photo credit: Richard Chenoweth*

---

[104]Id. s. 809.10.c.

[105]Id., s. 809.10.d.

[106]Id., s. 809.1.

[107]Id., s. 809.10.c.

[108]This phrase is a legislative "finding" concerning the park.

[109]Parts of this case study were taken from an unpublished paper by Michael L. Robbins and Sean C. Ahern, "The Price of Wilderness and Scenic Beauty: A Methology for the Inventory and Appraisal of Wilderness and Scenic Land," undated. Used with permission of the authors.

[110]16 U.S.C. § 1132 (1988).

[111]It was the hope of Congress and the intent of ALMA that compensation agreements could be negotiated that included exchange of other federally owned property or donations. Timber trades for national forest lands were considered probable. However, when PRMC sold its saw mill operations in the Wenatchee, Washington, area of the intended wilderness, the Forest Service found it expedient to withdraw trade offers from PRMC.

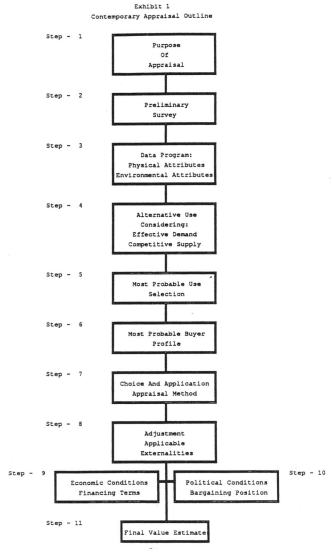

FIGURE 9.10   Contemporary Appraisal Outline

use for the subject property, this case study illustrated how transactions between informed buyers and sellers were structured so that the sales comparison approach (market inference) could be employed to price the subject property.

The contemporary appraisal process (Figure 9.10) is generally divided into eleven steps; however, the principal focus of this study will be Step 7, Choice and Application of Appraisal Method, and the inclusion of nontraditional aesthetic analysis as part of this step. Steps 1 through 6 are described briefly to provide context.

The Valuation Process

Step 1: The Appraisal Issue

The issue for which fair-market value was required stemmed from the Alpine Lakes Management Act of 1976, Section 4 (Land Acquisition and Exchange),[112] which authorized and directed the Secretary of Agriculture to acquire more than 41,000 acres of nonfederal lands in the Alpine Lakes Wilderness and the "intended wilderness."

One of the unique features of ALMA was that it gave the owners within the intended wilderness special rights that modify the appraisal rules affecting condemnation. For example, since ALMA provided three years for negotiated purchase, the Forest Service saw one of their alternatives to be no action at all in order to prompt landowners to force a purchase by court action (USDA FS 1978, p. iv).

While ALMA used the term "just compensation," there was no condemnation action at the time of appraisal. The actions of attorneys for the property owners were not adverse condemnation actions, but rather suits to proceed with negotiation of purchase in which the court would set the price should negotiations stalemate.

Step 2: Preliminary Survey

An initial survey of the unique physical attributes of the subject property suggested to the appraisal team that the most probable use could be wilderness, with a significant component for scenic quality conservation. The initial survey also suggested that this traditional public use concept (wilderness conservation) could be identified as a private market phenomenon in which there was an organized market acquiring land without right of eminent domain for the specific purpose of wilderness and scenic preservation.

Step 3: Data Program

To be sensitive to the attributes affecting economic value, the economic land unit is analyzed by collecting relevant data according to five categories:

1. *Physical attributes* such as size, shape, soils, geology, slope, water, flora, and fauna.
2. *Legal and political attributes* affecting use and degree of decision-making within the private sector, including federal, state, county, and private land use control relevent to the parcel.
3. *Linkage attributes* that tie the site to infrastructure sys-

then ranked in terms of economic benefit, physical suitability, political suitability, effective demand, and financial viability at a particular point in time. The resulting matrix of choices suggests scenarios of possible use for the parcel. The determination of most possible use, in turn, suggests the nature of the most probable buyer.

To estimate what the most probable buyer would pay in terms of market value, or most probable price, the appraiser must either find direct case equivalent sales of comparable property between fully informed parties or, in the absence of current market information, simulate the economic logic and pricing calculus of the most probable buyer, given political constraints and available market alternatives.

After determination of wilderness as the most probable

---

[112]16 U.S.C. pp. 1131–1136 (1988).

tems such as roads and sewer, or to peripheral activities and establishments that may generate demand for the parcel.

4. *Dynamic attributes* related to how people perceive a site — for instance, as prestigious, dangerous, attractive, enjoyable, beautiful.

5. *Environmental attributes* related to off-site effects of the subject property, for example, storm water runoff or destruction of a viewshed.

Step 4: Alternative Use Determination

The detailed property analysis resulted in two sets of uses being identified for PRMC: (1) lands for logging, intensive recreation, and recreation lot development; and (2) lands for wilderness and recreation. These are conflicting uses in that logging or development precludes the use of the land as wilderness.[94] Appraisal theory suggests that the most probable use of the land will be that which yields the highest present value within the practical constraints of public policy, market demand, physical resource base, and financial viability when sold on the open market, in a negotiated purchase, by a knowledgeable buyer and seller, neither acting under duress and given a reasonable time for sale (ILAC 1973, 25–28). While the economic ranking of PRMC land had been established for its timber value, the economic ranking for its use as wilderness and recreation had to be established in order to determine the most probable use.

Step 5: Most Probable Use Determination

While the appreciation and preservation of wilderness and scenic lands have been well accepted, the market valuation of such lands has received little attention (Robbins 1983, pp. 3–7). Wilderness and scenic lands are bought and sold every day, but the valuation process has yet to recognize the attributes associated with wilderness lands as economic commodities. When valuing a single-family house, the appraiser is able to assign adjustments to differences between attributes of the house (number of bathrooms, square footage, etc.) and a comparable value because the motivation and behavior of buyers indicate that such attributes have economic importance to them. Wilderness and scenic beauty attributes had been considered intangibles that could not be priced in the marketplace, in part, because the tie between buyer motivation and the physical attributes had not been established. The underlying principle of this research is that the market (both buyers and sellers) recognize that wilderness consists (at least in part) of tangible attributes that are capable of interacting with people in a way as to make them desirable and in demand.

Step 6: Most Probable Buyer Determination

The selection of the most probable use of the subject property by the appraiser leads to identification of the most probable buyer. Most probable buyer identification then enables the appraiser to begin the search for sales with a most probable use similar to that of the subject property. Wilderness land purchases, or comparables, could then be used to determine the fair-market value of the subject property based on the application of the sales comparison approach to value (Graaskamp 1985: pp. 7–8).

After careful matching of the attributes making up the subject property with previous buyer history along similar attributes, it was determined that the most probable use of the subject property was for wilderness and the most probable buyers would be those motivated to protect the unique condition of the subject property.

The appraiser has determined in his opinion that highest and best use of each cluster shall be allocated between, certain acres appropriate as trailhead and public corridor to the back country, and certain acres shall be allocated as wilderness for public purposes as these uses have not only immediate and higher present value than alternatives, but are in addition most compatible with community environment and development goals. *These uses presume a probable buyer or buyers motivated to preserve high priority wilderness tracts and representing collective private citizens financing.* (Graaskamp and Robbins, 1982, p. III-21 (emphasis added).

Step 7: Choice and Application of Appraisal Method

Choice of Appraisal Method

Once the most probable use has been determined, the best approach to valuation is to estimate value from what the most probable buyers have done in prior transactions of similar properties (inference). This method of determining most probable price involves inferring future market behavior from recently completed market transactions. The method implies that a prudent person will not pay more for a property than a comparable substitute property would cost.

Land appraisal depends primarily on the sales comparison approach as opposed to an income capitalization or cost approach to valuation (Graaskamp 1985, p. 9). The goal of the research was to establish a methodology enabling the sales comparison approach to be applied in the pricing of the subject property. The PRMC appraisal is unique because one of the potential uses was wilderness, a use that had not previously been appraised as a market commodity and whose attributes had been poorly defined.

The sales comparison approach preferred to compare the subject property in terms of specific, physically ascertained attributes to broadly similar properties that had been sold to a class of buyers with similar motivation. Therefore, it is necessary to describe the physical attributes of the subject property that may be significantly related to alternative uses for the selection of the best use. In the case of the Alpine Lakes Wilderness, where the subject property was owned in a checkerboard pattern adjoining both government and privately owned properties, it was also necessary to place the subject property within the context of a regional pattern and subenvironmental systems (Figure 9.11). Comparison of scale, physical diversity, ruggedness, and quality of the property in question created a data problem of unusual proportions (Table 9.1). Nevertheless, the distinctions between subject property and comparables had to be retained if pricing inferences were to be equitable.

The dual objectives of needing to maintain consistency in the application of pricing methodology while remaining sensitive to the diversity within and among the comparables and the subject property led the appraisal team to determine that a geographic information system (GIS) would be necessary to manage the data. In addition, it was determined that the automated data management function of the GIS would need to

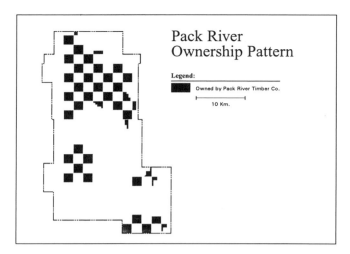

FIGURE 9.11   Typical Ownership Pattern

be tied directly to the automated pricing process so that individual components of the subject could be priced with selected units from comparable properties.

The automated selection and pricing process of this research fits the basic strategy of the sales comparison approach, which is to search for properties that might have served the same uses as the indicated most probable use for the subject property, on the principle that buyers' top price will be only as much as they would pay for reasonable substitutes.

In general, there are three major conditions for executing the sales comparison approach (even for wilderness lands) (Robbins 1987, p. 232):

1. There is an orderly market for parcels of wilderness and scenic attributes in which arm's length transactions occurred without recourse to eminent domain.

2. Adequate information is available to adjust sales prices of transactions meeting the first condition for external factors such as; time of sale, financial terms, and unusual sales conditions. The appraiser must have enough information to make reasonable adjustments for differences in location, or for imbalances in the market, to the degree that these differences are unique to only some of the comparables.

3. The subject property and the comparables need to have some common denominator with respect to both size and quality or suitability, for the presumed use, for comparison of the subject property and the comparables.

Determination of comparability based on a most probable use of wilderness was a fundamental challenge of this research. Two problems were encountered: (1) wilderness is a condition that is not defined by a single set of attributes but one that is a result of the synergy among various combinations of attributes; and (2) there was no established methodology to inventory the wilderness attributes once they were defined.

Establishing Comparative Wilderness Scores

Following the preliminary survey (Step 2) indicating wilderness as a potential most probable use, an assessment of the attributes associated with wilderness (Step 3) as a most probable use is the next step based on physical, dynamic, and environmental attributes. Of the three, definition of the dynamic attributes for wilderness posed the most difficult problem. As discussed above, the two problems confronted were how to identify wilderness attributes and once identified how to inventory them. The more general issue, however, was how to develop a scoring system for wilderness attributes that provided for a relevant unit for comparison — a unit that measures the kinds of utility buyers think they are purchasing when they buy wilderness lands.

In the search for wilderness and scenic attributes that

TABLE 9.1   Alternative Use Considerations

	Timber Potential	Lot Potential	Park Potential	Damage Potential to Other Alpine Areas Views and Ecosystems	Wilderness/ Public Access Route Potential	Acres Allocated to Trailhead Corridor	Acres Allocated to Wilderness
Public Benefits	Long term damage	Permanent damage	Long term damage	—	Long term benefits	—	—
*Cluster 1	Modest	Insignificant	Good	Serious	Established	640	1,909
*Cluster 2	Insignificant	None	Modest	Modest	Firmly Established	1,028	00
*Cluster 3	Fair	Modest	Excellent lakes, mt. peaks, high scenic quality scores	Serious	Established	640	3,057
*Cluster 4	Good East half only	Good	Excellent west half, lakes, mt. peaks, high scenic quality scores, good east half	Serious	Potential alternative to overcrowded Enchanted area; less hiker pressure currently	1,280	13,903
						3,588	18,869
Total Subject Property Acres							22,457

*As part of a strategic ploy by the appraisal team (in anticipation of possible court rulings) the subject property was organized into four separate clusters.

Source: James A. Graaskamp and Michael L. Robbins, *The Appraisal of the Pack River Lands* (Madison, WI: Landmark Research, 1982), p. III-17.

could be used for the valuation of the PRMC lands, two systems were identified that attempted to categorize lands based on their wilderness and scenic beauty quality: the Wilderness Attribute Rating System (WARS) (USDA, FS 1977, p. 1) and the Variety Class Assessment System (VCAS) (USDA, FS 1974). Both systems were developed by the U.S. Forest Service to rank lands for their wilderness and scenic quality by identifying the attributes that described these phenomena. These two systems provided a point of departure for the geographically based information system developed for the appraisal described in this case study.

The Wilderness Evaluation System (WES)

The term given the combination of GIS-based wilderness evaluation with automated sales-comparison-price estimating was the Wilderness Evaluation System (WES). WES was designed to extract the best aspects of WARS and VCAS for use in a spatial approach to wilderness evaluation (Table 9.2). WES augments the systems discussed above by using the additional tools provided in a spatial data base and the information gleaned from visitor employed photography (Chenoweth and Neimann 1982). WES was designed to provide a mechanism for a site-specific comparison of the subject property's

TABLE 9.2   The Scenic Quality Criteria*

I. Physiography
    1. Sharp dissected uneven slopes
    2. Moderately dissected slopes
    3. Irregular landscape
    4. Ridged landscape
    5. Peak
II. Rockform
    1. Avalanche chute (rock)
    2. Avalanche chute (snow)
    3. Talus slope or boulder field
    4. Rock outcrop < 2 acres
    5. Rock outcrop 2–5 acres
    6. Rock outcrop 5+ acres
    7. Cliff
    8. Pinnacle
    9. Cirque
    10. Permanent snow field
    11. Glacier
    12. Rock dome
III. Vegetation
    1. Stocking 10 to 39%
    2. Stocking 49 to 69%
    3. Stocking 70%+
    4. Large old growth timber
    5. West meadow
IV. Waterform
    1. Unusual shoreline configuration (lakes)
    2. Falls
    3. Rapids
    4. Meander

*These factors reflect elements of diversity revealed by the visual study to be prominent in scenic quality ratings of people who make the effort to enter the area on foot and selected for the fact that data could be gathered from air photos.

Source: James A. Graaskamp and Michael L. Robbins, *The Appraisal of the Pack River Lands* (Madison, WI: Landmark Research, 1982), p. II-22.

wilderness/scenic attributes with comparable properties' attributes in accordance with the sales comparison approach to value.

WES has several features that distinguish it from other approaches to wilderness evaluation: (1) evaluation is done on a site-specific basis; (2) it provides an understanding of the spatial relationships and attribute variability within a wilderness area; (3) it uses a standardized unit of evaluation, enabling retesting and comparative analysis to be performed; and (4) it is a programmatic approach that is specific in application.

System Structure

WES contains the four major components of wilderness: (1) natural integrity/apparent naturalness, (2) opportunity for solitude, (3) opportunity for primitive recreation experience, and (4) scenic beauty (Scenic Quality System).

Natural integrity was defined as the extent to which physical development has affected long-term ecological processes. The ratings were based on the same physical impacts used in WARS but geared toward impacts on the natural processes as perceived by the nonexpert typical user. Rating was done on individual cells (spatial unit of analysis) starting with 10 points. The value of any physical impacts contained within the cell's boundary was added. Values ranged from 10 (paved road) to 0 (no impact). A weighting factor was applied to each cell to account for the physical impact from surrounding cells. Therefore, the final natural integrity score for each cell reflected both internal and external physical development.

Opportunity for solitude was rated for each cell using four attributes: (1) distance perimeter to core, (2) view-from the cell, (3) view-to the cell (both from the same selected viewing platforms), and (4) vegetative screening. The first attribute was generated using a simple distance function in the GIS, and the second and third attributes were generated using viewshed algorithms (Travis et al. 1975). The last attribute was derived from the density information collected in the landscape attribute inventory. A rating system was devised that combined the four components into a single solitude score.

Opportunity for primitive recreation experience was made up of three attributes: (1) challenge, (2) diversity of terrain, and (3) diversity of landscape. Challenge was scored on the basis of several environmental attributes, such as the presence of various types of rock forms and the density of vegetation. Diversity of terrain used the percent slope as a measure of challenge (more elaborate measures could be made, e.g., fractal dimension). Diversity of landscape was measured by the number of different landscape features contained within a single cell (physiography, vegetative, rockform, waterform). Each cell was scored with respect to this component.

Scenic quality system (SQS) was based on many of the attributes described in the VCAS utilized by the Forest Service, which translates to a variety of rockforms, landforms, water, and vegetation per unit of area. The primary difference is that SQS used an inventory procedure based on individual cells using aerial color photographs for the inventory procedure and a visual interpretative key for each of the environmental attributes (Ahern 1982). In addition, SQS relied on the visitor employed photography study (Neimann and Chenoweth 1982) to augment those environmental attributes identified by users that were not delineated by wilderness and scenic experts. Scoring of each cell was done using the number of landscape attributes found in each cell (diversity) and the exposure of the cell to viewing platforms (as determined by view shed analysis).

The diversity measure was derived by correlating the scenic score that users gave to scenes they photographed with an inventory of the WES landscape attributes that occurred in each picture. Correlations had an r^2 of 94 percent using 800 + samples. The rationale behind using view-from as the other component of the scenic score is that a scenically beautiful region is even more valuable if it is visible from a variety of vantage points.

As stated previously, a complicating factor in the assessment of wilderness lands is that no one set of environmental attributes (those relating to the physical characteristics of the land) constitutes wilderness. WES addresses this problem (as does WARS) by defining four components of the system whose subattributes can be applied regardless of the region of the landscape on which the analysis is performed. The identification and interpretation of the environmental attributes used to score those components will vary from region to region. For example, the attribute challenge in a mountainous region with steep slopes may have a high score (indicating a significant challenge) because of the difficulty of traversing such terrain, whereas in a relatively flat terrain with no visible mountains, the score may be high due to orientation problems. This consistency of the wilderness components and their attributes in WES allows for comparison of wilderness areas regardless of their geographic region or characteristics. Site-specific information for each new study area is obtained from the environmental attributes for each set of components and interpreted on a case-by-case basis.

The other key feature of WES is its spatial approach to wilderness evaluation. Wilderness scores are calculated for each of the four components in a defined spatial unit (for the PMRC appraisal a ten-acre cell was used). This unit forms the basis for comparison of the subject and comparable properties. This unit is, however, not evaluated in isolation. The viewshed analysis in the GIS permits including off-site effects that influence the wilderness score of a cell. This spatial approach to wilderness evaluation has the advantages of site specificity, repeatability, context (visual exposure), and comparability (with other wilderness areas).

Data Sources

The WES component attributes were scored using environmental attributes obtained from map and photographic data and spatial operations of a GIS. The map data (7.5 minute US Geological Survey quadrangles) yielded information on physical development, human impact (roads and buildings), topography, and surface water. The photographic data (1 : 11,000 color aerial photographs) were used to derive the landscape attributes defined in WES. Derived data sets were generated using the spatial operations of the GIS and the Forest Service's VIEWIT Program (Travis et al. 1975). The derived data set included view-from and view-to each cell (from the same selected viewing platforms), distance perimeter to core, and slope for each cell.

Attribute Weighting

WES consists of ten attributes scored on an ordinal basis, each attribute having a minimum possible score of 10. The ten attributes were grouped into the four components of wilderness. It was decided that the most defensible weighting scheme, from a legal standpoint, would be one in which each attribute would be weighted equally, relative to the component in which it is assigned. This type of weight distribution is consistent with contemporary valuation theory in that it attempts to remove any biases. The Wilderness Act of 1964 identified three primary wilderness components — wilderness quality, solitude, and primitive recreation experience. It also permitted use of any of four supplemental attributes, including scenic quality, if present to a significant degree. For a detailed description of the application of the appraisal method see Robbins (1983 and 1987).

Significance and Results

This case study shows that spatial data base concepts can be used to value individual appraisal units, explicitly recognizing the unique combinations of ascertainable facts present in each appraisal unit. Rather than assigning average values for only limited amounts of the total site (e.g., by valuing the site for timber or recreational lot development by either the aggregate or multiple regression methods), the techniques utilized in this project allowed valuing each individual appraisal unit making up the subject property.

The development of the WES enabled the use of physical attributes and user attitudes in establishing proxies for recognized wilderness characteristics. Having established the wilderness proxies, the wilderness scores were evaluated and processed using an attribute-matching methodology, which was not dependent on inferential statistical reliability for accuracy. In addition, the attribute-matching pricing methodology provided for testing of alternate pricing models, allowing internal consistency and appraisal goals to be evaluated and maintained. Finally, the derived price estimate was provided in a format that was easy to follow and explain, thus greatly enhancing the defensibility of the price estimate.

This research demonstrated that there is an active and informed market for a natural landscape that contains significant concentrations of attributes associated with wilderness. By bringing together acceptable market transactions between knowledgeable buyers and sellers, where wilderness was recognized as a significant component of the transaction, with a systematic and detailed inventory of the subject and comparable properties, market inference could be employed to estimate the value of the subject under a wilderness use scenario.

The research concluded that:

1. The highest and best use of the Pack River lands in the Alpine Lakes Management Area was wilderness.
2. The complex issue of wilderness evaluation could be addressed by building a foundation of knowledge and guidelines as laid out by the U.S. Forest Service in the years since the Wilderness Act of 1964.
3. A comprehensive WES necessitated modification of the U.S. Forest Service's systems of wilderness and scenic beauty evaluation, for inclusion into a GIS, to provide an effective data structure for site-specific analysis.
4. A Fair-market evaluation ($37 million) of the Pack River property in the ALMA could be attained by building on well-established wilderness evaluation and real estate appraisal techniques.

References

Ahern, S. C. 1982. The dynamic attributes used in the appraisal of Pack River lands. In *The appraisal of the Pack River lands,* App. B. Landmark Research.

Blair, B., Jr. 1987. The Columbia River Gorge National Scenic Area: The act, its genesis and legislative history. *Environmental Law,* 17: 863–969.

Bonnhoff, H. M. 1982. *California v. Bergland*: A precarious victory for wilderness preservation. *Columbia Journal of Environmental Law,* 7: 179–212.

Booth, N. 1975. The Adirondack Park Agency Act. A challenge in regional land use planning. *George Washington Law Review* 43: 612.

Burke, J., and Twiss, R. 1976. Quantitative method in the wilderness: The selection of wilderness areas by the U.S. Forest Service. *Design Methods and Theories,* 10(1): 50–61.

Chenoweth, R. and Niemann, B. 1982. Alpine Lakes area user visual employed photography survey study. In *The appraisal of the Pack River landscape,* App. D. Landmark Research.

Coggins, G. C., and Phillips, J. D. 1977. Legal avenues and obstacles to wild and scenic river preservation III: Opportunities for citizen participation under state law. In *Pre-Symposium Compilation of Papers, Scenic River Programs, 1977 Scenic Rivers Symposium.* Louisiana State University.

Compton, R. L. 1975. Scientific and Scenic Rivers Act: Commentary and model statute. *Earth Law Journal,* 1 (3): 241–256.

Cornish, V. 1934. The scenic amenity of Great Britain. *Geography,* 19: 195.

Costley, R. J. 1972. An enduring resource. *American Forests,* 78(6): 8–11.

Curran, D. 1978. BLM begins wilderness review. *Conservation News,* 9(16): 8–10.

Cutler, M. R. 1972. A study of litigation related to management of Forest Service administered lands and its effect on policy decisions. Part two: A comparison of four cases. Unpublished Ph.D. dissertation, Michigan State University.

Davis, G. D. 1976, Meeting recreational, park and wilderness needs. *American Forests.* March: 12–13, 63.

Davis, J. S. 1986. The National Trails System Act and the use of protective federal zoning. *Harvard Environmental Law Review,* 10: 189–255.

Draper, J. B. 1974. The Rainbow Bridge Case and reclamation projects in reserved areas. *Natural Resources Journal,* 14(3): 431–445.

Dubey, R., and Zimmerman, K. 1975. Power v. the environment: Who wins and why? Hudson River Fisherman's Association v. Federal Power Commission, latest chapter in the Storm King controversy. *New England Law Review,* 10(2): 279–303.

Dutton, C. E. 1880. *Geology of the high plateaus of Utah with Atlas.* Dept. of the Interior. U.S. Geological Survey of the Rocky Mountain Region Monograph. U.S. G.P.O.

———. 1882. *Tertiary history of the Grand Canyon District.* U.S. Geological Survey Monograph. U.S.G.P.O.

EDAW. 1978. *Hells Canyon National Recreation Area Visual Resource Inventory and Imnaha Valley Study.* Prepared for USDA, Forest Service, Region 6, Portland, OR.

Everhart, W. C. 1972. *The National Park Service.* Praeger, New York.

Foote, J. P. 1973. Wilderness — A question of purity. *Environmental Law.* 3(2): 255–266.

Foster, J. D. 1976. Bureau of Land Management primitive areas — Are they counterfeit wilderness? *Natural Resources Journal,* 16(3): 621–663.

Frieson, B. F., and Day, J. C. 1977. Hydroelectric power and scenic provisions of the 1950 Niagara Treaty. *Water Resources Bulletin,* 13(6): 1175–1181.

Frome, E. 1974. *Battle for wilderness.* Praeger.

Goodman, W. M. 1972. Scenic Hudson revisited: The substanial evidence test and judicial review of agency environmental findings. *Ecology Law Quarterly,* 2: 801–865.

Graaskamp, J. A. 1985. *The Appraisal of 25 North Pinckney: A demonstration case for contemporary appraisal methods.* Landmark Research.

Graaskamp, J. A., and Robbins, M. L. 1982. *The appraisal of the Pack River lands.* Landmark Research.

Haight, K. 1974. The Wilderness Act: Ten years after. *Environmental Affairs,* 3(2): 275–326.

Hendee, J. C. 1974. A scientist's views on some current wilderness management issues. *Western Wildlands,* Spring (1974): 27–32.

Henning, D. H. 1971. The ecology of the political/administrative process for wilderness classification. *Natural Resources Journal,* 11(1): 69–75.

Interagency Land Acquisition Conference. 1973. *Uniform appraisal standards for federal land aquisition.* U.S. G.P.O.

Juday, G. P. 1975. *Oregon's natural area resources program.* Natural Area Resources Advisory Committee. Salem. OR.

Kusler, J. 1980. *Regulating sensitive lands: a guidebook.* Cambridge, MA: Ballinger.

Louisiana State University. 1977. *Pre-symposium compilation of papers, Scenic rivers symposium.* Baton Rouge.

Lucas, R. C. 1989. A look at wilderness use and users in transition. *Natural Resources Journal,* 29: 41–55.

Manning, R. E. 1989. The nature of America: Visions and revisions of wilderness. *Natural Resources Journal,* 29: 25–40.

Marsh, G. P. 1864. *Man and nature.* D. Lowenthal, ed. Harvard University Press, 1965.

McCabe, J. M. 1971. A wilderness primer. *Montana Law Review,* 32(1): 19–44.

McCloskey, M. 1966. The Wilderness Act of 1964: Its background and meaning. *Oregon Law Review,* 45(4): 292–294.

Nature Conservancy. 1976. *Preserving our national heritage, Vol. 1 Federal activities.* Prepared for USDI, National Park Service, and U.N. Man and Biosphere Program. U.S.G.P.O.

Note. 1975. Preserving scenic areas: The Adirondack Land Use Program. *The Yale Law Journal* Vol 84: 1705–1721.

Open Lands Project. 1971. *National symposium on trails.* U.S. G.P.O.

Palmer, J. F. 1976. The conceptual typing of trail environments: A new tool for recreation research and management. *Landscape Journal,* 2(1): 3–12.

Pinchott. G. 1910. *The fight for conservation.* Doubleday Page.

Poland, S. P. 1969. Development of recreational and related resources at hydroelectric projects licensed by the Federal

Power Commission. *Land and Water Law Review,* 4(2): 375–398.

Powell, W. 1957. *The exploration of the Colorado River,* abridged. University of Chicago Press.

Reynolds, C. C. 1989. Protecting Oregon's free-flowing water. *Environmental Law,* 19: 841–877.

Robbins, M. L. 1983. Methodology for evaluating, ranking and pricing mountainous wilderness lands. Unpublished Ph.D. dissertation, University of Wisconsin, Madison.

———. 1987. The valuation of large-scale natural landscapes using contemporary appraisal theory. *Appraisal Journal,* April (1987): 232.

Rohlf, D., and Honnold, D. L. 1988. Managing the balances of nature: The legal framework of wilderness management. *Ecology Law Quarterly* 15: 203.

Runte, A. 1972. How Niagara Falls was saved: The beginning of aesthetic conservation in the United States. *The Conservationist,* 26: 32–35, 43.

Sax., J. L. 1977. Freedom: Voices from the wilderness. *Environmental Law,* 7(3): 565–574.

Scott, N. R. 1974. Toward a psychology of wilderness experience. *Natural Resources Journal,* 14(2): 231–237.

Sive, D. 1976. Some thoughts of an environmental lawyer in the wilderness of administrative law. *Yale Law Review,* 70(4): 612–651.

Smardon, R. C. 1977. Research strategy for assessing visual impact from management and land development activities on wild and scenic rivers. In *Pre-symposium compilation of papers, scenic rivers symposium,* Louisiana State University.

Sokol, J. D. 1976. Geothermal leasing in the wilderness areas. *Environmental Law;* 6(2): 489–514.

Stankey, G. H. 1989. Beyond the campfire's light: Historical roots of the wilderness concept. *Natural Resources Journal,* 29: 9–24.

Steinitz, C., et al. 1978. *Simulating alternative policies for implementing the Massachusetts Scenic and Recreational Rivers Act: The North River demonstration project.* Landscape Architecture Research Office, Graduate School of Design, Harvard University.

Strong, D. H. 1970. The rise of the American aesthetic conservation: Muir, Mather and Udall. *National Parks Magazine,* Feburary: 4–9.

Tarlock, A. D. 1967. Preservation of scenic rivers. *Kentucky Law Journal,* 55(4): 745–798.

Tarlock, A. D., and Tippy, R. 1976. The Wild and Scenic Rivers Act of 1968. *Cornell Law Review,* 55(2): 707–739.

Tippy, R. 1968. Preservation values in river basin planning. *Natural Resources Journal,* 8(2): 259–278.

Travis, M. R. et al. 1975. *VIEWIT computation of seen areas, slope and aspect for land use planning.* USDA, Forest Service, Gen. Tech. Report PSW-11, Pacific SW Forest and Range Experiment Station, Berkeley, CA.

Turner, R. C. 1974. The preservation of rivers as wild and scenic. In *Environmental planning,* ed. Reitz, A. W. Chapter 8. North American International.

USDA, Forest Service. 1974. National forest landscape management, vol. 2. The *visual management system,* Chap. 1. U.S.G.P.O.

———. 1977b. *RARE II wilderness attribute rating system: A user manual, wilderness attribute rating system.*

———. 1977a. *Proceedings Symposium River Recreation Management and Research.* Gen. Tech. Report NC-28, North Central Forest Experiment Station, St. Paul, MN.

———. 1978. *Final environmental impact statement, Alpine Lakes Area acquisition.* USDA-FS-FES Administration 78-06.

USDI, Bureau of Outdoor Recreation. 1973. *National recreation trails: Information and application procedure.*

USDI. Bureau of Outdoor Recreation, and USDA, Forest Service. 1975. *National Scenic and Recreation Trails.*

———. 1977. Wild and scenic rivers. *Outdoor Recreation Action,* 43(Spring): 1–6.

USDI, National Park Service, 1971. *Guidelines: Appalachian Trail, National Scenic Trail, Maine to Georgia.*

Utter, J. G., and Schultz, J. D. 1976. *A handbook on the Wild and Scenic Rivers Act.* School of Forestry, University of Montana.

Vogelman, H. W. 1969. *Vermont natural areas.* Central Planning Office and Interagency Committee on Natural Resources.

Watson, R. A., and Smith, P. M. 1971. Underground wilderness, A point of view. *International Journal of Environmental Studies,* 1971(2): 217–220.

Williams, D. A. 1975. The National Park Service's master plan: An unconstitutional delegation of legislative power? *New England Law Review,* 11: 7–24.

Wolcott, E. S., III. 1973. Note: *Parker v. United States:* The Forest Service role in wilderness preservation. *Ecology Law Quarterly,* 3(1): 145–172.

Zube, E. H. 1973. Scenery as a natural resource: Implications for public policy and problems of definition, description and evaluation. *Landscape Architecture,* January: 126.

———, ed. 1978. *A Report prepared for the Heritage Conservation and Recreation Service, USDI, on scenic heritage classification and evaluation.* University of Arizona.

Chapter 10

Regulation of Environmentally Sensitive Areas and Resources

INTRODUCTION

Aside from wilderness areas, roadless areas, parks, preserves, mouments, wild and scenic rivers, and national and state trail systems, there are other areas of the landscape that are especially sensitive but are not publicly owned, assessed, or controlled. Areas such as the coastal zone of oceans and lakes, wetlands, mountain tops, ridges, and steep slopes pose special problems and risks for development, are ecologically sensitive, and are often key aesthetic resources (Figure 10.1). In this chapter we first outline the existing programs that protect these areas and their aesthetic values. Then we address specific programs and measures to protect air quality, water quality and quantity, archeological resources, and wildlife resources.

SENSITIVE AREA MANAGEMENT AND REGULATION

There is some broad-ranging federal and state legislation designed to deal with the unique problems of specific geographic areas. A number of states have used this "critical area" approach by setting up specific state agencies to control the use of land in particular sections of the state. The most prevalent types of critical area programs are coastal zone management, or shoreline regulation.

Coastal Zone Management/Shoreline Regulation

With the Coastal Zone Management Act of 1972[1] Congress authorized funding of states to develop planning and regulation programs for their coastlines. In its statement of purpose the act included: "to encourage states to achieve wise use of the land and water resources of the coastal zone, giving full consideration to ecological, cultural, historic and aesthetic values as well as needs for economic development."[2] Many states developed coastal zone management plans under sponsorship of this Act (Figure 10.2).

In one of the most famous coastal environment "disasters," the Santa Barbara, California oil spill, local public opposition to leasing in the Santa Barbara Channel for oil and natural gas development was based on aesthetic grounds. Following the spill, the offshore platforms were perceived as ugly (Baldwin 1970). According to Baldwin; "Aesthetic arguments did win the two-mile wide buffer zone. However, once Interior determined that such a zone outside the state sanctuary would be sufficient to forestall state leasing in the sanctuary, no further aesthetic arguments were successful" (Baldwin 1970, p. 38). The strong aesthetic grounds against oil and natural gas development were stated in terms of the alleged damage to natural beauty in a complaint for mandatory injunction[3] to stop future drilling in the Santa Barbara Channel.

---

[1]16 U.S.C. 1451 et seq. (1988).
[2]Id.
[3]County of Santa Barbara v. Hickel, Civ. No. 69-636 H (D.C. Cal. filed April 4, 1969).

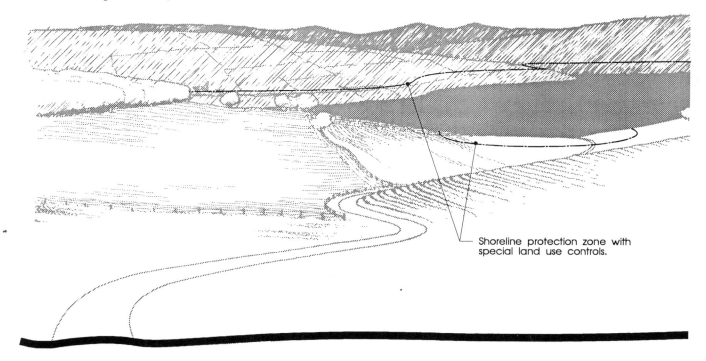

Shoreline protection zone with
special land use controls.

FIGURE 10.1   Generic landscape with stream/wetland protection zone. Graphic credit: Scott Shannon

One landmark occurred when aesthetic considerations were incorporated into coastal zone/shoreland management by the Tahoe Regional Planning Compact[4] in California and Nevada.

The 1969 compact formed an agency empowered to control all land development in the Tahoe Basin. One of the prime purposes of the agency was to protect the aesthetic value of the lake (Figure 10.3) with its deep-blue color, according to Bosselman and Callies (1971). Tahoe's land use ordinance delineates use districts and limitations on building heights, and refers to the need to "maintain the natural scenic quality of the Lake Tahoe region"[5] and the "protection of views."[6] A special shoreland ordinance requires permits for all construction and alteration on that shoreline, underlying land, or within the lake. Section 5 of that ordinance stipulates that before a permit is issued there be proof that the natural beauty of the area will not be destroyed.[7] As we have seen in Chapter 9, this approach was not successful in controlling development or scenic impacts in the Tahoe Basin.

A third example is the San Francisco Bay Conservation and Development Commission, which was created by the California Legislature in 1965 to plan for the development of San Francisco Bay (Bosselman and Callies 1971), the Bay Plan has evolved beyond Proposition 20[8] into the California Coastal Act of 1976.[9] The commission was formed partly to prevent the filling in of the bay and partly for scenic reasons. As Bosselman and Callies (1971, p. 109) have stated:" The fact that the Bay is seen so frequently by so many people made it very easy for the average person to visualize its reduction to a 'river'."

The California Coastal Zone Conservation Act[10] established a state coastal commission, six regional commissions, and a permit review process for coastal development (Figure 10.4). In a study of the permit process, 43 percent of the permits appealed from the regional to the state commission included aesthetics, view corridors, and facility design (Sabatier 1976, p. 148).

The 1976 act, which evolved from the San Francisco Bay experience has specific language that addresses aesthetic issues:

---

[4]Tahoe Regional Planning Compact Pub. Law No. 91-148, 83 Stat. 340 (1969).
[5]Land Use Ordinance #13, adopted 1972, amended 1973, ss. 7.10 et seq.
[6]Id.
[7]Id. Ordinance #6.
[8]California MacAteer Act of 1969, Cal. Nat. Res. Codes. 666000.
[9]Calif. Res. Code., Div. 20, Art. 6 (1976).
[10]Id.

a.

c.

d.

e.

b.

FIGURE 10.2 a, b, c, d, e Coastal zone mosaic. *Photo credit: R. C. Smardon*

True scenic and visual qualities of coastal areas shall be considered and protected as a resource of public importance. Permitted development shall be sited to protect views to and along the ocean and scenic coastal areas, and where feasible, to restore and enhance visual quality in visually degraded areas.[11]

Other coastal management/shoreline management programs of note include Delaware's Coastal Zone Act,[12] which restricts manufacturing and industrial uses along the coast. The Delaware State Planning Office takes aesthetic as well as other effects into consid-

[11]Id., s. 30251.
[12]Ch. 70, Title 7 Del. Code. Ann. ss. 7001 et seq. (1968).

FIGURE 10.3   Lake Tahoe scene. *Photo credit: Mathew Potteiger*

FIGURE 10.4 a, b   California coast scene. *Photo credit: R. C. Smardon*

eration when reviewing permit applications. Connecticut, Maryland, Michigan, Mississippi, New Hampshire, New Jersey, New York, North Carolina, Rhode Island, Virginia, and Texas also have statutes with aesthetic provisions.[13]

Wisconsin authorized all counties to enact shoreland zoning ordinances to preserve the beauty of its lakes and rivers.[14] The state's Model Shoreland Protection Ordinance[15] delineated land into districts, including conservancy districts, and has restrictions on tree cutting to screen structures as seen from the water.

The Coastal Barrier Resources Act (CBRA)[16] represents the first comprehensive attempt to link federal fiscal policy with natural resources conservation.

---

[13]Respectively, Conn. Ch. 440 s. 22a-28; Del. Ch. 66 ss. 6602 and 6604; Md. Title 9 s. 9-102: Mich. Inland Lakes and Streams Act of 1972, s. 281.957; Miss. Title 49, Ch.27; N.H. Ch. 483As.1-b; N.J. Title 13 Ch. 19 s. 2; N.Y. Tidal Wetlands Act. 483 Ch. 25 s. 0101(h); N.C. Ch. 13A-102; R.I. Title 2-1.13; Va. Code s. 62.1-13.1; and Tx. Ch. 33 ss. 001.

[14]Wisc. Stat. Ann. s. 144.25(1).

[15]Dept. of Nat. Res., Div. of Res. Develop., Wisconsin's Shoreland Protection Ordinance (1967).

[16]16 U.S.C. s. 3501 (b) (1988).

CBRA attempts to minimize loss of human life, wasteful expenditures of federal revenues, and damage to natural resources associated with development on coastal barriers along the Atlantic and Gulf Coasts. Noted for their natural beauty, wildlife habitat, and recreational opportunities, the coastal barriers also are prized sites for intensive residential development. The barriers are becoming urbanized at about twice the national rate, in part because of massive aid from numerous federal programs for development and redevelopment. Federal aid, by encouraging development, has often contributed to landscape degradation, destruction of natural resources of the barriers, and increased risk to human life.

CBRA limits new federal expenditures or financial assistance within the designated coastal barrier areas. Subject to certain limited exceptions for activities unrelated to development, CBRA prohibits federal financial assistance for the construction or purchase of structures, roads, bridges, facilities, and the related infrastructure. The intent of Congress was to eliminate federal development assistance so as to shift the financial risk and burden of development from the federal government and the taxpayer back to the developers and users of coastal property. Shifting the costs of development back to those who build and live on coastal barriers furthers two objectives: the conservation of natural resources of the coastal barriers and efficient use of limited government funds. South Carolina is also attempting to address restrictions on redevelopment on coastal barriers and coastal wetlands. (For a more detailed review of CBRA, the reader is referred to a comprehensive article by Kuehn 1984.)

Legal Decisions on Shoreland Protection

Many of the aforementioned programs have been upheld in court decisions. The California Supreme Court upheld the constitutionality of the Tahoe Regional Planning Agency in *People ex rel. Younger* v. *County of El Dorado*.[17] The California Court of Appeals upheld the decision of the San Francisco Bay Conservation and Development Commission in *Candlestick Properties Inc.* v. *San Francisco Bay Conservation and Development Commission*.[18] The Supreme Court of Wisconsin decided in favor of Marinette County ordinances under the Wisconsin Protection Act in *Just* v. *Marinette County*.[19] In the last case, the court specifically referred to the need to preserve the scenic beauty and other natural resources of the shorelands.

On November 3, 1977, in *Dept. of Ecology* v. *Pacesetter*,[20] the Washington State Supreme Court upheld the use of the police power, under Washington's Shoreline Management Act (SMA), to regulate development on a private waterfront lot on the grounds of protection of aesthetic values alone (Washington DOE 1977). In response to the plaintiff Pacesetter's argument that it was entitled to compensation because protection of aesthetics was not a proper exercise of police power without compensation, the court said:

Much decisional law upholds a government regulation protective of aesthetic values whether or not accompanied or combined with the protection of economic values. . . . Many cases hold protection of aesthetic values alone justify the exercise of police power without payment of compensation. . . . Moreover, the legislature has given expression to this state's public policy of supporting protection of aesthetic values by the enactment of the SMA and similar statutes.[21]

Finally, the shoreline development restrictions implemented by the Adirondack Park Agency in New York State have been upheld in a court decision. The court decided that the agency prohibition against boathouses on shoreline of Oseetah Lake was properly based on aesthetic considerations pursuant to the police power and constituted proper exercise of its discretion.[22]

Wetland Regulation and Aesthetic Values

Wetland laws and policies as they specifically relate to aesthetic values (Figure 10.5) are an important concern. Wetland regulation has become a major issue at the national, state, and local levels of government. The values of wetlands were documented in a multidisciplinary symposium held at Lake Buena Vista, Florida, in 1977 (Greeson, Clark, and Clark 1978), and the definition of visual-cultural or aesthetic values of wetlands was heralded in a U.S. interagency task force report (CEQ 1978) as well as in a book edited by one of the coauthors (Smardon 1983).

Law and policy affecting how wetland land use decisions are made occur at the federal, state, and local levels. Pertinent laws, programs, and policies at all three are briefly reviewed here but only in regard to aes-

---

[17]96 Cal. Rptr. 553, 11 Cal. App.3d 557 (1971).
[18]89 Cal. Rptr. 897 (1970).
[19]56 Wisc.2d. 7, 201 N.W.2d 761 (1972).
[20]511 P.2d. 196 (Wash. 1977).
[21]Id.
[22]McCormick v. Lawrence 83 Misc.2d. 64, 372 N.Y.S.2d 156 (1975).

FIGURE 10.5 a, b   Wetlands mosaic. *Photo credit: R. C. Smardon*

thetic values. A broader review of such laws and programs is comprehensively treated by Kusler (1978 & 1980).

Federal Programs Affecting Wetlands

Community wetland programs are encouraged by a number of federal programs. Two of the best known are the Coastal Zone Management Act of 1972, and the Rivers and Harbors Act of 1899.

1. The Coastal Zone Management Act of 1972.[23] This act applies to all states bordering on the oceans and the Great Lakes. To qualify for federal grants-in-aid for administration of a coastal zone program, a state must adopt land use regulatory and acquisition powers for coastal zone areas and either directly regulate uses or establish standards for local regulation

of these uses. The act also authorizes federal grants-in-aid for purchase of esturaine sanctuaries, although these provisions have not been funded. States are required to inventory coastal zone areas of "particular concern." These have been defined in the administrative guidelines to include wetland areas.

2. Corps of Engineers Permit Procedures. A permit is required from the U.S. Army Corps of Engineers for most fills and dredging of U.S. waters pursuant to the Rivers and Harbors Act of 1899[24] and the Federal Water Pollution Control Act Amendments of 1972.[25] Under a judicially broadened definition of Army Corps jurisdiction, a permit is required for fills and dredging in lakes larger than five acres, rivers to the point of headwaters (the point at which flow is five cubic feet per second), coastal areas to the high-water mark, and associated wetlands. Permits will not be issued unless proposed uses are consistent with state coastal zone programs and local regulations. These requirements give community wetland protection programs a strong veto power over Army Corps permits.

In addition to the Army Corps general guidelines, the Environmental Protection Agency (EPA) has published "Guidelines for Specification of Disposal Sites for Dredged or Fill Material" under Section 404 of the Water Pollution Control Act Amendments of 1972.[26] Within "Subpart G, Human Use Characteristics of These Guidelines," the EPA has included sections on recreation, aesthetics, and amenities. These provisions are quoted in full here to show the breadth and depth of concerns included in these regulations:

230.62 Recreation

Recreation encompasses activities undertaken for amusement and relaxation. Water related outdoor recreation requires the use, but not necessarily the consumptive use, of natural aquatic sites and resources, including wetlands.

(a) **Values.** Much of our outdoor recreation is water-dependent. A host of activities, including fishing, swimming, boating, water skiing, racing, clamming, camping, beachcombing, picnicking, waterfowl hunting, wildlife photography, bird watching and scenic enjoyment, take place on, in, or adjacent to water. In many parts of the country, space and resources for aquatic recreation are in great demand. Water quality is a vital factor in determining the capacity of an area to support the various water oriented outdoor recreation activities.

(b) **Possible loss of values.** One of the more important

---

[23]16 U.S.C.S. 1451 et seq. (1988).
[24]33 U.S.C. s. 403 (1988).
[25]35 U.S.C. § 1251 et. seq. (1988).
[26]Id.

direct impacts of dredged or fill disposal is on aesthetics; more serious impacts impair or destroy the resources which support recreation activities. Among the water quality parameters of importance to recreation that can be impacted by the disposal of dredged or fill material are turbidity, suspended particulates, temperature, dissolved oxygen, dissolved materials, toxic materials, pathogenic organisms, degradation of habitat, and the aesthetic qualities of sight, taste, odor and color. Changes in the levels of these parameters can adversely modify or destroy water use for several or all of the recreation activities enjoyed in any given area.

(c) **Guidelines to minimize impacts.** In addition to the consideration of alternatives in 230.10(a), Guidelines to minimize impacts as described in 230.10(d), and to minimize impacts as described in 230.10(d), and water dependency in 230.10(e) and the specific measures described in Subparts E and F, where appropriate, specific measures to minimize impacts on recreational resources include, but are not limited to:
  (1) Selecting discharge sites removed from areas of recognized recreational value.
  (2) Selecting time periods of discharge that do not coincide with seasons of periods of high recreational use.
  (3) Use of procedures and methods as described in 230.31(c) and 230.32(c) to minimize and contain the amounts of suspended particulates and dissolved contaminants, including nutrients, pathogens, and other contaminants released in the water column.

(d) **Special determinations.** In addition to the determination required by 230.20 and the special determinations required by Subparts E and F, where appropriate, special determinations where recreational areas may be affected by the discharge of dredged or fill material include whether the discharge will:
  (1) Change or affect the suitability of an area of high recreational value to provide recreational opportunities.

230.63 Aesthetics

Aesthetics associated with the aquatic ecosystem, including wetlands, consist of the perception of beauty by one or a combination of senses of sight, hearing, touch and smell. Aesthetics of aquatic ecosystems apply to the quality of life enjoyed by the general public as distinct from the value of property realized by owners as a result of access to such systems (see 230.64).

(a) **Values.** The aesthetic values of aquatic areas are usually the enjoyment and appreciation derived from the natural characteristics of a particular area. Aesthetic values may include such parameters as the visual distinctiveness of the elements present, which may result from prominence, contrasts due to irregularity of form, line, color, and pattern; the diversity of elements present including topographic expression, shoreline complexity, landmarks, vegetative pattern diversity, waterform expression, and wildlife visibility; and the compositional harmony or unity of the overall area. . . .

(b) **Possible loss of values.** The discharge of dredged or fill material can mar the beauty of natural aquatic ecosystems by degrading the water quality, creating distracting disposal sites, inducing nonconforming developments, encouraging human access, and by destroying vital elements that contribute to the compositional harmony or unity, visual distinctiveness, or diversity of an area.

(c) **Guidelines to minimize impacts.** In addition to the consideration of alternatives in 230.10(a), Guidelines to minimize impacts as described in 230.10(d), water dependency in 230.10(e), and specific measures described in Subparts D, E, and F, where appropriate, specific measures to minimize impacts on aesthetic values include, but are not limited to:
  (1) Selecting discharge sites and following discharge procedures that will prevent or minimize any potential damage to the aesthetically pleasing features of the aquatic site, particularly with respect to water quality.
  (2) Following procedures that will restore the disturbed area to its natural condition.

(d) **Special determination.** In addition to the determinations required by 230.20 and the special determinations required by Subparts E and F, where appropriate, special determinations where aesthetic values in aquatic areas may be affected by the discharge of dredged or fill material include whether the discharge will change or affect the elements of an aquatic or wetland area which contribute to its aesthetic appeal.

230.64 Amenities

Amenities derived from a natural aquatic ecosystem, including wetlands, include any environmental feature, trait, or character that contributes to the attractiveness of real estate, or to the successful operation of a business serving the public on its premises. Aquatic resources which are unowned or publicly owned may provide amenities to privately owned property in the vicinity.

(a) **Values.** Persons or institutions claiming amenities of the unowned or publically owned aquatic ecosystem have monetary investments in property, a portion of which can be realized only because of the existence of unowned but accessible public amenities. The added property value attributable to natural amenities varies with the quality, use, and accessibility of aquatic and wetland areas.

(b) **Possible loss of values.** The discharge of dredged or fill material can adversely affect the particular features, traits, or characters of an aquatic area which make it valuable as an amenity to property owners. Dredge or fill activities which degrade water quality, disrupt natural substrata and vegetational characteristics, deny access to the amenities, or result in changes in odor, air quality, or noise levels may reduce the value of an aquatic area as an amenity to private property.

(c) **Guidelines to minimize impacts.** In addition to the consideration of alternatives in 230.10(a), the Guidelines to minimize impacts as described in 230.10(d), water dependency in 230.10(e), and specific measures described in Subparts E and F, where appropriate, specific measures to minimize impacts on amenities include, but are not limited to:
(1) Selecting discharge sites which are of lesser value to nearby property owners as natural aquatic or wetland amenities.
(2) Timing the discharge to avoid interference during the seasons or periods when the availability and accessibility of aquatic or wetland amenities are most important.
(3) Following discharge procedures that do not disturb features of the aquatic ecosystem which contribute to the value of an aquatic amenity.
(d) **Special determination.** In addition to the determinations required by 230.20 and the special determinations required by Subparts E and F, where appropriate, special considerations where aquatic amenities may be affected by discharges of dredged or fill material include whether the discharge will change or affect any feature of an aquatic area which contributes to its value as an amenity to property owners.[27]

Note that EPA has written guidelines treating three distinct classes of visual-cultural values: recreational, aesthetic, and amenities. There are a number of interesting points in the characterization of these values. First, recreational values include those recreational activities that "Take place on, in, or adjacent to water."[28] Thus, the adjacent upland is seen as contributing to the enjoyment of the value. Second, aesthetics includes "perception of beauty by one or more of a combination of senses of sight, hearing, touch and smell."[29] Thus, aesthetics is not limited to the visual only. Note also that the "enjoyment and appreciation [are] derived from the natural characteristics of a particular area."[30] Many of these "characteristics" have been treated in recent work by one of the co-authors (Smardon 1983, Shiyam & Smardon 1990). Third, there is the special treatment of amenites, which, in contrast to values enjoyed by the special public, are "derived from a natural aquatic ecosystem, . . . include any environmental feature, trait, or character that contributes to the attractiveness of real estate, or to the successful operation of a business serving the public on its premises."[31] Thus, the economic attributes of aesthetic values through their contribution to property values and operation of certain amenity-dependent businesses are recognized.

In addition to these distinct classes of visual-cultural values, the EPA guideline even specifies a procedure for "site appearance determinations," which includes photographic documentation of the site in question. The following passage from the EPA guideline specifies procedures for visually documenting site conditions:

230.20

(g) **Proposed disposal site appearance determinations.** A determination shall be made of the appearance of the proposed disposal site and appropriate parts of its surrounding environment prior to the initiation of discharge activity. Photographic determinations are preferable to narrative descriptions, provided they are accompanied by pertinent data such as exact location of photographer and direction of exposure, time of year and day and weather conditions affecting film exposure, the kind of camera, lens, etc. used, and the photograph clearly depicts those aspects of the aquatic environment and wetlands that will be impacted or modified by the discharge activity. Comment: The appearance of the proposed disposal site and its surroundings prior to any discharge activity is relevant to the findings required in 230.10 and 230.11. Sufficiently detailed information concerning the appearance of the disposal site before discharge occurs will aid in predicting the impact of the discharge, assessing the adequacy of measures to minimize impacts, monitoring compliance with the permit and restoring the site where appropriate.

(h) **Special determinations.** A determination shall be made of whether the material to be discharged will disrupt any special disposal site characteristics, taking into consideration the resource values, possible loss of these resources, and these guidelines, as well as special determinations described in Subparts E through G of the proposed disposal site.[32] The specific procedure in 230.20 was suggested by Smardon to EPA to ensure adequate records of the site before an activity had taken place, and to be used as visual information for assessing the adequacy of mitigation procedures and whether they had taken place.

State Programs Affecting Wetlands
State programs pertaining to wetlands include coastal wetland acts, inland wetland acts, critical area acts, coastal management acts, navigable water acts, shoreline and lake management acts, open-space acts, and landuse planning acts.

---

[27]40 C.F.R. 230, (1991).
[28]Id.
[29]Id.
[30]Id.
[31]Id.
[32]Id.

Specific state statutes that mention the aesthetic enjoyment or scenic value of wetlands, or the preservation of the natural landscape character include coastal wetland acts for Delaware,[33] Maryland,[34] New York,[35] Rhode Island,[36] and Virginia[37]; inland wetland and navigable waterways acts for New Hampshire,[38] Vermont,[39] and Wisconsin;[40] critical area legislation for Alabama,[41] Arkansas,[42] Minnesota,[43] and Virginia;[44] coastal management acts for New Jersey,[45] Rhode Island,[46] and Texas;[47] shoreline and lake management acts for Maine,[48] Michigan,[49] and Washington;[50] an open-space act for Pennsylvania;[51] and a land use planning act for Vermont.[52]

Specific state statutes that mention recreational values or enjoyment include coastal wetland acts for Delaware,[53] Mississippi,[54] and New Jersey;[55] an inland lakes act in Michigan;[56] and a freshwater wetland and coastal management act for Rhode Island.[57] The critical area acts for Minnesota[58] and Alabama[59] include cultural and historical values of wetlands. New York state's Tidal Wetlands Act[60] is the most comprehensive, including educational and research values of wetlands as well as recreational and aesthetic values.

Local Regulation of Wetlands

Local regulation of wetland activities is authorized by state wetland protection acts in Virginia, Massachusetts, Connecticut, and New York. The Wisconsin and Washington shoreland zoning programs and the Florida critical area program, which has been interpreted to apply to Big Cypress and Green swamps, also require local controls. More than 1,000 local communities in these states have adopted wetland protection regulations (Kusler 1980). A larger number of other communities have adopted land use regulations for wetland areas pursuant to coastal zone or flood plain regulatory efforts, or to broader land use zoning or subdivision control programs.

As noted earlier, local adoption of wetland regulations has been encouraged not only by state wetland acts, but also by the National Flood Insurance Program, which requires local regulation of the 100-year-frequency flood plain (area flooded by a 100 year frequency storm) area in order to qualify for federally subsidized flood insurance. More than 14,000 communities have adopted or indicated an intent to adopt flood plain regulations in order to qualify for this program. Other federal incentives to promote wetland protection by localities include the Coastal Zone Management Act of 1972 and the U.S. Army Corps of Engineers section 404 permit requirements.

Strong local incentives also exist for the regulation of wetland areas. These incentives include the achieving such common land and water use planning objectives as reasonable minimization of natural hazards, provision for open space and recreation areas, prevention of septic tanks in unsuitable areas, allocation of lands throughout a community to their most appropriate uses, and protection of water supplies. However, sufficient funds are rarely available at the local level to

---

[33]Coastal Wetlands, Del. Code Title 7 s. 6602.
[34]Coastal Wetlands, Md. Ann. Code Title 9 s. 9–102.
[35]Tidal Wetlands, N.Y.S. Env. Cons. Law Title 46, Ch. 23, s. 25-0101.
[36]Coastal Wetlands, R.I. Gen. Law Title 46, Ch. 23, s. 1.
[37]Coastal Wetlands, Va. Code Ann. 62.1-63.1 et seq.
[38]N.H. Rev. Stat. Ann. 483-A:1-b.
[39]Navigable Waters, Shorelands, Vt. Stat. Ann. Title 10 s. 1421.
[40]Shoreland Areas, Wisc. Stat. Ann. 144.26.
[41]Coastal Areas, Ala. Code Title 9, s. 2.
[42]Environmental Quality Act, Ark. Stat. Ann. Ch. 9, s. 1401.
[43]Comprehensive Critical Areas Act, Min. Stat. Ann. s. 1166.02.
[44]Critical Environmental Areas, Va. Code. Ann., ss. 10-187 to 10-196.
[45]Coastal Wetlands, N.J. Stat. Ann. Title 13 Ch. 9A-1.
[46]Coastal Wetlands, R.I. Gen. Laws Title 46, Ch. 23, s. 1.
[47]Coastal Act, Tex. Stat. Ann. Art. 33.001.
[48]Shorelands, Maine Rev. Stat., Title 12, s. 4811.
[49]Shoreland Protection, Mich. Comp. Laws Ann., s. 281.957.
[50]Shoreline Areas, Rev. Code Wash., Ann Title 90.58.
[51]Open Space, Penn. Stat. Ann. Title 16 s. 11941.
[52]Large-scale Development Site Act., Vt. Stat. Ann. Title 10 ss. 6001-89.
[53]Coastal Zone, Del. Code Title 7 s. 7004.
[54]Coastal Wetlands, Miss. Code Ann. Ch. 49, s. 27-1.
[55]Coastal Areas, N.J. Stat. Ann. Title 13, Ch.19.
[56]Inland Lakes, Mich. Comp. Laws. Ann. 281.951.
[57]R.I. Gen. Laws, s. 2-1-13 et seq. and ss. 46-23-1 to 46-23-16.
[58]Comprehensive Critical Areas Act., Minn. Stat. Ann. s. 116.02.
[59]State Critical Area, Ala. Code Title 9 ch. 9 s. 1.
[60]Tidal Wetlands, N.Y.S. Env. Cons. Law s. 25-0101.

purchase more than a small portion of community wetlands to serve these objectives. In addition, it is often politically unacceptable to remove large tracts of land from the tax rolls and from economically preferable uses. For this reason, several types of land use regulation have been commonly adopted to restrict land uses that have the most severe impact on wetlands while permitting continued private use of lands.

Regulatory Approaches and Techniques

The two main regulatory approaches applied to wetland areas are: (1) complete prohibition of all fills, dredging, and structural uses; and (2) application of performance standards to uses that reduce flood losses, reduce impact upon wildlife, and serve a wide range of other objectives. The second approach is more common, although a considerable number of communities have adopted restrictive controls. Explicit wetland protection provisions are typically incorporated in several types of local regulations:

1. **Local wetland zoning regulations.** These are the most common kinds of wetland protections and are adopted as a primary or overlay zone within a broader comprehensive zoning ordinance or, alternatively, as a separate wetland ordinance. The regulations may be based upon a special wetland regulatory statute; a coastal zone, shoreland, or scenic and wild river statute; or a broader zoning authority. Zoning regulations consist of a map showing wetland boundaries as well as a text listing prohibited and permitted uses and establishing general standards for special permit uses. Usually a zoning board of adjustment, planning board, or special board (e.g., a conservation commission) is authorized to evaluate applications for special permits within wetland areas.

2. **Special wetland protection bylaws or ordinances.** These may be adopted pursuant to special wetland protection statutes (e.g., a Massachusetts statute authorizes local units of government to regulate directly or comment upon wetland uses), or to statutes authorizing local control of grading and filling, tree cutting, and other activities; or they may be included within the home rule powers of the municipality. Typically, they contain a text setting forth prohibited, permitted, and special uses. Wetlands may be defined by description or with a map reference.

In addition to these two principal types of wetland regulations, control of wetland development may be achieved through several other types of special and general ordinances and bylaws. Rarely do any of these measures include specific provisions for consideration of aesthetic or heritage values.

Critical Wetland Court Cases

What is most interesting and significant in the implementation of local government wetland regulation is the number of court cases that have generated disputes about appropriate decision-making by local units of government. These court cases have gone in two distinct directions.

One direction is a conservative environmental attitude. In wetland regulation cases, the courts found landowners who were deprived of their property rights by local government bodies when they tried to restrict uses of the wetlands. Such was the basic attitude in the cases of *Turnpike Reality Co.* v. *Town of Dedham*[61] in Massachusetts, *Dooley* v. *Town Planning and Zoning Comm'n.*[62] in Connecticut and *State of Maine* v. *R. B. Johnson.*[63] In these older cases, the courts tended to diminish the importance of the natural functions of wetlands; they stressed the individual property rights of wetland owners or questioned procedural practices of local wetland regulation bodies in their respective actions. This attitude seems to be receding.

On the other hand, there is the liberal environmental attitude. The decisions in these cases advance the protection of wetlands based on the public trust doctrine; that is, certain lands like wetlands, beaches, shorelands, and river bottoms are held in trust by the state for the benefit of the public. Other cases use a theory based on the prevention of public harm, or nuisance theory, that supports the protection of wetlands. These cases are characterized by *Rowe* v. *Town of North Hampton Commission,*[64] *Just* v. *Marinette County,*[65] and *Carter* v. *South Carolina Coastal Council.*[66]

Just v. *Marinette County* in Wisconsin is the most interesting of the three in that it articulates both approaches. First, the court states the context for the case and notes the changing sense of value of wetlands in general:

This case causes us to re-examine the concepts of public benefit in contrast to public harm and the scope of an owner's right to use of his property. In the instant case we have a restriction on use of a citizen's property, not to

---

[61]362 Mass. 221, 284 N.E.2d 891, (1972).

[62]151 Conn. 304, 197 A.2d 770 (1964).

[63]265 A.2d 711 (1970).

[64]553 A.2d 1331 (N.H. 1989).

[65]56 Wisc.2d 7 201 N.W.2d 761, (1972).

[66]314 S.E.2d 327 (S.C. 1984).

secure a benefit from the public, but to prevent a harm from the change in the natural character of the citizen's property. . . . What makes this case different from most condemnation or police power zoning cases is the relationship of the wetlands, the swamps and the natural environment of shorelands to the purity of water and to such natural resources as navigation, fishing, and to scenic beauty. Swamps and wetlands were once considered wasteland, undesireable, and not picturesque; but as the people became more sophisticated, an appreciation was acquired that swamps and wetlands serve a vital role in nature, are part of the balance of nature and are essential to the purity of water in our lakes and streams. Swamps and wetlands are a necessary part of the ecological creation and now, even to the uninitiated, possess their own beauty in nature.[67]

Next, the court states the owner's rights and what is and is not a reasonable use of the area in question:

An owner of land has no absolute and unlimited right to change the essential natural character of his land so as to use it for a purpose for which it was unsuited in its natural state and which injures the rights of others.

The exercise of the police power in zoning must be reasonable and we think it is not an unreasonable exercise of that police power to prevent harm to public right by limiting the use of private property to its natural use.[68]

The court continues:

The changing of wetlands and swamps to the damage of the general public by upsetting the natural environment and the natural relationship is not a reasonable use of the land that is protected from police power regulation.[69]

The court acknowledges the precedence of its decision, but it presents a balancing test to weigh the interests in any given situation.

We realize no case in Wisconsin has yet dealt with shoreland regulations and there are several cases in other states which seem to hold such regulations unconstitutional; but nothing this court has said or held in prior cases indicates that destroying the natural character of a swamp or a wetland so as to make that location available for human habitation is a reasonable use of that land when the new use, although of a more economical value to the owner, causes harm to the general public.[70]

The balancing test is to weigh the magnitude of the personal economic loss to the particular landowner against the magnitude of the harm to the general public, which is usually the infringement or elimination of the natural functions and character of the wetlands. Finally, the court cites the case of *Muench* v. *Public Service Commission*[71] in Wisconsin in articulating the public trust mandate for the state and in including protection of recreation and scenic beauty in that mandate.

The active public trust duty of the State of Wisconsin in respect to navigable waters requires the state not only to promote navigation, but also protect those waters for fishing, recreation and scenic beauty.[72]

Following *Just* v. *Marinette County*, courts in Florida,[73] South Carolina,[74] New Hampshire,[75] and North Carolina[76] have approved of the natural use theory (as termed by Hunter 1988), with New Hampshire contributing most of the doctrine, beginning with *Sibson* v. *State*[77] and progressing to *State of New Hampshire Wetlands Board* v. *Marshall*.[78]

It seems inevitable that the liberal environmental view of decision-making concerning the fate of U.S. wetlands and other sensitive areas will prevail. Just as zoning upheld merely on aesthetic considerations has gradually been accepted in most states, so will aesthetic considerations in wetland management.

---

[67]Just v. Marinette County, 56 Wis.2d 7, 10, 201 N.W.2d 761, 767–68 (1972).

[68]Id. at 11, 12, 201 N.W.2d at 768.

[69]Id. at 13, 201 N.W.2d at 768.

[70]Id.

[71]55 N.W.2d. 40 (Wis 1952).

[72]Just v. Marinette County, 201 N.W.2d. 761, 768 (1972).

[73]Graham v. Estuary Props. Inc. 399 So.2d 1374 (Fla. 1981).

[74]Carter v. South Carolina Coastal Council, 281 S.C. 201, 314 S.E.2d 327(1984).

[75]Claridge v. New Hampshire Wetlands Bd, 5 N.H. 745, 485 A.2d 287 (1984): Sibson v. State, 115 N.H. 124, 336 A.2d 239 (1975), overruled on other grounds, Burrows v. City of Keene, 121 N.H. 590, 601, 432 A.2d 15, 21 (1981), State v. McCarthy 117 N.H. 799, 379 A.2d. 1251 (1977).

[76]Smithwick v. Alexander, 17 Env't. Rep. Cons. BNA 2126 (E.D.N.C. 1982).

[77]115 N.H. 124, 336 A.2d 239 (1975), overruled on other grounds, Burrows v. City of Keene, 121 N.H. 590, 601, 432 A.2d 15, 21 (1981).

[78]127 N.H. 240, 247–48, 500 A.2d. 685, 689 (1985).

FIGURE 10.6 a, b   Hillside scene. *Photo credit: R. C. Smardon*

Hillside Protection

Several communities have special provisions for hillside preservation either for scenic view protection (Figure 10.6), as mentioned in Chapter 8, or for environmental hazard protection from steep slopes and excessive water runoff and erosion. The prominent examples include the cities of Cinncinati and Scottsdale, Arizona. As we have seen, the legal problems with restricting all use of hillsides can result in a taking as illustrated by the *Corrigan* v. *Arizona* case. Many of the same legal treatments and issues that apply to hillside protection ordinances apply to wetlands. The difference is that the multifunctional values of wetlands have been well established, whereas hillsides have a more limited set of functions. Also, the economic incentive of spectacular views is still a very strong incentive to develop such hillsides throughout the country. This very probably will be one of the next major battlegrounds for aesthetic resource regulation and protection.

RESOURCE-SPECIFIC LEGISLATION AND PROGRAMS

Some programs and legislation are resource-specific rather than activity-specific. This discussion addresses laws and programs of maintenance or preservation of aesthetic values connected with air quality, water quality and quantity, archeological resources, and wildlife resources.

Air Quality

Although there is federal legislation dealing with air quality with attendant federal and state regulations,[79] there is no clearer articulation of aesthetic values (see Figure 10.7) related to air quality than Section 128 of the Clean Air Act Amendments of 1977, Public Law 95-95,[80] enacted August 7, 1977. This act declares as a national goal the prevention of visibility impairment from manmade air pollution and the restoration of nat-

[79]Clean Air Act of 1967, 42 U.S.C. s. 7401 et seq. (1988).
[80]Id. at § 7428.

FIGURE 10.7 a, b   Air quality—Los Angeles basin. *Photo credit: R. C. Smardon*

ural visibility in mandatory Class I federal areas. Analysis of the legislative history of the visibility protection provision shows that Congress was primarily concerned with preserving "grand vistas" and "breathtaking panoramas" for the enjoyment of the public visiting mandatory Class I federal areas possessing such values.[81] The criteria used in the Federal Register to identify areas where visibility is an important value are:

1. Does the legislation for the area indicate that scenic value was an important consideration for establishing the area? or Is the area possessed of scenic values that are important to public enjoyment?
2. Are scenic values of the area primarily in the form of panoramas, background, intermediate or foreground views?
3. Do natural sources of visibility impairment seriously affect the ability of the public to appreciate visibility as an important value?

4. For those areas in which natural resources of visibility impairment seriously affect public appreciation of scenic values, is the magnitude of scenic value sufficient to warrant protection from man-caused sources?[82]

Class I federal areas are mainly wilderness areas, national parks, and national memorial parks, but they also include national primitive areas and national wildlife refuges. According to a staff person in the National Park Service involved with the act's regulations: (1) legislative intent or purpose in the Act's establishing the areas, (2) proof of public values related to visibility at the areas, and (3) a statement of management citing visibility as an important attribute were all important criteria used to identify these areas.[83]

Key problems in implementing this act, as pointed out by a National Park Service staff member, are: (1) how to measure visibility, which is a subjective judg-

---

[81]42 Fed. Reg.: 552280 (Oct. 14 1977).
[82]Id. at 552281.
[83]Phone interview with David Biderman, National Park Service, Washington, D.C., July 17, 1978.

ment; (2) what is "impairment" of air quality; and (3) who is responsible for the impairment.[84] There has been some research done on perceptions of air quality and how much people value clear and expansive views sponsored by the U.S. Environmental Protection Agency (1979).

The Clean Air Act Amendments of 1977 provide two directives to the Environmental Protection Agency (EPA) and federal land managers:

1. A directive to federal land managers (primarily the secretaries of Interior and Agriculture) that they have an affirmative duty to protect the air quality values (including visibility) of Class I areas from impairment due to emissions from new sources; and a further directive to identify those mandatory Class I areas where visibility is an important value, and where additional measures may be needed in order to prevent its impairment or to correct existing impairment.
2. A directive to the EPA to protect air-quality–related values in its prevention of significant deterioration (PSD) regulations, and to develop a program to protect the visibility in and around mandatory Federal class I areas.

Regarding the second area, the EPA was supposed to promulgate PSD regulations for other criteria (important) pollutants, besides establishing increments (allowable levels) for particulates and sulfur dioxide. Applicants for new source permits must show that Class I increments will be met, but it is the duty of the federal land managers to investigate whether air-quality–related values would be adversely affected.

One mechanism for doing this is the preconstruction review process, which includes requirements that air-quality–related values apply to federal lands in all Class I areas, not just mandatory federal Class I lands. In contrast, Section 169A on visibility protection is limited to federal mandatory Class I areas only.

Following the EPA's identification of a final list of mandatory Class I federal lands, it was to promulgate regulations within two years for the revision of Standard Implementation Procedures. These regulations are to include the requirement that each major stationary source existing at the time of enactment of the Clean Air Act Amendments, and not more than fifteen years old, is to install the best available retrofit technology (BART) as expeditiously as practicable. EPA regulations are also to include a "long-term" (ten- to fifteen-year) strategy for making reasonable progress toward meeting national goals of remedying any exist-

ing impairment of visibility in a mandatory Class I federal area. The EPA published proposed PSD regulations in November 1977[85] and issued final regulations promulgating implementation plans in early June 1978.[86]

No source has yet been affected by the BART requirement, since the EPA and the states have been unable to link any particular existing source to visibility impairment (Oren 1989). Much of the program has been criticized, for instance, shortcomings of the increments as site-shifting devices as they relate to nondegradation, overly restricting the scope of Class I protection, and ad hoc development of the PSD program (Oren 1989). The PSD program, in fact, was in response to a lawsuit, *Sierra Club* v. *Ruckelshaus*,[87] that was initiated by the Sierra Club to move EPA toward program development at a quicker pace.

Oren (1989) and others maintain that a partial solution to these problems are contained in the AQRV ("air-quality–related values") test. Section 165(d)(2)(C) of the Clean Air Act Amendments provides that Class I increments are not absolute but merely determine who has the burden of proof on whether a source could be built. If the Class I increments would be violated, then a source may build if the applicant shows that the source would not affect the AQRV of the area. A source could be prevented from building even if the Class I increments would not be violated, if the federal land manager shows a "potential adverse impact" on the Class I areas. In practice, the AQRV test has proven to be of little importance. No source has ever been denied a permit under the AQRV test.

Sections 110(a)(2)(J) and 161 of the amendments do not merely obligate states to include the specific provisions of the PSD program in their state implementation plans but also give the EPA the authority to impose further requirements in the name of preventing significant deterioration. In *Alabama Power* v. *Costle*,[88] the leading judicial interpretation of the PSD provisions of the act, lends some support to this view. The court held that Section 161 gave the EPA the authority to establish rules to abate interstate pollution in clean air areas but refused to allow EPA to go beyond that letter of the statute.

Much of research on perception of air quality was done in the Southwest since one of the largest and most controversial projects proposed for that area, the so-called Four Corners (Figure 10.8), or Kaiparowits, Power Complex, concerned air quality. Three environ-

[84]Id.
[85]42 Fed. Reg. 54741 et seq. (Nov. 3, 1977).
[86]43 Fed. Reg. 26388 et seq. (June 19, 1978).
[87]344 F. Supp. 253 (D.D.C. 1972).
[88]636 F.2d 373 (D.C. Cir. 1979).

FIGURE 10.8   Four corners scene. *Photo credit: USDI, Bureau of Land Management*

mental cases[89] were related to various aspects of the gigantic power complex under development. Ten electric companies proposed to construct a network of six coal-fired electric generating stations in the Four Corners area of Utah, New Mexico, Arizona, and Nevada that would ultimately produce as much as 13,000 megawatts, about as much power as the entire output of the Tennessee Valley Authority. Virtually none of the power was to be used in the region, but was to be shipped to distant load centers such as Los Angeles, San Diego, Las Vegas, Phoenix, and Tuscon. The coal for four of the six plants would come from underground mines. Altogether, the plants would burn about 144,000 tons of coal a day. Cooling water would be drawn from the Colorado River at the rate of 250,000 acre-feet (about 80 billion gallons) per year, more than twice the annual consumption of the entire city of San Francisco. Estimates of the air pollution associated with the power complex were staggering, over 200 tons of particulates, 1,350 tons of sulfur oxides, and 1,000 tons of nitrogen oxides would be produced every day — more than Los Angeles, the nations's smog capitol.

The situation is even more appalling when one considers that the Four Corners region is one of the last areas of relatively clean air left in the country. It contains some of the most prized scenic, recreational and cultural treasures: the Grand Canyon, Mesa Verde, Zion, Bryce Canyon, Lakes Mead and Powell and Canyon de Chelly. (Brecher 1972)

In this area, too, lived some of the last groups of Native Americans who had succeeded in maintaining tra-

ditional ways of life against the relentless pressures toward assimilation presented by modern American technology. Besides the conflict with Native American value systems, the authors wish to draw attention to the direct conflict over scenic area air quality degradation. The Kaiparowits Power Complex has been built with attendent air quality degradation.

In addition to the Kaiparowits Power Complex, another group of Southern California, Nevada, and Utah municipally owned utilities are drawing up engineering plans for another mammoth coal-burning plant, this one to be situated only ten miles from Capitol Reef National Park in southeast Utah (Conservation News 1978).

The location of the proposed Intermountain Power Project (IPP) is not the only similarity to Kaiparowits. The capacity of plant would be about the same — 13,000 megawatts, the largest coal-fired plant in the world; it would cost as much as $4 billion; it would emit about the same amount of pollutants; it would require about the same amounts of coal and water; and its social impacts would likely have the same boom-and-bust syndrome effect on a sparsely settled rural region. Predictably, it raises many of the same issues as Kaiparowits.

IPP was initiated after the U.S. Bureau of Reclamation stopped development of additional power supplies from the Colorado River Storage Project for a group of Utah and Nevada utilities, the Intermountain Consumers Power Association. Deciding it would be cheaper to produce their own power than to turn to the region's predominant private utility, Utah Power and Light, the small municipal utilities joined influential Los Angeles Power and Water Department and undertook an engineering feasibility study of a site in southern Utah.

A critical factor, water was available from two major sources, the Escalante and Fremont rivers. At both sites, IPP would have to build its own reservoir and drill wells. But, most importantly, it would not have to buy any water rights. The plant would be downwind from the park, and the two 700-foot-high stacks would be hidden from view behind a bluff. But the plant would need a variance to the requirements of the Clean Air Act and would run straight into the PSD air quality provision and the specifications of Section 128 of the Clean Air Act Amendments of 1977, mentioned earlier. Capitol Reef National Park,[90] which IPP would be near, is a federal Class I area designated under provision of Clean Air Act Section 162(a). The final decision under the AQRV test regarding a source violating the

---

[89]Jicarilla Apache Tribe v. Morton, 471 F.2d 1275 (1971); Lomayaktema v. Morton, Civ. No. 974-71 (D.D.C. filed May 14, 1971); Yazzie v. Morton, 59 F.R.D. 377 (1973).

[90]Fed. Reg. 42 (199):552286 (Oct. 14, 1977).

increments rests with the federal land manager. This is because it emerged from a congressional conference as a limited concession to the developers of the proposed Intermountain Power Project.

Capital Reef National Park is mountainous, and the emissions from the plant would at times be blown directly into the mountains. Air quality modeling showed that there would be violations on some days even with strict emission controls. As enacted, the AQRV provision allows the state's governor to permit the Class I short-term increments to be exceeded at high altitudes up to eighteen days per year. Thus, any federal land manager has the power to override the state and reject issuance of a permit under the AQRV test.

According to Oren (1989), Congress, in drafting the Clean Air Act Amendments, failed to give either EPA or the federal land manager the unambiguous responsibility or authority to protect air quality in Class I areas. Congress also failed to give the federal courts appropriate authority. In one case, *United States* v. *Atlantic Richfield*,[91] the district court held that a nuisance suit by the government against a large source of flourides near Glacier National Park should be decided on the basis of federal common law. The establishment of PSD has not only failed to provide substantive criteria for park protection but has prevented the federal courts from doing so. Instead, under the Supreme Court's decision in *Ouellette* v. *International Paper*,[92] any nuisance action would be resolved on the basis of the law of the state in which the source is located, even if the source is located across state boundaries from the place of injury. In effect, then, the source state would be able to define through its substantive law the scope of any obligation to protect a national park's air quality.

EPA regulations implementing the other major section of the amendments, Section 169A, also give states carte blanche to decide whether a new source affecting national park visibility should be allowed. For a source whose effects come from "nonattainment" emissions, or which affects an "integral vista," the state may decide that its own economic development is more important than protecting the view looking into or looking out of a Class I area. While the state must consider the federal land manager's analysis, it is in the state's control to decide whether the source will have an adverse impact on visibility. The departments of Agriculture and Interior have declined to designate "integral vistas," effectively eviscerating that portion of the program. EPA has confined the application of Section 169A to states that contain mandatory Class I areas in which visibility has been identified as an important value rather than encompass states with sources that might contribute to visibility degradation in the identified areas. Even if the vistas were to be designated, EPA regulations would give them little protection against new sources. EPA rules allow states to determine whether the vista should be protected by comparing the costs of compliance and other factors against park protection. Since integral vistas are views looking out from a park, their protection involves the regulation of sources whose impacts fall outside the parks. The scope of the visibility program seems to focus on reaching only new sources affecting visibility within a park in Class I areas.

Water Quality

There are some legal tools available to maintain certain levels of water quality and quantity. The federal government is also being urged to use, and appears to have adopted a policy of using, its general contract powers as a means of air and water pollution control, and to conserve aesthetic values. Edward Weinberg states that as early as 1937 the Interior Department began to take positive steps to control water pollution.[93] He notes that the Bonneville Project Act, adopted in 1937, contemplated that contracts for the sale of power would contain a provision that would assist in maintaining the water quality of the Columbia River and the aesthetic beauty of the Columbia River Gorge. Accordingly, from the inception, the Bonneville Project Act contracts carried an article that provided for the conservation of natural resources:

The Government will not be obligated to deliver power pusuant to this contract, whenever, in the judgement of the Administrator, the purchaser's plans or operations would harm or detract from the scenic beauties of the Columbia River Gorge, or the waste products from such plants or operations would harm or destroy the fish or other aquatic life or otherwise pollute the waters of drainage basins of the Pacific Northwest (16 U.S.C. § 832 et. seq.; (1988)).

The main piece of federal legislation affecting water quality, and thus aesthetic water quality, are the federal Water Pollution Control Act Amendments of 1972.[94] This act requires the EPA administrator to

---

[91]478 F. Supp. 1215 (D. Mont. 1975).

[92]479 U.S. 481 (1987).

[93]See address by Edward Weinberg, Deputy Solicitor, entitled "Federal Contracts as a Means of Water Pollution Control," Fed. B. Ass'n. Briefing Conference, Wash., D.C. (Feb. 17, 1967).

[94]33 U.S.C. s. 1251 et seq. (1988).

publish criteria for water quality accurately reflecting the latest scientific knowledge on the kind and extent of all identifiable effects on health and welfare that may be expected from the presence of pollutants in the water. Proposed water quality criteria, including aesthetic criteria, were developed by EPA and notice of their availability was published on October 26, 1973 (38 FR 29646). These criteria were again revised in 1976 in an EPA report entitled "Quality Criteria for Water" (U.S. EPA 1976). The criteria for aesthetic water qualities (Figure 10.9) are:

All waters free from substances attributable to wastewater or other discharges that:

(1) settle to form objectionable deposits:
(2) float as debris, scum, oil, or other matter to form nuisances:
(3) produce objectionable color, odor, taste and turbidity;
(4) injure or are toxic or produce adverse physiological responses in humans, animals and plants; and
(5) produce undesirable or nuisance aquatic life (U.S. EPA 1976, p. 10).

The rationale for these criteria from the 1976 report are as follows:

Aesthetic qualities of water address the general principles laid down in common law. They embody the beauty and quality of water and their concepts may vary within the minds of individuals encountering the waterway. A rationale for these qualities cannot be developed with quantifying definitions; however, decisions concerning such quality factors can portray the best in the public interest.

Aesthetic qualities provide the general rule to protect water against environmental insults; they provide minimal freedom requirements from pollution; they are essential properties to protect the nation's waterways." (U.S. EPA 1976, p. 10).

FIGURE 10.9   Water quality impacts. *Photo credit: R. C. Smardon*

Actually these criteria are very similar to those developed by the National Federal Advisory Committee in their "Water Quality Criteria" report to the Secretary of the Interior (NTAC 1968). The requirements for aesthetics as suggested by the committee were:

A. General Requirements
   I. All surface waters should be capable of supporting life forms of aesthetic value.
   II. Surface waters should be free of substances attributable to discharges of wastes as follows:
      (a) Materials that will settle to form objectionable deposits.
      (b) Floating debris, oil, scum, and other matter.
      (c) Substances producing objectionable color, odor, taste and turbidity.
      (d) Materials including radionuclides, in concentrations or combinations which are toxic or which produce undesireable physiological responses in human, fish, and other animal life and plants.
      (e) Substances and conditions or combinations thereof in concentrations which produce undesirable aquatic life.
B. Desireable Additional Requirements
   I. The positive aesthetic values of water should be attained through continuous enhancement of water quality.
   II. The aesthetic values of unique or outstanding water should be recognized and protected by development of appropriate criteria for each individual case (NTAC 1968, p. 3).

The criteria are substantially the same with the exceptions of parts A.I, B.I, and B.II added to the NTAC report. Criterion A.I was the committee's acknowledgement of the linkage of water quality to wildlife (NTAC 1968, p. 5), a linkage that has since been given little recognition or attention. Criterion B.I. was probably an overly optimistic and visionary goal of enhancement as contrasted to maintenance of the status quo and a recognition of the need for positive steps to be made to improve water quality for aesthetic consumption as well as ecological rationales (NTAC 1968, p. 6). Criterion B.II recognizes that certain bodies of water in the U.S. merit special consideration, such as Lake Tahoe, Crater Lake, portions of Biscayne Bay, and other coastal and estuarine areas, wild and scenic rivers, reservoirs, and lakes — "waters which by reason of clarity, color, scenic setting, or other characteristics provide aesthetic values of unique or special interest." (NTAC 1968, p. 6).

Certainly the standards of 1968 and their rationale are somewhat richer and more stimulating than the 1976 EPA standards. The 1968 committee also realized that aesthetic water quality standards were contextualistic or regional in character when they stated that:

The Subcommittee wishes to emphasize that aesthetic qualities — noticeably color and clarity — of natural waters vary sharply among regions and within regions or even on specific streams, lakes, reservoirs, bays, and esturaries. The recommended criteria are intended to be applied in the context of natural conditions (NTAC 1968, p. 6).

So again we find the need to use a contextual standard for aesthetic conditions that is sensitive to local conditions. The contextual concept seems to have been lost in the muddle of hurrying to meet quantitative water quality standards based primarily on health and biological indicators at the federal and state levels.

Research has been conducted on how people perceive water quality (Coughlin 1976). There is also a good aesthetic overview of the role of water in the landscape; it was originally prepared by Litton et al. (1974) for the National Water Commission.

Water Quantity

There are also some legal tools that may affect the flow, or quantity, of water for aesthetic purposes, especially during low-flow periods in Western states. These tools lie in the area of water rights and more specifically in the "reserved rights" doctrine. This doctrine holds that land owners do not have riparian rights but have appropriation water rights. Briefly, the doctrine states that upon the creation of a federal reservation on the public domain — whether by treaty, legislation, or executive order — the reservation has appurtenant to it the right to divert as much water from streams within or bordering upon it as necessary to serve the purposes for which the reservation was created. In *Arizona* v. *California,*[95] reserved water rights were decreed for Indian reservations, national recreation areas, national wildlife refuges, and national forests.

As Meyers (1966, pp. 65–66) points out, several aspects of the reserved rights doctrine have significant, operative consequences:

(1) The priority date is the date the reservation is created. State-created water rights in existence before this date are superior; those arising thereafter are subordinate.
(2) The reserved right, unlike state — created appropriative rights, does not depend upon diversion from the stream and application to beneficial use. The reserved right arises when the reservation is established even though the water right is not exercised for decades thereafter. In this respect the

right is like a riparian right. In time of shortage, however, it is unlike a riparian right, for it does not share the available supply pro rata but rather takes its place on the priority schedule and receives water ahead of all rights of later date.

(3) As may be inferred from the above statement, the federal reserved right need not be created or exercised in accordance with state law. Not only does its creation not depend on diversion of water and application of it for beneficial use, but the right does not depend upon filing with the state agency or upon recording of the claim. And it is not subject to state laws on forfeiture and abandonment.
(4) The quantity of water to be enjoyed under a reserved right is measured by the quantity necessary to fulfill the purposes of the reservation, both at the present time and in the future.

This reserved rights doctrine is extremely complex when federal versus state priority of water rights is considered, or when the doctrine is mixed with riparian and/or prior appropriation water rights system. Meyers points out that "only if the doctrine (reserved rights) is limited to Desert Land Act states and to streams subject exclusively to the law of prior appropriation is a coherent system of law on reserved rights achieved." (1966, p. 69).

In one of the most important water law cases in the West, *Arizona* v. *California,* the decree reserved water rights for the Lake Mead National Recreation Area, the Hvasau Lake and Imperial National Wildlife Refuge on the main stream of the Colorado River and the Gila National Forest on a tributary,[96] besides Indian reservation water rights. No differences were seen in principle between reserving water for Indian reservations and reserving water for other federal reservations.[97] Meyers points out that no guidance was given as to the amount of water that is to be withdrawn. What is an acceptable standard for national forests, parks, recreation areas, and wildlife refuges? The only standard given was "a quantity reasonably needed . . . for appropriate purposes."[98]

Meyers poses the problem that what may be an adequate or minimally reasonable amount for a national forest today may be an extremely large amount for a forest turned recreation area in the future. This may create uncertainty and may cloud potential dealings with private water rights.

Hammond proposes that the reserved rights doctrine be used to control mining operations in wilderness areas by allowing any such appropriation of waters in

[95]376 U.S. 340, 350 (1963) C.
[96]373 U.S. at 601 (1963).
[97]Report of the Special Master 12–14 (1960), Arizona v. California 373 U.S. 546 (1963).
[98]Id. at 295.

streams passing through the wilderness area that is compatible with a low level of stream pollution and a reasonable consumption of water. He uses *Federal Power Commission* v. *Oregon,*[99] or the *Pelton Dam* case to assert that federal control is preeminent over any water located in the boundaries of federal reservations, and that the need of the reservation (Glacier Peak Wilderness Area) is preservation of wilderness (Hammond 1968). Outside of wilderness areas or other areas with specifically designated protective statutes, the reserved rights doctrine may not do much to protect or reserve water flow for aesthetic purposes.

In 1978 the U.S. Supreme Court, in *United States* v. *New Mexico,*[100] affirmed the decision of the New Mexico State Supreme Court concerning water claims by the Forest Service in the Rob Mimbres Adjudication. The question before the Court concerned the original purposes for establishing forest reserves. The Supreme Court ruled, in application of the Reserved Water Doctrine, that the Organic Act of 1897 established two purposes for creating forest preserves: (1) to secure a favorable condition of water flow, and (2) to furnish a continuous supply of timber.

According to the Supreme Court, water claims for managment of aesthetics, recreation, wildlife, fisheries, or livestock are not legitimate claims under the reservation doctrine. In the Court's opinion, the Multiple-Use Sustained Yield Act of 1960 does not modify the purposes of forest preserves to include these claims even with a 1960 priority date. The court stated that although the Multiple-Use Act broadened the purposes of administering the national forests, Congress did not expand reserved rights to the U.S. Forest Service. The implications of this decision include: formidable barriers to claimed reserved rights arising by implied intent, and possible problems for federal land management agencies such as the Forest Service and BLM. The problems would be less for the National Park Service because of the specific authorization legislation existing for each national park and monument. The Court denied claimed reserved rights by reading a narrow construction of original legislation for the Gila National Forest and further specified that:

(1) the right must relate to the original purpose of the withdrawal of the reservation;
(2) the implication must be necessary to prevent the frustration of the original purpose of the reservation; and
(3) the distinction between primary and secondary purposes of reservations, stating that the court will

find a reserved right to effect the former but will draw the contrary inference for the latter.[100]

In 1979 the U.S. solictor general attempted an end run around *New Mexico* by issuing an opinion that made extensive federal reserved and on-reserved claims but which was repudiated by a subsequent solicitor general opinion. However, case law on parks and related reservations seems to be developing consistent with the 1979 opinion (Solicitor General 1979). A federal district court in Colorado[101] held that the protection of in-stream flows in wilderness areas, as opposed to multiple-use forest lands, is a primary purpose of the Wilderness Act of 1964 and applies equally to National Park Service areas. The Colorado Supreme Court recognized reserved rights for the benefits of the Rocky Mountain National Park for the protection of watershed and timber resources and the conservation of scenery, historic, and scientific objects and wildlife.[102] The court, however, applied the primary-secondary distinction and refused to recognize in-stream flows to support recreational boating in the Dinosaur National Monument. Many legal scholars are adocating that it is the public land managers responsibility to protect in-stream flows and water rights just as they should protect air quality of parks, wilderness areas, and national monuments (Leshy 1988; Marks 1987; Reynolds 1989; Sherton 1981; Tarlock 1986; and Vassallo 1986).

Another interesting situation is the Mono Lake controversy in California that also involves water rights issues. Los Angeles diverts four of five streams feeding Mono Lake for the Los Angeles area water supply. Preservationists maintain that diminishing water levels of Mono Lake affects the hydrology and ecology of the lake as well as causing aesthetic impact. After numerous lawsuits and political battles the city of Los Angeles agreed in September 1989 to surrender some of its water rights in order to reduce environmental damage. In fact, EDAW, an environmental planning firm, was retained to assess whether people could perceive changes in water level on the shore edges of Mono Lake over time. This was linked to an English water law concept of gradual versus sudden changes in water courses and bodies. The visual simulations of changed water levels and the accompanying testimony were some of the most powerful evidence submitted supporting the ecological and aesthetic impact of lowered water levels of Mono Lake (see Figure 10.10). The key court case in-

---

[99]349 U.S. 435 (1955).
[100]430 U.S. 696 (1978).
[101]Sierra Club v. Black, 622 F. Supp. 842 (D. Colo. 1985).
[102]Sierra Club v. City and County of Denver 656 P.2d 1 (Colo. 1982).

a.

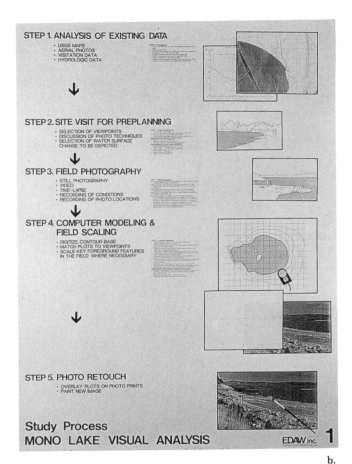

STEP 1. ANALYSIS OF EXISTING DATA
· USGS MAPS
· AERIAL PHOTOS
· VISITATION DATA
· HYDROLOGIC DATA

STEP 2. SITE VISIT FOR PREPLANNING
· SELECTION OF VIEWPOINTS
· DISCUSSION OF PHOTO TECHNIQUES
· SELECTION OF WATER SURFACE
  CHANGE TO BE DEPICTED

STEP 3. FIELD PHOTOGRAPHY
· STILL PHOTOGRAPHY
· VIDEO
· TIME-LAPSE
· RECORDING OF CONDITIONS
· RECORDING OF PHOTO LOCATIONS

STEP 4. COMPUTER MODELING &
        FIELD SCALING
· DIGITIZE CONTOUR BASE
· MATCH PLOTS TO VIEWPOINTS
· SCALE KEY FOREGROUND FEATURES
  IN THE FIELD WHERE NECESSARY

STEP 5. PHOTO RETOUCH
· OVERLAY PLOTS ON PHOTO PRINTS
· PAINT NEW IMAGE

Study Process
MONO LAKE VISUAL ANALYSIS   EDAW inc. 1

b.

LAKE ELEVATION

6379.86'   6380.08'

VIEW A Black Point · Negit

VIEW B County Park

VIEW C Highway

Perceptibility of Changes in Lake Level
MONO LAKE VISUAL ANALYSIS

d.

FIGURE 10.10 a, b, c, d, e, f (pages 170–171)   Mono
Lake study of perceived change of water levels. *Photo credit:*
EDAW Inc., San Francisco

c.

MONTHLY CHANGES IN LAKE LEVEL
(INCREASES & DECLINES)

0.0-0.2' CHANGE
58% OF ALL OCCURRENCES

0.2-0.25' CHANGE
9% OF ALL OCCURRENCES

0.0-0.25' CHANGE
67% OF ALL OCCURRENCES

0.25' OR MORE
33% OF ALL OCCURRENCES

WEEKLY CHANGES IN LAKE LEVEL
(INCREASES & DECLINES)

GREATER THAN 0.22'
0.6% OF ALL OCCURRENCES
14 OCCURRENCES IN 44 YEARS

0.0-0.22'
99.4% OF ALL OCCURRENCES

WEEKLY CHANGES IN LAKE LEVEL
(DECLINES ONLY)

ALL WEEKLY DECLINES HAVE
BEEN AT OR BELOW 0.22'

RATIONALE FOR DEPICTING
0.22' CHANGE IN LAKE LEVEL

0.22'
ACTUAL
SCALE

Hydrologic Data Summary
MONO LAKE VISUAL ANALYSIS   EDAW inc. 2

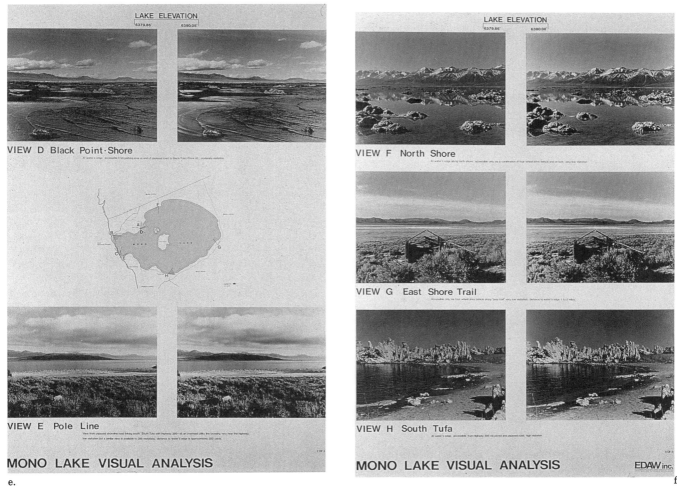

FIGURE 10.10 *(Continued)* Mono Lake Study of perceived change of water levels. *Photo credit: EDAW Inc., San Francisco*

volved with this dispute, *National Audubon Society v. Superior Court,*[103] was truly precedent-setting as no court had previously held that public trust doctrine affected riparian or appropriate water rights; the case expanded such rights to any public use associated with navigable waters to include recreation and aesthetics (Casey 1984; Conway 1984; Stevens 1989; and Walston 1987).

Archeological Resources

Federal acts that provide for protection of archeological resources are the Antiquities Act of 1906[104] and the Historical and Archeological Data Preservation Act of 1974.[105] The Antiquities Act provides for the protection of historic and prehistoric remains or "any object of an-

tiquity" on federal lands; establishes criminal sanctions for unauthorized destruction or appropriation of antiquities; authorizes presidential proclamation of national monuments; and authorizes the scientific investigation of antiquities on federal property, subject to permit and regulation. The Historical and Archeological Data Preservation Act of 1974 amended the Reservoir Salvage Act of 1960 to broaden the scope of the earlier act. It authorizes the temporary delay of any federally financed construction project or federally licensed activity or program while publicly financed recovery, protection, and preservation of historical and archeological resources, including relics and specimens, is undertaken. Many projects have been delayed due to archeological salvage activities under this provision.

[103]33 Cal.3d 419, 445, 658 P.2d 709, 727, 189 Cal. Rptr. 346 (1983).
[104]16 U.S.C. s. 431 (1988).
[105]16 U.S.C. s. 469 (1988).

Tying many historical and archeological provisions together is Executive Order 11593, "Protection and Enhancement of the Cultural Environment."[106] This executive order stated that it would be the policy of the federal government "to provide leadership in preserving, restoring, and maintaining the historic and cultural environment of the Nation."[107] The order added that federal agencies shall "administer the cultural properties under their control in a spirit of stewardship and trusteeship for future generations,"[108] and institute procedures to carry out these goals.

Wildlife Resources

Wildlife is not often thought of an an aesthetic or visual resource, but often wildlife, especially large mammals (Figure 10.11), will tend to dominate the landscape or seascape and "steal the show." Although ephemeral, wildlife is a major part of rural natural and wilderness landscapes as well as one of the main reasons for recreational activities in the landscape such as nature watching, and photography. Wildlife biologists refer to such values as the nonconsumptive values of wildlife. There has been little perceptual research on aesthetic values of wildlife.

Although wildlife usually belong to the states in which they are found, and state wildlife agencies are primarily responsible for their management and protection, there are a few key federal statutes that call attention to the aesthetic aspects of wildlife and their habitat. These are the Endangered Species Act of 1973[109] and the Marine Mammal Protection Act of 1972.[110] The purpose of the Endangered Species Act is stated as: "to provide a means whereby the ecosystems upon which endangered species and threatened species depend may be conserved, (and) to provide a program for the conservation of such species and threatened species"[111] Section 1531 of the act declares: " — (3) these species of fish, wildlife, and plants are of *esthetic,* ecological, educational, historical, recreational, and scientific value to the Nation and its people."[112] (Emphasis added.)

Section 2 (6) of the Marine Mammal Protection Act states that:

(6) marine mammals have proven themselves to be resources of great international significance, esthetic and

FIGURE 10.11 a, b   Wildlife stealing the show

recreational as well as economic, and it is the sense of the Congress that they should be protected and encouraged to develop to the greatest extent feasible commensurate with sound policies of resource management and that the primary objective of their management should be to maintain the health and stability of the marine ecosystems. Whenever consistent with this primary objective, it should be the goal to obtain an optimum sustainable population keeping in mind the optimum carrying capacity of the habitat.[113]

Thus, we have seen that there are many federal and state statutes that can be utilized for the protection of aesthetic or visual resources manifested in air and

[106]39 Fed. Reg. 8921 (May 18, 1971).
[107]Id.
[108]Id.
[109]16 U.S.C. s. 1531–1543 (1988).
[110]16 U.S.C. § 1361 et seq. (1988).
[111]16 U.S.C. s. 1531 (1988).
[112]Id.
[113]16 U.S.C. § 1361 (1988).

water quality, archeological resources, and wildlife resources.

Other Acts Protecting Aesthetic Rights

Aesthetics, or aesthetic rights, are also mentioned specifically in some state constitutions or separate statutes. For example, Article I, Section 27, of the Pennsylvania Constitution provides:

The people have a right to clean air, pure water, and to the preservation of the natural, scenic, historic, and aesthetic values of the environment. Pennsylvania's public natural resources are the common property of all the people, including generations yet to come. As trustee of the resources, the Commonwealth shall conserve and maintain them for the benefit of all the people.[114]

Case Study: Assessment of Amenity Wetland Values in Juneau, Alaska

This case study summarizes part of the findings of a larger study to determine human-use values associated with wetlands near Juneau, Alaska. (Palmer and Smardon 1989; Smardon et al. 1987). Criteria for rating potential value are based on available literature. A random survey was used to systematically assess existing human-use values. This approach allowed the collection of value-oriented data that could not be inferred from visitor counts. In a sense, a survey is a plebiscite that allows a richer investigation of the public's views than is possible through a single question on a ballot. The results of the survey were then analyzed and interpreted with decision rules so as to be integrated with the overall procedures used to assess and manage Juneau's wetlands (see Adamus et al. 1983 and 1987).

Juneau's Situation

The settlement of Juneau, Alaska (Figure 10.12), was determined by the location nearby of gold deposits rather than by its suitability as a site to build a community. In general, there are two types of building sites in Juneau, those on steep or avalanche-prone uplands and those in wetlands. For a time, desirable building sites were located on the most suitable upland areas or created by using discarded mine material to fill wetlands.

During the 1960s active development extended north of Juneau into the Mendenhall Valley, an area that was predominately wetland. This area is shown in Figure 10.13, which indicates the location of the major wetland systems immediately north of the original settlement. By the early 1980s the population of the Mendenhall Valley had reached 7,500 people, with an annual growth rate of nearly 10 percent. The comprehensive plan for the valley adopted in 1973 forecast an ultimate population of 18,700 residents on the east side and 9,600 on the west side of the river. A similar rate of growth was projected for Douglas Island if a second channel crossing were constructed.

In 1976 the U.S. Army Corps of Engineers was authorized under Section 404 of the Clean Water Act to regulate the discharge of dredged or fill material into navigable waters and adjacent wetlands, as described earlier in this chapter. Pressure for rapid residential and commercial development accompanied the economic boom associated with oil development in Alaska. After a decade of weak enforcement and poor compliance, a federal injunction halted development on wetlands until the city/borough of Juneau determined which of the remaining wetlands were most effective in performing certain natural functions in the public interest. An intractable situation was established between the mandate of the federal agencies to protect the natural environment and needs of the population of Juneau to grow and develop. Both perspectives, pro-development and pro-protection, were recognized as having a significant public support.

In May 1986 a contract was let to Adamus Resource Assessment, Inc., to evaluate wetland functions. In the past, wetland functions had been viewed primarily as part of the natural ecosystem. However, the city/borough of Juneau insisted the "public interest" also required the human-use functions of wetlands be evaluated.

This case study briefly reviews the findings of assessing the visual amenity values (Palmer and Smardon, 1988b) associated with wetlands near Juneau, Alaska. The approach chosen used a random survey to systematically determine these values. The larger human-use survey is described by a companion paper (Palmer and Smardon 1988a).

Methods

Scoping workshops were convened during June 1986 to better understand the public's perception of the issues. In addition, site visits were made to the major wetland areas, and a photographic inventory compiled. Based on the workshop results, a survey was prepared to assess public perceptions of (1) special issues and concerns, (2) the importance of wetland functions and attributes, (3) recreation use, and (4) wetland scenic quality. While scenic values were part of the first three sections, they were principally assessed through the evaluation of wetland scenes in the fourth section of the survey.

During October 1986 questionnaires were mailed to 1,560 residences that were randomly identified from the Juneau City Directory. A second mailing was made in December to all those who had not responded by that time. Of these, 197 were returned because there was no mail receptacle at the address. These were replaced by 199 randomly selected residential postal boxes. An additional 568 questionnaires were returned by the Postal Service for other reasons. A total of 431 responses were received out of a possible 994, for a total response rate of 43 percent.

---

[114]Pa. Const. Art. 1, s. 27.

FIGURE 10.12 a, b, c Juneau setting. *Photo credit: R. C. Smardon*

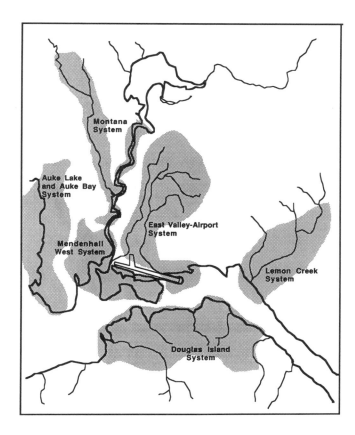

FIGURE 10.13 Map of Juneau study area. *Graphic credit: James F. Palmer*

FIGURE 10.14 (pages 175, 176, 177)   Juneau Study Photoquestionnaire. *Credit: J. F. Palmer*

Visual Presentation

The sixteen scenes selected to represent the range of visual character and intensity of development among Juneau's wetlands were evaluated by respondents for their scenic quality. The procedure used a nine-point rating scale ranging from 1 (very high scenic quality) to 9 (very low scenic quality). The scenes were offset-printed in black and white and included in the survey (see Figure 10.14).

These wetland scenes represent three visual conditions: open water, low vegetation, and high vegetation. In Juneau, saturated areas with unconsolidated bottoms, beds of floating vascular aquatic plants, and nonpersistent and persistent emergent vegetation are found in open-water wetland areas. Low vegetation areas include deciduous (broad leaf) and evergreen (needle leaf) which are scrub-shrub wetlands. Forested deciduous and evergreen wetlands represent a high vegetation condition. Filled wetlands were also evaluated, since they were the significant alternative condition proposed for

much of the wetlands being studied. The effect of development within a view on wetland scenic quality is evaluated by comparing four development intensities represented among wetland scenes: natural or undeveloped, roads or ground freshly broken for construction, residential, and commercial or industrial areas.

Results

Wetland Scenic Quality

The visual character and development intensity of each evaluated scene is listed in Table 10.1, which also shows their mean ratings and 95 percent confidence intervals. While there are clearly scenic differences among the scenes, they are difficult to evaluate without considering the general attributes of the Juneau area. The results of the analysis of variance indicate significant differences that are attributable to both development intensity and visual character as well as to the interaction between the two.

FIGURE 10.14   (*Continued*) Juneau Study Photoquestionnaire.

FIGURE 10.14   (*Continued*) Juneau Study Photoquestionnaire.

TABLE 10.1   Visual Preference Survey Results. Credit: J. F. Palmer

Photograph	Visual Character	Development Intensity	Mean Visual Quality	95% Confidence Interval				
2	Low vegetation	Undeveloped	2.49	.18	*			
1	High vegetation	Undeveloped	3.25	.21		*		
9	Low vegetation	Residence	3.47	.18			*	
12	Low vegetation	Residence	4.48	.18				*
4	Low vegetation	Construction/Road	4.70	.21	*			
14	Open water	Construction/Road	4.89	.20		*		
6	High vegetation	Residence	5.04	.18			*	
7	Open water	Residence	5.05	.20				*
15	Filled	Construction/Road	5.41	.21	*			
3	High vegetation	Residence	5.69	.17		*		
16	Filled	Construction/Road	5.88	.21			*	
11	Filled	Construction/Road	6.67	.18				*
13	Low vegetation	Commercial	6.74	.17	*			
10	Low vegetation	Commercial	6.93	.18		*		
5	Filled	Residence	7.13	.16			*	
8	High vegetation	Construction/Road	7.23	.21				*

Note: There are about 400 survey respondents from the sample survey. The photographs were rated on a 9-point scale where 1 was very high scenic quality and 9 was very low scenic quality.

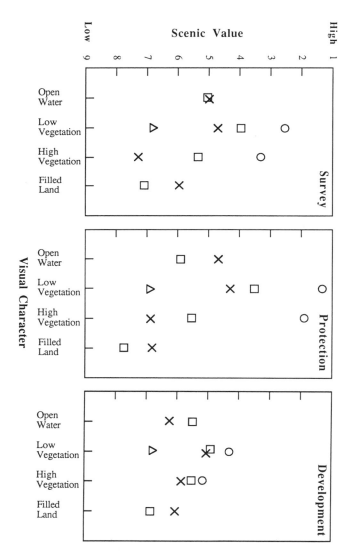

FIGURE 10.15   Plot of scenic values and survey results.
Credit: J. F. Palmer

The results are more easily interpreted by referring to Figure 10.15, which is the plot of the scenic value for each combination of visual character and development intensity represented by the scenes. Generally speaking, the highest quality areas are either open water or low vegetated. A posterior multiple-comparison Scheffe test of the four visual character types indicates that the scenic quality of open water and low vegetation wetlands is not significantly different. However, they are of significantly higher quality than high vegetation wetlands, which are in turn of higher quality than filled wetlands. The Sheffe test comparing development intensities found significant differences among four levels. The natural condition is of distinctly higher quality, followed by residential areas, then roads or construction disturbance, and finally commercial areas.

Criteria Ratings

The method of wetland functional assessment developed by Adamus et al. (1983) rates wetland areas as either high, moderate, or low, according to their importance for the various functions. The survey results clearly indicate that open water or saturated wetlands, as well as those with low vegetation, are very important to Juneau's scenic quality. In an undisturbed state, wetlands with high vegetation, especially when it is deciduous, have the potential for high scenic quality but may also be of moderate scenic quality. Once filled, wetlands lose much of their scenic quality. In addition, wetland scenic quality is particularly sensitive to deterioration from development within the scene. The results of the scenic quality survey are reinterpreted in Figure 10.16 to indicate the appropriate ranking for each wetland character.

Comparison with Other Wetland Functions

It is not intended that the ratings for a wetland's functions be given equal weight. Their relative importance may be determined by their abundance or scarcity in relation to their observed need. Alternately, the public may contribute to identifying their relative value.

Survey respondents indicated how they valued various wetland functions and attributes based on a standard value of

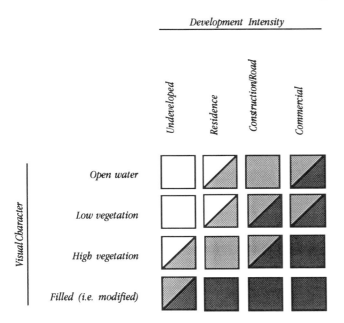

Development Intensity

Undeveloped Residence Construction/Road Commercial

Open water

Low vegetation

High vegetation

Filled (i.e. modified)

Visual Character

FIGURE 10.16   Relation of scenic quality to wetland visual character and levels of development intensity. Scenic quality is indicated as □ high, ▨ moderate, ■ low.

wetland biological productivity. One suspects the very high value placed on having litter-free wetlands is directly related to the significant trash problem, which had become a constant eyesore in Juneau's wetlands.

Among the remaining attributes are eight that are valued as more important then open space. Among these eight attributes are three that indicate an important desire for visible indications that Juneau's wetlands are healthy: clarity and condition of the water, scenic features, and undisturbed area of wetlands. These results show that the public can place significant value on scenic quality when compared to other wetland functions, even though it may be difficult to quantify in dollars and cents.

Conclusions

This case study describes a successful approach to meaningfully incorporate visual amenity values along with other wetland functions in a comprehensive assessment (Smardon et al. 1987). In reflecting upon the value of the overall study, Adamus et al. (1987, p. 7) note that:

The accuracy of the study's ratings of particular functions depended not only on manpower expended by topic, but on the general amenability or intractability of meaningfully measuring the function in the course of a field season.

Adamus et al. go on to indicate that the human-use functions are second or third from the top, based on their professional subjective evaluation of the relative confidence they have in the ten rated functions (Adamus et al. 1987, p. 11).

100 points for open space. The results in Table 10.2 show mean importance and 95 percent confidence intervals for twenty functions. Three attributes are clearly valued by residents as most important. The high value placed on wildlife and fisheries habitat indicate the perceived importance of

TABLE 10.2   Ranking of Overall Wetland Values. Credit: J. F. Palmer

	Mean	95% Confidence Interval
Most Important		
Wildlife habitat	229.2	17.5
Being free of litter	226.7	18.7
Fisheries habitat	212.6	15.5
More Important		
Water condition (e.g., clarity, color, litter, etc.)	192.0	14.9
Scenic features	180.8	14.4
Undisturbed areas of wetlands	171.2	15.2
Public ownership of selected wetland areas	158.9	17.4
Opportunities for solitude	147.3	13.8
Opportunities to fish	141.7	11.6
Opportunities for passive recreation (bird watching)	138.7	13.0
Opportunities for nature walks	134.1	11.7
Important		
Flood protection	112.3	12.3
Accessibility of wetlands	108.6	10.3
Opportunities to hunt	107.6	11.9
Area for children to play	104.8	10.8
Open space	100.0	—
Having some wetlands near to your home	97.5	12.0
Food gathering opportunities	88.2	10.2
Less Important		
Area for economic development	73.9	11.7
Area for residential development	66.8	9.7

Note: All importance ratings are calibrated to an open space value of 100. The highest value accepted as credible is 1000.

Those of us involved with visual assessments have reason to be reassured from this evaluation. It is time we became more comfortable with having the validity and reliability of our work compared to other scientific environmental assessments. Finally, it should be noted that the city/borough of Juneau is developing a comprehensive wetland management plan that incorporates the results of this study plus public input. Such a management plan also includes appropriate controls applied to a prioritized system for wetland protection.

References

Adamus, P. R. et al. 1983. *A method for wetlands functional assessment*, vol. 1 and 2. U.S. DOT, FHA.

Adamus, P. R. et al. 1987. *Juneau wetlands: Functions and values*, final draft. Adamus Resource Assessment.

Baldwin, M. F. 1970. The Santa Barbara oil spill. *University of Colorado Law Review*, 42(1): 33–76.

Barker, M. L. 1976. Planning for environmental indices: Oberver appraisals of air quality. In *Perceiving environmental quality: Research and application*, ed. K. H. Craik and E. H. Zube, pp. 175–204. Plenum Press.

Bosselman, F., and Callies, D. 1971. *The quiet revolution in land use control*. Council on Environmental Quality. U.S. GPO.

Brecher, J. J. 1972. Venue in conservation cases: A potential pitfall for environmental lawyers. *Ecology Law Quarterly*, 2(1): 91–117.

Casey, E. S. 1984. Water law — Public trust doctrine. *Natural Resources Journal*, 24: 809–825.

Conservation News. 1978. 43(13): 1–3.

Conway, T. J. 1984. *National Audubon Society v. Superior Court*: The expanding public trust doctrine. *Environmental Law*, 14: 615–640.

Coughlin, R. F. 1976. The perception and valuation of water quality. In *Perceiving environmental quality: Research and application*, ed. K. H. Craik and E. H. Zube, pp. 205–227. Plenum Press.

Council on Environmental Quality. 1978. *Our Nation's wetlands: An interagency task force report*. U.S. GOP.

Greeson, P.E., Clark, J. R., and Clark, J. E. 1978. *Wetland functions and values: The state of our understanding*. Water Resources Association.

Hammond, 1968. The Wilderness Act and mining: Some proposals for conservation. *Oregon Law Review*, 47(4): 456–548.

Hunter, D. B. 1988. An ecological perspective on property: A call for judicial protection of the public's interest in environmentally critical resources. *Harvard Environmental Law Review*, 12: 311–383.

Kuehn, R. R. 1984. The Coastal Barrier Resources Act and the expenditures limitation approach to natural resources conservation: Wave of the future or island unto itself? *Ecology Law Quarterly*, 11: 583–670.

Kusler, J. A. 1978. *Strengthening state wetland regulations*. USDI, Fish and Wildlife Service, Office of Biological Services FWS OBS 78/98.

———.1980. *Regulating Sensitive Lands*. Ballinger.

Leshy, J. D. 1988. Water and wilderness: Law and politics. *Land and Water Law Review*, 23(2): 389–417.

Litton, R. B., Jr. et al. 1974. *Water and landscape: An Aesthetic overview of the role of water in the landscape*. Water Information Inc.

Marks, J. 1987. The duty of agencies to assert reserved water rights in wilderness areas. *Ecology Law Quarterly*, 14: 639–683.

Mead, K. L. 1986. Comment: Wyoming's experience with Federal non-Indian reserved rights: The Big Horn adjudcation. *Land and Water Review*, 21: 433–453.

Meyers, C. J. 1966. The Colorado River. *Stanford Law Review*, (1): 1–75.

National Technical Advisory Committee. 1968. *Water quality criteria, Report of the National Technical Advisory Committee to the Secretary of the Interior*. Federal Water Pollution Control Administration, U.S. GPO.

Note. 1975. Preserving scenic areas: The Adirondack land use program. *Yale Law Journal*, 84: 1705–1721.

Oren, C. N. 1989. The protection of parklands from air pollution: A look at current policy. *Harvard Environmental Law Review*, 13: 313–421.

Ostrov, J. 1982. Visibility protection under the Clean Air Act: Preserving scenic and parkland areas in the Southwest. *Ecology Law Quarterly*, 10: 397–454.

Palmer, J. F. and Smardon, R. C. 1988a. Human-use values of wetlands: An assessment in Juneau, Alaska. In *Proceedings of the national wetland symposium: Urban wetlands*. ed. J. A. Kusler, S. Daly, and G. Brooks, pp. 108–114. Association of Wetland Managers.

———. 1988b. Visual amenity value of wetlands: An assessment in Juneau, Alaska. In *Proceedings of the national wetland symposium: Urban wetlands*, ed. J. A. Kusler, S. Daly and G. Brooks, pp. 104–107. Association of Wetland Managers.

———. 1989. Measuring human values associated with wetlands. In *Intractable conflicts and their transformation* ed. L. Kriesburg, T. A. Northrup, and J. Thorsen, pp. 156–179. Syracuse University Press.

Reynolds, C. C. 1989. Protecting Oregon's free-flowing water. *Environmental Law*, 19: 841–877.

Sabatier, P. A. 1976. Regulating development along the California Coast: A review and evaluation of the coastal commissions. *Journal of Soil and Water Conservation*. July-Aug: 146–151.

Sherton, C. C. 1981. Preserving in-stream flows in Oregon's rivers and streams. *Environmental Law*, 11: 379–419.

Shiyam, C. A., and Smardon, R. C. 1990. *Wetland Heritage assessment: Methodology and literature review as part of wetland evaluation technique*. IEPP Report 90-4, prepared for U.S. Army Corps of Engineers Waterways Experimental Station by Institute for Environmental Policy and Planning, SUNY/ESF.

Smardon, R. C., ed. 1983. *The Future of Wetlands; Assessing Visual-Cultural Values*. Allenheld-Osmun.

Smardon, R. C. et al. 1987. *Assessing human-use values of wetlands within the city/borough of Juneau, Alaska*. IEPP report ESF-EIPP-87-1, prepared for ARA by Institute for Environmental Policy and Planning, SUNY/ESF.

Stevens, J. S. 1989. The public trust and in-stream uses. *Environmental Law*, 19: 605–621.

Tarlock, D. 1986. Protection of water flows for national parks. *Land and Water Law Review*, 22(1): 29–48.

Tundermann, D. W. 1978. Protecting visibility; The key to preventing significant deterioration in Western air quality. *Natural Resources Lawyer,* 11(2): 373–383.

U.S. Environmental Protection Agency. 1976. *Quality criteria for water.* U.S. EPA, Office of Water Planning and Standards.

——. 1979. *Protecting visibility research.* EPA 450/5-79, 008 U.S. EPA.

U.S. Solicitor General. 1979. *Federal water rights of the National Park Service, Fish and Wildlife Service, Bureau of Reclamation, Bureau of Land Management,* 86 Interior Dec. 553, 594-602 (1979) Solicitor Opinion M-36914 (June 25, 1979).

Vassallo, N. 1986. Comment: Federal reserved water rights in National Forest Wilderness Areas. *Land and Water Law Review,* 21: 381–396.

Walston, R. E. 1987. The public trust and water rights: *National Audubon Society v. Superior Court. Land and Water Law Review,* 22(2): 701–724.

——. 1989. The public trust doctrine in the water rights context. *Natural Resources Journal,* 29: 585–592.

Washington State Department of Ecology. 1977. Supreme Court emphasis on aesthetics makes "Pacesetter" a landmark decision. *Shoreline Coastal Zone Management,* 2(5).

Chapter 11

Aesthetic Project Review

INTRODUCTION

Most people think of aesthetic impact in terms of review of specific project proposals such as construction of dams, roadways (Figure 11.1), structures, or some other massive undertaking involving public or private expenditures and much controversy. The controversy may be generated by the nature of the project or by the landscape on which it may have an impact. This chapter addresses basic legal procedural issues and approaches for reviewing the aesthetic impacts of such projects. Much of the information in the Chapters 9 and 10 is useful because one of the major issues in aesthetic impact assessment is the effect on recognized or sensitive scenic landscape resources. Chapters 12, 13, and 14 will address particular kinds of projects and activities that bring about specific aesthetic impacts on the landscape. That portion of environmental review involving aesthetics is now often called aesthetic or visual impact assessment (VIA). Methods for VIA are becoming well developed and are treated in detail in another volume (Smardon, Palmer, and Felleman 1986).

This chapter will first look at some important court cases and projects that set procedural guidance for review of major federal projects and clarified the issue of standing — when individuals or groups have the ability to intervene to review or stop major projects. Second, the chapter covers major federal and state programs for

aesthetic project review. Third, the chapter provides a section on procedural and methodological advances for aesthetic project review.

PROJECT REVIEW HISTORY: DEVELOPMENT OF PUBLIC INJURY AND STANDING

Beginning in 1966 procedural obstacles to environmental suits, such as standing to sue, were reduced. Courts abandoned the requirement that plaintiffs suffer significant personal damages before they had standing to bring a suit. The issue culminated in the U.S. Supreme Court decision in *Association of Data Processing*[1] in 1970, and now plaintiffs can have standing by proving injury in fact, economic and otherwise. The "otherwise" includes recreational, conservational, and aesthetic harm. The breadth of the Court's language swung the doors of the federal courts open to individual and organizational environmental plaintiffs.

The Supreme Court stated that[2] the Administrative Procedures Act[3] allows individuals or groups standing in order to sue for damage to the public aesthetic interest.

The "legal interest" test goes to the merits. The question of standing is different. It concerns, apart from the "case" or "controversy" test, the question whether the interest sought to be protested by the complainant is arguably within the zone of interests protected or regulated by the

---

[1]Association of Data Proc. Serv. Org. Inc. v. Camp, 397 U.S. 150, 153–54 (1970).
[2]Id.
[3]5 U.S.C. s. 702 (1988).

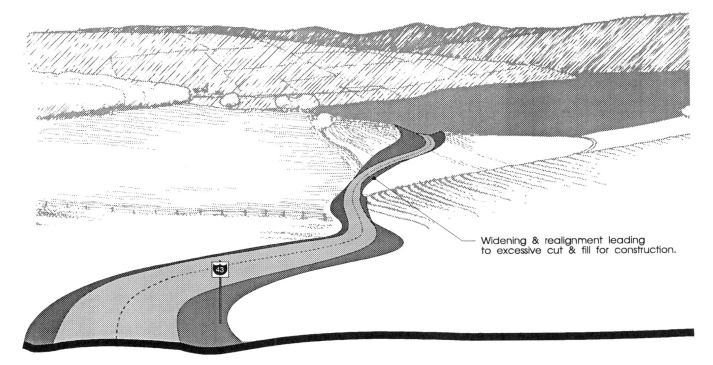

Widening & realignment leading
to excessive cut & fill for construction.

FIGURE 11.1   Generic landscape with new road in place. *Graphic credit: Scott Shannon*

statute or constitutional guarantee in question. Thus the Administrative Procedures Act grants standing to a person "aggrieved by an agency action within the meaning of the relevant statute" 5 U.S.C., s. 702 (1964) ed., Supp IV). That interest at times may reflect "aesthetic, conservational, and recreational" as well as economic values.[4]

In addition, the plaintiff must assert an injury to a value ("right," "concern," or "interest") that is within the zone of interest protected by law. Especially note that the Supreme Court has further elaborated that this value may be aesthetic, conservational, or recreational.[5]

STANDING RULE ANALYZED

The test for standing devised in the *Mineral King*[6] case may be legally and administratively desirable, but it causes some serious conceptual problems from an environmental aesthetics perspective. The standing test restated is that one who is "injured" "in fact" also had to prove "injury" by proof of "use" of the area in question.

The first conceptual dilemma is whether individuals have a stake in publicly owned resources, like Yosemite Valley or Mineral King Valley, even if they do not use these areas personally, that is, existence value. Was not the court in the *Mineral King* (*Sierra Club* v. *Hickle*) case really using a personal injury test for a "public" environment? The court's concept of "use," to some critics, caters to special interest groups who have caused problems in managing public areas by exerting an excessively unrepresentative influence on managing agencies. Thus the courts have limited the "user" who may claim "injury" to minority special interest groups, even though there may be a larger group (the American public) who may claim injury due to the degradation of the "public" resource and to future possibilities of experiencing the resource in a relatively undegraded state. With the advent of media exposure, through films and documentaries of publicly owned resources, the potential number of indirect public "users" has increased dramatically.

The second conceptual dilemma is that present standing requirements encourage tours, camping, and an unspecified number of uses of a landscape, which may potentially physically degrade the area and/or perceptually degrade it in the eyes of many existing and potential users. In order to have standing to preserve an

[4]Association of Data Proc. Serv. Org. Inc. v. Camp, 397 U.S. 150, 153–54 (1970).
[5]Sierra Club v. Hickle, 433 F.2d 24 (9th Cir. 1970). cert. granted, 401 U.S. 907 (1971); Sierra Club v. Morton, 401 U.S. 907 (1971), quoting Assoc. of Data Proc. Serv. Org. Inc. v. Camp.
[6]Sierra Club v. Hickle, 433 F.2d 24 (9th Cir. 1970). cert. granted, 401 U.S. 907 (1971).

area must we degrade the area? The actuality of this happening is minimal, but the logic is nevertheless disturbing.

Professor Stone's solution to these dilemmas is that natural objects themselves should have standing to sue on their own behalf and should have "rights" of their own. In his landmark paper, Stone (1972) outlined his arguments in detail. It should be noted as an important element in the sociology of law that this paper was purposefully and timely written to influence the Supreme Court justices in their review of *Mineral King* (Stone 1973, pp. xii–xv).

Stone points out that some natural objects and landscapes are treated differently under common law from other natural objects or landscapes. For instance, river, lakes, oceans, dunes, air, streams (surface and subterranean), and beaches are held in common trust under the "public trust doctrine"[7] for the public to have legal access to or enjoy certain uses of the area. These common trust resources are treated quite differently from natural objects on traditionally private land—for instance, a pond in a farmer's field or a stand of trees on a suburbanite's lawn. However, communal resources notwithstanding, Stone, (1973, p. 16) maintains:

None of the natural objects, whether held in common or situated on private land, has any of the three criteria of a rightholder. They have no standing in their own right, their unique damages do not count in determining outcome, and they are not beneficiaries of awards.

Stone laments that even when measures have been taken to conserve natural objects, it is for "our benefit" or "our use," an anthropocentric philosophy. He advocates that the environment gain recognition for its own injuries through use of a guardian appointed solely to represent its interests. Stone's arguments have ecological merit in their implications for the "rights" and "benefits" of the environment but do little directly for environmental aesthetics. The reason is that environmental aesthetic values are dependent upon the interaction of people with the environment, that is, we must feel it, see it, experience it, and so on. However, the argument does make sense if we think about how we would be better able to account for cumulative adverse effects (costs) on the environment if it were a holder of rights and could receive awards. Continuing this line of reasoning, suppose we were able to "buy," in some sense, cumulative "benefits" from the environment in the form of aesthetically pleasing experiences for "consumption" by present and future generations.

As Stone (1973) points out, "traditional legal institutions have a more difficult time 'catching' and confronting us with the social costs of our activities." This is why such innovative legal concepts as the "public trust doctrine" and "nature having rights of its own" are needed to enable the legal system to better address (some of the difficult environmental aesthetic valuation issues presented in this book). It is somewhat disheartening that we have not progressed beyond the level of Stone's thinking in 1972. There have been some uses of Stone's arguments though, the most famous application appearing in Justice Douglas's dissent to the Supreme Court decision on *Mineral King*:

The critical question of "standing" would be simplified and also put neatly into focus if we fashioned a federal rule that allowed environmental issues to be litigated before federal agencies or federal courts, in the name of the inanimate object about to be despoiled, defaced, or invaded by roads and bulldozers and where injury is subject to public outrage. Contemporary public concern for protecting nature's ecological equilibrium should lead to the conferral of standing upon environmental objects to sue for their own preservation. (See Stone, "Should Trees Have Standing? Toward Legal Rights for Natural Objects," 45 S.Cal. L. Rev. 450 (1972). This suit would therefore be more properly labeled as Mineral King v. Morton.

There are court cases where the environment has sued on its own behalf, for example, *Death Valley National Monument et al.* v. *the Department of the Interior.*[9] Aesthetic issues figured prominently in this case (Figure 11.2), in which disfigurement of desert landforms from mining activities is one of the major issues. Generally, however, individuals who can document "injury in fact" through actual use of a landscape affected by proposed projects is still required for standing to intervene on behalf of the environment.

FEDERAL AND STATE STATUTES GUIDING AESTHETIC PROJECT REVIEW

Probably the National Environmental Policy Act,[10] which affects federal agency actions and statewide mini-NEPA's, has had more potential for affecting aesthetic considerations than any other statute. NEPA acts as a wide-ranging net, catching many other appli-

---

[7]Public trust doctrine could be used to achieve environmental protection. See Gould v. Greylock Reservation Comm'n., 350 Mass. 410, 215 N.E.2d 114 (1966), discussed in Sax 1970.

[8]Sierra Club v. Morton, 405 U.S. 727, 741 (1972); J. Douglas, Dissenting opinion.

[9]Death Valley National Monument v. the Dept. of Interior. Civ. Action No. 76-401 (D.N.D. Cal. filed Feb. 26, 1976).

[10]42 U.S.C. s. 4321 et seq. (1988).

cable statutes when it assesses the environmental impacts of projects and activities. A federal agency not only has to comply with NEPA itself but with many other interconnected federal statutes as well as executive memoranda and federal regulations.

The language in NEPA incorporates aesthetic considerations. The act requires the "Federal government to use all practical means . . . to . . . assure all Americans safe, healthful, productive, and *aesthetically and culturally pleasing surroundings* . . . and to . . . preserve important historical, cultural, and natural aspects of our national heritage, and maintain, whenever possible, an environment which supports diversity and variety of individual choice" (emphasis added).[11] Furthermore to accomplish this, federal agencies are directed to "utilize a systematic, inter-disciplinary approach which will insure the integrated use of natural and social sciences and the *environmental design arts,* in planning and in decision making which may have an impact on man's environment" (emphasis added).[12]

Besides NEPA itself, the Council on Environmental Quality and individual agencies have regulations that furnish further direction. Most of these regulations produce little specific guidance for consideration of aesthetic effects, if they are mentioned at all. From the authors' own experience, most agency regulations are given minimal consideration by agency personnel or consultants because of their lack of specificity. Some federal agencies have developed their own methods to facilitate incorporation of aesthetics into their environmental impact assessments or statements as well as into general planning. Some of the leading agencies in this regard are the U.S.D.A., Forest Service (1973, 1974), U.S.D.O.T., Federal Highway Administration (1971, 1981), U.S.D.I., Bureau of Land Management (1975, 1980), U.S.D.A., Soil Conservation Service (1979), and the U.S. Corps of Engineers (Smardon et al. 1988). The U.S. Environmental Protection Agency (1979) and the U.S. Department of Energy (Jones et al. 1975) have sponsored research that may lead to assessment methods. The Stanford Research Institute's EPA report (Bagley et al. 1973) included an earlier review of

FIGURE 11.2 Mining activity in Death Valley National Monument. *Photo credit: National Park Service*

many agency procedures in relation to NEPA and aesthetics. A more recent review has been done by the co-author (Smardon 1986).

Some states have mini-NEPA's or statewide environmental quality/protection/policy acts. Many are similar to NEPA and include language that addresses consideration of aesthetics in impact assessment. State mini-NEPA's exist for the states of Arkansas,[13] California,[14] Connecticut,[15] Florida,[16] Hawaii,[17] Indiana,[18] Maryland,[19] Massachusetts,[20] Michigan,[21] Minne-

---

[11]Id., s. 4321.

[12]Id., s. 4322.

[13]Ark. Stat. Ann. ss. 8-1-101 (1987).

[14]California Environmental Quality Act, Cal. Pub. Res. Code s. 21000 et seq. (West 1982).

[15]Connecticut Environmental Review Process, Conn. Gen. Stat. Ann. ss. 22a-14 to 22a-20 (West Supp. 1974–1975).

[16]Florida Environmental Land and Management Act of 1972, Fla. Stat. ss. 380.92 et seq.

[17]Hawaii Rev. Stat. ss. 343-1 to 343-8 (1985).

[18]Indiana's Environmental Policy Act, Ind. Code Ann. ss. 13-1-10-1 to 13-1-10-8 (West 1987).

[19]Maryland Environmental Policy Act of 1973, Md. Nat. Res. Code Ann. ss. 1-3001 to 1-3005 (1983 Ann. Supp. 1987).

[20]Massachusetts Environmental Policy Act, Mass. Ann. Laws ss. 61-62H (Law Co-op 1986).

[21]Michigan Executive Order 1974-4.

sota,[22] Montana,[23] New Jersey,[24] New York,[25] North Carolina,[26] Puerto Rico,[27] South Dakota,[28] Virginia,[29] Utah,[30] Washington,[31] and Wisconsin.[32] City NEPA's exist for Bowie, Maryland,[33] and New York City.[34] Specialized or limited EIS project review requirements include the Delaware Coastal Zone Act,[35] a Georgia statute for highway project review,[36] a Kentucky statute for power plant review,[37] a Nevada statute for power line review,[38] and the New Jersey Coastal Area Facility Review Act.[39] Vermont has had considerable experience with Act 250,[40] which calls for review of large development projects and includes a specific criterion for aesthetics. Maine is in the process of developing aesthetic guidelines for their site location law[41] for large development review.

Meeting Legal Issues — The National Environmental Policy Act

A few NEPA cases have dealt with substantive aesthetic issues. One such case was *Public Service Company of New Hampshire* v. *NRC*.[42] In this case, the NRC had placed the condition for the Seabrook nuclear power plant's permits on the rerouting of power transmission lines around the Pow Wow Cedar Swamp (the utility's proposed route was right through the swamp). NRC justified the rerouting condition in the permit under NEPA because transmission lines through the swamp would cause significant environmental damage to increasingly scarce and valuable stands of Atlantic white cedar, and to the wildlife habitat of this important river-marsh ecosystem. NRC also determined that the 200-foot-high steel lattice work towers would constitute a "visual insult" to the relatively pristine area; and that practical alternative routes existed. Citing NEPA Section 101(b), the court held that: "Once having found that the Commission has jurisdiction over the transmission lines, we think it clear that, under the dictates of NEPA, it was obliged to minimize adverse environmental impact flowing therefrom."[43] This is significant in that aesthetic issues were directly addressed, and that it was recognized that ancillary parts of projects, such as transmission-line impacts, need to be addressed and mitigated as well.

Under NEPA, court decisions concerning the obligation of federal agencies to evaluate the visual beauty impact of their projects have ranged from requiring thorough consideration[44] to flat statements such as "aesthetic considerations alone may (not) be used as a basis for requiring an [environmental impact statement]."[45] A fairly recent case illustrates some of the typical problems. In *River Road Alliance, Inc.* v. *Corps of Engineers*[46] the plaintiff attempted to compel the

[22]Minnesota Environmental Policy Act, Minn. Stat., Ann. ss. 116D.01 to 07 (West 1977 and Supp. 1981).

[23]Montana's Environmental Policy Act of 1971, Mont. Code ss. 75-1-101 to 75-1-105; 75-1-201 (1981).

[24]New Jersey's Exec. Order No. 53 (1973).

[25]New York State Environmental Quality Review Act, NY Envtl. Conserv. Law ss. 8-0101 to 8-0117 (McKinney 1984).

[26]North Carolina Environmental Policy Act of 1971, N.C. Gen. Stat. ss. 113A-1 to 10 (1978).

[27]Puerto Rico's Environmental Policy Act, Law No. 9 of June 18, 1970, PR Laws Ann. Title 12 ss. 1121-1127.

[28]South Dakota Environmental Policy Act of 1974, S.D. Codified Laws Ann. ss. 34A-9-1 to 34A-9-12.

[29]Virginia Environmental Quality Act of 1973, Va. Code ss. 10-17.107 to 10-17.112.

[30]State of Utah Exec. Order (Aug 27, 1974).

[31]Washington's State Environmental Policy Act of 1971, Wash. Code ss. 43.21C.010-43.21C.910 (1974); Wash. Adm. Code R.197-11.

[32]Wisconsin Environmental Policy Act of 1971, Wis. Stat. s. 1.11 (1971, Supp. 1981-1982).

[33]Bowie, Maryland, Env. Policy and Impact Statement Ordinance (1971).

[34]New York City Executive Order No. 91, June 1, 1977.

[35]Delaware Ch. 175, vol. 58, Laws of Delaware (June 28, 1971).

[36]Ga. L. 1972-179 (March 10, 1972), Ga. Code Ann. Ch. 95A-1.

[37]Ch. 278.025 Ky. Rev. Stats. (April 1, 1979).

[38]Nevada Ch. 311, Laws of 1971, 58 N.R.S. Ch. 704 (1971).

[39]New Jersey Ch. 85 (1973) N.J.S.A. 13: 19-1 et seq. (Cam. Supp. 1974-1975).

[40]Vt. Act 250, Title 10, Ch. 151.

[41]Maine Stat. Title 38, s. 481 et seq.

[42]582 F.2d 77 (1st Cir. 1978).

[43]Id. at 85.

[44]Ely v. Velde, 451 F.2d 1130, 1134 (4th Cir. 1971).

[45]City of Columbia v. Solomon, 13 Env't. Rep. Cas. (BNA) 1301, 1307 (1979).

[46]764 F.2d 445 (7th Cir. 1985), cert. denied, 475 U.S. 1055 (1986).

U.S. Army Corps of Engineers to prepare an environmental impact statement (EIS) in connection with the grant of a permit to construct a barge fleeting facility, or "maritime parking lot," along the Illinois shore of the Mississippi River north of St. Louis. The Corps conceded that the proposed site and surrounding area "clearly provide some of the most impressive and unique vistas of any area along the Mississippi River."[47] Opponents of the project wanted a full EIS prepared and not just an environmental assessment, but the judge found that the costs of preparing the impact statement would outweigh its benefits because "aesthetic values do not lend themselves to measurement or elaborate analysis."[48] In addition to obviously ignoring specific provisions of NEPA, the judge felt that aesthetics was subjective to the perceiver, not subject to rigorous analysis and, as Linder (1990) has suggested, the judge did not feel it was a weighty enough issue to merit preparation of a full EIS. The situation is ironic because at the time this case was in court, the author was developing an elaborate visual impact analysis methodology for the U.S. Corps of Engineers (Smardon et al. 1988). This is a sad commentary on interpretation of acts such as NEPA when judges use their own biases to prejudge substantive issues without knowledge that methods of aesthetic analysis do exist.

LEGAL REQUIREMENTS: SECTION 4(f) LANDS

The Federal Highway Administration (FHWA) has provided much of the funding to states for construction of interstate, primary, and secondary roads, using different cost-sharing formulas. As part of this process, FHWA has had to respond to a number of federal environmental legislative mandates.

The Federal-Aid Highway Act of 1966[49] which contains Section 4(f) of the 1966 Department of Transportation Act[50] in conjunction with the National Environmental Policy Act[51] provide that no highway project requiring the use of publicly owned land from parks, recreation areas, and wildlife and waterfowl refuges, or any land from historical sites of national, state, or local significance, (called section 4(f) lands) can be approved unless there are no feasible and prudent alternatives to use of such land, and unless all possible planning to minimize harm to such land is taken.

Under federal law, any transportation project that requires the use of "Section 4(f) lands" must undergo a stringent review procedure, provided the lands affected or used are significant in the opinion of the officials having jurisdiction over them. A letter is sent by the project-initiating agency to officials having jurisdiction over these areas, requesting the information necessary to start a formal review process.

The Section 4(f) report will be included as part of the draft EIS required by the EPA. The combined EIS/Section 4(f) statement will then be circulated to appropriate public agencies and private groups for comment. Following the public hearing on the various transportation alternatives, one will be selected for implementation, and a final EIS/Section 4(f) statement will be prepared that responds to all comments received on the draft report and at the public hearing.

Some 4(f) statements were required before NEPA was implemented and set some major precedents in terms of aesthetic impact review of transportation projects. After NEPA, Section 4(f) areas combined with housing relocation had major impacts on the feasibility of highway projects in general, especially in urban areas.

In addition to the statement of significance, those preparing the 4(f) statement must contribute enough information about the area in question to permit those not acquainted with the project to understand the relationship between the proposed facility and the 4(f) area and the extent of impact. In the case of a highway, the federal Department of Transportation requires at minimum the following information:

1. Size (acres or square feet) and location (maps or other exhibits such as photographs, slides, and sketches, as appropriate).
2. Type (recreation, historic, etc.).
3. Available activities (fishing, swimming, golf, etc.).
4. Facilities existing and planned (description and location of ball diamonds, tennis courts, etc.).
5. Usage (approximate number of users for each activity if such figures are available).
6. Patronage (local, regional, and national).
7. Relationship to other similarly used lands in the vicinity.
8. Access (both pedestrian and vehicular).
9. Ownership (city, county, state, etc.).
10. If applicable, deed restrictions or reversionary clauses.
11. The determination of significance by the federal,

---

[47]Id. at 447.
[48]Id. at 451.
[49]23 U.S.C. s. 138 (1988).
[50]49 U.S.C. s. 1653 (f) (1988).
[51]42 U.S.C. s. 4321 et seq. (1988).

state, or local officials having jurisdiction of the Section 4(f) land.

12. Unusual characteristics of the Section 4(f) land (flooding problems, terrain conditions, or other features that either reduce or enhance the value of portions of the area).

13. Consistency of location, type of activity, and use of the Section 4(f) land with community goals, objectives, and land use planning.

14. If applicable, prior use of state or federal funds for acquisition or development of the Section 4(f) land.

Also required is a description of the manner in which the highway will affect the Section 4(f) land, such as:

1. The location and amount of land (acres or square feet) to be used by the highway.

2. A detailed map or drawing of sufficient scale to discern the essential elements of the highway/Section 4(f) land involvement.

3. The facilities affected.

4. The probable increase or decrease in physical effects on the Section 4(f) land users (noise, fumes, etc.).

5. The effect upon pedestrian and vehicular access to the section 4(f) land.

Another requirement is a specific statement (with supporting reasons) that no feasible and prudent alternative is available as well as information to demonstrate that all possible planning to minimize harm is or will be included in the highway proposal. Such information should include:

1. The agency responsible for furnishing the highway right-of-way.

2. Provisions for compensating or replacing the Section 4(f) land and improvements thereon, including the status of any agreements. (Include agreed-upon compensation, replacement acreages, and type land, etc. when known.)

3. Highway design features developed to enhance the Section 4(f) land or to lessen or eliminate adverse effects (improving or restoring existing pedestrian or vehicular access, landscaping, esthetic treatment, etc.).

4. Coordination of highway construction to permit orderly transition and continual usage of Section 4(f) land facilities (new facilities constructed and available for use prior to demolishing existing facilities, moving of facilities during off-season, etc.).

The most important Section 4(f) case was *Citizens to Preserve Overton Park* v. *Volpe,*[52] in which the district court granted a motion for summary judgment in favor of the defendants. The question raised in this case was whether the district court should have made its decision on the basis of the administrative record rather than affidavits as it did. Stated another way, can the court find that the Secretary of Transportation was not arbitrary and capricious in determining that there was no other "feasible and prudent alternative" route than the one through the park without reviewing the administrative record upon which that decision was based? The Federal-Aid Highway Act provides:

It is hereby declared to be the national policy that special effort should be made to preserve that natural beauty of the countryside and public park and recreation lands, wildlife and waterfowl refuges, and historic sites. The Secretary of Transportation shall cooperate and consult with the Secretaries of the Interior, Housing and Urban Development, and Agriculture, and with the states in developing transportation plans and programs *that include measures to maintain or enhance the natural beauty for the lands traversed.* After the effective date of the Federal-Aid Highway Act of 1968, the Secretary shall not approve any program or project which requires the use of any publicly owned land from a public park, recreation area, or wildlife and waterfowl refuge of national, state, or local officials having jurisdiction thereof, or any land from an historic site of national, state or local significance as so determined by such officials unless (1) there is no feasible and prudent alternative to use of such land, and (2) such program includes all possible planning to minimize harm to such park, recreational area, wildlife and waterfowl refuge or historic site resulting from such use.[53] (Emphasis added.)

The Supreme Court indicated unusual interest in this case by allowing oral argument on petitioner's request for a stay, which was granted. Right-of-way acquisition was authorized in 1967 prior to the passage of 23 U.S.C s. 138, and most of it was purchased and cleared. The city of Memphis was paid $2 million for the 26 acres of needed parkland, and $1 million has been invested to acquire a 160-acre golf course. The highway was not built.

In *San Antonio Conservation Society* v. *Texas Highway Department, Volpe et al.,*[54] a case factually similar to *Overton Park,* the state of Texas contended it has the right to proceed with construction of the project in the face of a Supreme Court stay order. Since the states own, build, and maintain the roads, and the federal government only participates in the cost of construction, the question arises: Can a state choose to proceed with

---

[52]309 F. Supp. 1189 (W.D. Tenn., 1970) aff'd. 432 F.2d 1307 (1970) rev. 401 U.S. 402 (1971).
[53]23 U.S.C. s. 138. (1988).
[54]446 F.2d. 1013 (1971).

the project utilizing only state money and thereby avoid federal requirements?

This question was substantially answered in a California case, *La Raza Unida* v. *Volpe*,[55] which involved the construction of the Foothills Freeway. California highway officials had failed to comply with the NEPA, DOT, and Federal-Aid Highway acts. The court held that the highway project had become subject to federal law at the time the DOT approved the location design for the highway. Federal involvement was deemed to commence even prior to any DOT authorization for federal funding, the event that was considered critical in *Conservation Society*.[56] The *La Raza* court stated:

[C]ommon sense dictates that the federal protective devices apply before federal funds were sought. It does little good to shut the barn doors after all the horses have run away. If the federal statutes and regulations are to supply any protection at all it must be prior to the time the residents have left and the deleterious effects to the environment have taken place. All the protections that congress sought to establish would be futile gestures were a state able to ignore the spirit (and letter) of the various acts and regulations until it actually received federal funds.[57]

One other Section 4(f) case that the co-author was involved with set a major substantive threshold for adequacy of 4(f) analysis. In the *Louisiana Environmental Society* v. *Claude Brinegar*,[58] the federal appeals court told the district court and defendents that "appropriate analysis of equivalent magnitude to potential harm" needed to be done as part of the 4(f) statement.

LEGAL ISSUES: STATE AND MINI-NEPA'S AND PROJECT REVIEW

At least one case under a state mini-NEPA statute dealt specifically with aesthetics. In *Urban Council on Mobility* v. *Minnesota DNR*[59] substantial evidence supported the determination that the highway route selected was superior to routing the highway across a lake because the selected route would have less of an impact on water quality, wildlife habitat, aesthetics, and area quietude.

No state has struggled more consistently with the issues of defining aesthetic standards for project development review than Vermont (Figure 11.3). Beginning in 1971, Criterion 8 of Act 250[60] required that in the review of proposed developments subject to its regula-

FIGURE 11.3   Typical Vermont landscape near Queechee, Vermont. *Photo credit: R. C. Smardon*

tions, a district commission or the state environmental board must make a finding that a proposed development "will not have an undue adverse effect on the scenic or natural beauty of the area, aesthetics, historic sites or rare or irreplaceable natural areas."[61] The state is still being assaulted by development, and there is a current effort to prepare proposed guidelines for interpretation of Criterion 8 (Williams et al. 1990).

Section 6042 of the "Capability and Development Plan" adopted by the legislature to implement Act 250 spells out legislative intent in more detail:

6042. Capability and Development Plan
(2) UTILIZATION OF NATURAL RESOURCES
Products of the land are the stone and minerals under the land, as well as the beauty of our landscape are principal natural resources of the state. Preservation of the agricultural and forest productivity of the land, and the economic viability of agricultural units, conversation of the recreation opportunity afforded by the state's non-renewable earth and mineral reserves, and protection of the beauty of the landscape are matters of public good. Uses which threaten or significantly inhibit these resources should be permitted only when the public interest is clearly benefited hereby.

.   .   .

(4) PLANNING FOR GROWTH
(B) Provision should be made for the renovation of village and town centers for commercial and industrial

[55]337 F. Supp. 221 (1971).

[56]446 F.2d 1013 (1971).

[57]337 F. Supp. at 221, 231 (1971).

[58]Louisana Environmental Society, Inc. v. Brinegar, 513 F. Supp. 179 (W.D. La. 1981).

[59]289 N.W.2d 729 (1980).

[60]Vt. Act 250, Title 10, Ch. 151.

[61]Id.

development, where feasible, and location of residential and other development off the main highways near the village center on land which is other than primary agricultural soil.

. . .

(12) SCENIC RESOURCES

The use and development of lands and waters should not significantly detract from recognized scenic resources including river corridors, scenic highways and roads, and scenic views. Accordingly, conditions may be imposed on development in order to control unreasonable or unnecessary adverse effects upon scenic resources.

The Vermont Environmental Board's summary of the legislative charge also provides guidance to the effort of developing guidelines for Criterion 8:

The term *undue* generally means that which is more than necessary — exceeding what is appropriate or normal. The word *adverse* means unfavorable, opposed, hostile. Scenic and natural beauty pertain to the pleasing qualities that emanate from nature and the Vermont landscape. In short, through Criterion 8 the legislature has directed that no project within our jurisdiction be approved if it has an unnecessary or inappropriate negative impact on the enjoyment of surrounding and scenic qualities[62] (emphasis added).

The terms *"adverse"* and *"undue"* are further spelled out by the board via the *Queechee* decision.[63] The process outlined in the *Queechee* decision requires that reviewers determine first if a proposed project has any adverse effects. In the words of the board, "will the proposed project be in harmony with its surroundings — will it fit the context within which it will be located?"[64] If there are indeed efforts to determine if the impact is adverse, then it must be determined whether or not the adverse impact is "undue." Not all adverse effects are undue. Any of three conditions may make the adverse effects of a proposed project undue: (1) violation of an expressed community standard regarding aesthetics, (2) effects that are potentially "offensive or shocking to the sensitivities of the average person," and (3) failure to reasonably mitigate adverse effects.

Five areas of questioning were identified by the board in an effort to determine if effects of the *Quee-chee* proposal were adverse. They are in brief:

FIGURE 11.4   Typical coastal Maine landscape. *Photo credit: R. C. Smardon*

1. What is the nature of the project's surroundings?
2. Is the project's design compatible with its surroundings?
3. Are the colors and materials selected for the project suitable for the context within which the project will be located?
4. Where can the project be seen from? and
5. What is the project's impact on open space in the area?[65]

Based on initial guidance and the *Queechee* regulatory decision, a design issues study committee, under the direction of Professor Norman Williams, is currently developing a evaluative process and guidelines for aesthetic review of projects under Vermont's Act 250.

Another ongoing struggle for clarification of aesthetic standards relates to Maine's Site Location of Development Law.[66] As part of the review process for large new developments (Figure 11.4), the Maine Department of Environmental Protection regulations contain a section on "No unreasonable effect on scenic character." The preamble to this section states: "The board considers scenic character to be one of Maine's most important assets. The Board also feels that visual surroundings strongly influence people's behavior."[67]

The key part of the regulations is the scope of review:

In determining whether the proposed development will have an unreasonable effect on the scenic character of the surrounding area, the Board shall consider all relevant evidence to that effect, such as evidence that:

[62]Brattleboro Chalet Motor Lodge, Inc. Land Use Permit Application # 4C0581-EB, issued Oct. 17, 1984.

[63]Queechee Lakes Corporation, Findings of Fact, Conclusion of Law and Order, Land Use Permit Applications # 3WO411-EB and #3WO439-EB, issued Nov. 4, 1985.

[64]Id., p. 18.

[65]Id.

[66]Me. Stat., Title 38, s. 481 et seq.

[67]Maine Board of Environmental Protection.

1. The design of the proposed development takes into account the scenic character of the surrounding area.
2. A development which is not in keeping with the surrounding scenic character will be located, designed and landscaped to minimize its visual impact to the fullest extent possible.
3. Structures will be designed and landscaped to minimize their visual impact on the surrounding area.[68]

The rest of the regulations contain guidelines for landscaping, parking lots, and planting specifications.

The co-author, Smardon, with Dr. James Palmer gave a informational legislative briefing to a group charged with studying the issue of developing more detailed guidelines in 1989. In 1990 there was a suit pending, *Diamond Cove Association* v. *Board of Environmental Protection et al.,*[69] which challenged among other things, the scenic impact provision of the site law as an unconstitutional delegation of authority and as unconstitutionally vague as applied.

As can be seen from the definitional struggles for Vermont's Act 250 and the Maine's Site Location and Development Law standards and guidance for aesthetic impact project review for such programs and legislation will continue to be debated at the State level.

VISUAL/AESTHETIC IMPACT ASSESSMENT: THE STATE-OF-THE-ART

We have NEPA, mini-NEPA's, Section 4(f)'s, and development review statutes. The question is: What type of aesthetic analyses have been done, and of what quality? Project site-scale studies have attempted to assess the detailed visual impact of project alternatives in environmental assessments, environmental impact statements, or in other similar studies that include visual impact mitigation. Rarely is any other aesthetic sense than visual dealt with in such studies. The co-authors have examined more than fifty projects in the United States, Australia, Canada, and the United Kingdom.

Project types for which detailed visual impact studies have been done include: coal strip mines, hard rock quarries, oil and gas development, oil pipelines and pumping stations, nuclear and conventional fossil-fueled power plants, refuse-burning power plants, windpower generators, electric power transmission lines, dams and reservoirs, flood control alternatives, coastal structures and dredging, mountaintop observatory, ski area development, highway development, urban development, port development, and industrial redevelopment. This is a limited sample of detailed visual impact assessment reports that have appeared in the literature and are executed mainly by private firms.

TABLE 11.1   Proportion of EIS's by Federal Agency Considering Visual/Aesthetic Impacts. Source: John Wiley and Sons

Agency	Number of EIS's
U.S. Army Corps of Engineers	77 (80%)
U.S. Department of Agriculture	
Forest Service	2
Soil Conservation Service	2
U.S. Department of Energy	
Federal Power Commission	3
Tennessee Valley Authority	1
U.S. Department of Interior	
Bureau of Land Management (OCS)	2
Bureau of Outdoor Recreation	1
Bureau of Reclamation	5
Environmental Protection Agency	2
Ohio River Basin Commission	1
Total	96

A content analysis of ninety-six EIS abstracts from the *Water Resource Abstracts* from 1968 to 1977 was done to see the types of aesthetic impacts identified, whether alternatives were considered, and whether measures to minimize harm were considered. The basic results of this analysis can be seen in Tables 11.1 and 11.2. The majority of the EIS's were done by the Corps of Engineers, which is not surprising since *Water Resources Abstracts* would key into water resource projects. Fifty-eight percent of EIS's described adverse aesthetic impacts. The degree of adversity generally increases as you read down Table 11.2. However, the vague and general terms used to describe visual impacts in most cases made judgment almost impossible in regard to severity of visual impact. The reader should also note that very few EIS's considered visual quality alternatives or detailed measures to minimize harm. Note that the three major types of adverse visual impacts encountered in these EIS's were: (1) unnatural intrusion of man-made appearance of disfigurement, or the general criterion of naturalness in relation to context; (2) partial degradation, reduction, or impairment of the existing level of visual quality; and (3) the complete loss of the visual resource, whether a natural stream, marsh, stand of trees, and so forth.

What can be seen from this analysis and other reports (Andrews and Waits 1978) is that, procedurally, visual considerations as treated in EIS's have rarely met the requirements as stated in NEPA and CEQ (Council of Environmental Quality) regulations. Thus, the treatment of visual and aesthetic considerations has not advanced, with a few notable exceptions in cer-

---

[68]Id.
[69]Law Docket No. KEN-90-567 Maine Sup. Ct. (1990).

TABLE 11.2   Treatment of Aesthetic Impacts. Source: John Wiley and Sons

		Actual #	% of EIS's Sampled
I. Identification of Impacts			
Enchancement of Aesthetics			
Environment unspecified		1	
Improved view		1	
Improved aesthetic appeal/improvement in aesthetic conditions/elimination of unsightliness/increase in recreational potential		12	15%
	Subtotal	14	15%
Adverse Effects on Aesthetics			
Adverse effects unspecified		2	
Temporary/short term		6	
Partial degradation/impairment		14	
Unnatural intrusion/man-made appearance/disfigurement		15	
Unsightliness		3	
Scale incompatibility		1	
Restriction of views		2	
Complete loss of resource		10	
Long-term irreversible effect		2	
Unavoidable adverse effect		2	
	Subtotal	57	58%
II. Consideration of visual alternatives/design treatments		4	
III. Consideration of measures to minimize harm		8	
	Subtotal	12	13%

tain EIS's and environmental assessments. The most notable exceptions in advanced state-of-the-art assessments often utilize different forms of visual simulation in order to better understand the visual aesthetic impacts for professional analysis and to better communicate these visual impacts to affected publics.

Development of Visual Resource Management (VRM) Systems

VRM is generally used in analyses and decisions about utilization of the publicly owned land areas, permitting activities to take place on the public landscape, and whether publicly financed activities should take place on private lands. VRM procedures generally facilitate the integration of scenic and/or visual values into the decision-making process, to be considered along with many other resource values. Visual or scenic resource values are rarely the major determining values in environmental decision-making but are becoming increasingly significant in some cases (Smardon 1984). As one can surmise, most of the activity regarding visual resource management is concerned with federal agency activities and management of federal lands. This emphasis is directly attributable to legal activity addressing the adequacy of environmental resource decision-making.

The need for development of VRM systems can be traced to certain public concern with aesthetic and environmental issues related to specific land management activities, for example, wilderness designation (as reviewed in Chapter 9), timber harvesting and strip mining practices (to be covered on Chapters 12 and 13), highway funding and construction (the 4(f) issues covered earlier in this chapter), park maintenance, and so forth. This concern is exemplified by several major federal court cases (see Table 11.3) in the last twenty-five years (Smardon 1982 and 1984). It is also exemplified by several major pieces of environmental legislation that call for explicit consideration of aesthetic or visual resources as part of environmental decision-making. (See Chapters 9–13 and Smardon 1982.)

Development of VRM systems have occurred only recently for five federal agencies in the United States. In fact, most developmental work was done in the 1970s and 1980s. Generally these systems were developed quite rapidly with little time for in-house research to meet multiple-resource management decision needs. However, incorporation of aesthetics into agency decision-making processes was often enthusiastically supported by key agency administrators (Smardon 1982 and 1986).

VRM systems were developed by federal agencies to deal with three classes of problems: (1) visual inventory and analysis systems for large areas needing landscape planning; (2) systems for scoping of potential visual impact or determining thresholds; and (3) systems for detailed evaluation of visual impact.

TABLE 11.3   Major Court Cases and Hearings Involving Aesthetic Issues. Source: John Wiley and Sons

Common Name	Legal Citation
Old Man in the Mountain, New Hampshire Highway Project	Soc. for the Protec. of N. H. Forests v. Brinegar. 394 F. Supp. 105 (1975)
Scenic Hudson, New York; Proposed Pumped Storage Power Plant	354 F.2d 608 (2nd Cir. 1965) Cert. denied 384 U.S. (1966)
Mineral King, California; Proposed Ski Resort	Sierra Club v. Morton 405 U.S. 727 (1972)
Rainbow Bridge; Reservoir	Friends of the Earth v. Armstrong 485 F.2d 1 (10th Cir. 1973)
Walton v. St. Clair Minnesota; Boundary Waters Canoe Area: Mining Activity	Walton v. St. Clair 313 F.Supp. 1312 (1970)
East Meadow Creek; Colorado Timber Cutting Activity	Parker v. U.S. 448 F.2d 793 (1971) Cert. denied 92 S. Ct. 1252 (1971)
Overton Park, Tennessee; Highway Project	Citizens to Preserve Overton Park v. Volpe 401 U.S. 402 (1971)
Death Valley Monument, California; Proposed Mining Activity	Death Valley National Monument v. Dept. of the Interior. Civ. Act. No. 76-401 (D.N.D. Cal. filed Feb. 26, 1976)
Ice Age National Monument, Wisconsin; Proposed Power Line	Wisconsin Public Service Commission (PSCW) 1977. Hearing record of case 6680-CE-13 and Wisconsin; Public Service Comm. Findings of fact & order. Case 6680-CE-13
Ogunquit, Maine; Dune Reconstruction	Ogunquit Village Corp. v. Davis. C.A. 76-1426 (First Cir. April 26, 1977).
Cross Lake, Louisiana I-220 Highway Bridge	Louisiana Environmental Society, Inc. v. Brinegar; U.S. Dept. of Transportation and Dept. of Highways, State of Louisiana, Civ. A. No. 17, 233 U.S. Dist. Ct., Western District of Louisiana, April 9, 1981
Santa Barbara Oil Spill; California	County of Santa Barbara v. Hickel Civil No. 69-636 D.C. Cal., filed April 14, 1969

TABLE 11.3   Major Court Cases and Hearings Involving Aesthetic Issues. Source: John Wiley and Sons (Continued)

Common Name	Legal Citation
Hells Canyon Dams. Washington, Idaho, Oregon; Proposed Dams and Reservoirs	Presiding Examiners Initial Decision on Remand, in Pacific Northwest Power Company, Project No. 2243 and Washington Public Power Supply System Project No. 2273, 1 E.L.R. 30017
Dept. of Ecology. Private Shoreline Development	Dept. of Ecology v. Pacesetter Construction Co. 571 P.2d. 196 (1977)
McCormick Oseetah Lake New York; Private Shoreline Development	McCormick *et al.* v. Lawrence 83 Misc.2d 64, 72 N.Y.S.2d 156, App. Div. 54 A.D.2d 153, 387 N.Y.S.2d 919 (1975)
Miners Ridge Case Washington; Glacier Peak Wilderness; Proposed Mining	
Grand Central Terminal; Proposed Highrise	Penn Central Transportation Co. v. New York City 438 U.S. 124 (1978)
Green County Nuclear Power Plant	

VRM Methods for Landscape Planning

VRM systems were utilized within the Forest Service (1973, 1974) and the Bureau of Land Management (1980) as part of broad regional planning and assessment. In the Forest Service, these exercises are known as regional guides and are prepared as part of the Resources Planning Assessment Act of 1974.[70] Regional assessments for BLM were either for special uses, for example, energy development in the state of North Dakota (USDI, BLM and ND 1978), or special areas, for example, the Desert Conservation Area Plan, which covers the southwestern one-third of California.

VRM was utilized forestwide for the preparation of ten-year timber management plans for the Forest Service. These plans were multiple-resource plans that arrayed the major resource groups against different goals of timber output from the forest. Timber management plans are supposed to (but do not always) interface with land use planning for specific geographic subareas of national forests. The VRM practitioners prepared their own visual inventory evaluations, sensitivity

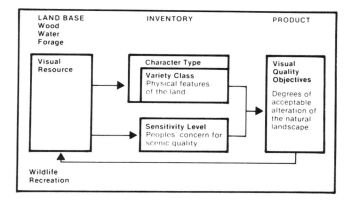

FIGURE 11.5   USFS Visual Management System. *Source: John Wiley and Sons*

analyses, and visual management objectives for these specific land areas (see Figure 11.5). Decisions concerning development and maintenance of the visual management objectives were worked out by an interdisciplinary land use planning team of which the VRM

[70]Forest and Rangeland Renewable Resources Planning Act of 1974, 16 U.S.C. s. 1601 et. seq. (1988).

practitioner was a member. The ultimate decision regarding visual management objectives rests with the forest ranger or a forest supervisor, depending on the scale of land area involved. Forest Service VRM practitioners also do visual corridor analyses for roads and visual absorption capability analyses for visual impacts for a range of activities.

BLM, like the Forest Service, is heavily involved with permit-processing activity to determine whether private parties should be allowed to do many different kinds of activities on federal lands. These activities include timber harvesting, vegetation conversion, recreational activities, water resource development, energy development and mining activity, agriculture, and range-related activities. For each permit action, both the Forest Service and the BLM need to check the existing visual quality or management objective of the site in question (see Figure 11.6) and do a visual impact analysis via an environmental assessment. A full environmental impact assessment may be needed if the project may cause significant environmental impact or is controversial. Even after the visual impact assessment work is done, visual mitigation work may have to be done to remedy the severity of visual impact. This is the range of situations in which the Forest Service and BLM would use VRM.

The U.S.D.A. Soil Conservation Service (1979) uses its landscape management system (LMS) on a similar geographic range of project scales, from very large to very small, but the activity types are much more restrictive. The landscape resource management system is used for water resource planning projects under the Small Watershed Development Projects Act of 1966,[71] or for local agricultural or soil conservation projects sponsored by a local conservation district. The LMS is used to identify visual resources of a land area that may be affected by planning alternatives, or those areas that need to be considered in an environmental assessment or environmental impact statement. These identified high-priority areas would then be analyzed by a landscape architect.

The U.S. Corps of Engineers has recently developed a visual resources assessment procedure (Smardon et al. 1988). VRAP includes a management classification system (Figure 11.7) that is utilized to map and classify large landscape areas by their inherent characteristics. Such a system would be used for broad brush studies, called reconnaisance studies, that the Corps often does initially, or for management of existing Corps reservoirs and other facilities. As part of VRAP each landscape area or zone ends up with a management objective similar to the Forest Service or the Bureau of Land Management.

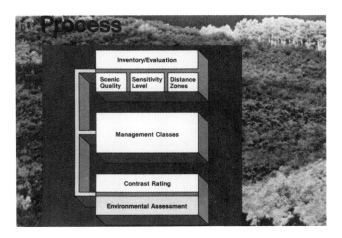

FIGURE 11.6 BLM Visual Resource Management. *Source: John Wiley and Sons*

Scoping the Visual Impact Assessment

A scoping approach is intended to help agency personnel identify visual effects, if any, that are likely to be significant on a particular project. This identification was intended to help determine the scope of visual impact assessments under NEPA as well as state mini-NEPA's and to suggest appropriate mitigation measures for study.

CEQ Regulations and Scoping

In 1983 revised regulations were issued for the implementation of NEPA by the Council for Environmental Quality (CEQ).[72] These are designed to increase the usefulness of environmental analysis in project decision-making as well as to reduce the paperwork and delays sometimes associated with the preparation and review of EIS's.

The regulations employ several means to achieve these purposes. The statute limits preparation of a full EIS to projects that are likely to have significant environmental effects. If the significance of a project's environmental effects is in doubt, agencies can perform a brief environmental assessment to determine whether a finding of no significant impact (FONSI) can be issued or a full EIS is needed. The regulations also allow agencies to establish categorical exclusions for actions that do not require environmental review except under extraordinary circumstances.

Another set of measures governs EIS preparation. Every EIS is to be "concise, clear and to the point." To this end, "there shall be an early and open process for determining the scope of issues to be addressed and for identifying the significant issues related to the pro-

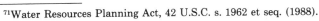

[71]Water Resources Planning Act, 42 U.S.C. s. 1962 et seq. (1988).
[72]40 C.F.R. § 1500 et. seq. (1991).

MANAGEMENT CLASSIFICATION SYSTEM

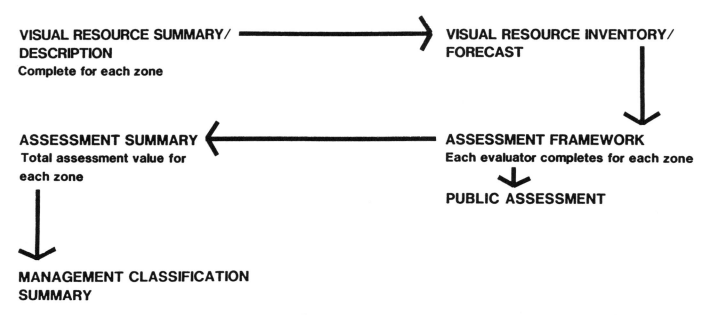

FIGURE 11.7   Corps of Engineers Visual Classification System

posed action. This process shall be termed scoping"
(CEQ 1979, p. 763).

A similar consideration applies to mini-NEPA's as
well. The following section outlines New York State's
visual scoping process under the state's Environmental
Quality Review Act. New York has one of the most
comprehensive scoping approaches of all the states,
and the basic forms and processes are broadly
applicable.

New York's State Environmental Quality Review Act: Visual Scoping Process

The New York State Environmental Quality Review
Act (SEQR) process calls for an EIS when an action
may have a significant effect on the environment. The
visual aspects of the environment, both manmade and
natural, are an important resource value. It is commonly held that determining significance based on aesthetic values is hopelessly subjective. Thus, one is dis-
couraged from addressing the visual resource when
considering potential environmental effects.

The following regulatory guidelines offer a model
process by which to preserve and enhance the visual resources of a community. The process is flexible, recognizing the inherent diversity in community values
across the state. The process provides simplified, practical tools for a lay person to evaluate potential visual
impacts and make a defensible determination of significance under SEQR. There are three basic stages:

Stage 1: *Conduct an inventory of visual resources* to establish or clarify community values, policies, and
priorities related to existing visual resources *before*
controversial projects arise.

Stage 2: *Establish practical visual criteria* to guide decisions related to the undertaking, funding, or approval of future projects.

Stage 3: *Use the visual–environmental assessment
form addendum* to supplement SEQR's full Environmental Assessment Form (EAF) and focus on a
project's potential visual impacts. Such impacts may
require preparation of a draft EIS. The form is an
orderly method that can be used to support a determination of nonsignificance.

Stage 1: Suggested Visual Inventory Process

A. Identify Community Visual Resource Values
   1. Describe and define the general character of the
      existing area.
   2. Document visual resource and/or visually sensi-
      tive land including:
      a. State parks or state forest preserves, munici-
         pal parks.
      b. wild, scenic, or recreational water bodies des-
         ignated by a state government agency.
      c. publicly or privately operated recreation
         areas.
      d. publicly or privately operated areas (includ-
         ing areas used for recreation) primarily de-

voted to conservation or the preservation of natural environmental features.

   e. hiking or ski-touring trails designated as such by a state or municipal government agency.

   f. architectural structures and sites of traditional importance.

   g. historic or archeological sites designated as such by the National Register of Historic Places.

   h. parkways, highways, or scenic overlooks and vistas designated as such by a federal, state, or municipal government agency.

   i. important urban landscapes including visual corridors, monuments, sculpture, landscape plantings, and urban "green space."

   j. important architectural elements and structures representing community style and neighborhood character.

B. Public Participation

  1. Notify the public of the proposed inventory process and its pupose.

  2. Conduct a survey of local resident/viewer perceptions:

    a. identify positive visual attractions.

    b. identify visual detractions or "misfits" (car dumps, gravel pits, waste disposal areas, and so forth).

    Results of the survey should indicate a preliminary consensus of the public's perceptions and values regarding its visual resources.

  3. Conduct public meeting(s) to inform residents of the public's perceptions and values regarding its visual resources.

  4. Adopt the municipal visual resource inventory.

  5. Formalize community visual standards through creation of sign ordinances, architectural boards of review adopted standards, or other appropriate techniques.

C. Establish "Critical Areas of Environmental Concern" in Accordance with SEQR

Special visual resources that are considered highly valued by the community and are sensitive to change may be established as Critical Areas of Environmental Concern under SEQR. Thereafter, any action that takes place within, partially within, or adjacent to the critical areas would be treated as a significant impact and receive a fully coordinated environmental review process.

Stage 2: Practical Visual Criteria

Agency decision makers can protect the visual character and quality of a project and its environmental setting by early consideration of the general siting and design criteria listed below. Muncipalities and agencies may wish to use these suggested criteria as a base, adding their own criteria to reflect community values.

1. Locate new facilities where they are intrinsically suitable to their visual environment.

2. Insure that agency decisions prevent the exposure or creation of visual misfits (such as car dumps or waste disposal areas adjacent to scenic vistas) unless visual mitigation measures are adequate.

3. Whenever possible protect the visual privacy of residential sites.

4. Actively preserve future access to public viewing points.

5. Emphasize shared infrastructure space for utilities.

6. In areas of high scenic quality, avoid commercial advertising, overhead utility service, and other manmade distractions.

7. Avoid development on steep slopes.

8. Take special care to enhance the visual quality of the physical entranceway to a community. The entranceway, usually a public roadway, sets the tone for the perceived visual expectation of the community.

9. Protect the integrity of visually important building facades by utilizing transfer of development rights techniques.

10. Promptly remove, refurbish, or replace abandoned facilities.

11. Be aware that visual spaces can be as important as physical objects. In this sense, air pollution can affect the visual quality of important spaces by obscuring or diminishing views.

12. Insure that transmission line corridors are not silhouetted against the skyline and traverse slopes on a diagonal rather than perpendicular basis.

13. As appropriate, either remove existing vegetation along travel corridors in order to create or enhance views or vistas, or retain existing vegetation along travel corridors to enhance natural character.

14. Consider all possible mitigation measures. Use vegetation, landforms, or structural techniques to screen visually intrusive characteristics of a proposed development.

15. Enhance views to bodies of water.

16. Avoid adverse visual effects caused by the introduction of materials, colors, and forms incompatible with the surrounding landscape.

Stage 3: Visual EAF Addendum

The following Visual EAF Addendum (Figure 11.8) is to be completed by the lead agency to provide information for determining whether a proposed action may have significant impacts on the visual resources.

The EAF Addendum focuses on four categories for measuring the visual significance of a project:

VISUAL EAF ADDENDUM

This form is to be used in conjunction with the SEQR Full EAF. Once the potential visual impacts have been identified by the following questions, proceed to Step 2 of the EAF.

Step 1

1. Is the project within or adjacent to a Critical Area of Environmental Cancer established under the State Environment Quality Review Act (see 617.4(j))?

Yes ☐   No ☐

Description of Existing Visual Environment

2. Area surrounding project site can be identified by one or more of the following terms:

	Within	
	*1/4 mile	*1 mile
Essentially undeveloped	☐	☐
Forested	☐	☐
Agricultural	☐	☐
Suburban residential	☐	☐
Industrial	☐	☐
Commercial	☐	☐
Urban	☐	☐
River, Lake, Pond	☐	☐
Cliffs, Overlooks	☐	☐
Designated Open Space	☐	☐
Flat	☐	☐
Hilly	☐	☐
Mountains	☐	☐
Other	☐	☐

3. Are there visually similar projects within:

*One Mile	Yes ☐	No ☐
*Two Miles	Yes ☐	No ☐
*Three Miles	Yes ☐	No ☐
Adjacent	Yes ☐	No ☐

*Distances from project site are provided for assistance. Substitute other distances as appropriate.

Degree of Project Visibility

4. Will the project be visible from outside the limits of the project site?

Yes ☐   No ☐

5. The project may be visible from:
   - Site or Structure on the National Register or State Register of Historic Places ☐
   - Palisades ☐
   - State or County Park ☐
   - Parkway ☐
   - Interstate Route ☐
   - State Highway ☐
   - County Road ☐
   - Local Road ☐
   - Bridge ☐
   - Railroad ☐
   - Existing Residences ☐
   - Existing Public Facility ☐
   - Adjacent Property Owners(s) ☐
   - Designated Scenic Vistas ☐
   - Other _____ ☐

6. Will the project eliminate, block, partially screen, or detract from views or vistas known to be important to the area?

Yes ☐   No ☐

7. Is the visibility of the project seasonal? (For example, screened by summer foliage, etc. but visible Fall/Winter/Spring)

Yes ☐   No ☐

If yes, which season(s) is project visible:
   - Summer ☐
   - Winter ☐
   - Spring ☐
   - Fall ☐

8. How many linear feet of frontage along a public thoroughfare does the project occupy?

_____ Feet

9. Will project open new access to or create new scenic views or vistas?

Yes ☐   No ☐

10. Does proposed project or action plan to:
   a. maintain existing natural screening

   Yes ☐   No ☐

   b. introduce new screening to minimize project visibility

   Yes ☐   No ☐

   If yes, is screening:
   1.) vegetative ☐
   2.) structural ☐

Viewing Context

11. Viewers will **likely** be in which of the following situations when the project is visible to them?

	Frequency			
			Holidays	
Activity	Daily	Weekly	Weekends	Seasonally
Travel to and from work	☐	☐	☐	☐
Involved in recreational activities	☐	☐	☐	☐
Routine travel by residents	☐	☐	☐	☐
At a residence	☐	☐	☐	☐
At worksite	☐	☐	☐	☐
Other _____	☐	☐	☐	☐

Visual Compatibility

12. Are the visual characteristics of the project obviously different from those of the surrounding area?

Yes ☐   No ☐

If yes the visual difference is because of:
   - Type of project ☐
   - Design style ☐
   - Size (including length, width, height, number of structures, etc. ☐
   - Coloration ☐
   - Condition of surroundings ☐
   - Construction material ☐
   - Other _____ ☐

13. Is there local opposition to the project entirely, or in part, because of visual aspects?

Yes ☐   No ☐

14. Is there public support for the project because of its visual qualities?

Yes ☐   No ☐

FIGURE 11.8 NY SEQRA Visual Environmental Assessment Form

Resource Inventory, there is a potential problem of having to conduct the inventory during a time of public controversy. This would make it even more difficult to establish a true consensus on community values. Conducting a visual resource inventory at an early stage would avoid this potential problem.

The Full EAF, Part 3, provides a series of questions to help determine the importance of each visual impact. These include:

1. What is the probability of the (visual) effect occuring?
2. What will the duration of the (visual) impact be?
3. Is the nature of the (visual) impact irreversible and will the (visual) character of the community be permanently altered?
4. Can the (visual) impact be controlled?
5. Is there a regional or statewide consequence to this (visual) impact?
6. Will the potential (visual) impact be detrimental to local goals and values?

The answers to these questions will indicate whether or not the potential impact is important. If one or more impact is found to be potentially large and important, sufficient reason exists to require the preparation of a Draft Environmental Impact Statement.

Step 2

By answering the questions in the Visual EAF Addendum, you have identified the visual relationship between the proposed action and its surrounding environment. With this information, return to the Full EAF, Part 2, Question 10, that addresses Visual Resources. Here you will identify the degree (size amount) of each significant visual impact. For example, the proposed action may only be visible after the leaves have fallen. This gives an indication of the time of exposure associated with a particular visual impact.

Once an impact's **magnitude** has been identified as potentially large, proceed to Part 3 on the SEQR Full EAF to determine the importance of the identified visual impacts. The community's established Visual Resource Inventory can be used as a practical measure of the importance of the potential impact. If the project will significantly affect a recognized visually sensitive area, facility, or site of visual importance, there should be sufficient information on the Visual Resource Inventory to warrant the preparation of a Draft Environmental Impact Statement.

FIGURE 11.8   (*Continued*) NY SEQRA Visual Environmental Assessment Form.

---

1. Description of the existing visual/scenic environment.
2. Identification of the degree to which the proposed action will be visible.
3. Determintion of who will see the project and in what context, for example, worker, tourist, or local resident.
4. Identification of the degree of visual compatibility or incompatibility of the project with the existing environment or the "projected" environment.

While the conceptual approach for determining visual significance relies heavily on objective measurements, there will always remain some degree of subjective discretion on the part of the decision maker. There are other scoping methods and forms used by the FHWA and the US Housing and Development (HUD) Agency (Smardon 1986b).

Detailed Visual Impact Assessment

There is an additional component to visual resource management that can assess the capability of specific landscape sites to absorb visual impacts of varying severity. BLM (1980) has used its contrast rating procedure for this purpose; the Forest Service has developed a process entitled Visual Absorption Capability (VAC) (Anderson et al. 1979); the FHWA (1981) has a visual impact guidance procedure; and the U.S. Army Corps of Engineers now has their own visual impact assessment (VIA) procedures that are part of Visual Resources Assessment Procedure (VRAP) (Smardon et

al. 1988). The philosophy behind the development of each of these systems is quite different.

VAC (Anderson, Mosier and Chandler 1979) is used to determine how much can be done to a landscape site before its visual absorption capability is exceeded. Contrast rating is used by BLM (1980) to determine whether a proposed change in the landscape would cause an acceptable or unacceptable level of contrast with that specific site, according to professional judgment. The FHWA system advocates public reactions to visual impact through simulations of the proposed project. The U.S. Corps VIA system incorporates many aspects of the previous ones but advocates use of multiple viewpoints, multiple raters, and simulations and public reactions to simulations as part of the assessment process to insure adequate reliability and validity.

VAC combines physical factors of the existing landscape, highly changeable perceptual factors, existing visual quality factors (form, line, color, and texture), and proposed activities factors (scale, configuration, duration, frequency, and so forth) to determine the VAC score for that particular landscape (see Figure 11.9). A low VAC score is very restrictive, and a high one means much more activity can be allowed. The VAC score range is then compared to the existing visual management objective(s) for that area (see Figure 11.10).

The contrast rating procedure for BLM operates in the following manner:

1. The landscape character as expressed by existing visual quality factors such as land features, water

LANDSCAPE MANAGEMENT GUIDE MATRIX				
I-Most Restrictive ↓ V-Least Restrictive	VISUAL QUALITY OBJECTIVE			
	Retention	Partial Retention	Modification	Maximum Modification
Visual Absorption Capability — Low	I	II	III	V
Inter-mediate	I	III	IV	V
High	II	III	IV	V

FIGURE 11.9   Visual absorption capability (VAC). *Source: John Wiley and Sons*

bodies, vegetation, and structures is described in terms of form, line, color, and texture.

2. The proposed activity for that particular locale is described in terms of introduced or modified form, line, color, and texture.

3. A contrast rating is then made by multiplying preestablished numerical values of form, line, color, and texture for land features, water bodies, vegetation, and structures by the estimated degree of contrast (strong = 3, moderate = 2, weak = 1, none = 0) to yield subtotals of contrast for land and water, vegetation, and structures (see Figure 11.11).

4. If the contrast ratings exceed "allowable" levels set according to the BLM manual, then the project feature/element of greatest contrast is redesigned, the basic presumption being in most cases that too much contrast is adverse or not desirable.

5. The process is repeated after the redesign.

This process is useful in that it provides a record of the landscape as it is and with the proposed project. It can be used to document which physical portion of the project needs to be reworked or redesigned, for example, landfill cuts reduced, less vegetation disturbed, structures reduced in size. If mitigation measures are not implemented, it can provide the legal documentation for taking action to ensure that they are. Thus,

from an administrative point of view, the process has many advantages.

For highway projects the approach suggested by U.S. Department of Transportation (1981) is flexible but is strongly related to the elements of visual experience. There are five general steps:

1. Define the visual environment of the project.
2. Analyze existing visual resources and viewer response.
3. Depict the visual appearance of project alternatives.
4. Assess the visual impacts of project alternatives.
5. Determine ways to mitigate adverse visual impact.

In practice, the content of these steps will depend on the visual issues specific to the project. Special considerations are the linear dynamic experience of the driver and/or passenger, which complicates the VIA analysis. This general approach should not be confused with the detailed Section 4(f) requirements covered earlier in this chapter.

For water resource projects, the U.S. Corps has supported the development of VIA within the new Visual Resource Assessment Procedure (Smardon et al. 1988). The steps for doing a detailed visual impact assessment appear in Figure 11.12, but in summary the procedure is:

Visual Quality Objective Matrix

		Distance Zone / Sensitivity Level						
		Fg1	Mg1	Fg2	Mg2	Bg1	Bg2	3
Variety Class	Class A	R	R	R	PR	PR	PR	RR
	Class B	R	PR	PR	M	M	M/MM	MM
	Class C	PR	PR	M	M	MM	MM	MM

Fg - Foreground   R - Retention   PR - Partial Retention
Mg - Middleground   M - Modification   MM - Maximum Modification
Bg - Background

FIGURE 11.10   Visual Quality Objectives

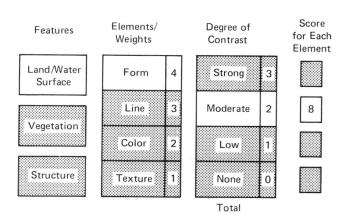

FIGURE 11.11   VRM contrast rating system

BASIC PROCEDURE

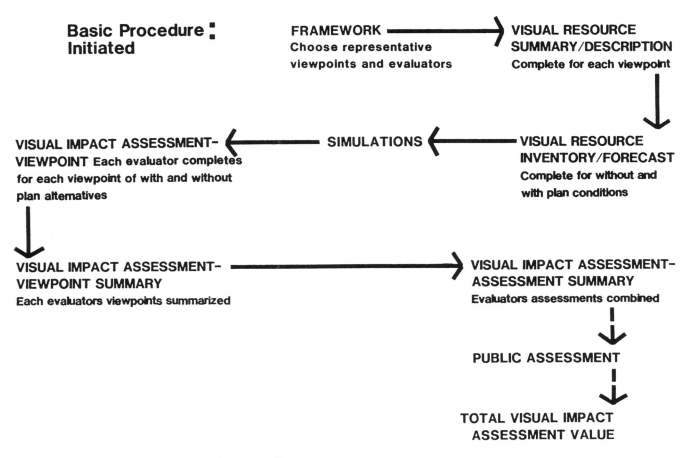

Basic Procedure :
Initiated

FRAMEWORK ──────────▶ **VISUAL RESOURCE**
Choose representative   **SUMMARY/DESCRIPTION**
viewpoints and evaluators   Complete for each viewpoint

VISUAL IMPACT ASSESSMENT- ◀──── **SIMULATIONS** ◀──── **VISUAL RESOURCE**
VIEWPOINT Each evaluator completes   **INVENTORY/FORECAST**
for each viewpoint of with and without   Complete for without and
plan alternatives   with plan conditions

VISUAL IMPACT ASSESSMENT- ──────────▶ **VISUAL IMPACT ASSESSMENT-**
VIEWPOINT SUMMARY   **ASSESSMENT SUMMARY**
Each evaluators viewpoints summarized   Evaluators assessments combined

PUBLIC ASSESSMENT

TOTAL VISUAL IMPACT
ASSESSMENT VALUE

FIGURE 11.12   Corps Visual Impact Assessment Process

1. Choose representative viewpoints and evaluators for the project.
2. Do a visual resource summary/description for each viewpoint.
3. Forecast the future landscape condition with and without the project.
4. Simulate both conditions for each viewpoint;
5. Have each evaluator assess landscape quality with and without the project.
6. Have each evaluator's viewpoint summarized numerically
7. Combine and average evaluator's assessments.
8. Combine professional assessment with public assessment (if it exists).

9. Obtain a total impact assessment value for the visual impact of the project or the alternative, which can then be compared with a predetermined visual quality management class (if it exists) or with other project alternatives.

Clearly, the U.S. Corps' approach is more complex than the previous methods discussed. The reason is that as more visual assessments are being challenged in courts and administrative hearings, any method used must be defensible from methodological and legal perspectives. Also, high-quality landscape simulations are being utilized for more and more VIA (Sheppard 1989 and 1986).

Case Study: Oregon Inlet Jetty Assessment

Background

Maintaining the Cape Hatteras National Seashore against erosion has always been a battle. This state of constant ecological and physical change is common to the barrier islands along many coastal waterways. The North Carolina barrier islands typically have a low vertical profile, are narrow, have a primarily sandy composition, and are exposed to high wave energy.

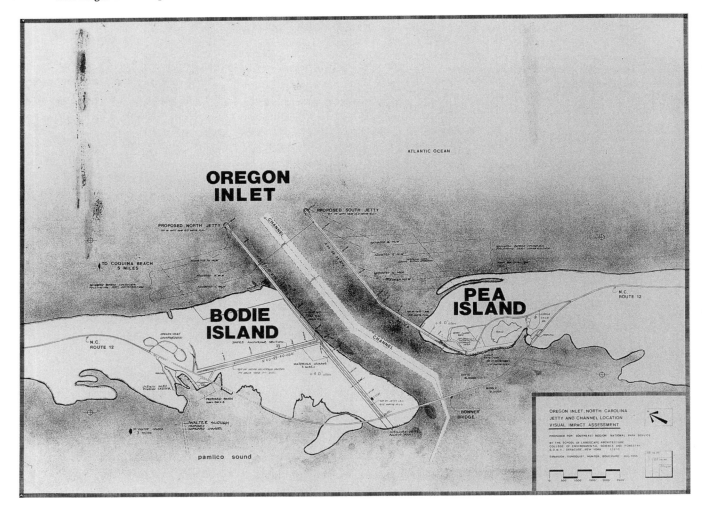

FIGURE 11.13   Oregon Inlet map

The channel at Oregon Inlet (see Figure 11.13) has been maintained by the U.S. Corps of Engineers for years. Concerned with the erosion of the islands to the north and south of this channel, the U.S. Corps proposed and designed a set of twin jetties to stabilize the area. The U.S. Corps prepared an EIS, but the project was appealed to an interagency council by the National Park Service and the U.S. Fish and Wildlife Service. To help settle outstanding questions on the visual and recreational impacts of the proposed project, the National Park Service, Southeast Region office, contacted the co-author, Smardon. We did a visual impact assessment and suggested mitigation measures. Visual impacts were especially critical because the area is a heavily used recreation area as well as a wildlife sanctuary for migrating shore and water birds.

Approach

The approach used for this study combined procedures the co-author was developing for the BLM (Smardon, Sheppard, and Newman 1979) and those used for similar coastal shoreline VIA's (Baird, Sheppard, and Smardon 1979; Mann 1979). It is made up of four steps:

1. Describing the physical and visual environment.
2. Ascertaining the type, number, and characteristics of recreational uses in the area.
3. Simulating the modifications at key viewpoints.
4. Evaluating the visual impact and discussing mitigating measures (Smardon et al. 1980).

The first step was to describe and visually document the visual landscape as it currently exists. The descriptive approach used a standard vocabulary of elements of form, color, line, texture, scale, and spatial dominance (Smardon, Sheppard, and Newman 1984). These same elements were later applied to the proposed modification to give a numerical rating to the impacts. The initial visual inventory was conducted on site through interviews with National Park Service employees and by taking 35-mm. slides. Care was taken to document the camera angles and viewpoint locations, and to provide scale clues so that simulations of the jetty structures would be accurate (see Figure 11.14).

The second step was to describe in detail the various recreational activities in the area and their general zones of occurrence. The recreational activities included swimming, sun-

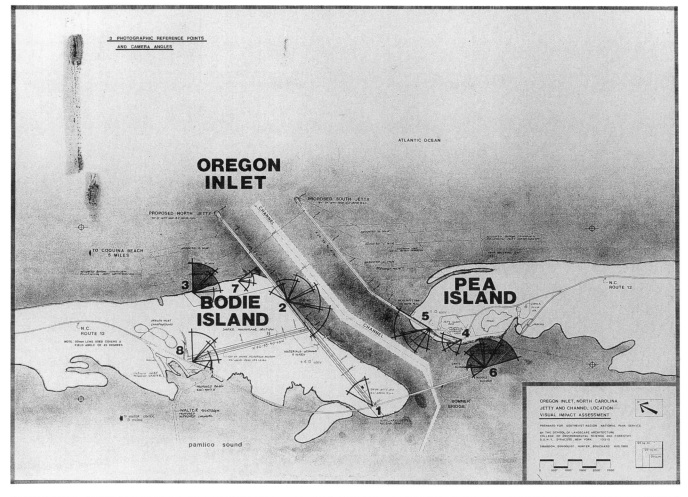

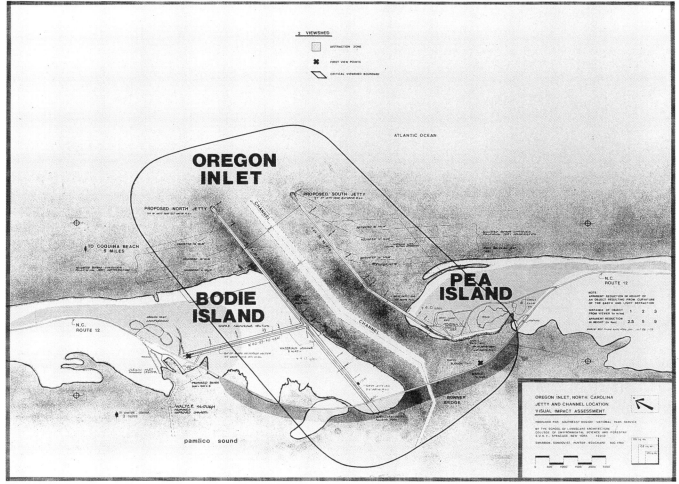

FIGURE 11.14 a, b Photopoints with foreground. *Graphic credit: Dan Sundquist*

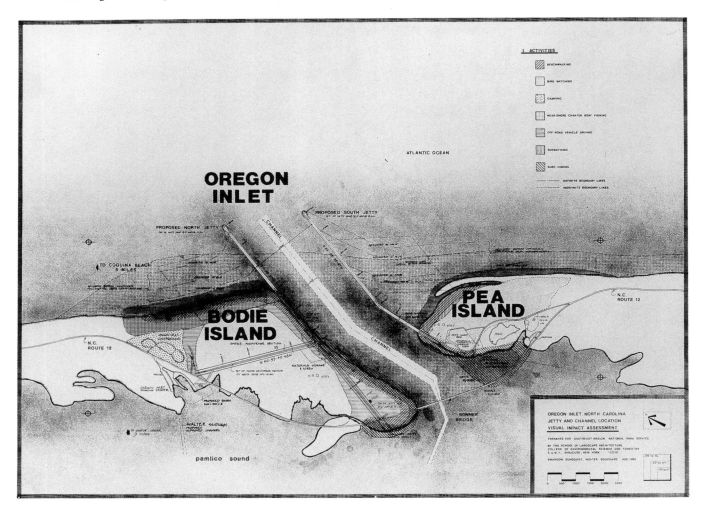

FIGURE 11.15   Recreation activity zones. *Graphic credit: Dan Sundquist*

bathing, charter boat fishing, surf fishing, off-road-vehicle driving, beach walking, bird watching, and camping (see Figure 11.15). This provided a working description of the impact of each user population in terms of annual use, time of day, mode of arrival, and average amount of time per day spent in the activity (see Table 11.4). Much of the information was derived from figures in the U.S. Corps EIS and was adjusted by information gathered from the on-site fieldwork.

The third step was to construct the simulations. The EIS provided for twin jetties built of either rough-cut rock transported by barge from nearby quarries from the north or of concrete dolos (looks like giant jumping jacks) made on site. Because of cost, the co-author assumed that rough-cut rock would be used for construction, and this material was rendered on the simulations.

The study team selected eight possible viewpoints and narrowed the choice to two critical ones (Figure 11.16). These were selected for simulation because they would have the largest number or duration of recreational viewers—the worst-case scenario. They also represented views in which the jetties would be in the viewer's middle ground to avoid biasing the view if the jetty were too close to the viewer.

Because views of Oregon Inlet were found to be panoramic, the simulations were constructed using a series of sequential matched color photographs of the interest area. An artist created the simulations on clear acetate overlays using color dyes, and they were mounted flip-style to provide "before" and "after" views for the evaluation of visual impacts (Figure 11.17).

The fourth step, impact evaluation, was conducted by two team members trained in the BLM (1980) procedure. This procedure involved making professional appraisals as previously described (that is, severe, medium, or no visual impact) with respect to the elements of form, color, line, texture, scale, and spatial dominance (Smardon, Sheppard, and Newman 1979). There were three consecutive steps:

TABLE 11.4 Viewer Activity Profiles Graphic

Recreational activity	Camping: Oregon Inlet Campground (Interdependent with all others)	Bird watching	Beach walking	Off-road vehicle driving	Surf fishing	Charter boat fishing	Sunbathing	Swimming
Viewing duration of activity	Seldom	Substantial	Substantial	Intermittent	Substantial	Intermittent	Occasional	Intermittent
Annual use	60,000 to 75,000 AVD			12,000 Veh./yr.	80,000 to 100,000 AVD	4,164 trips	11,000 AVD	11,000 AVD
ORV Average activity		3.2 hours	2.1 hours	3 hours	6 hours	8 hours	3.8 hours	3.8 hours
NON per day Time/day		1.4 hours	1.9 hours		3.5 hours	8 hours	4.4 hours	4.4 hours
Time/year	March 15 to Dec. 14	Late fall peak, all year	All year	All year	Spring/Fall	7 AM to 3:30 PM		8 AM to 4 AM May 30 to Sept. 1
Short-term (3-year) construction	Heavy equipment creates noise and dust. 50% reduction. Attractive nuisance.	Incompatible noise, dust. Disturbance of wildlife.	Heavy equipment creates noise and dust.	Access to some areas restricted or prohibited.	Access restricted or prohibited to surf-fishing areas.	Safety hazard to boaters from movement of construction materials by barge. Attractive nuisance.	Heavy equipment creates noise and dust. Reduced by 50%.	
Operation and maintenance	Noise associated with dredging for sand bypassing operation.		2,000 ft. of beachfront removed. Overcrowding. Sand bypassing.	2,000 ft. of beachfront removed from ORV use. Overcrowding. Sand bypassing.	7,000 linear feet of jetty crown for fishing off jetty.	Attract more boat fishermen near jetties.	Noise associated with dredging for sand bypassing operation.	
Cumulative long term	Additional pressure on NPS to expand campground.	Increased incompatibility to bird watching activity.	Overcrowding. Decrease in quality experience.	Encourage illegal ORV use/vandalism.	Potential increase in fishing activity with attendant management problems.	Increasing incidence of small-boat accidents.		

(Header arrows indicate "interdependent" relationships between Bird watching / Beach walking, Off-road vehicle driving / Surf fishing, and Sunbathing / Swimming.)

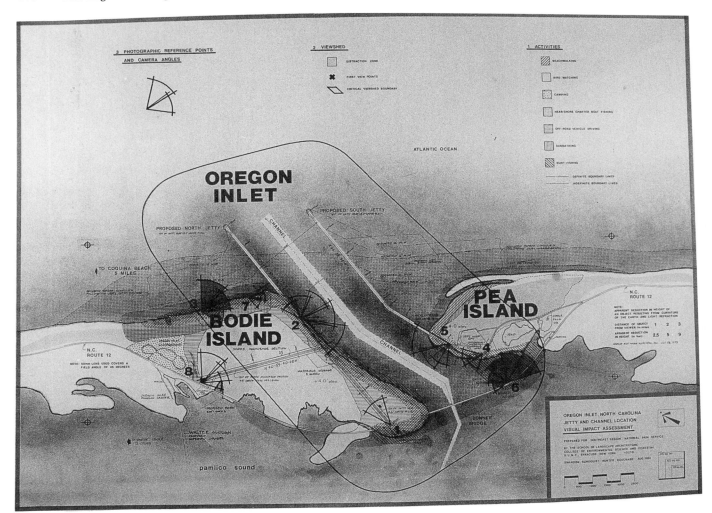

FIGURE 11.16   Composite analysis

1. Describing the existing landscape.
2. Describing the landscape with the projects in place using the simulations.
3. Contrasting the ratings for the existing and proposed conditions.

Results

One view had moderate-to-severe visual impact and another had low-to-moderate visual impact. Key visual problems were blocking the ocean horizon and the contrast of the tex-

FIGURE 11.17   Simulation from viewpoint 3. *Graphic credit: Dan Sundquist*

ture and color of the jetty material to the ocean and beach environment. Measures to minimize harm were suggested such as laying the armor stone flat against the jetty side to reduce contrast, providing guidelines for landscape treatment of spoil areas, (where dredged material is dumped) and paving the top of the jetties to enhance recreational fishing. The key finding was that the project would "urbanize" a natural area by providing more hard surface and encouraging a concentration or recreational users. This project did not go forward in 1980–1981, but it may be reviewed shortly due to economic and political pressures to maintain the Oregon Inlet channel for fishing interests. Although the U.S. Corps did not have a VIA methodology or process at the time the interagency conflict occurred, they now have a Visual Resources Assessment Procedure (VRAP) (Smardon et al. 1988) that includes VIA. Thus, they will be in a better position to address such issues in the future.

References

Anderson, F. R. 1973. *NEPA in the courts: A legal analysis of the National Environmental Policy Act.* Johns Hopkins University Press.

Anderson. L, Mosier, J., and Chandler, G. 1979. Visual aborption capability. In *Our national landscape,* ed. G. Elsner and R. C. Smardon, pp. 164–171.

Andrews, R. N. L., and Waits, M. J. 1978. *Environmental values in public decisions: A research agenda.* School of Natural Resources, University of Michigan.

Atkins, J. T., and Blair, W. G. E. 1983. Visual impacts of highway alternatives. *Garten und Landshaft,* 8(83): 632–35.

Bagley, M. D., Kroll, C. Clark, K. 1973. *Aesthetics in environmental planning.* EPA-600/5-75-009, U.S. G.P.O.

Baird, B. E., Sheppard, S. R. J., and Smardon, R. C. 1979. Visual simulation of offshore liquified natural gas (LNG) terminals in a decisionmaking context. In *Our national landscape,* ed. G. Elsner and R. C. Smardon, pp. 636–644.

Baldwin, M. F. 1970. The Santa Barbara oil spill. *University of Colorado Law Review,* 42(1): 33–75.

Broughton, R. 1972. Aesthetics and environmental law: Decisions and values. *Land and Water Review,* 7(2): 451–500.

Council on Environmental Quality. 1970–1985. *Environmental quality annual reports,* U.S. G.P.O.

Cutler, M. R. 1972. A study of litigation related to management of Forest Service administered lands and its effects on policy decisions. Part two: A comparison of four cases. Unpublished dissertation, Michigan State University.

Draper, J. B. 1974. The Rainbow Bridge case and reclamation projects in reserved areas. *Natural Resources Journal,* 14(3): 431–445.

Elsner, G. E., and Smardon, R. C. tech. compilers & eds. 1979. *Proceedings of our national landscape: A conference on applied techniques for analysis and management of the visual resource.* Gen. Tech. Rpt. PSW-35, USDA, Forest Service Pac. SW. Forest and Range Experimental Station, Berkeley, Calif.

Ferguson, A. B., Jr, and Bryson, W. P. 1972. Mineral King: A case study in Forest Service decision making. *Ecology Law Quarterly,* 2: 480–531.

Ferguson, F. E., and Haggard, J. L. 1973. Regulation of mining land activities in the National Forests. *Land and Water Review,* 8: 391–427.

French, J. 1975. Barreling through the notch. *Sierra Club Bulletin,* 60: 8.

Frey, C. 1978. The old man is smiling. *Conservation News,* 43(4).

Giorgio, J. W. 1972. Parklands and federally funded highway projects: The impact of Preservation Society v. Texas. *Environmental Affairs,* 1(4): 882–901.

Haggard, J. L. 1975. Regulation of mining law activities on federal lands. *Rocky Mountain Mineral Law Institute,* 12: 349–391.

Hanson, D. and Ristau, T. 1979. A case study: Death Valley National Monument California–Nevada. In *Our national landscape,* ed. G. Elsner and R. C. Smardon, pp. 693–699.

Johnson, G. G. 1974. *Mineral King visual analysis.* Landscape Architecture Group, USFS, Reg. 5, San Francisco.

Jones, G. et al. 1975. A method for the quantification of aesthetic values for environmental decisionmaking. *Nuclear Technology,* 25(4): 682–713.

Leighty, L. L. 1971. Aesthetics as a legal basis for environmental control. *Wayne Law Review,* 17: 1347–1396.

Leopold, L. B. 1969. Quantitative comparison of some aesthetic factors among rivers. *U.S.G.S. Circular 620,* U.S. G.P.O.

Linder, D. O. 1990. New direction for preservation law: Creating an environment worth experiencing. *Environmental Law,* 20: 49–81.

Mann, R. 1979. A technique for the assessment of the visual impact of nearshore confined dredged materials and other built islands. In *Our National Landscape,* ed. G. Elsner and R. C. Smardon, pp. 654–659.

McCloskey, M. 1967. A landscape policy for public lands. *Denver Law Journal,* 45(2): 149–166.

Murray, B. H. and Neimann, B. J. 1979. Visual quality testimony in an adversary setting. In *Our national landscape,* ed. G. Elsner and R. C. Smardon, pp. 693–699.

Note. 1970. Mineral King Valley: Who shall watch the watchmen? *Rutgers Law Review,* 25(1): 103–144.

Petrich, C. H. 1979. Aesthetic impact of a proposed power plant on an historic wilderness landscape. In *Our national landscape,* ed. G. Elsner and R. C. Smardon, pp. 474–484.

Poland, S. S, 1969. Development of recreational and related resources at hydroelectric projects licensed by the Federal Power Commission. *Land and Water Law Review,* 4(2): 375–398.

Redding, M. J. 1971. *Guidelines for incorporating factors of aesthetic and visual impact into the planning process of transportation systems.* U.S. D.O.T.

Sax, J. L. 1970. The public trust doctrine in natural resource law: Effective judicial intervention. *Michigan Law Review,* 68: 473.

———. 1973. Standing to sue: a critical review of the Mineral King decision. *Natural Resources Journal,* 13(1): 76–88.

Schauman, S. 1982 On a clear day in Ogunquit, Maine. In *Coastal Zone Management Journal,* 9(3/4): 313–322.

Sheppard, S. R. J. 1986. Simulating changes in the landscape. In *Foundations for Visual Project Analysis,* ed. R. C. Smardon, J. F. Palmer, and J. P. Felleman. John Wiley, Ch. 11, pp. 187–199.

———. 1989. *Visual simulation.* Van Nostrand Reinhold.

Sive, D. 1970a. Securing, examining, and cross-examining expert witnesses in environmental cases. *Michigan Law Review,* 68(5): 1175–1198.

———. 1970b Some thoughts of an evironmental lawyer in the wilderness of administrative law. *Yale Law Review,* 70(4): 612–651.

Smardon, R. C. 1982. An *organizational analysis of federal agency visual resource management systems.* PhD. dissertation, University of California, Berkeley, and University Microfilms International.

———. 1984. When is the pig in the parlour?; The interface of aesthetic and legal considerations. *Environmental Review,* 8(2): 146–161.

———. 1986a. Historical evolution of visual resource management within three federal agencies. *Journal of Environmental Management,* 22(1986): 301–317.

———. 1986b. Review of agency methodology for visual project analysis. In *Foundations for Visual Project Analysis,* ed. R. C. Smardon, J. F. Palmer, and J. P. Felleman, John Wiley. Ch. 9.

Smardon, R. C. et al. 1988. *Visual resources assessment procedure of the U.S. Army Corps of Engineers.* Instruction Report 88-1, U.S.A.C.O.E., Environmental Research Lab., Vicksburg, MS.

Smardon, R. C., Palmer, J. F., and Felleman, J. P. eds. 1986. *Foundation for visual project analysis,* John Wiley.

Smardon, R. C., Sheppard, S. R. J., and Newman, S. 1984. *Visual Impact Assessment Manual.* School of Landscape Architecture Occasional Paper ESF-009, SUNY/ESF.

Smardon, R. C., Sundquist, D. Hunter, M., and Bouchard, V. 1980. Visual impact assessment of the Manteo (Shallowbag) Bay Project on the Oregon Inlet area in Dane County, North Carolina. Prepared for the National Park Service, Southeast region, Atlanta.

Stone, C. D. 1972. Should trees have standing? Toward legal rights for natural objects. *Southern California Law Review,* 45: 459–501.

———. 1973. *Should trees have standing? Toward legal rights for natural Objects.* William Kaufman.

Thompson, R. H. 1973. Decision at Rainbow Bridge. *Sierra Club Bulletin,* 58: 8–9, 30–31.

U.S.D.A., Forest Service. 1973. *National Forest Landscape Management System,* vol. 1. U.S. G.P.O.

———. 1974. *National forest landscape management system,* vol. 2, Ch. 1. U.S.D.A. Handbook 462. U.S. G.P.O.

U.S.D.A., Soil Conservation Service. 1979. *Procedure to establish priorities in landscape architecture.* U.S.D.A., S.C.S. Technical release 65, U.S. G.P.O.

U.S.D.I., Bureau of Land Management. 1975. *Visual resources management manual.*

———. 1980. *Visual resources management program.* U.S. G.P.O., Stock No. 0024-011-000116-6.

U.S.D.I., Bureau of Land Management and the State of North Dakota. 1978. *Draft: West-Central North Dakota regional environmental impact study on energy development.* B.L.M. State Office, Bismarck, ND.

U.S.D.O.T., Federal Highway Administration. 1981. *Visual impact assessment for highway projects.*

U.S. Environmental Protection Agency. 1979. *Protecting visibility research.* Report 450/5-79, U.S. E.P.A., Research Triangle, N.C.

Williams, N. et al. 1990. *Interim report draft to the Agency of Natural Resources, State of Vermont.* Design Issues Study Committee, Vermont Law School.

Chapter 12

Surface Mining

INTRODUCTION

A number of specific land and resource uses have caused either a great deal of controversy or an extreme aesthetic disruption of the landscape throughout the country. One such activity is surface mining in all its various forms (Figure 12.1). Much of the discussion in this chapter will relate to these activities as practiced on federal lands or through federal permits (such as those given by the Bureau of Land Management), but the basic principles will also apply to private lands as regulated by federal and state statutes.

Rarely is there a more blatant conflict between economic and aesthetic values in the landscape than with surface mining. It is generally agreed that surface-mined land is considered "unaesthetic" (P.L.L.R.C. 1970, p. 122), "aesthetically undesirable" (Bosselman 1969) and "downright wicked" (Graham 1948), but it also may be the most economic use of the land. As Bosselman (1969, p. 143) so aptly states the case: "Perhaps the most serious but least tangible effect of surface mining is in the amorphous area of aesthetics."

The problem is to determine how aesthetic values should be considered in siting and location questions concerning various forms of surface mining, and the weight these values should be given in the decision process. There is ample legal literature on surface mining: (See Dietrich 1971; Larson 1972; Mintz 1976; Binder 1977; Haggard 1975; Kidd 1974; Renkey 1969; and Brooks 1966.) However, few journal articles consider aesthetics per se for any serious treatment. (See ASLA 1983; Bosselman 1969; Hubbard 1969; Clyde 1976; Down; and Stocks 1977; McCloskey 1968; and Kidd 1974.)

TYPES OF SURFACE MINING

The term "surface mining" refers to processes by which minerals are uncovered from the surface of the earth and then extracted. It is distinguished from "deep mining" in which a shaft is constructed to the mineral vein and the mineral is extracted through the shaft. The best-known type of surface mining is variously referred to as strip mining, surface mining, or open-cut mining; it currently accounts for about 50 percent of the coal mined. Although surface mining is used to remove many types of minerals, its most common use, and the one that has created the greatest problems, is the mining of coal, sand, gravel, and stone.

There are at least five distinct types and subdivisions of surface mineral mining: generally taken from the U.S. Forest Service (1977) "Anatomy of a Mine."

1. In the **hydraulic method**, high-pressure water jets are used to wash the land from its original location over riffles or some other mechanism where the mineral is trapped, as in gold mining in some of the Western states.

2. **Strip mining** consists of mining a relatively shallow deposit by removing one parallel strip of "overburden" after another; the overburden is then placed on the adjacent strip from which the mineral has been removed. It is useful to distinguish between three broad types of strip mining: contour mining, which takes place in hilly terrain; area mining, which is performed on relatively flat land; and auger mining, which may occur in both types of terrain.

   a. In **contour mining** (Figure 12.2) earth-moving machinery cuts a section out of a hillside to ex-

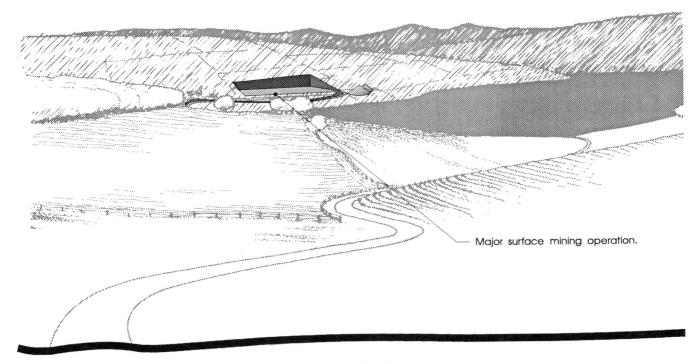

FIGURE 12.1   Generic landscape image with surface mine. *Credit: Scott Shannon*

pose the coal seam and, as the name implies, follows the contour of the seam along the hill. What is left is a long vertical "highwall," sometimes over a hundred feet high, at the point of furthest penetration into the hill, and a horizontal "bench" from which the coal has been removed. In the simplest technique of contour mining, the removed overburden, now "spoil," is placed downslope of the bench as mining proceeds. With "contour stripping," used in mountainous areas, the strips resemble looped shoestrings as they follow the sinuous outcrop of a coal seam, leaving

a gash of one hundred feet or so in the hillside. The resulting cut can be viewed as a triangle cut out of a hill. From a distance the cut looks like a road (or series of parallel roads if successive cuts have been made) running around the side of a hill.

b. In **area mining** (Figure 12.3) coal is uncovered by digging what is essentially a huge trench. After the overburden and coal are removed, another cut is made next to the first, and the spoil from the new one is placed in the previous trench. The process creates a series of high ridges and furrows—

FIGURE 12.2   Contour mining. *Photo credit: R. Burton Litton, Jr.*

FIGURE 12.3   Area mining. *Photo credit: USDI Bureau of Land Management*

resembling "a gigantic washboard" — with an exposed trench, often a hundred or more feet deep, marking the last cut. In both contour and area mining explosives are commonly used to fracture and loosen the overburden prior to removal.

c. **Auger mining** is a relatively new technique in which the augurs are used to get any remaining coal that contour mining cannot economically reach. Drills as large as seven feet in diameter bore into a seam (often into a highwall left by stripping) from the surface, leaving a perforated series of holes from which the coal has been removed. Any of these methods may cause extensive pollution and erosion damage downslope and downstream of the mine site unless the mine is carefully managed.

3. **Open-pit mining** (Figure 12.4) is used to mine ore bodies that may be large masses or bodies of irregular wandering configuration. It generally requires the removal of large amounts of material from an ever-expanding pit and the deposit of waste in separate dump areas near the pit. This type of mining is more common with metaliferous ores, such as iron or copper.

4. **Dredge mining** is generally done by a machine floating (Figure 12.5) in a pool of water and is used to mine shallow mineral-bearing gravels. Tailings from the dredge are placed behind it in piles as it moves.

5. **Underground mining** may leave spoil piles on the surface of the land even though the actual mining activity is not seen.

Any of these methods of mining may result in changes to the surface. Dumps of waste material and tailings from undergound mines are generally deposited on the surface, and if the block-caving method of underground mining is used, there may be large-scale

FIGURE 12.5   Dredge. *Photo credit: R. C. Smardon*

subsidence of the surface. The results to the surface from the other mining methods are obvious. Much of the visual impact may be due to ancillary facilities and equipment such as roads, processing centers, and large excavating equipment.

This is a brief sketch of mineral mining methods and some of their visual impacts, but accurate delineation of the activity is needed to assess the types of visual or aesthetic impacts involved (see U.S.D.A. FS 1977; Law 1984; ASLA 1978). It is evident from law journal and popular articles that there is much confusion and misconception about the actual mining techniques used and their effects on the environment.

VISUAL IMPACTS AND PROBLEMS FROM SURFACE MINING

There is still very little literature relating to the visual impacts due to surface mining activities. This is ironic, given the wide geographical scope of activity and the amount of public concern. One study on methodology for visual reclamation of surface mining is based primarily on eastern Appalachian conditions (Cole et al. 1976), while the only other in-depth studies are descriptive approaches for assessing northern Great Plains (Litton et al. 1979) and northeastern British Columbia (Tetlow and Sheppard 1977) landscapes. Some good summary material of mining impacts and approaches has been released (ASLA 1978; Adams 1983), and the Oak Ridge National Laboratory has been looking at surface mine reclamation and post-use possibilities as well (Seddon and Petrich 1983a and 1983b).

Visual management problems from surface mining break down into three basic types: First is the cumulative visual impact of unreclaimed surface mining activity on the unexceptional everyday landscape. Second is

FIGURE 12.4   Open pit mining. *Photo credit: USDI Bureau of Land Management*

the direct conflict over surface mining activity for rare locatable, (valuable minerals located at specific deposits or sites) minerals that affects landscapes of high visual quality or social significance (Figure 12.6) — for example, national parks, wilderness areas, or monuments. Examples of the last category include phosphate mining in Caribou National Forest in Idaho (Figure 12.7) and borax mining in the Death Valley National Monument in California and Nevada. The third problem is the visual impact of surface mining adjacent to or within viewing distance from a highly scenic area.

The next step is to see how these visual or aesthetic concerns are addressed at the state and federal levels. The third problem is well illustrated by the Miners Ridge case in the Northern Cascades where Kennecott Copper Corporation proposed to develop an open-pit mine within Washington's Glacier Peak Wilderness. McCloskey (1968, p. 82) describes the situation quite graphically:

FIGURE 12.7   Phosphate mining in Idaho. *Photo credit: USDI Bureau of Land Management*

The Miners Ridge case is a flagrant example of conflicting values. The mine site is the center of the wilderness on broad high meadows which look out on breathtaking alpine panoramas. Treasured Image Lake, mirroring Glacier Peak, is but a short distance away. Digging a 2,000 foot-wide hole in these meadows is like punching out the eyes of the Mona Lisa. The damaged area may be small, but the damage changes the importance of everything in sight for miles around. It is no longer a glorious, remote, and untouchable area. In a psychological as well as visual sense, the open pit will rob the area of the meaning it now has as wilderness.

The first type of visual problem is found throughout the U.S.: Appalachia, the northern Midwest, the northern Great Plains, the Southeast, Southwest, and so on. The second and third types of visual problems have become increasingly common in publicly owned environments in which protection is significant and also have valid mining claims. These values conflict directly and indicate many of the wilderness/mineral resource development conflicts that have never been amicably resolved. These conflicts may be expected to increase to some degree as certain rare (in location) minerals are found in publicly protected areas, and as the scale and physical intensity of mining (large scale-more impact) technology increases and more publicly owned areas are designated for protection — for instance, wilderness, roadless, primitive, or scenic area.

STATE SURFACE MINING CONTROL STATUTES

There are a number of state surface mining control statutes that specifically provide for consideration of aesthetic values. In the Wyoming Environmental Quality Act,[1] which was drafted to regulate surface

FIGURE 12.6   Wilderness and mining — Holyoke Range. *Photo credit: R. C. Smardon*

---

[1]Wyo. Laws, Ch. 250, ss. 35–487.1 et seq. (1973).

mining specifically, an operating permit for mining exploration or production on unique quality lands can be denied under certain conditions. The criteria for classification is whether "the proposed mining operation would irreparably, harm, destroy, or materially impair any area that has therefore been designated by the council to be of a unique and irreplaceable historical, archeological, *scenic* or natural value."[2] (Emphasis added.) The act also provides that the agency created by the act should inventory sites deemed as unique and irreplaceable, and of archeological, historical, scenic, or natural value. The intent of the provision was stated by Governor Hathaway before a U.S. Senate committee:

With our vast energy fuel resources Wyoming wishes to do its part to help alleviate the nation's energy crisis. But in the development and use of these resources we desire, indeed, we insist, that we have appropriate and adequate protection for our clean air and water and for our scenic and inspirational landscapes. . . . The number of visitors to our two great national parks in Wyoming, Yellowstone and Grand Teton, and to our lakes and streams, our big game areas and to our historical and geological attractions is each year more than 30 times the resident population of Wyoming.[3]

The concern voiced here is for a balance, including conservation of the Wyoming landscape, which contributes to Wyoming's third most profitable industry — tourism.

Montana also has a surface mining act, entitled the Montana Reclamation of Mining Lands Act,[4] which mentions that priorities should be given to "the aesthetics of our landscape, waters and ground cover."[5] Other state acts may not mention aesthetic values per se, but may still imply maintenance of aesthetic values through reclamation provisions.[6] For example, a North Dakota act requires that before the commission gives a permit, they must consider, among other things, whether the mining activity will result in "the permanent destruction of consequential aesthetic values."[7]

The West Virginia Strip Mine Control Act[8] provides that the director of their department of natural resources can refuse altogether to issue a permit to a strip mine if the activity will unreasonably and irreparably interfere with the property rights of others. Included among such property rights is the aesthetic value of potentially damaged property. Broughton (1972, p. 498) comments that the professional training and value system of the head administrator of the act is key to the success to protection of environmental values. According to Broughton, one permit was refused on the grounds of damage to aesthetic values, where the action contemplated was to physically sever the top of a ridge immediately adjacent to Grandview State Park.[9]

The following states have active surface mining statutes, permit programs, and some form of enforcement: Alabama,[10] Arkansas,[11] California,[12] Colorado,[13] Florida,[14] Georgia,[15] Idaho,[16] Illinois,[17] Indiana,[18] Iowa,[19] Kentucky,[20] Maryland,[21] Michigan,[22] Minnesota,[23] Mississippi,[24] Missouri,[25] Montana,[26] New Hampshire,[27] New York,[28] North Carolina,[29] North Dakota,[30] Ohio,[31] Oklahoma,[32] Oregon,[33] Pennsylvania,[34] South Carolina,[35] South Dakota,[36] Tennessee,[37] Texas,[38] Utah,[39] Virginia,[40] Washington,[41] and West Virginia.[42]

---

[2]Id. s. 35–487.24.

[3]Hearings on S. 768 before the Senate Committee on Interior and Insular Affairs, 93rd Cong., 1st Sess., part 1 of 9 (1973).

[4]Mont. Rev. Codes. Ann. ss. 50–1201 to 50–1224 (Supp., 1971).

[5]Id., s. 50–1202.

[6]See Open Cut Land Reclamation Act of Colorado, Colo. Rev. Stat. Ann., ss. 92–13–2 to 92–13–78m (supp. 1972) and New Mexico Coal Surface Mining Act of 1972, N.M. Stat. Ann., ss. 63–34–1 to 63–34–20 (Supp. 1972).

[7]N. Dak. Cent. Code s. 38–14–05.1 (Supp. 1975).

[8]W. Virginia Ann. s. 20–C–11 (Supp. 1971).

[9]Petition of Sparks Coal Company before the West Virginia Coal Reclamation Board.

[10]Surface Mining Act of 1969, Code of Ala. s. 9–16.

[11]Open Cut Land Reclamation Act of 1977, 52 Ark. Stat. Ann. ss. 917–934.

[12]Surface Mining and Reclamation Act of 1975, Ch. 9 Ann. Calif. Pub. Res. Code, ss. 1710–2795.

[13]Colorado Mined Land Reclamation Act of 1976, Col. Rev. Stat. s. 34–23.

[14]Fla. Stat. Ann. s. 211.32.

[15]Surface Mining Act of 1969, Code Georgia Ann. Ch. 43–14.

[16]Dredge and Placer Mining Restoration Act and Surface Mining Act, Title 47, Chs. 13 and 15 Idaho Code.

[17]Strip Mined Land Conservation and Reclamation Act 1971, 96 1/2 Ill. Ann. Stat. ss. 4501–4520.

[18]Indiana Stat. Ann. Title 13, Art. 4, Ch. 6 ss. 1–13.

[19]Code of Iowa s. 83A.

[20]Kentucky Rev. Stat. Ch. 350.

[21]Surface Mining Law of 1975, Ann. Code of Maryland Nat. Res. Title 7, subtitle 6A.

[22]Mine Reclamation Act of 1970, 18 Mich. Stat. Ann. s. 594.

[23]93 Minn. Stat. ss. 44–51.

[24]Surface Mining and Reclamation Act 1977, Miss. Code Ann. Title 53, Ch 7.

Eight states do not have a statewide regulatory program applicable specifically to surface mining. These states include four Eastern states where little surface mining occurs, except for sand and gravel: Connecticut, Delaware, New Jersey, and Rhode Island; three Western states with substantial mining activity and large amounts of public lands: Alaska, Arizona, and Nevada; and Nebraska. Hawaii's statute is inactive and is not being used.

Even among states with permitting statutes, there are differences. For example, California's permits are granted by local governments within the context of state policy. In Maine[43] and Vermont[44] permits are granted within the context of the statutes regulating the location of all developments having major impact on land resources. (For a more detailed discussion of state surface mining statutes and programs the reader is referred to Bloom 1980.)

FEDERAL SURFACE MINING STATUTES AND PROGRAMS

The most wide-ranging federal legislation passed on this type of mining is the Surface Mining Control and Reclamation Act (SMCRA) of 1977.[45] This act is the result of many previously proposed pieces of legislation that failed in Congress (Mintz 1976). The findings section of the act states that "many surface mining operations result in disturbances of surface areas that burden and adversely affect commerce and public welfare . . . by impairing natural beauty,"[46] among other

things. Aesthetics is not heavily emphasized elsewhere in the act, whose other major intent seems to be to provide a very detailed program for states to develop their own "ecologically sound" surface mining programs and to provide federal resources to promote surface mine land reclamation to restore the ecological functions of the landscape. Several aspects of the act will be emphasized here as they relate to aesthetics.

Environmental protection performance standards contained in the act that are to be utilized by approved state and federal programs include provisions for restoring the "approximate original contour"[47] of the land. This phrase is defined as:

Approximate original contour means that surface configuration achieved by backfilling and grading of the mined area so that the reclaimed area, including any terracing or access roads, closely resembles the general surface configuration of the land prior to mining and blends into and complements the drainage pattern of the surrounding terrain, with all highwalls and spoil piles eliminated; water impoundments may be permitted where the regulatory authority determines that they are in compliance with section 515(b)(8) of this Act.[48]

The implied criterion is that the land be restored to a "natural" or prior landform configuration. This leaves little room for alternative landform treatment as some have proposed, although there may be some provision for experimental aesthetic landform treatments of reclaimed surface mine sites under the section of the act dealing with experimental practices.[49]

[25]Land Reclamation Act of 1971, 444 Missouri Stat. Ann. ss. 760–786.

[26]Mont. Code Ann. Title 82, Ch. 4.

[27]N.H. Stat. Ann. Ch. 12-E.

[28]Mined Land Reclamation Law 1976, Envtl. Cons. Laws of NY Ann. Art. 23, Title 27.

[29]Mining Act of 1971, N.C. Gen. Stat. Ch. 74, Art. 7.

[30]N.D. Cent. Code Title 38, Ch. 16.

[31]Ohio Rev. Code Ch. 1514.

[32]Mined Lands Reclamation Act of 1971, 45 Ok. Stat. Ann. ss. 721–738.

[33]Or. Re. Stat. ss. 750–900.

[34]Surface Mining Conservation and Reclamation Act 1971, 52 Penn. Stat. Ann. s. 1396.

[35]Mining Act 1973, Code of Law of S. Carolina Title 48, Ch. 19.

[36]Surface Mining Land Reclamation Act of 1971, S.D. Cons. Laws s. 25–6A.

[37]Mineral Surface Mining Law of 1972, Tenn. Code. Ann. Title 59, Ch. 8 ss. 201–228.

[38]Uranium Surface Mining and Reclamation Act, Texas Nat. Res. Code Ch. 131.

[39]Mined Land Reclamation Act 1975, Utah Code Ann. Title 40, Ch. 8.

[40]Code of Virginia Ch. 16, Title 45.1.

[41]Rev. Code of Wash. Ch. 78.44.

[42]W. Va. Code, Ch. 20, Art. 6D.

[43]38 Me. Rev. Stat. Ann. ss. 481–490.

[44]Vt. Stat. Ann. Title 10 Ch. 151.

[45]30 U.S.C. s. 1201 et seq. (1988).

[46]Id., s. 1201(c).

[47]Id., s. 1265.

[48]Id., s. 1291 (2).

[49]Id., s. 1301.

The environmental protection performance standards relating to revegetation also imply a strong return to a natural situation. The operation should:

establish on the regraded areas, and all other lands affected, a diverse, effective, and permanent vegetative cover of the same seasonal variety native to the area of land to be affected and capable of self-regeneration and plant succession at least equal in extent of cover to the natural vegetation of the area; except, that introduced species may be used in the revegetation process where desirable and necessary to achieve the post-mining land use plan.[50]

The act exceeds most previous ones in the specificity of its procedures and duration pertaining to performance and monitoring of reclamation measures. There are even separate standards for steep-slope surface coal mining.[51]

There are some procedural deterrents to the bringing of many potential environmental cases: (1) the case must be "brought only in the judicial district in which the surface coal mining operation complained of is located,"[52] that is, no change of venue strategies allowed; and (2) the plaintiff may be liable for court costs of the litigation or may be required to file a bond or equivalent security if a temporary restraining order or preliminary injunction is sought.[53] These two provisions may act to discourage most environmental groups from litigation under the act.

The act also prohibits future mining activities on certain federal lands:

After the enactment of this Act and subject to valid existing rights no surface coal mining operations except those which exist on the date of enactment of this Act shall be permitted—

(1) on any lands within the boundaries of units of the National Park System, the National Wildlife Refuge System, the National System of Trails, the National Wilderness Preservation System, and Wild and Scenic Rivers system, including study rivers designated under section 5(a) of the Wild and Scenic Rivers Act and National Recreation Areas designated by Act of Congress:

(2) on any Federal lands within the boundaries of any national forest: *Provided however*, That surface coal mining operations may be permitted on such lands if the

Secretary finds that there are no significant recreational, timber, economic or other values which may be incompatible with such surface mining operations and—

(A) surface operations and impacts are incident to an underground coal mine; or

(B) where the Secretary of Agriculture determines, with respect to lands which do not have significant forest cover within those national forests west of the 100th meridian, that surface mining is in compliance with the Multi-Use Sustained-Yield Act of 1960, the Federal Coal Leasing Amendments Act of 1975, the National Forest Management Act of 1976, and the provisions of this Act; *And provided further*, That no surface coal mining operations be permitted within the boundaries of the Custer National Forest;

(3) which will adversely affect any publicly owned park or places included in the National Register of Historic Sites unless approved jointly by the regulatory authority and the Federal, State, or local agency with jurisdiction over park or historic site."[54] (Emphasis added.)

The act also allows states to designate lands that have values that would be incompatible with surface mining. One of the criterion used is that surface mining not

(B) affect fragile or historic lands in which such operations could result in significant damage to important historic, cultural, scientific, and *esthetic values* and natural systems.[55] (Emphasis added.)

LEGAL AND CONSTITUTIONAL ISSUES

SMCRA's legislative history reflects congressional thinking (see Eichbam and Buente 1980; Kite 1978; and Waters 1979). Congress observed that surface mining seriously impaired the post-mining usefulness of the land, then concluded that this important problem required a federal solution. Finally, it found that a relatively detailed regulatory scheme governing post-mining land use was necessary.

SMCRA requires that all land disturbed by surface coal mining operations be restored to a condition capable of supporting the potential uses of the land prior to any mining, or to higher or better uses if certain conditions are met. This standard is imposed in both the initial and permanent phases of the SMCRA regulatory

---

[50]Id., s. 1265 (b)(19).
[51]Id., s. 1265(d).
[52]Id., s. 1270 (c).
[53]Id., s. 1270(d).
[54]Id., s. 1272(e).
[55]Id., s. 1272 (a)(3)(B).

program. During the initial program, the Office of Surface Mining directly enforces the standard on individual mine operators under Section 515 (b)(2) and the implementing regulations. During the permanent program, the standard may be enforced directly by the states if they qualify for delegation by the Secretary of the Interior. A permanent program must institute federal procedural mechanisms, principally permitting and performance bonding, to ensure compliance by the industry. Section 515(b)(2) and the implementing regulations form a land use regulatory scheme that is national, uniform, and mandatory.

There was much hostility and resentment from states that were already implementing stringent surface mining regulation programs, from states that needed to mesh federal standards with already existing standards, and from other states, where the requirements were so different. Some saw procedural hardship deriving from the specificity of the regulations.

Two constitutional amendments could potentially limit the federal government's power to enact and enforce SMCRA's land capability requirements. First, land use regulation under Section 515(b)(2) may constitute a "taking" under the Fifth Amendment, entitling affected persons to just compensation. Second, these requirements may violate the Tenth Amendment because they inappropriately interfere with state land use regulation. However, in *Hodel* v. *Virginia Surface Mining and Reclamation Association, Inc.*[56] and *Hodel* v. *Indiana*,[57] the U.S. Supreme Court reversed the decisions of the two separate federal district courts, in Virginia and Indiana, that had found several provisions of SMCRA unconstitutional and had permanently enjoined their enforcement.

The Virginia district court found that the acts' reclamation requirements for steep-slope mining interfere with traditional state government functions and thus violate the Tenth Amendment. The Indiana district court enjoined SMCRA's prime farmland provisions, finding that they regulate activities having no substantial impact on interstate commerce and so are beyond the power of Congress under the commerce clause. The Indiana court also held that the prime farmland provisions violate the Tenth Amendment by usurping state functions, and that both they and the steep-slope "approximate original contour" provision violate the substantive due process and equal protection guarantees of the Fifth Amendment. Both district courts held that the provisions for issuing cessation orders and impos-

ing civil penalties for their violation transgress the procedural due process of the Fifth Amendment.

The lower courts also found that several provisions of SMCRA are impossible to comply with and are economically prohibitive, thus taking from the mine operators all use of their land in violation of the just compensation clause of the Fifth Amendment. In reversing, the Supreme Court held that SMCRA is a legitimate exercise of commerce clause power and that it does not violate the Tenth Amendment. The Court also rejected appellant's equal protection argument. The Court held, however, that the due process and just compensation questions were not ripe for decision, leaving mine operators free to litigate these issues later if SMCRA's provisions adversely affect specific property interests. (For more detailed discussion of the Supreme Court cases and lower court cases leading up to these decisions, see Conner 1982; Eichbaum and Buente 1980; and Wadsworth 1980.)

EARLIER FEDERAL ACTS

There were other, earlier federal statutes, prior to the Surface Mining and Reclamation Control Act of 1977, that also have a potential impact on visual resources. The General Mining Law of 1872[58] is the statutory authority used by the mining industry and the federal land management agencies to provide the industry with a right to mine on public lands. Hard-rock mining on public lands as authorized by the 1872 mining law refers primarily to mining metals such as gold, silver, copper, molybdenum, lead, zinc, and uranium. It does not include mining for coal, oil shale, sodium, and phosphate or common varieties of certain building materials. Most of the nation's nonferrous metal deposits are located in the vast public lands in twelve Western states, especially in desert and mountainous areas, managed mostly by the U.S. Forest Service and the Bureau of Land Management.

Although the 1872 mining law states that mines on the public lands must comply with regulations prescribed by law, it does not explicitly vest the Forest Service or BLM with authority to regulate mining activities. However, organic acts of the Forest Service and BLM give these agencies specific authority to regulate mining. The Forest Service Organic Act of 1897[60] requires that miners in national forests comply with rules and regulations issued by the Secretary of Agriculture.

[56]452 U.S. 264 (1981).
[57]452 U.S. 314 (1981).
[58]30 U.S.C. ss. 22–54 (1988).
[60]43 U.S.C. § 1701 et. seq. (1988).

Section 302(b) of the Federal Land Policy and Management Act (FLPMA) grants BLM a sweeping mandate to prevent undue degradation of the public lands "by regulation or otherwise."[61] BLM's mandate is strengthened by the fact that, although hard-rock mining is not governed by most FLPMA provisions due to a savings clause preserving the miners rights under the 1872 law, Section 302(b) is explicitly exempted from this savings clause.

These provisions provide the Forest Service and BLM with sufficient authority to impose environmental regulations on hard-rock mining. BLM and the Forest Service do have regulations in force. In addition to requiring compliance with the Clean Air Act, the Clean Water Act, and Resource Conservation and Recovery Act RCRA,[62] the Forest Service imposes requirements designed to harmonize operations with scenic values "to the extent practicable."[63] The emphasis on "practicable" means the Forest Service regulations do not eliminate environmental degradation from the mines in the national forests, but require only those measures the miner can afford.

To block mining activity, the land agencies have resorted to reserve public lands and thus remove them from the purposes of mineral exploration. In 1910 Congress passed the Pickett Act granting to the president the power to "temporarily" withdraw public lands and reserve them for public purposes specified in the withdrawal orders, such withdrawals to remain in force until revoked by the president or act of Congress.[64] In 1914 the Supreme Court, in the case of United States v. Midwest Oil Company,[65] declared that, for the eighty years prior to the passage of the Pickett Act, the president had had an implied grant of power to make withdrawals without express statutory authority. By Executive Order No. 10355 of May 1952, the president's powers of withdrawal were delegated to the Secretary of the Interior.

All units in the National Park System and the National Wildlife Refuge System that contained wilderness areas were closed to mining before any of their lands were designated as wilderness. The mining exception thus has no application to these areas. Eastern national forests and their wilderness area are not subject to the mining laws.

The mining exception was incorporated into most Western forest wilderness areas as they were added to the system, but there were some exceptions. The Saw-tooth and Hells Canyon wilderness areas and their surrounding national recreation areas were withdrawn from operation of the mining laws on the date they were established. The Boundary Waters Canoe Area in northern Minnesota was withdrawn from mining in 1978. The Misty Fjords and Admiralty Island national monuments of Alaska and their wilderness areas, administered by the Forest Service were established on December 2, 1980, and withdrawn from mining the same day.

In two Idaho wilderness areas, the mining exception went to the advantage of the mining industry. In the Gospel Hump Wilderness, created by the Endangered American Wilderness Act of 1978, withdrawal was not until January 1, 1988. The River of No Return Wilderness was created with a "special management zone" within which there will be no withdrawal from mining with respect to cobalt and associated minerals.

For the most part, mineral exploration in wilderness areas ceased on January 1, 1984. The withdrawal (from mined utilization) is "subject to valid rights then existing," however. In 1976 Congress responded to political opposition to withdrawals by enacting the Federal Land and Management Act, which limits BLM's traditional authority to withdraw land from mineral entry.[66] It requires notification to Congress of withdrawals over 5,000 acres, and such withdrawals are subject to a one-house congressional veto which would prevent withdrawal from mineral utilization. The act also limited the duration of withdrawals and mandated review of existing withdrawals before 1991.

If land is not withdrawn from mining law application, it is still subject to the mining law of 1872 as well as to Forest Service and BLM review. The critics (see Noble 1980; Toffenetti 1985) charge that current Forest Service and BLM practices that are intended to regulate and control hard-rock mining activities on public lands are too timid or too brutal. On the one hand, regulations to protect surface resources do not sufficiently protect public lands from degradation, while on the other, withdrawal power is too blunt and sweeping. Other options include denying the existence of a valuable deposit, denial of other necessary permits, or proposals for new procedures addressing more stringent environmental regulation. The last is espoused most often; for a more detailed treatment of the mining law of 1872 and its impacts on public lands, see Noble (1980) and Toffenetti (1985).

[61] Id. 1732(b).
[62] 36 C.F.R. ss. 252.4 (e) (1)-(5) (1991).
[63] Id., s. 252.8(d).
[64] 43 U.S.C. ss. 141, 142 (1988); see also 37 op. Att'y. Gen. 433 (1934); 40 op. Att'y. Gen. 73 (1941).
[65] 236 U.S. 459 (1915).
[66] 43 U.S.C. s. 1714 (1988).

Many of the minerals located in the public domain are controlled by the Mineral Leasing Acts (MLA's),[67] which cover mining and exploration activities for minerals that are not hard rock — such as phosphorus, sodium, oil shale, oil and gas, and coal as well as geothermal development. The MLA's delineate the broad terms of a lease, the qualifications of applicants, and the acreage that may be leased. A tremendous amount of discretion is given to the Secretary of the Interior under the MLA's, including rule-making authority, which must consider other environmental statutes, and the general directive to manage public lands in the public interest.

Under these acts the federal government is able to insert clauses into a mining lease that will provide for the preservation of aesthetic values and will require restoration of the surface. Also, many of the leasing statutes provide for the renegotiation of the terms of the lease at stated intervals. The federal government is inserting clauses in its lease renewals requiring restoration of the surface. In the *Montana Power Company* case,[68] where the federal government owned mineral rights but not the surface, the Secretary of the Interior inserted such a clause on December 3, 1965. The surface rights were held by the Northern Pacific Railway, which was the assigner of the coal lease. According to the appellants, Northern Pacific had waived restoration of the surface rights. Nevertheless, the BLM required restoration, and this was one of the main grounds for the appeal. The decision states, in upholding the insertion of the restoration clause:

The appellant stresses that the Northern Pacific Railway has no interest in the restoration of the surface. It contends that the restoration provision should be limited in acreage, the surface of which is owned by the United States. Although it is true that the United States has a greater interest in its own lands, it also has a substantial concern with the lands of others in which it has reserved the minerals. Furthermore, by the end of the twenty-year lease terms, the ownership of the surface of the land may well have changed, and the new owners may have a different attitude from the railroad's.[69]

Administration of the forest reserves was transferred from the Secretary of Interior to the Secretary of Agriculture in 1905, but responsibility of all mineral entries within the national forests remain with the Department of Interior. The Forest Service has the authority to manage only the surface resources of national forests. The BLM exercises authority for the secretary of interior for all oil and gas leasing as well as for other minerals that call for leasing of public lands under the MLA's. But, the relevant land management agency, often the Forest Service, prepares the environmental assessment for the proposed leasing activity.

The final authority over the granting of oil and gas leases and locatable minerals leases resides with the Secretary of the Interior through the Department of the Interior Board of Appeals (IBLA). In a critical case, *Duncan Miller*,[70] the IBLA abandoned the departmental policy of accepting the recommendations of the land management agency — in this case, the Forest Service. The IBLA rejected the agency's stipulations or recommendations because they would have made all oil and gas exploration and development so difficult as to render the leases nugatory. The new departmental policy is that Forest Service leasing recommendations are considered but are not conclusive. This is a major issue and has been at the center of more recent disputes, such as phosphate mining in the Osceola National Forest (see Pell 1984) and offshore leasing for gas and oil (see Martin 1982). The only counterweight that the land management agency has is their assessment as to whether surface environmental impacts from mineral exploration and development are significant and whether remediation is possible.

Both the mining act of 1872 and the Mineral Leasing Acts have caused extensive litigation, much of which focuses on the relationship with environmental legislation as stated in the Wilderness Act and the National Environmental Policy Act, among others.

WILDERNESS AND MINING

In 1929 the Secretary of Agriculture and the chief of the Forest Service, by administrative action, set aside within the national forests eighty-eight wilderness-type areas. These areas were divided into "primitive," "wilderness," "wild," and "canoe" categories. In 1964 the Wilderness Act[71] took the last three categories and designated them as "wilderness" areas (see Chapter 9). The most important provisions of the Wilderness Act relating to mining activities are found in Subsections 4(b) and 4(d). The last sentence of Subsection 4(d) sets forth the general rule:

---

[67]Mineral Lands Leasing Act 30 U.S.C. ss. 181–287 (1988); Mineral Leasing Act for Acquired Lands 30 U.S.C. ss. 351–359 (1988); Right of Way Leasing Act of 1930 30 U.S.C. ss. 301–306 (1988), the Geothermal Steam Act of 1970 30 U.S.C. ss. 1001–1025 (1988); Outer Continental Shelf Lands Act 43 U.S.C. ss. 1331–1356 (1988).
[68]72 Inter. Dec. 518 (1965).
[69]Id.
[70]Duncan Miller, 79 Interior Dec. 416 (1972).
[71]16 U.S.C. 1133 (b) (1988).

Except as otherwise provided in this Act, wilderness areas shall be devoted to the public purposes of recreational, *scenic*, scientific, educational, conservation, and historical use.[72] (Emphasis added.)

Subsection 4(d)[73] sets forth the exceptions to this general rule. The most important exception is in Subsection 4(d)(3):[74]

Notwithstanding any other provisions of this Act, until midnight December 31st, 1983, the United States mining laws and all laws pertaining to mineral leasing shall, to the same extent as applicable prior to the effective date of this Act, extend to those national forest lands designated by this Act as "wilderness areas."[75]

Thus, mineral claims could be located in wilderness areas until 1984, and all further exploration for mineral development ceased in 1984. However, any claim validly located by that date could be worked indefinitely thereafter (Comment 1968 and Toffenitti 1985). As pointed out by Toffenetti (1985), viable mineral claims established before 1984 will have to pass several economic tests, and actual logistical working operations may prove impossible in many wilderness locations.

It should be noted, however, that in the interval between the effective date of the act and 1984, certain restrictions were placed upon mining and mineral leasing activities. First, patents issued on claims located in the interval conveyed title only to mineral deposits within that claim. The only timber and surface rights acquired were those reasonably required for conducting mining and prospecting activities. Second, the Secretary of Agriculture could prescribe reasonable regulations governing ingress to and egress from mining operations.[76] Third, the Secretary of Agriculture could promulgate regulations governing the use of motorized equipment in connection with exploration, drilling, and production of mineral deposits. Fourth, the Secretary could require that upon termination of mining operations, the surface of the land disturbed by those operations be restored as nearly as is practicable to its condition prior to mining activities.

The greater limitations upon leases for mineral exploration are a consequence of the differences between the mineral leasing acts and the federal mining location laws. Under the latter, citizens are free to explore as a matter of right, while under the leasing laws they must apply for the "privilege," as one case puts it.[77] Citizens have no vested interest until the privilege is granted through the issuance of a permit. However, no application for a lease or permit covering lands within a wilderness area can be denied solely because the lands are within a wilderness area. Such a decision would appear to abuse discretion, which would emasculate the express provisions of the Wilderness Act allowing such activity.

The other major "exception" to the general plan of the Wilderness Act is found in Subsection 4(d)(1).[78] This provision states that where the use of aircraft or motorboats within a wilderness area has already been established, that use "may be permitted to continue," subject to any restrictions that the Secretary of Agriculture may promulgate. This does not mean, however, that if these modes of transportation were used prior to the Wilderness Act permission to continue such use was automatically established. On the contrary, in *United States* v. *Gregg*,[79] the court held that after the act's passage the Secretary of Agriculture had to give express permission to continue flights into wilderness areas even where such use had already been established. The court pointed out that the Wilderness Act provides "that the landing of aircraft *may*, not *shall*, be permitted where such use has become established."[80] (emphasis added).

The court then looked to Subsection 4(d)(4),[81] which states that "the grazing of livestock . . . shall be permitted to continue,"[82] and concluded that that language "clearly shows that Congress knew how to write an exception if they had intended one."[83] The court also held to be criminal acts any violations of valid regulations promulgated by the Secretary of Agriculture under the authority contained in the Wilderness Act.[84]

---

[72]Id.
[73]Id.
[74]Id., s. 1133(d)(3).
[75]Id.
[76]Id.
[77]Wilber v. United States ex rel Barton, 46 F.2d 217, 221 (D.C. Cir. 1930), aff'd. 283 U.S. 414 (1931).
[78]16 U.S.C. 1133(d)(1) (1988).
[79]290 F. Supp. 706 (W.D. Wash. 1968).
[80]Id. at 707.
[81]16 U.S.C. 1133 (d)(4) (1988).
[82]Id.
[83]Id. 290 F. Supp. 706, 708 (W.D. Wash. 1968).
[84]Id.; 16 U.S.C. s. 551 (1988) provides: "[A]ny violation of . . . rules and regulations (promulgated by the Secretary of Agriculture to protect national forests) shall be punished by a fine of not more than $500 or imprisonment for not more than 6 months or both."

Confusion abounds as to when certain mining activities are allowed in national forests, wilderness areas, primitive areas, and roadless areas, and also what degree of regulation is deemed appropriate by the agency. In this area of openly conflicting laws, court opinions, and agency regulations, there are very few clear guidelines. The Surface Mining and Control Act of 1977 eliminates some of these questions, but it does not clarify questions relating to previous or existing mineral rights. The cessation of mineral exploration in wilderness areas after 1984 also clears up other questions. However, there are still viable mineral claims in national forests, national monuments, wilderness areas, and even national parks, with little guidance as to what are allowable mining extraction activities and land-space impacts, or whether mining operations have to calculate environmental mitigation as part of their feasibility costs are lacking.

MINING AND THE NATIONAL ENVIRONMENTAL POLICY ACT

Beside the Wilderness Act, the National Environmental Policy Act (NEPA) is the other far-reaching federal act affecting federal actions regarding surface mining. Although NEPA is abroad (see Chapter 11), some factors limit its application to mining activities on federal lands and in regard to certain Federal agency actions.

First, NEPA's effect on existing mining laws is limited, depending on whether a restrictive or liberal view is adopted.

A conservative interpretation of NEPA proceeds as follows. Section 102 of NEPA provides, in part:

The Congress authorizes and directs that, to the *fullest extent possible*: (1) the policies, regulations and public laws of the United States shall be interpreted and administered in accordance with the policy set forth in this act.[85] (Emphasis added.)

The Senate-House Conference Committee added the words emphasized above and explained their purpose:

The purpose of the new language is to make clear that each agency of the Federal government shall comply with the directives set out in such Subparagraphs (A) through (H) unless the existing law applicable to such agency's operations expressly prohibits or makes full compliance with one of the directives impossible. If such is found to be the case, then compliance with the particular directive is not immediately required.[86]

NEPA provides further: "The policies and goals set forth in the Act are supplementary to those set forth in existing authorizations of Federal agencies."[87]

The conference committee explained this section to mean: "The effect of this section . . . is to give recognition to the fact that *the bill does not repeal existing law*."[88] (Emphasis added.)

Therefore, NEPA does not require the impossible, nor does it change any existing laws, including the mining law. These conclusions were applied in *United States* v. *Kosanke*[89] in which the IBLA decided that the above provisions of NEPA[90] exempted mineral patent application proceedings from NEPA environmental impact statement procedures.[91] *Kosanke* holds that a federal agency decision that does not involve the exercise of discretion but requires only the application of fixed objective rules to the facts establishing statutory rights need not be preceded by an environmental study.[92]

The question now arises as to what mining law activities other than mineral patent proceedings may be exempted from NEPA procedures. Additional language in Kosanke is useful in applying this exemption to such activities as mineral exploration and development under the existing Forest Service regulation system[93] and the prospective BLM regulation system:

Moreover, to condition the full enjoyment of an existing right upon the filing of an informational statement by the executive branch of the federal government, the adequacy of which statement is subject to attack by third parties and ultimate determination by the courts, would seriously impair that right.[94]

---

[85]42 U.S.C. s. 4332 (1988).

[86]Conf. Rep. No. 91–795, 1969 U.S. Code Cong. and Adm. News, 91st Cong., 1st Sess. 2767, 2770 (1969). Hereinafter cited as Conf. Rep. No. 91–765.

[87]42 U.S.C. s. 4335 (1988).

[88]Conf. Rep. No. 91–765 at 2771.

[89]12 IBLA 282 CFS (Min) 79 (1973).

[90]42 U.S.C. s. 4332, 4335 (1988).

[91]The board came to this conclusion notwithstanding the fact that it also found that the secretary may consider costs added by environmental requirements in determining whether the claimant can satisfy the marketability test.

[92]Another attempt was made to apply NEPA to mineral patent application proceedings in the United States v. Pittsburg Pacific Company, IBLA 74–271.

[93]36 C.F.R. Part 252 (1991).

[94]12 IBLA 282 CFS (Mn) 79 (1973) at 297.

To the extent that mining laws give the individuals the right to enter the public domain, to locate claims thereon, to discover minerals therein, and to extract and remove those minerals therefrom, all without prior approval of the United States, the development of a mining claim cannot be tortured into "Federal action" major, minor or otherwise.[95]

The result reached by the ILBA in Kosanke is supported by at least two circuit court decisions. The Court of Appeals for the Fifth Circuit has held that the qualifying words "fullest extent possible" Section 102 of NEPA mean that the act does not require a NEPA statement of its preparation would lead to the violation of a statutory duty of the agency concerned.[96] However, any such agency that decides that its statutory duties preclude application of NEPA procedures must make express findings of the exigencies and conflicts preventing compliance.[97] Under this interpretation, it may be concluded "that the NEPA procedures cannot be applied to any Mining Law activities, including mineral exploration, development or mining, if such application would interfere with existing rights under the Mining Law or with an agency's duty to provide for those rights" (Haggard 1975, p. 355) — in other words, ministerial functions of the secretary mandated by the mining law.

One court confirmed that NEPA does indeed permit the secretary to "establish lease terms that, to the fullest extent possible, assure protection of environmental quality."[98] The courts have consistently held that the secretary does not have discretion to reject preference right lease applications if the requisite showing has been made, and that NEPA does not operate to transform a previously ministerial task into a discretionary one.[99] Nevertheless, the courts have also determined that issuance of a lease in these cases is not a purely ministerial act, in light of NEPA; two statutory provisions afford a degree of discretion to the secretary.

First, one of the MLA's provides that "each lease shall contain provisions . . . for the protection of the interests of the United States."[100] This affords the secretary broad discretion in setting the terms and conditions of leases, including preference right leases. Second, the secretary has an obligation "to interpret and administer the Mineral Lands Leasing Act in accordance with NEPA 'to the fullest extent possible. '"[101] The result of construing the MLA and NEPA together is that the secretary has discretion to condition the terms of the lease for protection of environmental values.

The preference right lease cases confirm that NEPA's application is limited. It does not enable the secretary to abrogate vested rights. For example, invocation of NEPA as authority for conditioning a lease may subvert the purposes and terms of MLA. NEPA cannot be extended that far. NEPA expands the secretary's powers incrementally but does "not justify [their] gross extension" (Martin 1982). Much sorting out of the interrelationship of the Mineral Leasing Acts and the General Mining Law of 1872 in relation to environmental statutes remains to be done.

SPECIFIC STATUTES FOR SPECIFIC LANDS

All the aforementioned federal acts apply to a general purpose for a geographic area, but there are specific statutory or regulatory provisions for certain federal lands. Most of these provisions are related to National Park Service lands such as the Coronado National Monument, Arizona,[102] Death Valley National Monument, California–Nevada,[103] Glacier Bay National Monument, Alaska,[104] Mount McKinley National Park, Alaska,[105] and Organ Pipe Cactus National Monument, Arizona,[106] all of which provide that the Secretary of the Interior shall prescribe regulations for surface mining. The secretary apparently relies on the regulations of the National Park Service as to surface use in these areas.[107] Another statute placed the burden of reclamation on the mining claimant, but that is also of limited effect. The Mining Claims Rights Restoration Act of 1955[108] opened to mineral location public

---

[95]Id. at 298.

[96]State of Louisiana v. Federal Power Commission, 503 F.2d 844 (5th Cir. 1974).

[97]American Smelting and Refining Co. v. F.P.C., 494 F.2d 925 (D.C. Cir. 1974).

[98]Utah Int'l. Inc. v. Andrus, 488 F. Supp. 962, 966 (D. Utah 1979).

[99]Id., plus Natural Resources Defense Council, Inc. v. Berklund, 458 F. Supp. 925, 928 (D.D.C. 1978), aff'd., 609 F.2d 553 (D.C. Cir. 1980).

[100]30 U.S.C. s. 187 (1988).

[101]Utah Int'l. Inc. v. Andrus, 488 F. Supp. 962, 966 (D. Utah 1979), quoting NEPA s. 102, 42 U.S.C. s. 4332 (1988).

[102]16 U.S.C. 450y-2 (1988).

[103]16 U.S.C. 447 (1970), 36 C.F.R. 7.26 (1991) 43 C.F.R. 3826.3 (1991).

[104]43 C.F.R. 3826.4-1 (1991).

[105]16 U.S.C. 3509 et seq. (1988); 36 C.F.R. 7.44 (1991); 43 C.F.R. 3826.1 (1991).

[106]16 U.S.C. 4502 (1988); 43 C.F.R. 3826.6 (1991).

[107]36 C.F.R. 7.26, 7.44 (1991).

[108]30 U.S.C. 621 to 625 (1988).

lands withdrawn for power development or power sites. This law also provides that the secretary of the interior may prohibit placer mining, or may permit it only upon condition that the surface be restored.

There is also statutory authority to regulate mining law activity in U.S. Federal Wildlife Service areas in the Custer State Park Game Sanctuary in South Dakota.[109] The Secretary of Agriculture is authorized to regulate mining operations and locations of claims. The Surface Mining Control and Reclamation Act of 1977 also states that no surface coal mining operations are permitted in the Custer National Forest.[110]

The prohibitions or restrictions in these individual areas are interesting because they often follow a pattern of events. In many of these areas, mining was allowed at one time to perpetuate the image of the single prospector with pick axe in hand. However, most of these areas have unique scenic values that conflict directly with large-scale high-technology mining allowed under the mine claims established prior to the protective statutes. The Death Valley National Monument cases are an illustration in point.

Plans to expand borate mining in Death Valley National Monument focused public attention in 1975 on mining in the national parks. Mining is generally prohibited, but in some parks preexisting rights under the 1872 mining law have been preserved; special legislation has opened other parks to mining.

Congress enacted special legislation opening Death Valley to mining under the 1872 mining law four months after the area was proclaimed a national monument by President Roosevelt in 1933. At that time, no one contemplated large-scale surface mining within the monument. Today there are seven talc mines and two borate mines operating.

A case decided in March 1975 by the U.S. District Court for the Eastern District of California provides reason to forecast even more serious difficulties than those experienced in the past for conducting mining activities in the few available areas under National Park Service jurisdiction. In *Kayser* v. *Morton*,[111] the court upheld a denial by the superintendent of the Death Valley National Monument of an application by holders of unpatented mining claims to construct a road to their claims for mineral exploration and min-

ing. The court found that Death Valley National Monument was open to mineral location pursuant to 16 U.S.C. s. 447 (1970) subject to regulations of the Secretary of the Interior as set forth in 36 C.F.R. 7.26, which requires road permits. The court expressed the following as a basis for its decision:

1. There was reason to doubt the validity of the mining claims.
2. The road would leave a permanent scar on the environment.
3. There are other means of access to the claims, for instance, foot trail, burro, and helicopter.[112]

This decision was quickly followed by a memorandum dated April 21, 1975, from the director of the National Park Service to the regional directors stating:

This order provides the legal authority for National Park Service management to refuse to grant permits concerning unpatented mining claims unless the claims are determined to be valid. You should request the Branch of Mining and Minerals of the Land Acquisition Division to investigate the validity of all unpatented mining claims before issuance of permits" (Haggard 1975, p. 384).

Haggard states that "the incorrectness of this order and the Court's decision should be clearly demonstrable by precedents holding that a valid mining claim is not a prerequisite to conduct mineral exploration in areas open to Mining Law activities" (Haggard 1975, p. 384).

In another case, the Sierra Club filed against the Department of the Interior, listing the Death Valley National Monument itself as a plaintiff[113] and stating that the secretary of the interior has a trust and a responsibility to protect the monument. The suit asked that this trust be fulfilled by such measures as the promulgation of regulations that would prohibit surface mining or require effective reclamation, prohibit the expansion of existing mines, and provide for the withdrawal of certain areas of the monument from the General Mining Law of 1872.[114]

One case that never went to trial resulted in a tempo-

---

[109]16 U.S.C. s. 678a(1988), 36 C.F.R. s. 251.10. (1991).

[110]16 U.S.C. s. 1276 (1988).

[111]Civ. Action No. f-75-10 (D.C.E.D., Calif. 1975).

[112]Id.

[113]Death Valley National Monument v. Dept. of Interior Civ. Act. No. 76–401 (D.H.D. Cal. filed Feb. 26, 1976).

[114]Id.

rary restraining order awarded to the National Park Service against American Borate.[115] The order restrained American Borate from doing exploratory work that would create a cumulative visual impact that would become visually significant when added to the previous mining activity in the area. The area would have straddled an interpretive drive that carried 25 percent of the monument's total visitor traffic. In still another incident, concern was raised over potential strip mining near the Zabriskie Point viewing area, "considered a premier scenic wonder of Death Valley, where ribboned waves of sand, stone and rock stand in a fragile frieze"[116] (see the case study below).

Incidents such as this one in the Death Valley National Monument, as well as others in the national parks mentioned before where mining was allowed, added impetus to passage of the Regulation of Park Mining Act of 1976 (PL. 94–429). The act imposes a moratorium on mining in Death Valley. The moratorium does not shut down ongoing mines, but permits no new land disturbance pending a study by the U.S. Department of the Interior to determine the validity of the existing rights to Death Valley National Monument, Mount McKinley National Park, and Organ Pipe Cactus National Monument, and to recommend to Congress whether any valid or patented claims should be acquired by the United States. The act also repeals the laws that permit the staking of new mineral claims in Coronado National Memorial, Crater Lake National Park, Death Valley National Monument, Glacier Bay National Monument, Mount McKinley National Park, and Organ Pipe Cactus National Monument.

The Forest Service also saw several forest areas promoted to the status of national issues by environmental groups. The first of these issues arose in early 1969 when a mining company applied for a permit to construct a road to explore and develop its mining claims in the White Clouds area of the Challis National Forest, Idaho. The issue was resolved by establishment of the Sawtooth National Recreation Area in 1972.[117] Still other conflicts over mineral development activity arose in the Stillwater complex in the Custer and Gallatin National Forests of Montana (see Burns 1972).

These types of conflicts lead to one point: Despite all the general legislation and regulation, there still are exceptions, for which protection is being lobbied, that do not fit the normal classification. The contextual rule as discussed earlier rises again. The legal system does not itself seem capable of dealing with the idiosyncratic conflicts of aesthetics versus economic values found in mining situations. This is pointed out by a landscape architect's testimony for the Surface Mining Control and Reclamation Act of 1977 (Franzman 1977) as to site-to-site differences affecting reclamation practices; and by Clyde (1967), when he stresses the need for flexibility in regard to slope practices, rainfall differences, and intensity of use or viewing differences. Another factor is the impact of future mining technologies and the need to limit the location of mining activities in the future. Examples are potential phosphate mining in the Caribou National Forest in Idaho, the Osceola National Forest in Florida, and the Los Padres National Forest in California, as well as vermiculite mining in the Green Springs Historic District, Virginia.

Case Study: Death Valley National Monument[118]

Background and Context

Death Valley National Monument was created February 1933 by presidential proclamation under the authority of the Antiquities Act of 1906. When President Roosevelt made the proclamation, special note was taken of the "unusual features of scenic, scientific, and educational interests therein contained," and the monument was closed to mineral entry. However, four months after creation of the monument, Congress reopened Death Valley to mining.

Two primary types of claims for minerals can be located under the mining law of 1872: placer and lode claims. Placer claims are filed on alluvium, an ore carried away from its original source, usually by the action of water. Lode claims are filed upon rock-in-place; the intersection of the mineral vein with the surface, or apex, is discovered, and the claim is filed upon that apex.

Placer claims can be up to 20 acres if filed by an individual, and up to 160 acres if filed by an association of eight individuals. On a placer claim, the miner must continue working within the stated boundaries of the claim.

Lode claims can be up to 20.66 acres, and are filed upon the apex of the vein or lode. Though the exact claim dimensions

---

[115]Phone interview with Larry May, USNPS Denver Service Center, August 1978.

[116]New York Times, 1976, Oct. 6, p. 1.

[117]16 U.S.C. § 460aa (1988).

[118]Previously presented by Dan Hamson and Toni Ristau as A Case Study–Death Valley National Monument California-Nevada as part of the National Conference on Applied Techniques for Analysis and Management of the Visual Resource, G. Elsner and R.C. Smardon, Tech. Coord. (Incline Village, Nevada, April 23–25, 1979). Reproduced with permission of the authors.

are dependent upon site restrictions, the idealized lode claim is 600 by 1,500 feet. The claim need not be rectangular, but the 600-foot end lines must be parallel; these end lines in turn are to be located parallel to the vein and not in excess of 300 feet from the center line of the vein. In a lode claim, the miner may not cross the end lines of the claim, but may follow the vein outside the lateral lines of the claim so long as the vein is continuous and remains within the parallel projection of the end lines.

Tunnel site claims are similar to lode claims but do not require that ore show upon the surface of the ground. The claimant has the right to any veins or lodes discovered within 3,000 linear feet of the tunnel face. Upon discovery, the claimant must show the location of the tunnel line upon the surface to create the mining claim.

In addition, the miner may claim up to 5 acres of nonmineralized land for use as a mill site. A valid or patented mill site entitles the owner to use of the surface, including such resources as water and timber, to support the mining or milling operations.

Death Valley has had a romantic history of prospecting and mining within its boundaries—images of the grizzled prospector moving across the desert with his faithful burro and the 20-mule-team borax wagon trains making the 250-mile trek across the Mojave Desert are an established part of Western lore. Early prospecting and mining operations were small-scale efforts; the mines themselves were underground. Despite continuing efforts to find untold mineral riches, the operations in Death Valley netted only about $2 million in the 60 years following the first flurry of prospecting activities in the 1880s. Small amounts of precious metals were discovered and mined out, but the most profitable commodities in the region proved to be borax and talc. Talc is a relatively common mineral, and it is mined in several parts of the country, but sizable amounts of borates in the U.S. are found only in southern California and Nevada. A few years after borates were found in Death Valley, much larger discoveries of sodium borates were made in the Searles Lake and Boron, California, area about 100 miles southwest of the monument (Cranston 1976). As a result, mining for borax in the monument was essentially shut down. As for talc, there was a brief rise in mining activity during World War II, but the operations since that time have been sporadic and small scale.

Increased demand for colemanite and ulexite (the sodium-calcium borates ores found in Death Valley National Monument) in the early 1970s prompted Tenneco Company to enter the monument and to stake claims for borates directly below Zabriskie Point. Internationally famous, Zabriskie Point is one of the prime scenic viewpoints within the monument; it was the view from Zabriske Point that, over one hundred years ago, prompted pioneer William Manly to write that he had "just seen all of God's creation." Upon completion of claim location, Tenneco announced plans to reopen a strip mining operation for borates. To the shock of both the National Park Service and the general public, it was discovered that the company was within its rights under the General Mining Law of 1872, and that the monument could do little to prevent such an operation within its boundaries. The loophole left by Congress in authorizing mineral entry allowed not only a prospector with burro, pick, and shovel but large-scale strip mining as well. The resulting public outcry

prompted Congress to take steps to prevent the desecration of Death Valley National Monument's natural, cultural, and scenic resources.

On September 28, 1976, Congress signed the Regulation of Park Mining Act (P.L. 94–429) into law. It provided, among other things, that national park system lands be closed to future mineral entry under the mining laws of 1872; that existing mineral rights be examined for validity; and that, upon determination of the extent of valid claims and their environmental consequences, the Secretary of the Interior will make a recommendation to Congress on allowing mining to continue, acquiring valid claims, or excluding significant mineral deposits by boundary adjustment in order to reduce the cost of acquisition. In order to ensure that damage would not continue during the time allotted for studies, a moratorium on further surface disturbance for the purpose of mineral extraction was imposed; this moratorium applied to Death Valley. The Secretary of Interior was given until September 28, 1978, to perform the required studies and formulate recommendations to Congress (Figure 12.8).

Analysis and Study Approach

The National Park Service was given the responsibility for producing the studies required. As there was little time available in which to perform fieldwork and produce the studies, two facets of the project—validity determination and assessment of environmental effects—proceeded simultaneously. Originally, 863 unpatented claims were registered with the

FIGURE 12.8   Map of area

superintendent (in compliance with P.L. 94–429); however, after completion of fieldwork by the mining engineers, only 19 were determined to be valid (workable) without contest. Within Death Valley, then, there are 118 patented claims and 19 valid unpatented claims. The valid and patented (registered) claims can be combined in various ways to offer a large number of alternatives for allowing mining on some claims, acquiring some claims, or excluding certain claims through adjustment. It was decided, in order to facilitate the choice of reasonable alternatives, the first step would be to study the environmental consequences of mineral extraction on all valid and patented claims.

As the proclamation creating the monument makes special note of the scenic resources of the monument, the impact on this was of major concern to the National Park Service. In analyzing this factor, the study team determined that "scenic quality" within the monument was already established when President Roosevelt signed the proclamation. The team specifically cited the unique scenic quality, which has been internationally recognized as a major scenic phenomenon. Most people visit Death Valley to view the spectacle of multicolored rock, magnificent desert vistas, stark salt pans, and majestic mountain ranges. Therefore, in assessing visual impact on visitors, there was no need to deal with subjective values attached to scenic quality. The study team's task was simply to determine which existing or potential mining operations (Figure 12.9) would likely be visible from the most heavily used visitor-use areas in the monument, and thus to identify those that might alter the scenic quality of the monument.

In order to objectively analyze an area as large as Death Valley National Monument — over 2.1 million acres — a computer-assisted program was needed. In consultation with the in-house Automatic Data Processing (ADP) unit, the study team decided to use a routine developed by Colorado State University that is designed to utilize the IMGRID cellular data system developed by Harvard University. The IMGRID system is a computer program designed to manipulate natural resource data that have been organized on the basis of a grid cell data structure. Visual Information System (VIS), the Colorado State University program, is a computer algorithm of IMGRID that analyzes the terrain visible from a single point or from multiple observer points. A search of 360 degrees is made from the observer point to delineate the viewshed for a given horizontal distance.

The IMGID-VIS program was chosen so that the terrain information already digitized by the Defense Mapping Service (DMS) and now distributed by the National Cartographic Information Center (NCIC) could be utilized. These tapes contain topographic maps interpolated to produce a data point for approximately every 208 feet on the ground. These data are accurate within ±100 feet vertically and ±400 feet horizontally. Using an existing routine, the DMS data were then integrated into the IMGRID format. Without the information available on these tapes, the team could not have carried out the analysis within the project's time and budget constraints.

The study area boundary selected encompassed the entire monument; it contained 54,540 cells, each approximately 83 acres in size. The overall study area thus included approximately 7,100 square miles. An elevation point was selected for each cell from information from the NCIC tapes. To ensure that the analysis would be on the conservative side, the lowest point inside each data cell was used, rather than the average or the highest point. Mining claims were then grouped according to certain geographical and mineral resource characteristics. This facilitated the analysis by eliminating the need to make a run from each individual mining claim. Selection of claims for grouping was thus important, as single data points were required both to represent claim groups and to fit the level of refinement mandated by the 83-acre cell size.

Mining claim locations were incorporated into the program according to information furnished by the mining office in Death Valley. To reduce computer time and save money, all searches or visual scans originated from the group of mining claims and scanned an arc with a horizontal distance of 79 miles and a vertical distance of 82.5 miles. A factor of 5 feet was added to each cell searched to obtain an average height for an observer looking into a mining area; the origin point was left at ground elevation.

A tabular format was chosen for the report. Thus, the value printed for any particular cell indicated the number of mining claim groups in each run that could be seen along a direct sightline from the location in the monument. If none of the claim groups was visible from a location, the cell was left blank. The program did not identify which claims within a group were visible. As a result, some groups were later split and run again in order to better define the claims with the highest visibility from sensitive visitor-interest areas. Also, factors such as horizon silhouetting of above-ground structures, dust/smoke plumes, and relative contrast between mined areas and adjacent lands (talc, for instance, is starkly white and offers a high degree of contrast with the natural colors of the surrounding rock, soil, and vegetation) were not included in the analysis. The visibility analysis was run to show which of the mining claims as likely to be visible and thus intrude on the monument's natural scenic resources. The analysis did not purport to include any information on the relative intrusiveness of different types of mining methods.

The data obtained from the computer model were plotted on monumentwide base maps (Figure 12.10) that delineated the areas within the monument from which one or more of a particular set of claims were visible. With the help of the monument staff, the most popular visitor-interest points were identified and plotted on base maps. To further assist the evaluation, a 25-mile radius was drawn from each claim group analyzed and the acreage affected totalled within the curve. After field checking, the team decided that the recognition factor would drop off dramatically from this point outward so that even if the area was visible from a great distance, the casual observer would not be able to identify a mining operation as such.

Results

The acreage within each viewshed was totaled both within the 25-mile-radius zone and for the entire monument; and the number of visitor-interest points that fell within the viewshed was identified. With this information, the team could estimate the number of visitors that annually might view the mining from those scenic spots in the monument and thus infer the mining impacts on visitation. In the exam-

a.

d.

b.

c.

e.

FIGURE 12.9 a, b, c, d, e Aerial and surface views of mining activity. *Source: National Park Service*

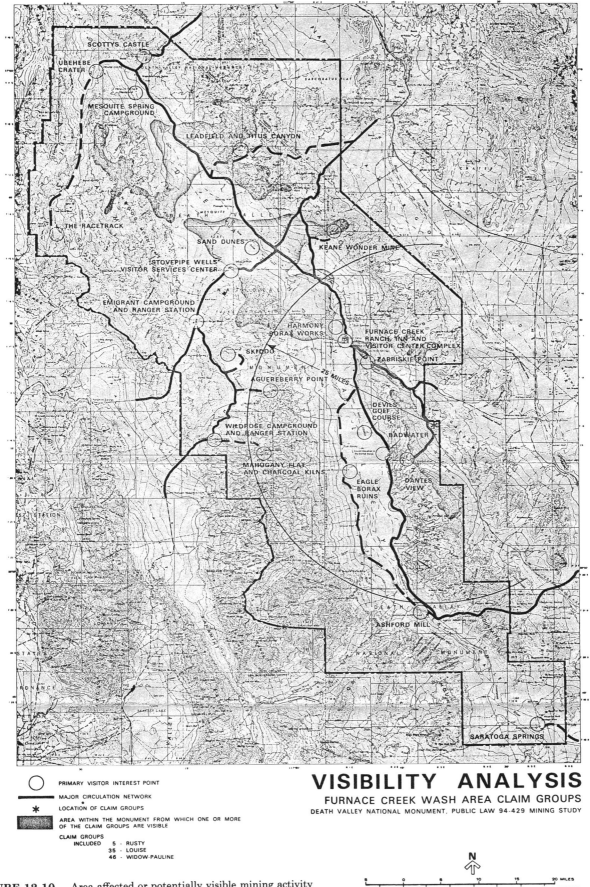

○ PRIMARY VISITOR INTEREST POINT

━━ MAJOR CIRCULATION NETWORK

∗ LOCATION OF CLAIM GROUPS

▨ AREA WITHIN THE MONUMENT FROM WHICH ONE OR MORE
OF THE CLAIM GROUPS ARE VISIBLE

CLAIM GROUPS
INCLUDED   5 - RUSTY
             35 - LOUISE
             46 - WIDOW-PAULINE

VISIBILITY ANALYSIS

FURNACE CREEK WASH AREA CLAIM GROUPS
DEATH VALLEY NATIONAL MONUMENT, PUBLIC LAW 94-429 MINING STUDY

N

FIGURE 12.10   Area affected or potentially visible mining activity

ple shown in this case study, the mining proposed for the three claim groups would disturb a maximum of 1,390 acres in the Furnace Creek area of the monument. However, the analysis revealed that those disturbed lands would be potentially visible from 86,000 acres within 25 miles of the claims and from 559,000 acres with the monument as a whole, and thus potentially affect some 310,000 visitors annually. Therefore, analysis of the severity of visual intrusion (in terms of area and viewers affected) caused by mining of the various claims was facilitiated (Figure 12.10).

The study for Death Valley National Monument was submitted to Congress in two parts; the first discussed the environmental consequences of mineral extraction, and the second presented alternatives to allowing mining, boundary adjustment, and acquisition of mining claims. Congress, in general, has restricted any future mining activities in the Central Parts, but has allowed mining in previous activity valid potential claims.

References

Adams, C. 1983. *Landscape design in mined land reclamation.* USDA, Soil Conservation Service, Landscape Architecture Note #1, U.S. G.P.O.

American Society of Landscape Architects. 1983. *Creating land for tomorrow: Landscape architecture technical information series, vol. 1, no. 3.* American Society of Landscape Architects in cooperation with Surface Environment and Mining Program, U.S. Forest Service.

Binder, D. 1977. Strip mining, the west and the nation. *Land and Water Law Review,* 12(1): 1–72.

Black, R. A. 1988. State control of mining on federal land: Environmental or land use regulation. *Natural Resources Journal,* 28: 873–881.

Bloom, C. R. 1980. *State Regulation of non-coal surface mining: A summary and comparison of state programs.* Office of Science and Natural Resources, National Conference of State Legislatures, Denver.

Bluechner, T. F. 1980. Mineral Leasing Act of 1920: Environmental standards set by departmental regulations. *Natural Resources Journal,* 20: 367–370.

Bosselman, F. P. 1969. The control of surface mining: An exercise in creative federalism. *Natural Resources Journal,* 9(2): 143.

Brecher, J. J. 1972. Venue in conservation cases: A potential pitfall for environmental lawyers. Ecology Law Quarterly, Vol. 2: 91–117.

Brooks, D. B. 1966. Strip mine reclamation and economic analysis. *Natural Resources Journal,* 6(1): 13–44.

Broughton, R. 1972. Aesthetics and environmental law: Decisions and values. *Land and Water Review,* 7(2): 451–500.

Burns, C. S. 1972. Legal problems imposed by requirements of restoration and beautification of mining properties. *Rocky Mountain Mineral Law Institute,* 13: 187–231.

Clyde, E. W. 1976. Preservationist pressure on the Forest Service. *Rocky Mountain Mineral Law Institute,* 17: 91–112.

Cole, N. F. et al. 1976. *Visual design resources for surface-mine reclamation.* Institute for Man and Environment and ARSTECHNIA; Center for Art and Technology, University of Massachusetts.

Comment. 1968. The Wilderness Act and mining: Some proposals for conservation. *Oregon Law Review,* 47: 447–448.

Comptroller General of the United States. 1972. Administration of *regulations for surface exploration mining and reclamation of public and Indian lands.* U.S. G.P.O.

Conner, T. 1982. *Hodel v. Virginia Surface Mining and Reclamation Association* and *Hodel v. Indiana.* Ecology Law Quarterly, 10: 69–86.

Cranston, A. 1976. The battle for Death Valley. In *National Parks and Conservation Magazine* Vol. 50, No. 1.

Cruickshank, N., and Gulley, D. A. 1987. Mineral rights in wilderness areas. *Environmental Policy and Law,* 17(3/4): 135–146.

Dietrich, C. C. 1971. Mineral land reclamation in the Western United States. *Rocky Mountain Mineral Law Institute,* 16: 143–205.

Down, C. C., and Stocks, J. 1977. Visual impact. In *Environmental Impact of Mining,* C. G. Down and J. Stodes, John Wiley.

Eichbaum, W. M., and Buente, D. T. 1980. The land restoration provisions of the Surface Mining Control and Reclamation Act: Constitutional considerations. *Harvard Environmental Law Review,* 4: 227–259.

Ferguson, F. E., and Haggard, J. L. 1973. Regulation of mining law activities in the national forests. *Land and Water Review,* 8(2): 391–427.

Franzman, C.A. 1977. Statement presented to Subcommittee on Public Lands and Resources within Interior and Insular Affairs. In *Surface Mining Control and Reclamation Act of 1977, Hearings before the Subcommittee on Public Lands and Resources of the Committee on Energy and Natural Resources,* U.S. Senate, 95th Congress, 1st Sess. on S.7. U.S. G.P.O. Pub. No. 95–32, pp. 119–152.

Graham, H. P. The *economics of strip coal mining.* Bureau of Economic and Business Research, University of Illinois Bulletin No. 66.

Haggard, J. L. 1975. Regulation of mining law activities in federal lands. *Rocky Mountain Mineral Law Institute,* 21: 349–391.

Hubbard, K. D. 1969. Ah wilderness! (but what about access and prospecting?). *Rocky Mountain Mineral Law Institute,* 15: 585–619.

Kidd, D. T. 1974. The effect of zoning and land use control on mineral operations. *Rocky Mountain Mineral Law Institute,* 19: 277–329.

Kite, M. S. 1978. The Surface Mining Control and Reclamation Act of 1977: An overview of reclamation requirements and implementation. *Land and Water Law Review,* 13(3): 703–745.

Larson, T. A. 1972. Federal regulation of strip mining. *Environmental Affairs,* 2(3): 533–561.

Law, D. L. 1984. *Mined-land rehabilitation.* Van Nostrand Reinhold.

Litton, R. B. et al. 1979. *Landscape inventory framework: Scenic analysis of the Northern Great Plains.* USDA Forest Service Research Paper PSW-135. Pacific SW Forest and Range Experimental Station, Berkeley.

Martin, J. B. 1982. Comment: The interrelationship of the

Mineral Lands Leasing Act, the National Environmental Policy Act, the Wilderness Act, and the Endangered Species Act: A conflict in search of resolution. *Environmental Law*, 12: 363–441.

McCloskey, J. M. 1968. Can recreation conservationists provide for the mining industry? *Rocky Mountain Mineral Law Institute*, 13: 65–85.

Mintz, D. 1976. Strip mining: A policy evaluation. *Ecology Law Quarterly*, 5(3): 461–530.

Noble, H. 1980. Environmental regulation of hardrock mining on public lands: Bringing the 1872 law up to date. *Harvard Environmental Law Review*, 4: 124–163.

Pell, H. A. 1984. Phosphate in the forest: Mandated or precluded by the Mineral Leasing Act. *Natural Resources Journal*, 24: 571–589.

Renkey, L. E. 1969. Local zoning of strip mining. *Kentucky Law Journal*, 57(4): 738–758.

Rochow, K. W. J. 1979. The far side of paradox: State regulation of the environmental effects of coal mining. *West Virginia Law Review*, 81: 559–593.

Seddon, J., and Petrich, C. H. 1983a. Case *studies: Developing land uses in surface mine reclamation.* Oak Ridge National Laboratory, USDI Office of Surface Mining, OSM/TR-1-83 ORNL/TM-8017.

———. 1983b. *Management of public impacts in surface mining.* Oak Ridge National Laboratory, ORNL/TM-7672.

Tetlow, R. J. and Sheppard, S. R. J. 1977. *Visual resources of the Northeast coal area study: 1976–1977.* Environment and Land Use Subcommittee on Northeast Coal Development, Analysis/Interpretation Division, Resource Analysis Branch, Ministry of the Environment, Province of British Columbia, Victoria.

Toffenetti, K. 1985. Valid mining rights and wilderness areas. *Land and Water Law Review*, 20(1): 31–66.

U.S.D.A., Forest Service. 1977. *Anatomy of a Mine from prospect to production.* General Technical Rpt. Imt-35; Intermountain Forest and Range Experimental Station, Ogden, Utah.

Unknown. 1967. Copper vs. conservation. *Science*, 157: 1021.

Viramantes, D. 1984. Status of mining claims within the national rivers of the United States. *Natural Resources Journal*, 24: 221–227.

Wadsworth, S. 1980. Surface Mining Control and Reclamation Act of 1977: Regulatory controversies and constitutional challanges. *Ecology Law Quarterly*, 8: 725–773.

Waters, R. A. 1979. A summary of the legislative history of the Surface Mining Control and Reclamation Act of 1977 and the relevant legal periodical literature. *West Virginia Law Review*, 81: 775–783.

Chapter 13

Timber Harvesting and Vegetation Protection

This chapter will review major legal developments and controls as they affect timber harvesting activity in the wildlands and rural areas of the country as well as vegetation or tree protection ordinances as they are being developed within urban areas. There has been strong public reaction to actions in both cases.

TIMBER HARVESTING

A specific land-based activity that has prompted wide public concern and resulted in specific legislation and programs is timber harvesting. During the 1960s and 1970s there was widespread criticism (see Behan 1976; Heyman and Twiss 1970; Devall 1973; Reich 1962a and 1962b; Siegal 1973; Rodgers 1969) of resource management and decision-making processes of the federal forest management agencies—mainly the U.S. Forest Service and, in lesser roles, the Bureau of Land Management and the National Park Service. Specific timber harvesting methods came to the forefront with the famous Virginia Division of the Izaak Walton League versus Butz[1] court decision. This decision applied the "plain meaning" of certain terms of the Organic Act of 1897,[2] which originally provided for the establishment and management of the national forest and park lands, to permanently enjoin clearcutting on the Monongahela National Forest in West Virginia (Figure 13.1).

Some have criticized the court's decision by examining the doctrines of statutory construction and analyzing the legislative history and administrative interpretation of the Organic Act (Bernstein, Hazelton, and Hubel 1974). Others have commented that the Monongahela decision was not really about clearcutting at all, but it was a small, albeit dramatic, skirmish in the continuing process of pressure and compromise over forest policy decisions." (Fairfax and Achterman 1977). All these points notwithstanding, our major reason for mentioning the Monongahela West Virginia decision here is to follow the train of events that led to the creation of the National Forest Management Act of 1976,[3] and specifically to examine the role that aesthetic values had in its formation.

Many of the aesthetic value questions were not dealt directly with in the Monongahela decision but precipitated the legal examination of a few key terms in the Organic Act. These questions were covered in greater detail by the 1972 "Church" subcommittee's report in the U.S. Senate.

The subcommittee found that the present concern with clearcutting in national forests resulted from a combination of factors, including:

1. General application of clearcutting to eastern hardwood stands in 1964. Before 1964 those forests were harvested primarily by partial cutting, for either the selection or shelterwood systems.
2. The increase in Forest Service allowable cuts over the

---

[1]367 F. Supp. 422 (W.D. W.Va. 1973).
[2]16 U.S.C. ss. 473–75 (1988).
[3]16 U.S.C. s. 600 et seq. (1988).

FIGURE 13.1   Monongahela National Forest. *Photo credit: Arthur Eschner*

last decade and the corresponding income in timber sales and harvesting activities.

3. The manner in which clearcutting is sometimes applied, including examples where there are large blocks or strips of 1,000 acres or more, close spacing of blocks, cutting on steep slopes, large amounts of slash and waste, accelerated erosion, and generally devastated appearances.
4. Increased national concern over the growth and protection of the environment by the public.
5. An increased desire to participate in decision-making by public administrations.
6. The alleged failure of the Forest Service in some instances to be responsive to concerns about the environmental impacts of timber harvesting and management practices. (U.S. Senate 1972, pp 3–4)

Clearly, aesthetic factors were there. Also note that the committee's recommendations on future clearcutting applications included aesthetic considerations:

Harvesting limitations
     Clearcutting should not be used as a cutting method on Federal land areas where . . .
     C. Aesthetic values outweigh other considerations . . .
Clear-cutting should be used only where . . .
     c. A multidisciplinary review has first been made of the potential environmental, biological, *aesthetic*, engineering, and economic impacts on each site area.
     d. Clearcut blocks, patches or strips are, in all cases, shaped and blended as much as possible with the natural terrain. (U.S. Senate 1972, p. 9) (Emphasis added.)

This language in the subcommittee report was adopted

almost verbatim in the National Forest Management Act of 1976 (NFMA)[4] as well as in regulations implementing the law.

Many laws affect the administration of the U.S. Forest Service, but none relates so explicitly to aesthetics as NFMA. Included here is a long excerpt from the act describing specific aesthetic considerations to be taken during "clearcutting, seed tree cutting, shelterwood cutting, and other cuts" as well as specific planning processes for including aesthetic values. The specificity of this act in regard to aesthetics is a drastic change from the indirect, ambiguous language of the 1970 Sustained Yield Act.[5] In NFMA specific procedures are listed for aesthetically sensitive timber harvesting practices.

(F) insure that clearcutting, seed tree cutting, shelterwood cutting and other cuts designed to regenerate an even-aged stand of timber will be used as a cutting method on National Forest lands only where—
     (i) for clearcutting, it is determined to be the optimum method, and for other such cuts it is determined to be appropriate, to meet objectives and requirements of the relevant land management plan;
     (ii) the interdisciplinary review as determined by the Secretary has been completed and the potential environmental, biological, *esthetic*, engineering, and economic impacts on each advertised sale area have been assessed, as well as the consistency of the sale with the multiple use of the general area;
     (iii) *cut blocks, patches or strips are shaped and blended to the extent practicable with the natural terrain*;
     (iv) these are established according to geographic areas, forest types, or other suitable classifications the maximum size limits for areas to be cut in one harvest operation, including provision to exceed the established limits after appropriate public notice and review by the responsible Forest Service Officer one level above the harvest proposal: Provided that such limits shall not apply to the size of areas harvested as a result of natural catastrophic conditions such as fire, insect and disease attack, or windstorm; and
     (v) such cuts are carried out in a manner consistent with the protection of soil, watershed, fish, wildlife, recreation, and *esthetic* resources and the regeneration of the timber resource.[6] (Emphasis added.)

Thus the Monongahela decision plus the Tongass case in Alaska[7] provided the impetus to include the sub-

---

[4]Id. at (v).
[5]16 U.S.C. ss. 528 and 529 (1988).
[6]16 U.S.C. s. 1604 (1988).
[7]Zieke v. Butz, 6 ELR 20129 (D. Alaska 1975).

stantive provision of the subcommittee's report into the NFMA. Stone (1978) notes that the act is the second time that federal legislation refers to visual or aesthetic aspects as resources and accepts them on an equal standing with other land-based resources. In addition, the more recently enacted Forest Stewardship Act of 1990 (Title XII, ss. 1201–1224) may have implications for aesthetic concerns and timber harvesting that extend to nonfederal lands.

Timber Harvesting Methods

There is probably as much confusion about timber harvesting methods and activities as about surface mining activities (see Chapter 12). The four principal methods discussed in the Monongahela decision are addressed specifically in the National Forest Management Act: (1) clearcutting, (2) seed tree cutting (around seed trees) (3) shelterwood cutting, and (4) intermediate and improvement cutting. Basic definitions of harvesting methods are important to have.

Intermediate cutting involves the selective removal of excess trees from a stand, either in the form of commercial thinnings, sanitation cuttings, or pre-logging activities. Commercial thinnings are designed to remove merchantable-size lumber (often poles and pulpwood) from a stand that has not yet reached final harvest age. The crop trees remain, better able to maintain their growth rates, because some of the members of the stand have been removed, making more nutrients and space available to the remaining trees. Sanitation cuttings remove individual trees that pose a threat to the health and quality of the unaffected trees in the stand. Disease and/or insects may be agents necessitating the removal of the trees. Pre-logging activities deal with the removal of commercial species just previous to the final harvest of the stand. The trees removed are the ones that would "break up," losing much of their merchantable value if harvested with the entire stand.

Salvage cutting is designed to utilize fallen trees, scattered dead and poor-risk trees, that will not be merchantable if left in the stand until the next scheduled cut. Trees may be in this category as a result of fire, blowdown, insects, and disease damage.

Regeneration cutting is any removal of trees to assist any present regeneration or to make future regeneration possible. There are many different methods available including shelterwood and clearcutting. Shelterwood cuts have limited use, while clearcutting continues to dominate harvest methods.

Shelterwood cutting involves the removal of most of the existing overstory stand. Enough trees are left to provide half-shade to the ground. After natural vegetation has fully established itself beneath the prospective trees, then the rest of the overstory trees are removed. Some damage to regeneration may occur at this time.

Clearcutting is the removal of an entire stand. The removal of cull trees and small stems is generally desirable, depending on regeneration and protection problems, resistance to wind, fire hazard, insect or disease prevalence, and aesthetics. There are many factors to consider when planning a clearcut, such as the biological, environmental, visual, economic, and managerial problems. The principal biological factor is the tolerance of the species to competition, especially in terms of sunlight. Intolerant species will not successfully establish themselves on low amounts of sunlight. Major environmental or resource protection factors to be considered are the damage resulting from mass soil movement, soil erosion, adverse streamflow, water quality characteristics, and excessive alteration of the forest floor. The visual factors involve effects of dispersion, size, and shape. Harvested areas can be located and shaped to blend with the natural topography. Economic factors include logging costs, stumpage values, supply and demand of forest products, and employment and income of forest industry workers. Major managerial factors concern keeping the sustained-yield harvest rates at a high level and the efficiency of performing current and future forestry practices.

Logging Systems

Besides the basic timber harvest methods, many types of logging systems can be used with each harvesting method, which may further aggravate or ameliorate visual effects. The logging systems include tractor, highhead, skyline, helicopter, and balloon (see Figures 13.2 a, b).

Tractor is a logging system in which diesel tractors, rubber-tired skidders, or low-pressure ground skidders are used to drag felled and bucked logs to a loading point where they are taken to mills by truck. This system is planned for areas in which it is uneconomical and difficult to harvest by other means. These areas are often part of a planned cable system (overhead or on the ground cables used to draw logs to loading point) sale, but would require the establishment of a new landing if logs were to be cable-yarded. Tractor-yarding is also used in stable soil areas where volumes or values are too low to pay the costs of other systems.

Highhead is a logging system using a powered unit that hauls a cable between two points. The term "highhead" comes from the fact that the mainline is elevated above the landing, thus providing some lift to one end of the logs. This system is used to haul felled trees above or along the ground to a point where a truck can then haul them to a mill.

Skyline is a logging system using a powered unit that hauls a carriage between two points elevated above the ground. It is used to haul felled trees above the ground,

FIGURE 13.2 a, b   Logging systems; tractor yarding and balloon systems. *Photo credit: David Kissel and James Palmer, respectively*

especially over steep slopes, to a point for a truck hauling to the mill.

Helicopter logging has not been used extensively. Sites planned for such operations are usually inaccessible by road or have unstable soils. In the case of unstable soils, disturbance resulting from road construction and/or yarding (gathering logs) would be unacceptable. Helicopter logging is not limited to clearcut harvests, but may also be utilized in thinning and salvage operations where other systems fail to provide environmental protection or access by road is limited.

Balloon is a logging system where cable systems are modified to include a large balloon that helps to lift logs above the ground. This system works well for downhill-yarding.

Site disturbance associated with harvesting focuses in three areas: road construction, log-yarding, and tree-felling. The impacts of the various systems are related to; (1) how many miles of road per harvest acre are constructed, (2) how much ground contact the logs have during yarding, and (3) the specifications for tree-felling (directional) or not. Helicopter, skyline, and balloon systems require the fewest miles of roads, while highlead is intermediate; tractor systems require the most (including well-used skid trails).

Development of Approaches for Forest Aesthetics

The U.S. Forest Service, in order to deal with the unusual number of variables just described, has developed a visual management system (U.S.D.A., Forest Service 1974). It is an inventory of the physical landscape character of the area involved that is mapped as a distinctive, common, or minimal variety class. Then the degree of sensitivity or exposure to the viewing public is rated on maps that are overlayed to determine the visual quality objective(s) for which the area is to be managed. The range of visual quality objectives includes preservation, retention, partial retention, modification, maximum modification, rehabilitation, and enhancement. The whole forest is mapped in terms of specific visual quality objectives. These objectives aid in the layout of timber sales in respect to dispersion, size, and shape of the cutting units. Harvest areas are located and shaped to harmonize with the natural topography and to meet visual quality objectives of that area.

The general impression left by environmental groups after the Monongahela decision is that clearcutting and aesthetics and/or recreation are mutually exclusive. As Bernstein, Hazelton, and Hubel (1974,

p. 123) point out this is a short-sighted over-simplification.

The appearance of clearings from a distance is aesthetic disaster if indiscriminate checkerboard cuts are used, but well-designed and located openings could add additional color and textural dimensions to the landscape. Clearcut openings can also provide scenic overlooks on horseback or cross-country skiing trails.

A number of key variables are critical to the aesthetic or visual impact of timber-cutting techniques. The experience that the viewer has is dependent on the type of activity engaged in, the viewing distance, comprehensiveness of the activity, the physical attributes of the forest stand, and the natural patterns of the overall landscape. For instance, a clearcut imitating the natural patterns rock talus slide paths on a mountain slope at a distance may be unnoticeable, but patch cuts in a thickly vegetated Eastern deciduous forest or a West Coast Douglas fir forest would be blatant. A clearcut as experienced by hikers may be a welcome diversion filled with wildflowers and berries, but from the air an opening in continuous forests would appear to be an unwelcome blotch in the overall pattern of the landscape (Figures 13.3 a and 13.3 b). It is as much contextual visual resource management as is surface mining and depends on the variation of local geographic conditions as well as the attitude of the landscape experiencers.

Unlike surface mining, however, research has been done on the reactions of people to timber harvesting techniques, on theories of visual impact from timber harvesting, and on methods of simulating these impacts as well as ameliorating visual timber harvesting activity (see Cook 1969; Murtha and Greco 1975; Elsner and Smardon 1979; and Smardon et al. 1981). Shafer (1967) first called attention to "forest aesthetics" as a productive research area. He even suggested that forest recreationists should be tested as to their perceptions of timber harvesting activities over time (Shafer 1967, pp. 62–66).

Early work in landscape description and inventories led the way for landscape architects, planners, and foresters to start to think about how to describe and inventory forest landscapes. Early innovators were Litton (1968, 1972, 1973) in the U.S. and Crowe (1966) in England. Much of this type of work is based on the landscape architect's vast experience in perceiving and working with forested landscapes, but is strongly modified by design training that emphasizes form, line, color, and texture.

There was also early innovative work that could be characterized as management prescription. Most of it proposed simple, easy-to-follow guidelines for mixing good forestry with enhancing aesthetics. It was aimed

FIGURE 13.3 a, b   Clear cuts in Idaho on the ground and aerial perspectives. *Photo credit: David Kissel*

at practitioners "on the ground" with advice on how to deal with slash (Noyes, 1969; Wagar 1974), roads (Noyes 1970), firebreaks (Gaidula 1976), and general forest practices (Noyes 1969).

In the 1970s much of the work shifted to three areas regarding forest landscape aesthetics: (1) perceptual and behavioral studies on how people reacted to different forests or forest practices as elicited from photographs, actual visits to forest areas, or other visual stimuli; (2) increased emphasis on developing quantitative indices for rating or ranking visual aspects of forest management practices; and (3) work on models or simulated forest environments that could be used as aids or tools in eliciting responses from professional or lay groups (see Cook 1969, Murtha and Greco 1975, Elsner and Smardon 1979, and Smardon et al. 1981). The most useful work for practitioners is the U.S. Forest Service's timber management handbook, which combines silvicultural practices with visual resource management for typical regional forest types in the continental U.S. and Alaska (Bacon and Twombley 1980).

STATE FOREST PRACTICE LAWS

Besides the federal statutes regarding timber harvesting, many states have forest practices acts that affect logging practices on private timber lands. States also have adopted forest practices acts because of Environmental Protection Agency's (EPA) enforcement of the Section 208 provisions in the Clean Water Act Amendments of 1972,[8] which were directed at controlling nonpoint (overland water pollution — not from a single discharge point) and indirect water pollution sources. At least seventeen states have legislation regulating forest practices, including: Alaska,[9] California,[10] Connecticut, Florida,[11] Idaho,[12] Louisiana,[13] Maryland,[14] Massachusetts,[15] Mississippi,[16] Missouri,[17] Nevada,[18] New Hampshire,[19] New Mexico,[20] New York,[21] Oregon,[22] Vermont,[23] Virginia,[24] and Washington.[25] Detailed provisions of these acts are found in Klein (1980), Lundmark (1987), and Ellefson and Cubbage (1980). Most of these acts cover practices needed to minimize fire damage and reestablish a stand after cutting, but some go much further. There have been major problems, however, in implementation, inspection, and enforcement of forest practices acts, as indicated by the California experience (see Comment 1974; Arola 1962).

The statutes in Mississippi, Virginia, and Washington specifically mention promotion of aesthetics among their goals, but most do not explicitly require the consideration of forest amenities in private timber land management (Lundmark 1987). Topics with specific restrictions that do promote aesthetics in many of these acts are slash and waste removal, riparian buffer zones, scenic road buffer zones, location of logging roads, silviculture (logging systems), tree species choice, and conversion of timberland to nontimber uses. No case law has been found specifically deciding the constitutionality of purely aesthetic restrictions on commercial timber management (Lundmark 1987; Ellefson and Cubbage 1980).

An owner of forest land who wishes to convert it to nonforest uses may not have a right to do so unless the nonforest uses are consistent with the character of the surrounding property. For example, the California Appellate Court upheld the state's Coastal Zone Conservation Commission's denial of a building permit for an owner to construct a house on his 2.32-acre parcel in the Del Monte Forest. The commission had denied the permit because the development would have damaged a fragment of primeval Monterey cypress forest of great value and would have partially destroyed an archeological site.[26]

Aside from these specific pieces of legislation, other federal and state laws affect forest practices. These include the Wilderness System Act[27] (see Chapter 9) and the National Environmental Policy Act[28] (see Chapter 11) for federal agencies and mini-NEPA's and critical area protection acts for the states. One of the most interesting acts in terms of its implications for private forestry lands is the Forest Stewardship Assistance Act of 1990, which amends the Cooperative Forestry Assistance Act of 1978. The general purpose of the 1990 act is to promote sustainable forestry practices on nonfederal forest lands in recognition that over half of U.S. forest lands need some type of vegetation conversion treatment.[29]

Most specifically, the act directs the Secretary of

---

[8]33 U.S.C. s. 1288 (1988).

[9]Alaska Forest Resources and Practices Act, Alas. Stat. s. 41.17010 (1984).

[10]Z'berg-Nejedly Forest Practice Act of 1973, Cal. Pub. Res. Code Div. 4, Ch. 8 ss. 4511-4628, and Cal. Adm. Code Title 14 subch. 4.1 Ch. 2 div. 2.

[11]Florida Seed Tree Law, Fla. Stat. Ann. s. 591.27 (West 1962).

[12]Idaho Forest Practices Act of 1974, Idaho Code ss. 38-1301 to 1312.

[13]Lousiana's Turpentine Seed Tree Law, La. Rev. Stat. Ann. s. 56.1493 (West 1952).

[14]Maryland Ann. Code art. 5, s. 101 (1985).

[15]Mass. Forest Cutting Practices Act, Mass. Gen. Laws Ann. Ch. 1322, s. 40 (West Supp. 1986).

[16]Miss. Forest Harvesting Law, Miss Code Ann. s. 49-19-53 (1972).

[17]Missouri State Forestry Law, Mo. Rev. Stat. s. 254.010 (1979).

[18]Nevada Forest Practices and Reforestation Act of 1955, Nev. Stat. s. 528.010 (1986).

[19]N.H. Rev. Stat. Ann. s. 221 (1985).

[20]N. M. Stat. Ann. s. 60-1-1 (1981).

[21]New York Forest Practices Act, 1946 N.Y. Laws s. 60-d.

[22]Oregon Forest Practices Act, Or. Rev. Stat. s. 527.610 (1983).

[23]Vt. Stat. Ann. Title 10 s. 2621 (1984).

[24]Va. Code Ann. ss. 10-74.1, 10-90.30 (1985).

[25]Washington Forest Practices Act. Wash. Code s. 76.90.010 (1983).

[26]Davis v. California Coastal Zone Conservation Commission, 57 Cal. App.3d 700, 129 Cal. Rptr. 417 (1976).

[27]16 U.S.C. s. 1133 et seq. (1988).

[28]42 U.S.C. s. 4321 et seq. (1988).

[29]16 U.S.C. s. 2101 et seq. (1988). The Food, Agriculture, Conservation and Trade Act of 1990, Title XII s. 1201-1224 (PL 101-624, Nov. 28, 1990).

Agriculture, in consultation with state foresters or equivalent state officials, to establish programs to encourage the long-term stewardship of nonindustrial private forest lands. Owners of such lands would be encouraged to more actively manage their forest and related resources by utilizing existing state, federal, and private-sector resource management expertise and assistance programs.[30]

Specific programs in relation to aesthetics within this act include: Rural Forestry Assistance, Forest Stewardship, Stewardship Incentives, Forest Legacy Program for threatened areas, and Urban and Community Forestry Assistance for urban and suburban areas. Let us look first at the sections of this comprehensive act detailing each program:

Sec. 3 RURAL FORESTRY ASSISTANCE

(a) Assistance to Forest Landowners and others— The Secretary may provide financial, technical, educational, and related assistance to State Foresters . . . to enable such officials to provide technical information, advice and related assistance to private forest land owners and managers, vendors, forest resource operators, forest resource professionals, public agencies, and individuals to enable such persons to carry out activities that are consistent with the purposes of the Act, including—

(6) managing the rural-land and urban-land interface to balance the use of forest resources in and adjacent to urban and community areas;

(7) identifying and managing recreational forest land resources;

(8) identifying and protecting the aesthetic character of forest lands.[31]

Sec. 5 FOREST STEWARDSHIP PROGRAM

(a) Establishment— The Secretary, in consultation with State Foresters or equivalent, shall establish a Forest Stewardship Program to encourage the long-term stewardship of non-industrial private forest lands by assisting owners of such lands to more actively manage their forested related resources by utilizing existing State, Federal and private sector resource management expertise and assistance programs . . .

(d) Implementation— . . . Such information and assistance shall be directed to help such owners understand and evaluate alternative actions they might take including—

(1) managing and enhancing the productivity of timber, fish and wildlife habitat, water quality, wetlands,

recreational resources and the aesthetic value of forest lands.[32]

Given the Forest Stewardship Program, the action-oriented complement is the Stewardship Incentive Program:

Sec. 6 STEWARDSHIP INCENTIVE PROGRAM

(a) Establishment— The Secretary in consultation with State Foresters or equivalent . . . shall establish a program with the Forest Service, to be known as the "Stewardship Incentive Program" to meet the objectives and goals of section 5. . . .

(4) Approved Activities—

(A) Development— The Secretary, in consultation with the State Coordinating Committees established pursuant to section 19(b), shall develop a list of approved forest activities and practices that will be eligible for cost-sharing assistance under the program with each state.

(B) Type of Activities— The Secretary in developing a list of approved activities and practices shall attempt to achieve landowner and public purposes including—

(i) the establishment, management, maintenance and restoration of forests for shelterbelts, windbreaks, aesthetic quality, and other conservation purposes. . . .

(iii) the protection, restoration and use of forest wetlands . . .

(vi) the management and maintenance of fish and wildlife habitat;

(vii) the development of outdoor recreational opportunities.[33]

The previous three programs are statewide. The Forest Legacy Program focuses on forested regions with threatened critical resources:

Sec. 7 FOREST LEGACY PROGRAM

(a) Establishment and Purpose— The Secretary shall establish a program to be known as the Forest Legacy Program, in cooperation with appropriate State, regional, and other units of government, for the purposes of ascertaining and protecting environmentally important forest areas that are threatened by conversion to nonforest uses and through the use of conservation easements and other mechanisms, for promoting forest land protection and other conservation opportunities. Such purposes shall

---

[30]16 U.S.C. s. 2103a (1988).
[31]Id.
[32]Id., s. 2105.
[33]Id., s. 2106.

also include the protection of important *scenic*, cultural, fish, wildlife, and recreational resources, riparian areas and other ecological values. . . .

(2) Initial program— Not later than 1 year after the date of enactment . . . the Secretary shall establish a regional program in furtherance of the Northern Forest Lands Study in the State of New York, New Hampshire, Vermont and Maine. The Secretary shall establish additional programs in each of the Northeast, South and Western Regions of the United States and the Pacific Northwest. . . .

(e) Eligibility— To be eligible, such areas shall have significant environmental values or shall be threatened by present or future conversion to nonforest uses. Of land proposed to be included in the Forest Legacy Program, the Secretary shall give priority to lands which can be effectively protected and managed and which have important *scenic or recreational values*; riparian areas; fish and wildlife values, including threatened and endangered species; or other ecological values.[34] (Emphasis added.)

Note that the Forest Legacy Program focuses on assessing regional forest areas of either high resource value or under threat of conversion. The Northern Forest Lands Study is already underway. The last significant program is really an urban extension and tree-planting program:

Sec. 9 URBAN AND COMMUNITY FORESTRY ASSISTANCE

(a) Findings— The Congress finds that
  (1) the health of forests in urban areas and communities, involving cities, their suburbs, and towns in the United States is on the decline;
  (2) forest lands, shade trees, and open space in urban areas and communities improve the quality of life for residents;
  (3) forest lands and associated natural resources enhance the economic value of residential and commercial property in urban and community settings;
  (4) urban trees are 15 times more effective than forest trees at reducing the buildup of carbon dioxide and aid in providing energy conservation through mitigation of the heat island effect in urban areas; . . .
  (6) efforts to encourage tree plantings and protect

existing open spaces in urban areas and communities can contribute the social well-being and promote sense of community in these areas.[35]

Specific purposes within this section of the act also include "understanding the benefits of preserving existing tree cover," "encouraging owners to maintain trees and expand forest cover," providing "education programs and technical assistance," establishing a competitive matching grant program and a tree-planting program, setting up demonstration projects, enhancing technical skills and understanding, and expanding "research and educational efforts."[36]

This last program is significant because it incorporates environmental forestry research on physical and sensory functions of urban greenery and trees and lays the framework for a massive urban forestry extension program throughout the United States. Overall, the Forest Stewardship Assistance Act of 1990 is like a large extension program for the whole country to encourage proper utilization and conservation of forest lands and trees in rural, urban, and natural areas that are primarily privately owned.

In addition, there are laws affecting timber harvesting for specific geographic areas. The most notable is the federal statute creating the Redwood National Park,[37] the purpose of which was "to preserve significant examples of the primeval coastal redwood . . . forest and streams and seashores with which they are associated for . . . public inspiration, enjoyment, and scientific study."[38] The history of the creation, maintenance, and enlargement of the park to protect the redwoods has probably been one of the most controversial sagas in the history of the National Park Service (Crabtree 1975; Hudson 1978). Currently, there are four California statutes[39] critical to the protection of the watersheds of the Redwood Region (Figure 13.4), which in turn will ensure the aesthetic maintenance of the "primeval coastal redwood."

Two major precedent-setting court cases addressed the issue of the National Park Service's responsibilities to protect the redwood forest from logging activities within and adjacent to the park. In *Sierra Club I*,[40] although the court's discussion of the "trust duty" is very brief, this holding is the most significant aspect of the litigation. The court found the basis for the public trust

---

[34]Id., s. 2107.

[35]Id., s. 1209.

[36]Id.

[37]16 U.S.C. s. 79a. (1988).

[38]Id.

[39]These statutes include the Z'berg-Nejedly Forest Practice Act supra note 10; the Porter-Cologne Water Quality Control Act, Cal. Water Code s. 13000 et seq. (west Supp. 1974); the Environmental Quality Act, Cal. Pub. Res. Code s. 21000 et seq. (West Supp. 1974); and the California Coastal Act of 1976 infra Ch. 10.

[40]Sierra Club v. Dept. of the Interior, 376 F. Supp. 90 (N.D. Cal. 1974) (Sierra Club I).

FIGURE 13.4   California Redwoods in John Muir Forest. *Photo credit: R. C. Smardon*

duty in the Organic Act of the national park system. *Sierra Club I* is the first reported case to hold that this trust relationship creates a *judicially enforceable* duty to protect a national park from threatened injury. The public trust doctrine requires that the Department of Interior exercise reasonable care to protect and preserve national parks in their natural state.

After summary judgment was denied, the Sierra Club suit proceeded to trial. The issue was whether the Department of Interior's administration of Redwood National Park was unreasonable, arbitrary, and an abuse of discretion in light of the secretary's trust and statutory duties to protect the park. Resolution of this issue required that three questions be answered.

First, the court had to determine if the park was suffering from threatened or actual damage as a result of logging on adjacent land. Second, the court had to evaluate the adequacy of actions already taken by the Department of the Interior to protect the park from possible future damage. Finally, based on the result of the

first two inquiries, the court had to decide whether the secretary's conduct, and particularly his failure to take remedial action to protect the park, was an abuse of discretion. In July 1975 the court issued its opinion *Sierra Club II*,[41] finding that the park was suffering damage as a result of logging upslope and downstream; that measures heretofore taken by the agency were inadequate to protect the park from the threat of future damage; and that the secretary's conduct was an abuse of discretion. Subsequent actions taken by the National Park Service included on-site actions and enforcement of federal and state statutes for off-site impacts.

LOCAL TREE PROTECTION ORDINANCES

Trees and greenery in urban areas serve many functions, including increase in property values, positive psychological reinforcement, shade and microclimate amelioration, children's play areas, and recreation; perceptual functions such as aesthetic quality and symbolic meaning (see Figures 13.5 a and 13.5 b); and cog-

FIGURE 13.5 a, b   Urban trees. *Photo credit: R. C. Smardon*

[41]Sierra Club v. Dept. of Interior 398 F.Supp. 284 (N.D. Cal. 1975) (Sierra Club II).

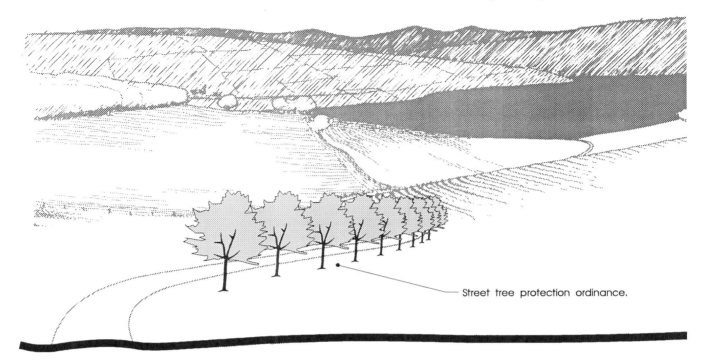

FIGURE 13.6   Generic landscape image with vegetation control. *Graphic credit: Scott Shannon*

nitive orientation in urban environments (Smardon 1988). Across the United States there is growing interest in protecting existing trees, both individual and stands, particularly in urban areas, for all the reasons previously listed. A number of local governments have adopted specific species of street trees as community hallmarks. Other communities have gone further, writing tree preservation ordinances and detailed landscaping requirements (Figure 13.6).

Legal Challenges to Tree Ordinances

There are very few challenges to local tree preservation ordinances and landscaping requirements. Courts have generally been sympathetic to tree protection efforts in cases that have reached them. In a case upholding a St. Petersburg tree ordinance,[42] a landowner challenged the ordinance as an unlawful delegation of authority because it gives the city managers the power to issue removal permits only if certain criteria were met and if there was not a "significant adverse impact" on the environment (e.g., the permit must be disallowed if tree removal adversely alters the water table). The court had no difficulty in upholding a summary judgment for the city.

In one case, however, a local tree protection ordinance requiring 15 percent of the trees on a site to be retained was struck down on the grounds that the state legislature had not authorized such an enactment.[43] Local governments should check to see if state zoning or site plan enabling legislation is broad enough to cover tree protection.

An emerging legal issue that has challenged tree protection in many areas is how to prevent an owner from clearing a site of trees before he applies for a building permit or site plan approval, thereby circumventing any restrictions. To avoid such situations, some communities are following the model land development code approach and include tree removal under the definition of development that must have a permit. Others enact separate regulations placing restrictions on land clearance, often as part of drainage and soil erosion ordinances.

Trees on Public Property

Many communities have enacted laws governing the removal or pruning of trees on public property, particulary street rights-of-way. The rationale behind these laws is not only to protect public property but to lead by example through careful stewardship. These programs vary from community to community. Progressive examples include ordinances in Cincinnati, Ohio, and Alexandria, Virginia.

[42]Watson v. City of St. Petersburg, 489 S50.2d 138 (Fla. 1986).
[43]Dunbar v. City of Spartansburg 266 S.C. 113, 221 S.E.2d 848 (1976).

Cincinnati has an appointed forestry board made up of citizens and heads of planning, public works, and other departments to administer a local ordinance that strictly regulates the removal of city-owned trees. A permit is required for their removal, and the developer must compensate the forestry division for the value of the tree removed or replace it with a tree of similar size. For any trees damaged during a project, a "devaluation" charge is assessed. Utility companies must obtain special permits for routine maintenance of trees in the community and, if trees are irreparably damaged, compensation must be paid to the city. In 1980, city voters overwhelmingly adopted a special levy on property owners (five cents per linear foot of property abutting a street) to be used for the care of street trees. This levy has enabled the city to establish a permanent urban forestry program.

Alexandria has enacted an ordinance regulating placement of trees on public property (e.g., median strips, public lands next to sidewalks and streets). A permit is required to remove or plant any tree, and only the fifty species set out in the ordinance may be planted.

Trees on Private Property

A number of jurisdictions, particularly in Florida, California, and Virginia, provide special protection for specimen trees on private property and regulate land clearance operations to retain trees in new developments (see Coughlin et al. 1984).

An Alexandria ordinance allows the city to designate "historic" and "specimen" trees. Any tree of notable historical association or of extraordinary value because of its age, size, or type can be so designated. Removal is not allowed without permission of the planning commission. More generally, no trees may be destroyed on private property without first securing a permit from the city arborist, who must consider such things as aesthetics and soil erosion when reviewing the case. Permission must be granted if the trees lie within the buildable area of the site plan.

Rapid development and the unnecessary destruction of trees were problems for many communities in the 1970s. This led Fairfax County, Virginia, to adopt one of the most comprehensive tree preservation laws in the nation. Among other factors the county ordinance establishes a tree commission to oversee the program

and requires the following (from Duerksen, 1986 p. 25):

a. Conservation plans that clearly set forth all trees over two inches in diameter with an indication of which trees will be cleared and which will be retained. All utility installations, retention ponds, etc. must be sited and carried out with a minimum of tree removal. Specimen trees and those important to wildlife are to be retained to the maximum extent possible.
b. Planting plan that clearly indicates the location and species of each plant as well as its size and other features.
c. Special protection for remaining trees from wind damage, soil compaction, and root zone damage.
d. Erosion control plans that outline existing trees and vegetation to the maximum extent possible to reduce runoff.
e. Conservation escrow to ensure that all vegetation, landscaping plans, and erosion control measures are undertaken.

Sanibel Island, Florida, has enacted tree protection provisions similar to those employed in many other Florida communities. Briefly, the Sanibel approach is to strictly limit destruction of trees during site preparation. The city has created a citizen vegetation committee to inspect all sites before a building permit is issued. The committee works with the developer to retain as many native trees as possible and requires transplanting of significant trees if they cannot be saved. Native plants must make up the predominant part of new landscaping. Vegetation that contributes to beach stability cannot be removed seaward of a coastal construction control line.

LANDSCAPING ORDINANCES

Many communities require extensive landscaping for developments along major public roads and as part of site plan review for any project. Some of these ordinances are quite specific as to the number and size of trees they require and the species to be planted. The New Orleans urban corridor zoning plan (Chapter 8) and the Lake Charles sign ordinance (Chapter 7) are good examples of specific requirements for perimeter and interior landscaping. The Maine site location law also has specific landscaping provisions for parking lots in its regulations. Several American Planning Association publications go into greater detail (Glassford 1983; Corwin 1978).

Case Study: Visual Project Analysis for the Allegheny National Forest[44]

The Allegheny National Forest in Pennsylvania felt it needed to develop a practical method of visual impact assessment of proposed vegetation alteration activities, following in the wake of the Monongahela decision and pressure mounting from various activities in the National Forest. Project Visual Analysis was designed for project impacts covering 100 acres or less that involved vegetative manipulation. It could be applied to projects such as timber cutting, right-of-way clearing, well-site clearing, and borrow-source clearing that are beyond the immediate distance. Removal of vegetation was chosen as the main thrust of the analysis because it was the most frequent and significant visual impact on the forest environment. Other project impacts, such as landform impacts, addition of structures, water impoundments, and recreation developments are not dealt with.

The results of the procedure are five landscape management guides determined through two key analyses: visual quality objective (U.S.D.A., Forest Service 1974), which establishes the degree of acceptable modification of the landscape; and visual absorption capability (U.S.D.A., Forest Service 1976), which indicates the capability of a specific project area to absorb certain kinds of management activities. One of five brief and simple sets of guides can be chosen and used either as an evaluation of a proposed impact's ability to meet the recommended visual quality objective or as an aid in mitigating a vegetative impact. With experience, other guides can be added as well as criteria for landscape inventory and guides for other, nonvegetative impacts.

Procedure

Project Visual Analysis for the Allegheny National Forest takes the user through a logical step-by-step assessment, requiring the completion of up to five forms and two maps. Under the premise that the level of analysis should be commensurate with the level of visual resource sensitivity and with the magnitude of the proposed impacts, the procedure was designed so that the actual number of steps will vary with the situation. The steps that may be completed are:

Step 1: Inventory
Step 2: Sorting Questions
Step 3: Visual Absorption Capability
Step 4: Visual Quality Objective
Step 5: Landscape Management Guide

In the following explanation each step assumes a project has been proposed by the land manager and a visual assessment must be made. The term "project area" refers to a general area within which several impacts may occur. The term "impact" refers to site-specific vegetative cutting impacts.

Step 1: Inventory

Inventory data based on existing ground conditions are gathered during the season in which the project area receives the most use. All existing view facilities and those proposed for the next ten years are identified through review of maps and approved plans. A view facility can be a road, trail, recreation site, water body, or residence. For each view facility, views are inventoried and mapped (Figure 13.7). The project area will be part of the immediate foreground, part of the distant landscape, or both. The sensitivity level, or a measure of peoples' concern of scenic quality, from each view facility is identified from maps prepared for the entire forest. Also important is the preparation of a work map (Figure 13.7). Information such as the project area, view facilities, proposed impacts, and sensitivity levels should be displayed. This map will be an important working tool for the rest of the analysis.

Emphasis is placed on field checking all data as future steps are dependent on valid information. The remaining analysis assumes the inventory to be comprehensive and utilizes the data as recorded. New data should be entered as they become available, prior to completing the entire process.

Step 2: Sorting Questions

The purpose of this step is to sort and drop from the remaining procedure any data that are not visually significant, such as the least-sensitive view facilities and impacts producing only minor contrast. For these impacts, the visual resource will still be recognized and the appropriate guidelines recommended. Also, projects that produce impacts as part of the immediate foreground contiguous to the view facility will be

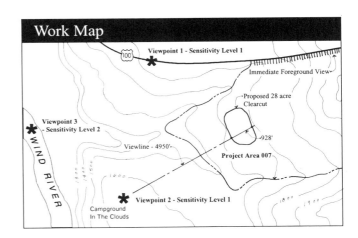

FIGURE 13.7   Generic map. *Graphic credit: Scott Shannon*

[44]Presented by Gary Kell, "Project Visual Analysis for the Allegheny National Forest," as part of *Our National Landscape: A Conference on Applied Techniques for Analysis and Management of the Visual Resource*, G. Elsner and R. C. Smardon, tech. coord. Incline Village, NV, April 23–25, 1979. Reproduced with permission of the author.

referred to expertise beyond the field level. The analysis will continue on only those remaining impacts that produce major contrasts and that will be seen from a senstive view facility.

Step 3: Visual Absorption Capability

The visual absorption capability is an assessment of the ability of a specific land area to absorb impacts. A rating system based on the needs of the Allegheny National Forest has been developed to measure this ability for impacts relating to vegetative manipulations (Figure 13.8). An overall rating of high, intermediate, or low is based on a sum of numerical ratings of observer position, observer distance, view duration, landscape composition description, and degree of slope.

To begin the process, up to three points that provide key views of a specific proposed impact need to be identified. Then data related to the above-listed factors are collected for each viewpoint and a visual absorption rating from a low of 1 to to high of 5 is assigned to each inventory factor (Figure 13.8). The most critical viewpoint can then be determined with the lowest overall rating. It is this key viewpoint and rating that will be used for further evaluation, since it has the lowest capability to absorb vegetative impacts. The assumption is made that if the impact is acceptable from the most

Visual Quality Objective Matrix

		Distance Zone / Sensitivity Level						
		Fg1	Mg1	Fg2	Mg2	Bg1	Bg2	3
Variety Class	Class A	R	R	R	PR	PR	PR	RR
	Class B	R	PR	PR	M	M	M/MM	MM
	Class C	PR	PR	M	M	MM	MM	MM
		R - Retention PR - Partial Retention						
		M - Modification MM - Maximum Modification						

FIGURE 13.9   Visual quality objective matrix. *Graphic credit: Scott Shannon*

critical viewpoint, then it will also be acceptable from the other viewpoints.

The factors chosen for the inventory (Figure 13.8) are those most relevant to visual absorption capability of the Allegheny National Forest. Others, such as vegetative height and recovery rate, are of relevance but, because of their uniformity in the Allegheny National Forest, have an effect on the resulting visual absorption capability rating. An effort was made to limit the number of variables used.

Step 4: Visual Quality Objective

The visual quality objective identifies to what level or degree the land manager is willing to alter the natural landscape. Using the Visual Management System developed by the U.S. Forest Service (1974), an objective is derived from the sensitivity of the viewer, the intrinsic variety of the land, and the distance from the viewer. In order to achieve uniformity, sensitivity levels and variety classes have been inventoried and mapped on a forestwide basis. The information identified from these maps, combined with the distance zone from the key viewpoint, will yield a recommended visual quality objective (Figure 13.9).

Step 5: Landscape Management Guides

Once the visual quality objective and visual absorption capability have been identified, the appropriate set of landscape management guides can be chosen (Figure 13.10). A total of five sets of guides have been conceived to adequately cover all possible combinations of visual quality objectives and visual absorption capabilities. Figure 13.11 shows an example of one set of guides and contains recommendations for shadow zone — size, shape, and line from timber cuts. Shadow zone is the

Visual Absorption Capability

Factors		Variables	Rating	V1	V2	V3
Observer Position	Superior	+300' - +500'		1		
	Normal	+100' - +300'		2	2	2
		+/-100'	3			
	Inferior	-100' - -300'	4			
		-300' - -500'	5			
Observer Distance	Foreground	0 - 1/4 mile	1			
	Middleground	1/4 - 1/2 mile	2			
		1/2 - 1 mile	3	3	3	
		1 - 2 miles	4			4
	Background	2 + miles				
View Duration	Long	30 + seconds		1		1
	Short	10 - 30 seconds	1		1	
		5 - 10 seconds	3			3
		3 - 5 seconds	4	4		
	Glimpse	0 - 3 seconds	5			
Landscape Description	Feature		1			
	Focal		2			2
	Enclosed		3	3	3	
	Panoramic		4			
	Other		5			
Slope	Very Steep	+45%	1			
	Steep	30 - 45%	2			
	Moderate	20 - 30%	3			
	Gentle	10 - 20%	4			
	Very Gentle	0 - 10%	5	5	5	5
		Lowest Rating is the Key Viewpoint		17	14	18
		Visual Absorption Capabilty		5 - 13	Low	
				14 - 16	Intermediate	
				17 - 23	High	

FIGURE 13.8   Visual Absorption Capability. *Graphic credit: Scott Shannon*

Landscape Management Guide Matrix

I - Least Restrictive V - Most Restrictive		Visual Quality Objective			
		Retention	Partial Retention	Modification	Max. Modification
Visual Absorption Capability	Low	I	II	III	V
	Moderate	I	III	IV	V
	High	II	III	IV	V

FIGURE 13.10   Landscape management guide matrix. *Graphic credit: Scott Shannon*

Landscape Management Guides

Landscape Management Guides III

Does the proposal meet this guide?

Shadow Zone - Design the depth of the cutting unit not to exceed 1.5 times the Shadow Zone length.

[Yes] [No]

Size - Maximum size of the cutting unit should be 24 acres.

[Yes] [No]

Shape - Edges should be varied. Use undulating free-form boundaries, not straight lines or geometric shapes. Cutting units should be patterned on the largely horizontal form and line of the ANF landscape, that is, generally two to three times as long as wide and parallel to the contours.

[Yes] [No]

Line - If cutting units approach a ridgeline, design to eliminate "notch effect." Provide a transition in height from forest cover to opening by selective cutting of adjacent stands or by location and shape of cutting unit boundaries. This transition should occur in a distance equal to one-half the width of the proposed opening at a minimum.

[Yes] [No]

FIGURE 13.11 Landscape Management Guides, an example. *Graphic credit: Scott Shannon*

area screened from view by foreground vegetation. A program has been developed for a pocket calculator to solve for shadow zone area. It calculates the portion of the proposed impact that would be actually viewed. In addition to inventory data from Step 3, such significant factors as vegetative height, view direction, and aspect are incorporated. The size guideline operates in conjunction with the shadow zone and sets an upper limit on the size of impact. The shape guide requires the form of visible openings to correspond to the horizontal line and form of the Allegheny National Forest landscape. The line guide insures recognition of potential contrasts when a project is located against the skyline.

To be acceptable, visually proposed impacts need not necessarily meet all guides. This allows flexibility in design and should encourage that the spirit rather than the letter of the guides be followed. Depending on the number of guides met, the proposals may proceed without change, may proceed with minor changes, or may require redesign and alternative development. If less than two guides are met, the user should recognize the need for expertise beyond the field level. Otherwise the project proponent, in response to the guides may develop mitigating measures or alternatives.

Conclusion

It must be emphasized that this procedure is not a land use decision but only a working tool for providing input. It attempts to answer the question of how an impact can be mitigated to meet the visual quality objective. The user is even encouraged to retrace the analysis steps and reevaluate the inventory factors. This retracing process enables the user to reduce the visual problem to specific items for which solutions can be developed.

Project Visual Analysis is a methodical, consistent approach that can be performed by adequately trained field personnel. Experience, after testing with selected field personnel on the Allegheny National Forest, has been positive. Adequate training was given to all involved in visual analysis, and a handbook (Kell 1978) describing in detail how to complete the forms has been developed and used as part of training. A more detailed timber harvesting visual impact assessment approach can be seen in the U.S. Forest Service's timber management handbook (Bacon and Twombley 1980).

References

Arola, 1962. Forest practice regulation in California. *Journal of Forestry* 60: 872–875.

Bacon, W. R., and Twombly, A. D. 1980. *National forest landscape management, Vol. 2, chap. 5 Timber*. U.S.D.A. Agriculture Handbook No. 559, U.S. G.P.O.

Behan, R. W. 1967. The succotash syndrome or multiple use: A heartfelt approach to forest land management. *Natural Resources Journal*, 7(4): 474–484.

Bernstein, J. E., Hazelton, P., and Hubel, D. J. 1974. Clearcutting, can you see the forest for the trees? *Environmental Law*, 1: 85–126.

Comment. 1974. Environmental protection: Z'berg-Nejedly Forest Practice Act of 1973. *Pacific Law Journal*, 5: 420–433.

Cook, W. L., Jr. 1969. Timber harvesting and forest aesthetics: A critical review of the literature. MS thesis, SUNY, College of Environmental Science and Forestry.

Corwin, M. A. 1978. *Parking lot landscaping*. American Society of Planning Officials, Planning Advisory Service Report No. 335.

Coughlin, R. et al. 1984. *Private trees and public interest programs for protecting and planning trees in metropolitan areas*. Department of City and Regional Planning, University Of Pennsylvania, Research Report No. 10.

Crabtree, T. J. 1975. The redwood: To preserve and protect. *Environmental Law*, 5(2): 283–310.

Crowe, S. 1966. *Forestry in the landscape*. Forestry Committee, Booklet 18, NMSO, London.

Devall, W. B. 1973. The Forest Service and its clients: Input to Forest Service decision-making. *Environmental Affairs*, 2(4): 732–757.

Ellefson, P. V., and Cubbage, F. W. 1980. State forest practice laws. *Environmental Policy and Law*, 6(1980): 125–133.

Elsner, G., and Smardon, R. C., technical coordinators 1979. *Proceedings of our national landscape: A conference on applied techniques for analysis and management of the visual resource*. USDA, Forest Service, Section on Timber Management, General Technical Report, PSW-35. Pacific SW Forest and Range Experimental Station, Berkeley.

Fairfax, S. K., and Achterman, G. L. 1977. The Monongahela controversy and the political process. *J. of Forestry*, August 1977, p. 485.

Gaidula, P. 1976. *Wildland fuel management: Guidelines for the California State Park System*. California Resources Agency, Department of Parks and Recreation.

Glassford, P. 1983. *Appearance codes for small communities*. American Planning Association, Planning Advisory Service Report No. 379.

Haines, R. W. 1977. Monongahela and the National Forest Management Act of 1976. *Environmental Law*, 7: 345–362.

Hall, J. F., and Wasserstrom, R. S. 1978. The National Forest Management Act of 1976. Out of the courts and into the forests. *Environmental Law*, 8: 523–538.

Heyman, I. M., and Twiss, R. H. 1970. Environmental management of the public lands. *California Law Review*, 58(6): 1364–1411.

Hudson, D. A. 1978. Sierra Club v. Department of the Interior: The fight to preserve the Redwood National Park. *Ecology Law Quarterly*, 7: 781–859.

Kell, G. W. 1978. *Project visual analysis Handbook for the Allegheny National Forest*. Allegheny National Forest, Warren, Pa.

Klein, S. B. 1980. *New state forest practice laws: A review of state laws and their natural resource data requirements*. National Resource Information Systems Project, National Conference of State Legislatures, Denver.

Litton, R. B., Jr. 1968. *Forest landscape description and inventories: A basis for land planning and design*. USDA Forest Service Research Paper PSW-49, Pacific SW Forest and Range Experimental Station, Berkeley.

——. 1972. Aesthetic dimensions of the landscape. In *Natural environments: Studies in theoretical and applied analysis*, Krutilla, J. V. pp. 191–262. Johns Hopkins University Press.

——. 1973. *Landscape Control Points: A Procedure for Predicting and Monitoring Visual Impacts*. USDA Forest Service Research Paper PSW-91, Pacific SW Forest and Range Experimental Station, Berkeley.

Lundmark, T. 1987. Visual impacts of forestry. *Columbia Journal of Environmental Law*, 12: 131–156.

Miller, M. 1971. The forest from the trees in the Tongrass. *American Forests*, 77(7): 16–19.

Murtha, P., and Greco, M. 1975. *Appraisal of forest aesthetic values: An annotated bibliography*. Information Report FMR-X-79. Forest Management Institute, Ottawa, Ontario.

Noyes, J. H. 1969. *Woodlands, highways and people*. Pub. No. 33, Planning and Resource Development Series No. 9, Cooperative Extension Service, University of Massachusetts.

——. 1970. *Timber Harvesting and Forest Aesthetics*. Coop. Ext. Bull. No. 170, Coll. of Agric., Univ. of New Hampshire, Durham.

Pardo, R. 1976. Forest law and policy. *Toledo Law Review*, 7: 420–433.

Reich, C. A. 1962a. *Bureaucracy and the forests*. Center for the Study of Democratic Institutions.

——. 1962b. The public and the nation's forests. *California Law Review*, 50(3): 381–407.

Rodgers, J. P. 1969. The need for meaningful control of the management of federally owned timberlands. *Land and Water Law Review*, 4(1): 121–143.

Shafer, E. L., Jr. 1967. Forest aesthetics — A focal point in multiple-use management and research, pp. 47–71. In *14th IUFRO Congress*, Paper 7, Section 26. September 4-9, Munich.

Siegel, W. C. 1973. Environmental law — Some implications for forest resource management. *Environmental Law*, 4(1): 115–134.

Smardon, R. C. 1988. Perception and aesthetics of the urban environment: Review of the role of vegetation. *Landscape Urban Planning*, 15: 85–106.

Smardon, R. C. et al. 1981. *Our national landscape: Annotated bibliography and expertise index*. Agricultural Sciences Publication, Division of Agricultural Sciences, University of California, Berkeley.

Stone, E. H., II. 1978. *Visual resource management*. Landscape Architecture Technical Information Series, vol. 2. American Society of Landscape Architects.

USDA, Forest Service. 1974. *National forest landscape management*, vol. 2, chap. 1, *The visual management system*. USDA Agriculture Handbook No. 462, U.S. G.P.O.

——. 1976. Visual absorption capability. *USDA Forest Service manual*, 2382.2–31.

U.S. Senate. 1972. *Report on clearcutting on federal timber lands*. Subcommittee on Public Lands of the Senate Committee on Interior and Insular Affairs, 92nd Congress, 2nd Sess. U.S. G.P.O.

Chapter 14

Facility Siting

INTRODUCTION

Chapters 12 and 13 dealt with the impact on the landscape of landform alteration and vegetation cover. Massive structures or facilities introduced into the landscape are another major impact (Figure 14.1). This is called facility siting, and it generally refers to the introduction of large structures such as power plants, dams, or other processing and/or manufacturing facilities as well as connected utility lines. Utility corridor impacts include those of electric power transmission lines and support structures and pipelines of all types. Aesthetic impacts from these activities can be considerable, and they can be highly charged issues to local populations, as evidenced by the following cases.

MAJOR POWER PLANT LITIGATION AND CONFLICT

In the early 1960s two power-plant–siting conflicts crowded the headlines across the country, one on each coast. The Pacific Coast fight involved the siting of a nuclear power plant at Bodega Head, north of San Francisco. The battle in the Northeast was over the proposed Cornwall hydroelectric plant at Storm King Mountain on the Hudson River, 40 miles north of New York City. In each case, the sponsors did not realize either the degree of concern or the specific concerns of significant public groups.

The Storm King Mountain pump storage hydroelec-

tric plant was called the Cornwall project by its sponsor, Consolidated Edison Company of New York, because of its location near the village of Cornwall on the Hudson River (see Figure 14.2). The company first filed for a Federal Power Commission (FPC) license in January 1963. Today the project is tabled.

Early protests centered on visual concerns; the protests were later expanded to include even earthquake hazards. The initial protest was led by people across the Hudson River from the proposed plant whose views would be altered, and by people who had second homes in the area of the plant who were concerned with the growth that might accompany the plant. They organized the Scenic Hudson Preservation Conference, which was supported by major conservation organizations. A public relations firm was hired, and the conflict turned into a national issue. The Hudson River Fisherman's Association also joined the fray. The principal points of contention were: impacts on scenic and historical qualities, growth inducement, possible fish kills, public safety, and the need for the project. The site had also been considered for inclusion in a state park. The FPC granted a license for the plant in the spring of 1965 but was promptly taken to court by the opposition. The second circuit court remanded the license in December of the same year,[1] with the judgment that FPC had not compiled an adequate hearing record, that aesthetic, conservation, and recreation aspects had to be protected in power development cases, and that a conservation organization could sue to protect the public in-

---

[1]Scenic Hudson Preservation Conference v. F.P.C., 354 F.2d 608 (2d Cir. 1965), *cert. denied*, 384 U.S. 941 (1972).

Power plant & transmission line

FIGURE 14.1   Generic landscape with power plant plus transmission lines. *Graphic credit: Scott Shannon*

terest in the environment under the Federal Power Act (as was discussed in Chapter 11).

The FPC reopened hearings in 1966, and in 1970 it reissued the license to build the power plant. The plant was originally proposed with an aboveground powerhouse. However, to soften the opposition the project was redesigned; it placed the powerhouse completely underground so as not to detract from the appearance of the mountain. Likewise, transmission lines from the plant were designed to run underwater and underground to an inland point on the opposite side of the river. Another appeal by Scenic Hudson to set the li-

FIGURE 14.2   Storm King on the Hudson River. *Photo credit: Peter Black*

cense aside was turned down by the court. In 1972 the Supreme Court refused to hear Scenic Hudson's appeal of this decision, clearing the last legal hurdle to construction after nine years of litigation.

Construction began in March 1974 but was suspended four months later following issuance of a U.S. circuit court decision that further hearings should be held by the FPC to examine the Cornwall project's effect on fish life in the Hudson River. In February 1977 Con Ed submitted a 1,100-page ecological report on the Hudson River to the FPC. The report summarized the findings of ten years and $20 million worth of ecological studies related to Hudson River power plants. Well-publicized demonstrations and citizen actions led to the legal decision of far-reaching importance. The second circuit court's 1965 decision set the basic guidelines for standing for citizen suits against federal agencies and contributed to the legal formulation of NEPA.

In the case of the Bodega Head plant, to be sited on a beautiful oceanside promotory near the San Andreas Fault, the widely representative opposition was led by conservationists and supported by biological scientists from across the country. The main issues were scenic beauty preservation (the state legislature had authorized purchase of the site for a state park) and safety. The public became thoroughly confused on the subject of safety when well-known marine biologists argued on both sides of the radioactive-contamination issues. Pacific Gas and Electric Company, the sponsoring company, settled the conflict by withdrawing its proposal in 1964, when detailed geological investigations revealed that the plant would be located on an active earthquake fault subsidiary to the major San Andreas Fault. Construction was well underway by the time of the decision.

An interesting follow-up to the Bodega Head case was the next siting attempt by the same company. In 1966 it bought property for a nuclear plant at Nipomo Dunes, about halfway between San Francisco and Los Angeles, on the oceanfront. Again conservationists, fresh from the Bodega Bay struggles, were alerted. The Nipoma Dunes site had previously been designated by the National Park Service as one of unexcelled scenic quality that should be acquired for public recreation. Before a full-scale conflict started, the company consulted with the opposition-leading Sierra Club and a special task force set up by the California Resources Agency. Negotiations resulted in the plant being shifted to Diablo Canyon, a site about 20 miles away.

The Diablo Canyon plant was completed in 1979 but still has not gone into operation. While the plant was under construction, geologists discovered an earthquake fault less than 3 miles off the coast from the facility. Also design errors were discovered which have to be rectified. Several pending lawsuits and administrative actions have produced an uncertain outlook for full operation of the plant.

These two power-plant–siting cases were celebrated in the media. They, plus the cases mentioned in Chapter 10 (with potential problems with the Clean Air Act Amendments of 1977[2]) and the proposed Greene County (New York State) nuclear power plant case study in this chapter, illustrate the potential for controversy in general and the significant role of aesthetics in plant-siting cases.

SITING PROBLEMS OF ELECTRIC POWER PLANTS

The basic problem is one of land use, where to put new generating facilities, and in what form (overhead vs. underground) to place transmission lines. In 1973 professionals in the field of power generation offered that most of the new electric generating capacity in the United States during the next 20 years would be obtained from about 250 very large power plants, each producing 2,000 to 3,000 megawatts. Fossel fuel power plants of this size require 900 to 1,200 acres of land, primarily for fuel storage, plus rights-of-way about 250 feet wide for utility lines. Nuclear plants of similar capacity require 2,000 to 4,000 acres plus similarly sized rights-of-way. Both types of plants also need access to large quantities of water for cooling, although atomic plants need considerably more than do fossil fuel plants (Figure 14.3).

FIGURE 14.3 a, b, c   Mosaic of power plants; hydroelectric, fossil fueled & nuclear. *Photo credit: USDI Bureau of Land Management*

---

[2]42 U.S.C. ss. 7401 et seq. (1988).

Both types of generating facilities need provision to bring in fuel and eliminate waste water. In the case of coal-burning plants, immense quantities of fly ash are produced. In any type of fossil fuel burning plant, other wastes are produced. These wastes had traditionally been vented as stack gases. Even with stack emission controls, fossil fuel power plants have major impacts of visible air quality (as discussed in Chapter 10). In addition, lands are required for fuel storage and handling facilities, docks and railroad trackage, pipelines for oil and gas, offshore facilities for oil and liquefied natural gas tankers, and in the case of coal-fired plants, ash removal facilities.

Today there is a trend toward smaller, co-generation plants in urban areas as well as experimentation with wood-fired power plants in some areas of the country as well as waste-to-energy plants. Even such seemingly benign power sources such as hydroelectric, wind power, geothermal, and solar have substantial visual impact on the landscape (see Figure 14.4) with large-scale operations. In summary, for power plant facility projects, visual impact includes the plant structure itself with plume, attendant air quality impacts, the fuel feeding system and stockpiling, the substation and distribution system of power lines, and other linear connections such as pipelines, roads, and railroads.

Electric power transmission lines are a source of visual problems (Figure 14.5). As a Library of Congress (1970) report put it:

> The most obvious environmental effect of electric transmission is the sight of the towers and their cables, and the accompanying withdrawal of land for other uses. Lesser effects include interference with reception of radio and television signals under certain conditions and, in the case of direct current lines, the possibility of corrosion of underground metal structures, such as sewer or water pipes, because of electrical currents within the earth.

The greater use of extra-high voltage transmission will minimize the total number of miles of overhead transmission. However, the wider rights-of-way, the more massive and higher towers, and the larger conductors could, in the view of the Federal Energy Regulatory Commission (FERC), compound the problems in seeking to preserve environmental values.

Through the 1990s it is expected that overhead transmission will dominate, for the technology because

FIGURE 14.4 a, b   Geothermal development and wind turbine. *Photo credit: USDI Bureau of Land Management*

FIGURE 14.5 a, b, c   Mosaic of transmission lines. *Photo credit: R. Burton Litton and USDI Bureau of Land Management*

high-voltage underground transmission is not expected to be available (EDAW 1975). A large 2,400-megawatt power plant typically would be the juncture of three rights-of-way, each 200 feet wide.

Two different approaches to mitigating the effects of transmission lines are possible. One is to put the lines underground, as mentioned. The other is to encourage multiple use of the land required for their rights-of-way. The first is very expensive (10 to 20 times the cost of overhead lines) and hindered by the technology. Multiple land use sometimes occurs, but in general it must be forced by planners and regulators.

FEDERAL LAWS AND PROCEDURES FOR FACILITY SITING

The major federal act affecting facility siting is the National Environmental Policy Act[3] (as reviewed in Chapter 11), which affects all federal funding, licens-

ing, and permits. In addition, specific federal agencies have additional guidance and/or special legislation for facility/utility corridor siting. The U.S. Forest Service (1975) has a special chapter/handbook within their visual management system that addresses utility corridor siting and is cross-referenced in the Forest Service manual.

The U.S. Army Corps of Engineers, as well as the Bonneville Power Administration, the Federal Energy Regulatory Commission, the Bureau of Reclamation, and U.S.D.A. Soil Conservation Service, all have to function under the Water Resources Planning Act,[4] which covers all federal and regional agency water resource projects. In addition, the Water Resource Council, of which all these agencies are members, has issued "Principles and Standards for Planning" (WRC 1973), which includes aesthetic resource evaluation as part of project development. Under these "principles and standards," the co-author developed the Corps of

---

[3]16 U.S.C. 470 et seq. (1988).
[4]42 U.S.C. s. 1962 et seq. (1988).

Engineers' Visual Resource Assessment Procedures (VRAP) (Smardon et al. 1988) that are applicable to all water resource projects, including hydroelectric-generating projects and related structures and activities. The Corps also has a host of environmental regulations (ER's) that include guidance for treatment of aesthetics as part of project planning.[5] The Bonneville Power Administration, part of U.S. Dept. of Interior, has developed an elaborate process for siting electric transmission lines from their hydroelectric facilities called PERMITS (a computerized siting process); was developed by Landscapes Limited in 1974 (Lewis et al. 1974) and has funded many visual studies and research on the visual impact of power lines (Hendrickson et al. 1974; Jones and Jones 1976a & 1976b; Murray, T. J. Biserius and Macotte 1979).

FERC, formerly the Federal Power Commission, issues licenses for the construction, operation, and maintaining of dams, water conduits, reservoirs, powerhouses, transmission lines, and the physical structures of hydroelectric power projects under the Federal Power Act of 1920.[6] In general, FERC tends to use the Bureau of Land Management's (BLM) visual impact procedures (USDI 1980) for utility corridors, or whatever methodology can be shown to be most appropriate.

The BLM issues all leases for mining and energy exploration activity on federal lands. It also follows special provisions of the Federal Land Policy and Management Act of 1976[7] for right-of-way corridors:

Sec. 505. Each right-of-way shall contain —

(a) terms and conditions which will
    (i) carry out the purposes of this Act and rules and regulations issued thereunder;
    (ii) minimize damage to scenic and esthetic values and fish and wildlife habitat and otherwise protect the environment . . .
(b) such terms and conditions as the Secretary concerned deems necessary to. . . .
    (v) require location of the right-of-way along a route that will cause least damage to the environment, taking into consideration feasibility and other relevant factors; and
    (vi) otherwise protect the public interest in the lands traversed by the right-of-way or adjacent thereto.[8]

In general BLM (1980) uses the visual contrast rating method (as covered in Chapter 11) to assess visual impacts of utility corridor and energy facility development projects.

The role of the Nuclear Regulatory Commission (NRC) is similar to that of FERC, but it is specific to nuclear power plant licensing. As part of the licensing process under NEPA, the NRC is supposed to consider aesthetic impacts of nuclear power plants. Although clearly the safety aspects of nuclear power plant construction are paramount, aesthetic impacts have played a major role in situations like Bodega Head and Nipomo Dunes, California, and Greene County, New York. Maybe this is why the NRC, through the Battelle laboratories in Richland, Washington, have sponsored research to develop a methodology for assessing visual impacts of nuclear power plants (see Gray, Ady, and Jones 1979; Jones et al. 1975).

Other facilities or federal projects are those dealing with transportation. Chapter 11 covered the effect of NEPA and Section 4(f) on highway projects and aesthetic review. The Airport and Airway Development Act of 1970[9] has sections that discuss how the Department of Transportation will consider community interests, local community land use planning goals, and Section 4(f) type resources and lands affected by proposed airport facilities. Finally, the Urban Mass Transportation Act of 1964[10] gives similar guidance to the Urban Mass Transportation Administration in reviewing federally financed mass transit projects.

In addition to all of the above, certain agencies function in an oversight role in reviewing federally funded projects. For example, the Environmental Protection Agency reviews projects with respect to air, water, and noise impacts; the Fish and Wildlife Service reviews projects with respect to their impact on fish and wildlife and their habitat; and the National Park Service reviews projects for their impact on historical and cultural resources.

STATE REGULATION OF FACILITY SITING AND CORRIDORS

Regulation by states of power plant siting or placement of transmission lines is far from uniform and is in a

---

[5]See ER 1165-2-500, "Environmental Guidelines for the Civil Works Program of the Corps of Engineers," Sept. 30, 1972; ER 1105-2-507, "Planning Preparation and Coordination of Environmental Statements," April 15, 1974; ER 1120-2-400, "Investigations, Planning and Development of Water Resources: Recreation Resources Planning," Nov. 1, 1971; ER 1130-2-400, "Policy on Fish and Wildlife Management"; and ER 1130-2-406, "Project Operation: Lakeshore Management at Civil Works Projects," December 13, 1974.
[6]16 U.S.C. 791a et seq. (1988).
[7]43 U.S.C. s. 1701 et seq. (1988).
[8]Id. at s. 1765.
[9]49 U.S.C. § 1716(C)(I)(A)&(C)(3).
[10]Urban Mass Transportation Act of 1964, 49 U.S.C1601 et seq. (1988).

condition of flux, as states continually add or amend regulation systems or initiate them. The first comprehensive state power-plant–siting review procedure was set up in Maryland in 1968, and amended in 1971. A few other states, including Vermont, New York, and Connecticut have similar plans and processes.

The Maryland plan[11] suspends a utility's use of public domain powers until the state public service commission issues a certificate of "public convenience and necessity." This certificate can be issued only after a public hearing, and after due consideration has been given to the need for the plant, its effect on the reliability of the entire system, economics, pollution, aesthetics, historical sites, and the wishes of local governments. This law applies to any power plant or transmission line with a capacity of 69 kilowatts or more.

A similar statute was adopted by Vermont in 1968.[12] It applies to plants or power lines that have a 48-kilowatt or greater capacity, and requires that approval be obtained before substantial investment is made, so as to avoid any possible bias in favor of the facility due to possible loss (including site destruction) if permission is refused. The Vermont act includes the Maryland provisions, but stiffened the standards by requiring that the plant and power lines "not unduly interfere with the development of the region; be needed, and not adversely affect system stability, reliability, or economics; and not have undue adverse effects on aesthetics, historic sites, the purity of air and water, the natural environment, or the public health and safety."[13]

The Maryland act was amended in 1971 in regard to the procedures to be followed in seeking a certificate, including a requirement of a minimum of two years between application and scheduled construction. Also added to the act was the provision for a surcharge on electricity users to pay for continuing research in site evaluation, and for purchase by the state of likely sites, which may be resold or leased to utilities. Lands already owned by power companies would be included in the site evaluations. Local zoning regulations would be superseded by the state law in respect to sites purchased by the state, but would remain in force in regard to all other sites.

In 1971 Arizona adopted a power plant and transmission line siting bill.[14] All the statutes discussed above provide for a state utility regulator to decide on siting, but Arizona created an eighteen-member committee to make the decision. Eleven are ex-officio and seven are appointees of the Arizona Corporation Commission, the utility regulator, appointed to represent certain enumerated interests. The act requires a firm consideration of the costs of proposals before the committee.

In 1970 Washington created the Thermal Power Plant Site Evaluation Council to review power plants and attendant transmission systems.[15] The act established this interdisciplinary committee to evaluate siting proposals. The council can develop regulations, but the final decision is made by the governor. Local laws are superseded by the act.

In 1971 Oregon adopted a siting bill[16] primarily for thermal power plants. Its council consists of appointed members, who outnumber ex-officio members. As in Washington, the governor is also given a clear role in the siting decision, and has a great deal of control over who is appointed to the council. A three-year period after the first filing is required before approval can be granted. However, the act requires the council to act within two years of the receipt of the application. It is possible for the procedure to take less than the three years.

In 1971 Connecticut adopted the Public Utility Environmental Standards Act[17] to provide a siting procedure for both generating plants and transmission lines. The act is similar to that in New York (see below), but includes a panel called the Power Facility Evaluation Council. Two of its members are appointed by the legislative leadership and two by the governor as experienced ecologists; there are also three general appointees. The other members of the nine-member panel are ex-officio members. Local laws under this statute are made binding, though certain powers of the municipalities to regulate the location of certified facilities are limited.

In 1970 New York provided a siting statute[18] for major utility transmission facilities including both gas and electric lines. The law also covers major power plants of over 50,000 kilowatts and resource recovery plants with over 80,000 kilowatts generating capability. The law provides detailed procedures for proposed

---

[11]Maryland Code Ann. Art. 78, Sec. 54A, Supp. 1970, Ch. 23, 1971 amended Ch. 31, 1971.

[12]Vt. Stat. Ann. s. 248 Supp. 1971.

[13]Id.

[14]Ariz. Rev. Stat. Ann. Title 40, Ch. 2, Art. 6.2, 1971.

[15]Wash. Rev. Code Ch. 80.50, 1970.

[16]Or. Laws, Ch. 609, 1971.

[17]Conn. Laws No. 575 1971.

[18]N.Y. Pub. Serv. Law, Art. VII, McKinney Supp. 1970.

projects, including consideration of aesthetics, as well as a hearing by the state Public Service Commission. The law is modeled after that of Vermont, but includes other features relating access to the courts, standards of decisions, the interrelation of local laws, and the development of the record. Detailed regulations have been adopted.

Other states that have special provisions for facility siting review include Delaware, whose Coastal Zone Act[19] restricts manufacturing and industrial uses along the coast; Vermont with its Large-Scale Development Site Review Act[20] (reviewed in Chapter 11); and Maine which enacted the Site Location Law.[21] Kentucky has a separate statute for power plant review,[22] and the New Jersey Coastal Area Facility Review Act[23] is also meant for review of large facilities.

Fewer than a dozen states report that they have significant jurisdiction over new transmission lines. The remainder either have no jurisdiction, or have jurisdiction in special cases only. Of the 50 state regulatory commissions plus Puerto Rico, 25 have no jurisdiction of any kind over the routing of transmission lines. Of the 51 regulatory commissions, 16 indicated that aesthetics and environmental matters were, or could be, among the factors taken into consideration. Others indicated their review was limited by law to matters such as safety, property of investment, and neccessity for

the line. In many states, transmission line construction is regulated piecemeal by local agencies.

A more detailed treatment of power facility siting can be seen in Stone (1971). During the 1980s attention focused more on siting questions related to waste facilities, landfills, waste-to-energy and hazardous waste facility siting, with little concern for aesthetics per se; however, there was a good deal of attention on public participation in the process.

METHODOLOGY DEVELOPMENT FOR FACILITY SITING

There was considerable development work in siting power plants and utility corridors during the 1970s. The environmental planning firm of EDAW even produced a whole volume on facility siting (Williams and Masa 1983). Specific methodology has been developed for visual impact assessment for nuclear (Gray, Ady, and Jones, 1979; Jones et al. 1975; Petrich 1979a) and fossil fueled power plants (Blau and Bowie 1979; Williams and Blau 1980) as well as visual air quality impacts (Tremain et al. 1979). There also has been a considerable amount of work on the visual impacts of power lines (EDAW 1975; Hendrickson et al. 1974; Jackson and Hudman 1978; Lewis et al. 1974; Miller, Jethra, and MacDonald 1979; Vaughn 1974).

Case Study: Greene County Nuclear Power Plant[24]

Introduction and Regulatory Context

As part of its federal licensing responsibilities under NEPA, the NRC performs independent environmental assessments of each application for a license to construct and operate a nuclear power plant. The NRC contracted with Oak Ridge National Laboratory to conduct an assessment of the projected environmental impacts of a $1.8-billion 1,200-megawatt nuclear power plant proposed by the Power Authority of the State of New York (PANSY) to be built in Greene County, on the west bank of the Hudson River about 40 miles south of Albany. The proposed Greene County Nuclear Power Plant (GCNPP) site was to be located at the base of the Catskill Mountains and the primary alternative site proposed was 10 miles north (see Figure 14.6). The engineering

designs called for a 450-foot-tall natural draft cooling tower and a 205-foot domed reactor containment structure. PANSY, a state-owned, tax-exempt utility, would transmit the electrical power produced by the plant to the New York City metropolitan area, where its principal customer would be the subway system.

Assessment Technique

The aesthetic experience is dependent on the environmental stimulus, that which is seen, and the background and context of the observers, those doing the seeing. Petrich (1979a, 1977b) employed three approaches, each centering on the landscape to be seen and the context within which it is seen. This context encompassed the viewer's immediate geograph-

---

[19]Delaware Coastal Zone Act, Ch. 70, Title 7 Del. Code Anno. ss. 7001 et seq. (1968).
[20]Vt. Stat. Ann. Title 10 ss. 6001-89. (1970).
[21]Me. Stat. Title 38 s. 481 et seq. (1970).
[22]Ky. Revised Stats. Ch. 278.025 (April 1, 1973).
[23]N.J. Ch. 85 (1973) N.J.S.A. 13:19-1 et seq.
[24]Portions taken from Carl Petrich, 1979. "Aesthetic Impact of a Proposed Power Plant on a Historic Wilderness Landscape," presented as part of *Our National Landscape; A Conference on Applied Techniques for Analysis and Management of the Visual Resource*. Incline Village, NV, April 23-25, 1979. Reproduced with permission of the author.

FIGURE 14.6 Computer graphic of landscape context.
Source: Carl Petrich Oak Ridge National Laboratory

ical setting, expectations, attitudes about nuclear power, and degree of affinity for and familiarity with local landscape, as well as a more detailed look at the historical and cultural context. The first two approaches, an analysis of the extent of visual quality and an analysis, in part through use of a visual preference survey, of the potential viewers, are heavily quantitative. The results of these two approaches did not help to determine which of the chief sites was preferable (see NRC 1979). The analysis of the historical and cultural context of the plant did point out a preferable site in terms of aesthetic impacts, according to Petrich (1979a). This represented an unusual twist in aesthetic impact analysis and is described later in the case study.

Evaluation of the Extent of Scenic Quality

This facet of the assessment considered the scenic quality of the area surrounding the two proposed sites. Petrich evaluated the unique scenic features as well as visual "misfits" in the landscape proximate to the proposed sites. Colleagues at the laboratory aided in developing a computer-assisted model of the scenic quality surrounding the two sites that helped assess the quality of the landscape in which potential viewers would stand. "Before and after" photographs assisted in simulating the visual changes likely to occur from critical viewing points surrounding the two sites.

Scenic Features and Misfits

Existing studies were the basis for assessing the relative quantity and quality of scenic features (e.g., waterfalls, scenic overlooks) or visual misfits (ill-placed visually noxious industries, unscreened junkyards) within 10 miles of either plant site. The primary site, near the hamlet of Cementon, because it is closer to the escarpment of the Catskill Mountains (Figure 14.6), had considerably more scenic features than the chief alternate site near the village of Athens.

Model of Scenic Quality and Visibility

Petrich assessed the existing scenic quality of the possible viewer settings surrounding the two sites and analyzed the results in terms of whether or not a proposed plant would be visible from an observer setting having a given level of scenic quality. Based on this criterion, an appropriate plant location is one with low visibility or, if visibility is high, the scenic quality of those lands with visual access is low. The assump-

tion is that the higher the scenic quality of the given location, the more sensitive viewers in that area are to any intrusion in their visual field.

Petrich used the criteria of landscape preference developed by Zube and his colleagues from their Connecticut River Valley research (Zube 1973, 1974; Zube, Pitt, and Anderson, 1974) to map scenic quality. Individual landscape variables (e.g., relative topographic relief, land use diversity, land use height contrast) were evaluated for sub-areas within a five-mile radius around each site and weighted, and the scores of each sub-area summed. By summing the scores of each sub-area within a given radius from each site, Petrich could, in part, assess the relative scenic quality of each site. Alternately, Petrich multiplied a given sub-area's score by the percent of land within it from which the cooling tower at either site could be seen. This assessed the relative scenic quality of that land having visual access to the cooling tower at each site.

Modeling Result

The results of the modeling effort were not definitive (from Petrich's perspective) in terms of suggesting which site was preferable. Results showed slightly higher scenic quality surrounded the Cementon site. When lands with visual access alone were considered, however, the Athens site had higher visual quality. Reliance on visibility impacts alone is of limited value in aesthetic analysis. Although people reside in a specific locale, their transportation patterns mean they live (work, shop, attend school) at a regional level. With people traveling widely across this modern scale landscape, topography cannot conceal features in the landscape very long or very well. The results of a visibility analysis alone could therefore be misleading.

Simulation of Plant and Plume

To superimpose the plant on photographs of the present landscape a professional artist airbrushed the plant and its visible plume (both appropriately scaled from calculations) on to photographs from critical locations. A computer model (Dunn et al. 1978) of a broad variety of visible plume alternatives provided the artist appropriate wind directions and dimensions for a "typical" (not worst case, but still visible) plume. Visible plumes consist of water droplets and are dependent on hourly as well as seasonal variations in a site's micrometeorology. The model's output also helped to characterize the frequency and extent of the visible plume throughout the year.

With the help of the simulated plant and plume superimposed on photographs from critical viewing areas, Petrich described the projected aesthetic impacts based on traditional criteria of visual analysis (changes in line, texture, form, color, scale, and so on) and on the changes Petrich felt likely to occur in the area's cultural and historical context.

Visual Preference Survey

A visual preference survey can assess, in part, how people feel about their environment and possible changes in it. People who live in the study area were surveyed because they were the prime group to be affected. In the survey, subjects expressed their preferences by rating (on a numerical scale, 1 to 5) 40 photographs of the local landscape; some photographs had cooling towers or cement plants superimposed on them. Cement plants were chosen as intrusions comparable to the power plant because they represent heavy industry, make sense in terms of the regional economic base, and represent a taxable industry. Additionally, respondents completed two pages of written questions to provide information about their attitudes regarding the proposed facility, nuclear power, their frequency of use of local recreation areas, their appreciation and use of the area's historical and cultural resources, and their individual backgrounds.

The professional artist assisted in superimposing the cooling towers and cement plants on 16 of the 40 photographs. The result was 8 groups of 3 photographs each (such as the triad in Figure 14.7) and 16 other photographs. All photographs were middle- to- long-distance shots of the local landscape. The photographs were reduced to 2-by-3 inches, randomized, and printed by offset process, 8 photographs per page. A total of 145 valid responses (from randomly approached respondents) comprised the survey. The survey had a very satisfactory distribution of respondents by age, sex, income, occupation, education, time lived in the region, present residence, and where respondents grew up. Twenty-four subgroups from the original sample were derived from demographic information supplied by each respondent or from the nature of their answers to certain questions. Statistical crosstabulations by sub-group pairs were made on all photographs.

The results of the survey were augmented by personal interviews with local residents and by a search of newspaper files for clues to attitudes toward the local environment. The conclusions reached were that the people most likely to view the proposed plant from roads or residences are likely to be strongly opposed to any type of power plant at either location; are likely to be strongly opposed to large natural draft cooling towers in their landscape; have apparently adjusted through familiarity or by some other mechanisms to the presense of cement plants in their landscape; preceive their area of the Hudson Valley as having the highest scenic quality of any area between New York City and Albany; value and frequent the area's historic and cultural sites; and strongly prefer the scenic quality perceived in natural and rural landscapes. Among other conclusions, they perceive the proposed facility at Athens to be less of an aesthetic impact than it would be at Cementon. From the local resident's perspective, the Greene Country Nuclear Power Plant appeared to be highly unwelcome and inappropriate.

Historic and Cultural Context

In exploring the historical and cultural context within which the proposed plant would exist, Petrich used an analysis that continually narrowed its scale from the larger New England landscape and nineteenth-century times down to the actual importance and present-day quality of the view from a historic site near the proposed GCNPP site. Each incremental step emphasized uniqueness or special quality. In this respect, all the steps began to interrelate and a cumulative uniqueness and special quality emerged. A detailed account of this study is presented in a separate document (Petrich 1979b).

In the mid-nineteenth century the mid–Hudson Valley was the seat of cultural inspiration in this country. From the Hudson River School of painters, who were the leaders of the

ORNL–DWG 79–11073

1 2 3 4 5   AS IS

1 2 3 4 5   WITH CEMENT PLANT

1 2 3 4 5   WITH COOLING TOWER

FIGURE 14.7 a, b, c   Sample triad of images. *Source: John Wiley and Sons*

romantic movement, one emerged as most popular and best able to give graphic image to the public's longings and feelings about nature and America's role in Western civilization. Frederic Edwin Church put his considerable talents to use in painting the icons of his time: archetypal New World images

FIGURE 14.8 a, b   Principal view from Olana, landscape painting and photo. *Source: John Wiley and Sons*

such as South American volcanos, north woods wilderness, North Atlantic icebergs, Niagara Falls, and so on. Church, who grew up in Hartford, Connecticut was a cousin of Frederick Law Olmsted and was Thomas Cole's only pupil. He learned landscape painting at Cole's home and studio (still existing) in Catskill, five miles from the proposed GCNPP.

After Church became a wealthy world figure in his early thirties he bought land atop a steep hill on the east side of the Hudson River. There he applied his design genius for the next 30 years in constructing a mansion and grounds that exist today. It is one of the few surviving Victorian estates in a setting comparable to its nineteenth-century environs. Art and architectural historians have called it the most spectacularly sited mansion in the country and termed it the best site in the Eastern United States. Olana, as the estate is known, is about 6 miles from the Cementon site (Figure 14.6). Theodore Stebbins, the curator of American painting at Boston's Museum of Fine Art, said that Olana "is the best place to feel the spirit of the artist coming together with nature as it was in the nineteenth century."

Olana is important to the present day. The goal of nineteenth-century landscape design was to create three-dimensional picturesque views which looked like two-dimensional painting. The American perception of what is "pretty" can be traced directly to the prototypical landscapes such as Olana's and other estates built along the Hudson Valley at this time, and indirectly to their European antecedents.

The landscaped views at Olana were created by Church, the master painter, a close relative of, and undoubtedly much influenced by Olmsted. The mansion itself was designed by Church in collaboration with Calvert Vaux, Olmsted's partner in the design of New York's Central Park. The principal view (Figure 14.8) that Church celebrated at Olana was to the southwest, a consciously developed motif of looking across the continent (part of the nineteenth-century idea, Manifest Destiny). This view has been universally acclaimed in both the art history world and in popular literature. It is a view of classic composition, one which Church painted at least 35 times.

Figure 14.9 shows the location of the proposed GCNPP relative to Olana's celebrated view. The making of views is historically the essence of the landscape architect's craft. The GCNPP would severely inhibit the appreciation of one of the few remaining American landscape prototypes, the original

FIGURE 14.9   Simulation of GCNPP from the same view. *Source: John Wiley and Sons*

source for understanding the beginnings of the landscape designer's profession, and a living embodiment of popular American landscape taste. Petrich foresaw the GCNPP at Cementon to be an unacceptable physical and symbolic intrusion into a unique national treasure.

Summary

The NRC's final environmental statement (1979) concluded that the GCNPP at Cementon would unacceptably diminish these national, historical, cultural, and scenic ressources. This is the first impact statement issued by NRC to ever recommend the denial of a license to construct a nuclear power plant. That this recommendation is primarily for aesthetic reasons documents the progress in credibility and defensibility that visual analysis has made.

References

Ady, J., Gray, B. A., and Jones, G. R. 1979. A visual resource management study of alternative dams, reservoirs and highway and transmission line corridors near Copper Creek, Washington. In *Our national landscape*, ed. G. Elsner and R. C. Smardon, pp. 590–597.

Baird, B. E., Sheppard, S. R. J., and Smardon, R. C. 1979. Visual simulation of offshore liquified natural gas (LNG) terminals in a decisionmaking context. In *Our national landscape*, ed. G. Elsner and R. C. Smardon, pp. 636–644.

Blau, D. H., and Bowie, M. V. 1979. Visual sensitivity of river recreation to power plants. In *Our National Landscape*, ed. G. Elsner and R. C. Smardon, pp. 499–506.

Brookshire, D. S., Ives, B., and Shulze, W. P. 1976. The evaluation of aesthetic preferences. *Journal of Environmental Economy and Management*, 3(1): 325–346.

Crowe S. 1958. *The Landscape of power*. Architectural Press.

Draper, J. B. 1974. The Rainbow Bridge case and reclamation projects in reserved areas. *Natural Resources Journal*, 14(3): 431–445.

Dunn, W. E. et al. 1978. *Mathematical modeling of plumes from proposed cooling Towers at Seabrook and alternative sites*. Division of Environmental Impact Studies, Argonne National Laboratories.

EDAW International. 1975. *Study of environmental impact of underground electric transmission system*. U.S. Department of Energy.

Gray, B. A., Ady, J., and Jones, G. R. 1979. Evolution of a visual impact model to evaluate nuclear power plant siting and design options. In *Our national landscape*, ed. G. Elsner and R. C. Smardon, pp. 491–498.

Hendrickson, P. L. et al. 1974. *Measuring the social attitudes and aesthetic and economic considerations which influence transmission line routing*. Battelle Northwest Laboratory Pub. No. BNML-1837, Richland, WA.

Jackson, R. H., and Hudman, L. E. 1978. Assessment of the environmental impact of high voltage power transmission lines. *Journal of Environmental Management* 6(2): 153–170.

Jones and Jones, 1976a. *Measuring the visibility of high voltage transmission facilities*. NTIS Pub. No. BPA-VIS-76-1, Springfield, IL.

———. 1976b. *Visual impact of high voltage transmission facilities in northern Idaho and northwestern Montana*. U.S.D.I. Bonneville Power Administration, Kalispell, MT.

Jones, G. R. I. et al. 1975. A method for quantification of aesthetic values for environmental decisionmaking. *Nuclear Technology*, 25: 682–713.

Lewis, P. H., Jr. et al. 1974. *PERMITS Methodology Phase II*. U.S.D.I., Bonneville Power Administration. Portland, OR.

Library of Congress. 1970. *The economy, energy and the environment: A background study proposed for use of the Joint Economic Committee, Congress of the United States*. Environmental Policy Division, Legislative Reference Service, Library of Congress, U.S. G.P.O.

Miller, C., Jethra, N., and MacDonald, R. 1979. Classification of the visual landscape for transmission planning. In *Our national landscape*, ed. G. Elsner and R. C. Smardon, pp. 507–513.

Murray, T. J., Bisenius, D. J., and Marcotte, J. G. 1979. Northwest Montana/North Idaho transmission corridor study: A computer-assisted corridor location and impact evaluation assessment. In *Our national landscape*, ed. G. Elsner and R. C. Smardon, pp. 470–476.

Note. 1969–1970. Legal conservation-thermal pollution from a nuclear power plant. *Journal of Urban Law*, 47: 895.

Note. 1971. Legal setting of nuclear power plant siting decisions: A New York State controversy. *Cornell Law Review*, 57: 80.

Petrich, C. H. 1979a. Aesthetic impact of a proposed power plant on an historic wilderness landscape. In *Our national landscape*, ed. G. Elsner and R. C. Smardon, pp. 477–484.

———. 1979b. *The historical and cultural context of the proposed Greene County Nuclear Power Plant*. Pub. ORNL/TM-6774, Oak Ridge National Laboratory.

Poland, S. P. 1969. Development of recreational and related resources at hydroelectric projects licensed by the Federal Power Commission. *Land and Water Law Review*, 4(2): 375–398.

Ramey, J. T. 1970. Planning for environmental protection in the siting of nuclear and fossil powered plants. *Atomic Energy Law Journal* 12: 59.

Smardon, R. C. et al. 1988. *Visual resources assessment procedure of the US Army Corps of Engineers*. Report 88-1, Environmental Research Laboratory, Vicksburg, MS.

Stone, L. B. 1971. Power siting: A challenge to the legal process. *Albany Law Review*, 36: pp. 1–34.

Tarlock, A. D., Tippy, R. and Francis, F. E. 1972. Environmental regulation of power plant siting: Existing and proposed institutions. *Southern California Law Review*, 45: 502.

Tremain, E. F. et al. 1979. Simulation of the visual effects of power plant plumes. In *Our National Landscape*, ed. G. Elsner and R. C. Smardon, pp. 485–490.

U.S.D.A., Forest Service. 1975. *National forest landscape management: Utilities*, vol. 2 no. 2. USDA Handbook No. 478, U.S. G.P.O.

U.S.D.I., B.L.M. 1980. *Visual resources management program.* Division of Recreation and Cultural Resources. U.S. G.P.O. (Stock no. 0024-011-000116-6).

U.S.N.R.C. 1979. *Final environmental statement for Greene County Nuclear Power Plant proposed by Power Authority of the State of New York.* Docket No. 50-549, NUREG-0512.

U.S. Office of Science and Technology. 1970. *Electric power and the environment.* Energy Policy Staff.

U.S. Water Resources Council. 1973. Water and related land resources: Establishment of principles and standards for planning. *Federal Register,* 38(174), September 10, 1973.

Vaughn, A. V. 1974. A *visual analysis system to assist in locating transmission corridors.* Ontario Hydroelectric and Forestry Department Toronto.

Williams, E. A. and Masa, A. K., with Blau, D. H., and Schoal, H. R. 1983. *Siting major facilities: A practical approach.* McGraw-Hill.

Willrich, M. 1972. Energy-environmental conflict: Siting electric power facilities. *Virginia Law Review,* 58: 257.

Zube, E. H. 1973. Rating everyday rural landscapes of the Northeastern U.S. *Landscape Architecture,* 63(4): 371–375.

———. 1974. Cross-disciplinary and intermode agreement on the description and evaluation of landscape resources. *Environment and Behavior,* 6: 69–89.

Zube, E. H., Pitt, D. G., and Anderson, T. W. 1974. *Perception and measurement of scenic resources in the southern Connecticut River Valley.* Institute for Man and Environment, Pub. No. R-74-1, University of Massachusetts.

IV
Law and Aesthetics
in Practice

OVERVIEW

The final section of the book, Part IV: Law and Aesthetics in Practice, incorporates much of the previously presented material to illustrate how legal and resource professionals can work together in the various legal situations. e.g., hearing and courtroom. Chapter 14, "Aesthetic Litigation," for example, illustrates how legal and aesthetic analysis professionals should deal with procedural issues,

appropriate levels of analyses in prelitigation, preparation and presentation of graphic materials, and the role of expert witnesses in hearings and trial situations.

The final chapter, 15, "Appropriate Roles," is a reflective review of the potential roles that can be played by all types of practitioners, and also summarizes some major procedural and legal-philosophical issues that will need continuing attention.

Chapter 15

Litigation and Aesthetic Analysis

INTRODUCTION

In many of the situations and most of the case studies in the previous chapters, the need for aesthetic analysts and legal counsel has been shown. Their critical skills and processes lead to the development of defensible visual analyses, ordinances, or other products that will withstand both methodological and legal scrutiny. The authors have been involved in a number of major court cases and hearings, and much of the material presented in this chapter is drawn from these experiences. In addition, several other works concern some aspects of aesthetic analysis for litigation (Atkins and Blair 1983; Brace 1980; Carruth 1977; Murray and Neimann 1979; Schauman 1982; and Stuart 1980) as well as legal counsel's perspectives (Sive 1970). Finally, there is a nicely written short book for planners in their role as expert witnesses (Dorram 1982).

THE ROLE(S) OF THE EXPERT WITNESS/ANALYST

When one performs a visual or aesthetic analysis for a specific project or planning study for a local ordinance, there is always the possibility of becoming an expert witness in trial or hearing. Therefore, in scoping the aesthetic analysis, this eventuality should be anticipated, especially for controversial projects.

Beside direct testimony or producing materials for trials or hearings, there are a number of other roles that expert witnesses and analysts play. The co-author Smardon has been involved in literature searches to substantiate defensible legal programs, such as putting electric utility lines underground in New York State or the protection of wetland heritage values as part of coastal zone planning in South Carolina. For this role, the critical skills needed are good access to and knowledge concerning the appropriate literature as well as the ability to screen for the most appropriate or relevant literature or case studies.

The opposite of developing the knowledge base for a regulatory program is critiquing and analyzing a legislative program as it is being implemented. The author Smardon did such for the California Coastal Act of 1976. This 90-page act was analyzed from the perspective of what local governments need to do to develop local coastal programs (Dickert and Smardon 1977). A step-by-step movable flowchart was developed to understand what local governments would have to do, and two glitches in the legal language describing review procedures were discovered.

Sometimes the visual analyst's role is to produce a written and graphic product that must stand on its own to be submitted to a judge or hearing officer. There is no direct testimony, thus the critical skill is the careful planning and preparation of self-explanatory exhibits linked with written prefiled testimony. An example of this is Figure 15.1, which shows the visual impact of off-road vehicle usage on Cape Cod National Seashore. These are two of several images that were used to elicit reactions of raters and then paired with the statistical analysis on the back of the image. Although depositions were taken from the author as part of this case,[1] there was never any direct testimony in federal court—thus

---

[1]Conservation Law Foundation of New England vs. Dept. of Interior and Conservation Law Foundation v. Clark Civ. Act. No. 81-1004-M Boston, deposition of Richard C. Smardon, April 15, 1982.

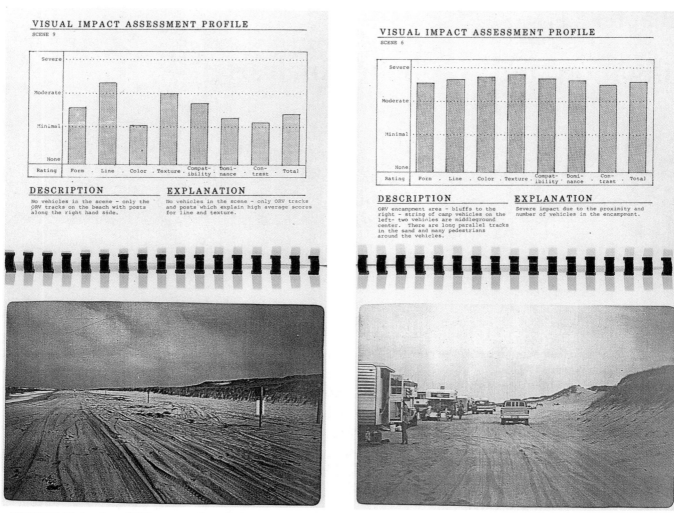

FIGURE 15.1 a, b   ORV usage on Cape Cod National Seashore used for litigation

one can see why self-explanatory exhibits are necessary.

Another role of the expert witness/analyst is to work with legal counsel to articulate points of potential testimony of lay witnesses. One may have lay expert witnesses by virtue of their substantial experience with specific uses of a resource such as fishing, sailing, boating, and so on. In the Shreveport I-220 Highway viaduct case,[2] the co-author Smardon worked with several lay expert witnesses to graphically articulate their key testimony points. Several of these points involved safety and risk of water-related recreational activities near highway viaduct structures. These points were summarized graphically and later became exhibits entered into the court record (see Figures 15.2). This can be an extremely valuable function when counsel is try-

ing to build a solid record of factual points that can be easily retrieved and reviewed later.

Probably the most valuable role of the experienced expert witness/analyst is advising other expert witnesses about what to expect on the witness stand or in the hearing room. It can be an unnerving experience for the uninitiated.

TYPICAL SEQUENCE OF EVENTS

The first step is the expert witness/analyst agreeing to work on a specific project. One is usually contacted by legal counsel, although there are now specialists whose sole activity is putting together teams of expert witnesses. The person or firm engaging you will want to know your background, education, training, and exper-

---

[2]Louisiana Environmental Society, Inc. V. Brinegar 513 F. Supp. 179 (1981).

FIGURE 15.2 a, b, c   Sample graphics of boating hazards used for litigation. *Graphic credit: Haynes, Popadre, and Abbey*

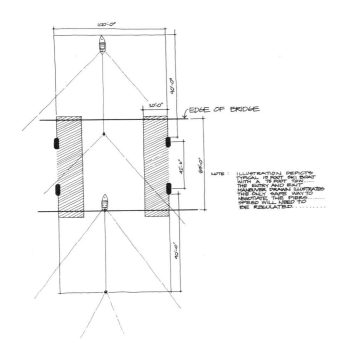

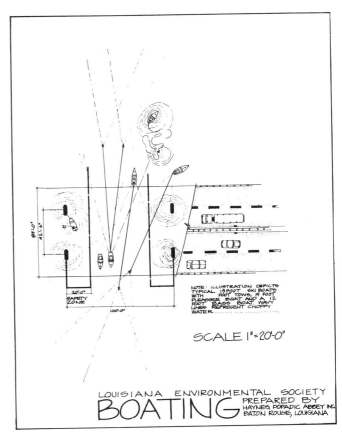

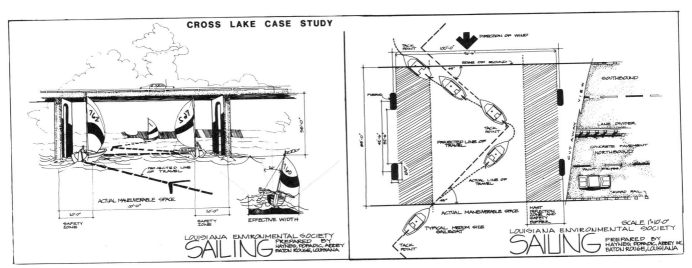

tise in working with similar projects and situations. This is very important, as it affects your stature as an expert witness in court. The analyst should carefully negotiate the scope of the work to be done, including establishing personal knowledge of the particular site or locale affected.

The next step is the actual study or background preparation prior to testimony. For an expert analyst, this is very important, as you will be asked to both present and defend your results. It is also important to build a step-by-step process or procedure that can be easily followed by a judge or hearing officer who is not an expert in aesthetic analysis. Thus the graphics — maps, photographs, charts, diagrams, and so on — should be extremely well prepared so as to be easily read and comprehended anywhere in the court or hearing room (Appleyard 1977; Murray and Neimann 1979).

Prior to actual testimony there is a little game played

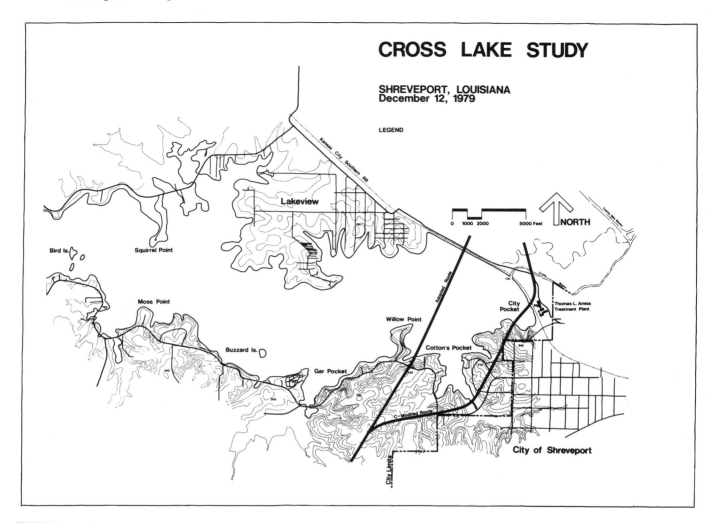

FIGURE 15.3   Map of Cross Lake I-220 viaduct alternatives. *Graphic credit: Dan Sundquist*

called the discovery process. The game is to discover what the opposition's testimony and exhibits are before they are presented in court. Tactics include taking lengthy interrogatories and depositions from opposite-side expert witnesses prior to direct testimony and reviewing all exhibits before they are brought into court. Countertactics include not finishing studies or exhibits until just before court date.

In the I-220 Shreveport case,[3] for instance, the Federal Highway Administration (FHWA) legal counsel was shocked to discover the quality and power of Stephen Sheppard's before and after rendered photographic simulations of the highway viaduct structures which were done for two alternatives from three viewpoints. (See Figures 15.3 and 15.4.) As a result of this early discovery experience, the FHWA counsel spent much effort and time trying to discredit the exhibits so they could not be entered into the court's record.

a.

FIGURE 15.4 a, b, c, d, e, f, g (above and page 265) Simulation of Cross Lake I-220 viaduct structures from three viewpoints. *Graphic credit: Stephen R. J. Sheppard*

---

[3]Id.

FIGURE 15.4 *(Continued)* Simulation of Cross Lake I-220 viaduct structures from three viewpoints

Setting a court or hearing date is often an exercise in strategic chess-playing, as each side jockeys for the advantage in preparation. Setting a date is also contingent on what is found out during the discovery process. If one side can offer "proof" that they will not get a favorable hearing from a specific court or hearing officer, they can argue, in some cases, for a change in venue, judge, or hearing officer.

Finally, we have the actual testimony, when the expert is sworn in with a brief prepared statement and presentation of professional qualifications. The presentation of qualifications is extremely important. Opposite legal counsel, if they are sharp, may attempt to prune your qualifications to a smaller domain, thus limiting the area of expertise that you are deemed qualified to testify on. Thus, as an analyst you want to use your qualifications and training to build a broad base for testimony since the opposite counsel will undoubtedly attempt to diminish your qualifications. Aesthetics is a particularly difficult area in this regard, as no one knows what adequate training, education, and experience is deemed to be that of an expert. Even well-trained landscape architects, architects, planners, and engineers may not have the appropriate education, training or experience in the area of aesthetic impact analysis.

The expert witness will then be asked about knowledge of the specific landscape or project in question. You will be asked whether you have visited the site and have personal knowledge of the area involved. This step can be very important, for if you have not visited the site involved in the litigation, then your credibility, or even the admission any of your testimony, is at risk.

Next you present your direct testimony so that it can become part of the court or hearing record. This is the payoff for all your preparation; you should present the information as clearly and succinctly as possible, without drawing it out or giving a lecture, or discussing tangential points. While you are presenting the results of your aesthetic analysis, you will also identify and introduce into the record your graphic exhibits with the aid of friendly counsel. This can be a critical step, as some of these exhibits can be quite powerful (as, for example, the "before and after" simulations presented during the discovery process, mentioned above). Legal counsel may attempt to keep such exhibits from being entered into the court record by questioning how they were produced. For instance, for a photograph of a landscape or project, you need to know how the photograph was taken, including camera type, lens, aperture, film type, exposure, time of day, and so on. Legal counsel may also question admission of exhibits, if you as an analyst did not personally prepare them, but hired or supervised others in doing so.

While you are giving your direct testimony and introducing your exhibits with the aid of friendly counsel, the opposing counsel and battery of experts are very busy taking and passing around notes about how to disassemble or discredit your direct testimony, or both. Before finishing your direct testimony you will be asked to give a summary: For example, does this project have an acceptable or unacceptable level of visual impact, or can it be mitigated?

During the cross-examination the opposing counsel gets to ask you questions about your direct testimony, in order to impeach or discredit that testimony. Or, if it is a quasi-judicial hearing as, for instance, under New York State's Environmental Quality Review Act, several interveners get to ask you questions in succession until they run out. Cross-examination is when you truly earn your fee as an expert witness, but you may not introduce any new exhibits at this time. The opposing counsel is trying to test your knowledge, procedures, and conclusions by various means, and you may feel as if you are in a verbal sparring match. The co-author has been on the witness stand for one and one-half days on cross-examination alone after direct testimony of one day's duration. Any vague points that you did not quite solidify during direct testimony may come back to haunt you during cross-examination. Also, at this time, expert witnesses on the other side use their collective wisdom to feed questions to cross-examining attorneys. Of course, you can do the same for the other side's expert witnesses too, which is part of your job as an expert witness.

Two general tactics are often used by legal counsel: (1) wear you down until you contradict yourself, and (2) find weak spots in your direct testimony and try to discredit those particular points in the record. Good expert witnesses avoid being backed into verbal corners and use the questions as an opportunity to provide more substantial points if possible.

Finally, the redirect is that portion of the testimony where you get back on the stand "to repair the damage" done during cross-examination. You cannot introduce new evidence or exhibits at this point, but you may provide clarification and rebuttal points if needed.

This is likely to be the full sequence of events in a trial in federal or state court. Some parts of the process, such as direct testimony and cross-examination, are used during regulatory hearings as well. Some hearing formats allow experts to sit together as a panel to answer questions. This is much easier than a single expert witness fielding all questions.

There are a few points about the process that may not appear in textbooks but the author recommends. Peter Dorram's (1982) book is quite engaging and hits some of the same points mentioned here. These items are critical for aesthetic analysis tied to litigation: These items are

1. The aesthetic analyst and legal counsel must have a clear idea of what is involved with the particular project or study scope, and each should know about

the other's professional requirements and processes.

2. Adequate resources are needed in order for on-site fieldwork and analyses to be defensible in court.

3. Careful analysis, logic, and exhibit preparation are needed, as there may be competing analysis methods and simulations on either side of the issue.

4. Adequate time and preparation should be allocated for rehearsal of the aesthetic expert witness and others so that the needed testimony and exhibits enter the court record in comprehensible fashion.

These are just a few points that can be made about the role of the expert witness/aesthetic analyst. This is a new and exciting field where electronic image-processing and computer simulation techniques for putting projects on the landscape are creating new thresholds of realism and battles over what is an admissible exhibit in court (see Appleyard 1977; Mertes, Smardon, and Miller, 1991; and Sheppard 1989). The case study by Bruce Murray and Bernard Niemann that follows ties together some of the points we have tried to make in this chapter.

Case Study: Ice Age National Reserve, Wisconsin[4]

Introduction and Background

The construction of a 69 kv transmission line in contrast to a larger transmission line, for example, 345 kv, is typically not a controversial item. Nor would it normally be expected that a facility of this type would attract institutional, legal, and professional interest. This was not the situation for this Wisconsin Public Service Commission (PSCW) case. The reasons for the interest in this case are important because they establish a set of opportunitistic conditions for a test of the importance of visual quality. The test was: Under what conditions would the PSCW commissioners be willing to rule for or against construction of a transmission facility solely on visual quality issues?

The following conditions were present. First, Murray and Neimann, as professionals, were asked by an attorney representing a private land owner to visit the site. They responded to two questions. One, if construction of the 69 kv line were to be completed, could there be a deleterious visual impact on the Cross Plains unit of the Wisconsin reserve system? Two, was the PSCW staff in error by not requiring an environmental impact statement because the Wisconsin Environmental Policy Act (WEPA) requires a two-step evaluation? The first step requires the agency staff to determine if a more comprehensive environmental impact statement is necessary. In this case, the PSCW staff determined that an environmental impact statement was not necessary.

Second, the institutional and political makeup of the PSCW appeared to support a test case. The PSCW chairman was a nationally known energy economist recognized for his innovative use of economics in resource-related issues; plus he had conducted research on economics in relation to environmental values.

Third, two competent, aggressive, and committed attorneys were involved. Previous experiences in adversarial settings had proven to be extremely counterproductive when Murray and Niemann had been involved with or represented by inferior and noninvolved counsel.

The adjacent landowner was represented by a tax attorney who typically represented settlement cases. The citizens of Wisconsin were represented by the public intervener, which is a public-supported office, whose responsibility is to intervene when the citizens' rights to environmental quality are not being represented by the Department of Natural Resources (DNR). Before becoming the public intervener, he was an aggressive criminal lawyer in the state attorney general's office.

Fourth, the geological uniqueness of the site would make the case for visual quality more straightforward. From a geological point of view the site was unique.

Fifth, Murray and Neimann's previous experiences in developing weighted, descriptive, and hierarchical transmission location models show that an array of experts concur that certain unique natural features should be avoided. These studies have documented that one should avoid: (1) areas of recognized national importance, (2) scientific areas, (3) significant scenic areas, (4) unique archeological and historic areas, (5) scenic roads, (6) ridge lines, (7) unique topographic features, and (8) unique geological formations. Also, because one of the studies had involved the utility proposing the construction of the 69 kv transmission facility, it seemed appropriate to determine that the previous conclusions would be admissible and prevail in an adversarial setting.

Sixth, additional conditions made this a compelling situa-

---

[4]Bruce H. Murray and Bernard J. Niemann, Jr. 1979. "Visual Testimony in an Adversary Setting." Presented as part of *Our National Landscape: National Conference on Applied Techniques for Analysis and Management of the Visual Resources.* Incline Village, NV., April 23-25, 1979. Reproduced with permission of the authors.

tion. The PSCW staff had erred, in Murray and Neimann's judgment, in not requiring an environmental impact statement. This, therefore, made the conclusions and recommendations for non-undergrounding suspect. The utility had chosen a highly visible site (the highest point in the region) for the substation; the selection was eventually shown to be insensitive to overall visual concerns. In addition, it was generally concluded that the utility had chosen their route only after being threatened with legal action. It was not their preferred route. Neither the utility nor PSCW had asked the DNR (who manages the reserve) for their opinion concerning the proposed 69 kv transmission facility. Also, the employee responsible for overall planning of the reserve system in Wisconsin was not allowed by his superior to speak out on this issue. This constraint for basically political reasons suppressed public discussion of this visual quality question.

Conditions of the Site

The reserve was created in May 1974 (U.S.D.I., 1973). The enacting legislation provided for a joint planning, management, and ownership arrangement between the National Park Service (NPS) and the Wisconsin DNR. The nine reserve sites were selected to represent different results caused by the glaciers in Wisconsin. The Cross Plains unit is a 160-acre site that includes a unique gorge created by melt water from the glacial ice. The regional condition makes the site unique. The site is located on the interface between the unglaciated (driftless) and glaciated landscape. The site is elevated and provides views of both landscapes.

The master plan calls for an interpretive center and self-guiding trails. The trails are intended to guide the visitor to both the internal and external glaciation features. The master plan calls for an interpretive center to be located on top of the site. DNR was unable to purchase this site and politically did not want to ask the state legislature for permission to use condemnation authority. This will require the interpretive center to be located in a different place, which would be visually much closer to the proposed 69 kv transmission line. This becomes an important issue in the case.

Procedure

Murray and Neimann used four objectives to assist and guide in the development of the case study materials:

Defensible:

The materials and techniques employed had to be able to withstand cross-examination. The techniques and resultant materials could not be construed as biased, arbitrary, or irrelevant.

Factual:

The data presented had to be factual. Interpretations and expert opinion had to be clearly identified and limited to the findings portion of the case.

Self-descriptive and logical in progression:

The case materials had to be developed and organized in such a way that the contents led the reviewer logically through the

materials in a self-describing format. Murray and Neimann assumed that the PSCW staff, the utilities, and the PSCW commissioners would review the materials in detail in private. Because the materials laid the foundation for Murray and Neimann's eventual findings as expert witnesses, they developed them to assist the self-reviewer to understand the basis of their conclusions.

Illustrative:

In addition to being self-descriptive and logical, the materials needed to be illustrative as much as possible to simulate the before and after conditions of the 69 kv transmission facility. The utilities were inadvertently quite helpful in assisting Murray and Neimann to simulate the before and after conditions. As soon as Murray and Neimann knew they were going to be involved, they photographed the site. The utility had been so sure they would eventually be allowed to construct the facility that they proceeded with construction. Thus, they photographed the site again with the facility in place. The presence of structures provided real rather than simulated conditions. Five guidelines were used to prepare case materials. The presentation graphics were to be visually communicative, flexible, interrelatable, attractive, and concise. These objectives were incorporated into the exhibit materials represented in Figure 15.5

The following is a list of the variables selected and the reasons for their selection. Figure 15.5 illustrates the dimensions of the reserve, the difference between authorized and actual public ownership, and the proposed transmission alignment. Areas within the dashed line are presently owned by DNR. Figure 15.5 also serves as a factual base for illustrating the following features:

Viewshed:

Because one of the primary functions of the site is to provide views of the glaciated and nonglaciated landscape, it was important to document factually the extent that it was possible to view both landscapes from the site (heaviest line).

Proposed and existing 69 kv transmission Route:

The inclusion of all existing 69 kv systems (line with dots) is important to document the extent of these facilities and the distances from which they can be seen from the site (see Figure 15.5).

Associated landscape features:

Relevant associated features were identified, such as adjacent land uses. These were delineated to document the expert witnesses familiarity with the site (see Figure 15.5).

Topography:

The portrayal of this variable was important for three reasons. One, it documents that the substation, to which the 69 kv line connects, is located on a prominent and highly visual elevation. Two, the reserve site is located on a prominent ele-

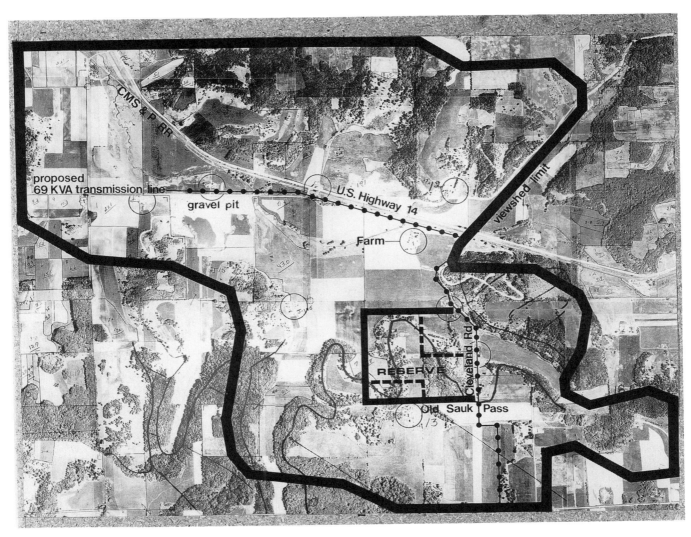

FIGURE 15.5   Site conditions and base map. *Source: Murray and Neiman*

vation overlooking two distinct landscapes. Three, the delineation of the viewshed shown on the photograph mosaic base can be verified if desired.

Land ownership:

This variable was included since it documented three things: one, that DNR owned only portions of the totally authorized area; two, the overall ownership patterns; and three, that the expert witnesses were aware of the litigant's property holdings. Murray and Neimann anticipated that the utility would attempt to cloud or discredit the expert witnesses' objectivity by implying that the adjacent landowner was only looking out after his long-term potential development interests and not necessarily the public good. As anticipated, the utility did raise the implication. Murray and Neimann responded by referring to this document.

Open-space corridor:

This variable was included to show that the reserve site was originally designated as an open-space corridor. It reinforced

the concept that the reserve site had special qualities that could possibly be altered by visual intrusions.

Photographic locations:

A series of before and after photographs were taken from the reserve, to the reserve, and along Cleveland Road, which parallels the route of the proposed 69 kv transmission line. The location and direction of each photograph were recorded. If the photograph was used in the quantitative change analysis, it was so noted. Murray and Neimann anticipated that the objectivity and representativeness of the photographs would be questioned. This proved to be true. The inclusion of this exhibit was quite important in illustrating the representativeness of the photography (Figure 15.6).

Panorama locations:

To assist further in illustrating the photographic coverage, the panoramic photographs were noted. This variable was in-

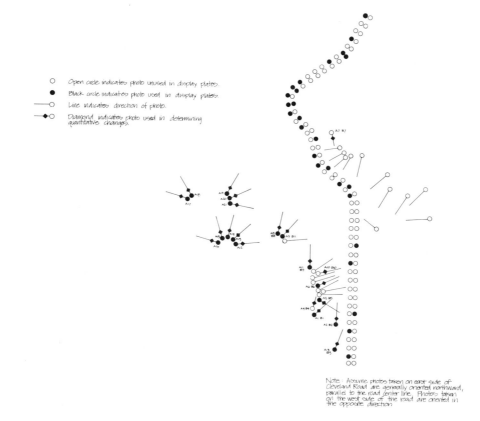

Note: Assume photos taken on east side of
Cleveland Road are generally oriented northward,
parallel to the road center line. Photos taken
on the west side of the road are oriented in
the opposite direction.

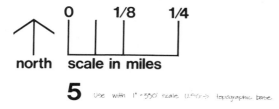

photograph locations

5   Use with 1"=350' scale U.S.G.S. topographic base.

FIGURE 15.6   Photographic locations. *Source: Murray and Neiman*

cluded to document the location of the scene and cone of visual coverage of each panorama (the land area included in the view). In addition, which the use of other overlay variables, the type of landscape elements visible in the panorama could be verified (Figure 15.7).

View locations with comments:

At this point in the case the type of information changes. The preceding material was straightforward and did not require professional or expert witness interpretation. The materials that follow do. They include the before and after photographs taken from the site with comments. The comments are Murray and Neimann's reactions, as experts, to visual change resulting from the proposed 69 kv transmission line. The comments were also used to verify again what features were visible from the reserve (Figure 15.8).

Quantitative changes:

This variable was used to document and verify the type and quantity of landscape elements presently visible and the type and quantity of landscape elements potentially visible after the construction of the proposed 69 kv transmission line. The results indicated that construction of the proposed 69 kv line would introduce new visual elements to the landscape. From Murray and Neimann's experience, it is important to document clearly that visual change will occur. How visually perceptible the change will be or what effect the change will have are separate questions. What is presented for the hearing record is what change will, in fact, occur. A nonverified theory, called a "cobweb" theory, was developed and applied to measure visual change, the assumption being that the combination of conductors created a "cobweb" effect between the viewer and the scene; the net visual change being equal to the distance between the top and bottom conductor. The utility attorney argued the contrary, which was that the net visual change was only equal to the net perceptual diameter of the conductor itself (Figure 15.9).

Photographic sequence along Cleveland Road with comments:

Cleveland Road was important because it served as the entrance road to the interpretive center and visitor parking lot.

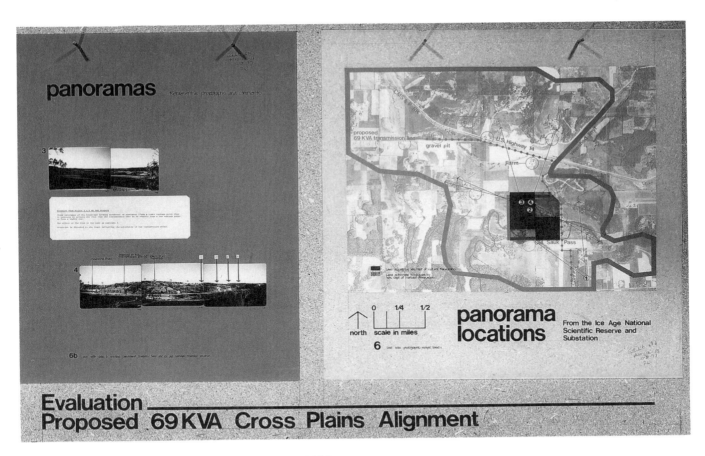

FIGURE 15.7   Panoramic locations. *Source: Murray and Neiman*

Proposed tour route: Effect of utility system traveling north with comments:

This material was included because the interpretive tour route is an official part of the master plan. Travel along the route is potentially affected by the 69 kv transmission line itself and the connecting substation. For example, emanating from the substation is a series of distribution lines parallel with the interpretive tour route and associated glacial features observable from the route (Figure 15.10).

FIGURE 15.8   View locations. *Source: Murray and Neiman*

Techniques Employed

The previous discussion covered the source and content of the base materials. We now discuss the techniques employed to ensure that the base materials would be accepted as relevant material. As separate techniques, they are not unusual, but as a composite group they represent the array needed in an adversarial setting. They include:

Site visit:

Familiarity with the site was essential. For example, the PSCW staff had never visited the site even though it was near their office. In addition, the utility's attorney was not familiar with the unique qualities of the site. More familiarity with the site proved to be of considerable advantage, particularly of a psychological advantage when the expert witness lacks experience in an adversarial setting.

Logical sequence of base materials:

The use of overlays and a common set of scales plus an ordered sequence proved to be very helpful. Knowing that the material was self-guiding provided a psychological lift during the more intense periods of testimony.

Graphic/overlay procedure:

To assist in conveying content of the base materials, various graphic and overlay techniques were employed. Also the base materials were self-contained and displayed on a mounted panel. All photographs were securely mounted on panels,

FIGURE 15.9 a, b Visual impact before and after. *Source: Murray and Neiman*

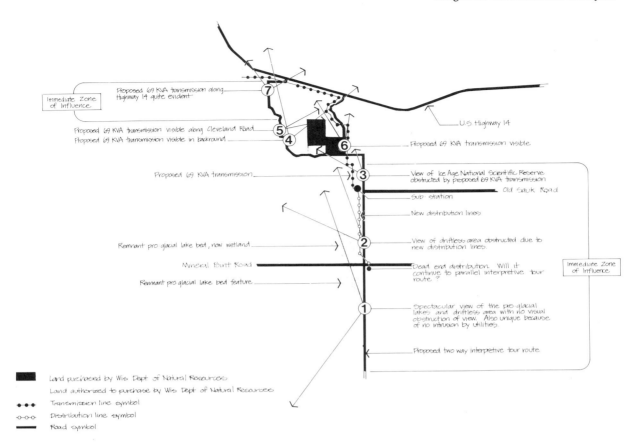

Land purchased by Wis. Dept of Natural Resources
Land authorized to purchase by Wis. Dept of Natural Resources
Transmission line symbol
Distribution line symbol
Road symbol

north   scale in miles

0   1   2

Proposed Interpretive Tour Route
Effect Of Utility System
Traveling North

10   with 1:24,000 scale USGS topographic base

FIGURE 15.10   Interpretive tour route. *Source: Murray and Neiman*

therefore requiring others to review the materials in relationship to the testimony.

Random photography:

Because Murray and Neimann anticipated that the utility's attorney would question the representativeness and objectivity of their photography, they employed a random photographic procedure along Cleveland Road. The technique consisted of segmenting the road into 100-foot segments. Numbered coins representing 10-foot intervals were used to assign randomly the photographic location within each 100-foot segment. Murray and Neimann's concern over non-biased photography proved to be very important. As anticipated, the utility's attorney asserted that the photography was purposefully taken to portray only the negative aspects of the 69 kv transmission line. In addition, the attorney argued that "artist's license" was used to accentuate further the negative aspects. Because Murray and Neimann anticipated this form of cross-examination, they were able to respond effec-

tively. It is essential for the expert witness to prevail at this point in the testimony as the photographs were an essential part of the case. If the photographs had been descredited, the case would have been severely damaged.

Before and after photography:

Because Murray and Neimann were able to actually photograph before and after conditions, the task of simulating the 69 kv transmission line was quite easy. The importance of representative simulation cannot be underestimated in an adversarial situation.

Quantitative measurement of change:

This technique consisted of projecting a 35mm slide on a grid. Within each square, the presence of manmade features was measured in percent of the whole grided picture. This procedure was conducted for selected before-and-after photographs. The accumulated cell differences between the before photograph and after photograph equal the quantitative measurement of change.

Documentation:

Again, to ensure that the base materials would be admissible, Murray and Neimann carefully documented their origins and currency. All maps were documented as to origin, date, and original or actual scale. The location and direction of all photographs were maintained. The type of film, type of camera, type of film processing, type of lens, characteristics of the lens, time of day, and the date of the year were also recorded.

Experience and the adversary mentality:

The experiences that Murray and Neimann have had indicate quite clearly that anticipation, preparation, documentation, and a sort of "gamesmanship" are important factors. The adversarial setting, in which the primary goal of the adversary is to discredit you as an expert, can be painful, particularly to the uninitiated who tend to react as if the cross-examination were a personal attack. In law classes the "art of selecting and using an expert witness" is discussed and taught. Unfortunately, the education of design professionals lacks preparation in the art and science of being an expert witness. Success in these adversarial settings is important. Professionally, it is important to perform well to ensure that your client has been represented effectively. Quite simply, success builds a reputation and credentials as an expert that lawyers and the courts consider fundamental.

Rehearsal:

Some form of "dress rehearsal" in which you and your lawyer develop the questions upon which you will give your testimony is essential. In addition, the lawyer can assist by asking questions expected during the cross-examination from the adversary, and you can assist the lawyer by developing questions to be asked of adversarial witnesses. Since most lawyers will have had no prior experience in visual-quality–contested cases, you will be expected (most likely) to provide the basic strategy. Be aware of other relevant cases, and be familiar with the relevant body of knowledge. The expectation of an expert witness is just what the term implies — an expert.

Findings

1. The quality of the views from the interpretive tour route to the pro-glacial lakes and the unglaciated landscape was adversely affected by the poles and lines.
2. The substation was located on the highest elevation in the area near the reserve, resulting in a visible and incongruous visual object.
3. The utility proposed erecting 69 kv lines adjacent to the reserve, creating a situation deleterious to the visual quality of the reserve.
4. The utility had constructed a 69 kv transmission line in the background adjacent to Highway 143, creating a visual

condition that is deleterious to the visual quality of the reserve.
5. The location of a substation strongly influences the route selected for a transmission line. In this case, there were several alternative routes that would have avoided the reserve.
6. The project was evaluated by the PSCW staff utilizing environmental assessment, and as a PSCW staff member stated, "the overall difference in impacts between routes is not environmentally significant".[5] This conclusion by PSCW staff, in Murray and Neimann's opinion, was not justified in the face of the evidence provided.
7. In Murray and Neimann's judgment, the PSCW lacked educational background and competence in visual quality assessment.
8. The information was known and, presumably, understood by the utility, but staff member chose to ignore the information when locating the transmission line adjacent to the reserve.

Recommendations

From the analysis Murray and Neimann carried out, the following recommendation was given:

Relocate or underground the proposed 69 kv transmission facility from where the Reserve is first visible from Cleveland Road (traveling south) to where the vegetation begins to mask the proposed transmission facility. The northerly burial point must be predicated upon the location of the interpretive center and the views from the potential interpretive hiking trails within the Reserve. This assures the DNR essential flexibility in determining the most representative and educational hiking trail experience for the visitor. This also provides essential flexibility in determining the location of the interpretive center.[6]

Epilogue: Commission Ruling

The findings of the PSCW commissioners were included in a document entitled "Findings of Fact and Order," which contains the following statements:

The commission finds that because of the special unique geological features of the Cross Plains Unit, its special significance at National, State and local levels to the public in appreciation and understanding the Ice Age, and the expected extensive use of the Cross Plains Unit by the public in furthering its knowledge of the Ice Age in Wisconsin, the Cross Plains Unit is particularly important from a public interest standpoint. The commission fully understands the relatively high cost of underground versus overhead construction and that underground construction will have some relatively small impact on rates paid by customers of Wisconsin Power and Light Company. Nevertheless, the Commission considers that in this particular case the public interest supports a requirement for underground construction in the vicinity of Cross Plains Reserve Unit.

The commission will accordingly herein require that

---

[5]P.S.C.W. 1977. Hearing record of case 6680-CE-13, Madison, WI, p. 5.
[6]Id., pp. 95–96.

Wisconsin Power and Light utilize underground instead of overhead construction. . . .

This determination is not considered to be precedent setting in terms of future transmission line projects, but rather one which reflects the uniqueness and importance of the Cross Plains Unit and the stated, significant public interest considerations involved.[7]

Regarding the precedent-setting, one commissioner dissented:

My decision is based on a test of balancing these interests (economic vs. environment) in a manner consistent with the overall general public interest which I feel requires undergrounding, considering the uniqueness of the Reserve. There is precedential value in this decision.[8]

References

Appleyard, D. 1977. Understanding professional media. In *Human behavior and environment*, ed. I. Altman and J. Wohwill, vol. 2. Plenum Press.

Atkins, J. T., and Blair, W. G. E. 1983. Visual impacts of highway alternatives. *Garten und Landschaft*, 8(83): 632–635.

Brace, P. 1980. Urban aesthetics and the courts. *Environmental Comment*, 1980 (June): 16–19.

Carruth, D. B. 1977. Assessing scenic quality transmission line siting. *Landscape*, 22(1): 31–34.

Dickert, T., and Smardon, R. C. 1978. California Coastal Act of 1976 — Procedural Steps. In T. Dickert and J. Sorensen, *Collaborative Land-Use Planning for the Coastal Zone*, vol. 1, A process of local program development. Institute for Urban and Regulatory Development, University of California, Berkeley.

Dorram, P. B. 1982. *The expert witness*. Planners Press, American Planning Association.

McCloskey, M. 1979. Litigation and landscape aesthetics. In *Our national landscape*, ed. G. Elsner and R. Smardon, pp. 674–675.

Mertes, J. D., Smardon, R. C., and Miller, A. J. 1991. Applications of video technology in landscape architecture and environmental design. *Design methods and theories*, 25(1): 1353–1368.

Murray, B. H. and Neimann, B. J. 1979. Visual quality testimony in an adversary setting. In *Our national landscape*, ed. G. Elsner and R. C. Smardon, pp. 693–700.

Palmer, J. F., and Smardon, R. C. 1982. Visual impact assessment of ORV activity on Cape Cod National Seashore Beaches. Prepared for Conservation Law Foundation of New England.

Schauman, S. 1982. On a clear day in Ogunquit, Maine. *Coastal Zone Management Journal*, 9(3/4): 313–322.

Sheppard, S. R. J. 1989. *Visual simulation: A user guide for architects, engineers and planners*. Van Nostrand Reinhold.

Sive, D. 1970. Securing, examining, and cross-examining expert witnesses in environmental cases. *Michigan Law Review*, 68: 1175–1198.

Stuart, N. H. 1980. Rosslyn: A monumental intrusion. *Environmental Comment*, 1980 (June): 4–7.

U.S.D.I., National Park Service. 1973. *The preliminary master plan for the National Ice Age Scientific Reserve*. Wisconsin Department of Natural Resources and U.S.D.I., National Park Service.

[7]P.S.C.W. 1978. Findings of fact and order, Case 6680-CE-13, Madison, WI.
[8]Id., p. 16.

Chapter 16

The Legal Landscape: Issues and Trends

INTRODUCTION

This chapter is an effort to put the previous legal discussion in a distinctly nonlegal perspective. Given the evolution of aesthetic value treatment by the legal system, some major philosophical issues and concepts should be mentioned. The theoretical perspectives utilized by the authors will include the "sociology of law" approach (Cutler 1972); the environmental psychology of environmental decision-makers (Craik 1970); and the political science of environmental administration (Caldwell 1970). All of these approaches have potentially valuable contributions to make to environmental aesthetics and the law.

REVIEW OF MAJOR PROGRESSIONS AND TRENDS

We can summarize the evolution of aesthetic value treatment by the legal system into three significant trends:

1. The shift from only a few states supporting use of aesthetics alone as a basis for exercising the police power for land use, architectural, and signage regulation to a majority of states supporting use of aesthetics only.
2. The gradual shift of the courts to facing issues with environmental aesthetic values. The evolution of this shift from (a) not facing aesthetics, to (b) fictionalizing or masking aesthetics under other issues, to (c) facing up to the right to address aesthetic injury to the present human users.
3. Increased legislation and regulation at federal,

state, and local levels that address aesthetic value protection with increasing specificity.

The previous trends are dependent upon a highly erratic legal pendulum swinging from conservative to liberal decisions across time. The liberal decisions are always labeled as "maverick" or the exception, but somehow they are also signposts for the overall general trend (see Figure 16.1). The legal system is generally conservative in its treatment of the aesthetic values of society, as most court decisions lag behind overall popular trends. Simultaneously, many legal scholars call upon the court system for leadership in an area they are loath to go into.

WILL THE LIBERAL TRENDS CONTINUE?

The general force behind consideration of aesthetic values in American society is its high level of affluence. Will future fiscal, energy, and food production constraints limit this rising affluence and possibly cause a downward trend in public support for protection of aesthetic values in the landscape? This last possibility may diminish interest in assimilating an "environmental land ethic," as originally proposed by Aldo Leopold (1949) and endorsed earlier in this book as a useful standard for local aesthetic regulation. An alternative scenario might present a society that has learned to "tighten its belt" by reduction in energy and material consumption and has refocused its attention on maintaining and regenerating environmental quality. In this scenario, educational, recreational, and aesthetic environmental attributes would be "consumed" experientially, with high informational and experiential quality becoming the desirable goal.

276

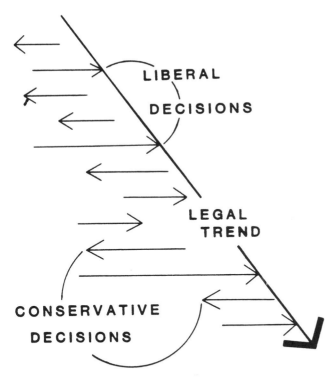

FIGURE 16.1 Environmental court cases and trends. *Source: John Wiley & Sons*

LEGAL-PHILOSPHICAL DILEMMAS

A number of key questions and dilemmas have arisen from the previous discussion: (1) elitisim versus the common man, (2) uniform precedent versus contextualism, and (3) administrative management stability versus shifting public value systems.

Elitism versus the Common Man

We have an elite minority dictating, by their value systems, the degree of consideration of environmental aesthetics in legal environmental cases. One can prescribe altrusim, but there are natural constraints for most individuals, who may attempt to extend themselves into other people's value systems. The challenge is to open the process, whether legal or planning, so that more value systems may be represented. The liberalized rules of standing do this for those groups or individuals who have the means to litigate. A more direct and less expensive approach is through agency administrative hearings and workshops. An even better approach is the use of mass surveys, which could tap the "silent" mass publics for their aesthetic values, such as what was done for the Juneau case study in Chapter 10 and the Greene County Nuclear Power Plant case study in Chapter 14. There are major restrictions for federal agencies to do mass surveying, as the Human Subjects Clearance process and Report Reduction Program as administered by the Office of Management and Budget create very few slots for annual or one-time surveys. Without using direct public participation and surveys to ascertain public aesthetic value sets, administrative agencies will be forever rebounding from the legislative bodies to the public and back again.

Uniform Precedent versus Contextualism

National legislation cannot be sensitive enough to deal with local contextual environmental aesthetic issues. That is, unless there is created a separate piece of legislation for every sensitive area of high aesthetic value in the country. This is not far from the present trend, as environmental groups are trying hard to get certain landscapes currently managed by federal agencies as multiple-use environments into more protected status of single- or limited-use environments (e.g., designated wilderness areas). In the local context, the prime example would be specific areas designated for architectural control or historic preservation.

The question is: Should one overload the legal system with specific pieces of legislation to protect separate and specific areas? Is this, in fact, a good way of protecting public aesthetic values for specific areas? Another related aspect of this issue is that specific areas, if they have survived highly visible court or administrative hearing battles over their fate, emerge with highly charged symbolic values that may or may not correlate with their physical aesthetic attributes (e.g., Overton Park, Knoxville, Tennessee).

A problem also appears in relation to legal precedents from court cases. Lawyers and judges are forever searching for that one clear precedent that will make sense out of the whole morass. Precedents are useful for clarifying legal procedures but may not be for substantive issues. If we adopt a contextual approach to environmental aesthetics, every place may be seen as qualitatively unique and have an essence of its own. Therefore, precedents dealing with substantive matters may be of little use if we are concerned with the essence or contextual uniqueness of environmental aesthetic values.

Administrative Management Stability versus Shifting Public Value Systems

The preceding situation is further aggravated by shifting public value systems. We know that in some cases the public's sensitivity to certain landscapes and landscape features has changed drastically in relatively short periods of time (see Glacken 1967; Nash 1967; Passmore 1971; Ress 1975). This presents a doubly perplexing problem for the administrative agency charged with visual resource or aesthetic management. First, the agency has to anticipate shifting public values so as not to get into a bind; for instance, trade off or allow development of a landscape of which the public thinks highly. Second, the agency must not appear to be shifting policy rapidly themselves and thereby precipitating uncertainty or anxiety in the public eye. Agencies may find themselves engaging in the perilous adventure of retaining a public image of confidence as to the certainty or consistency of its actions while simultaneously being flexible enough to account for contextual aesthetic values.

IN SEARCH OF CONTEXTUAL HARMONY

In summary, public regulation and control through legislative mandate for the public environment and, recognizing certain constitutional tests, for the private environment seem to be the most hopeful prescription of environmental aesthetics. In assessing the roles of the different actors in environmental aesthetic control, a number of conclusions could be drawn. Judges, legislatures, and administrative agencies need to make better use of existing aesthetic theory and information so that theoretically compatible approaches are developed for environmental aesthetic protection. Many of the legal tests are of a contextual nature, and there is a corresponding contextual theory of aesthetics. They could reinforce each other. Legal professionals need to work with aesthetic analysts, such as landscape architects, planners, and social scientists, and vice versa. There needs to be a better meeting of the minds over environmental aesthetics. If this happens, better theory will be provided for legal test foundations, there will be a more orderly evolution of aesthetics and law, and methodologists will be confronted with more realistic environmental aesthetic questions and dilemmas.

References

Beck, R. E. 1967. Book reviews: A wilderness bill of rights. *Natural Resources Journal,* 7(3): 456–460.

Brecher, J. J. 1972. Venue in conservation cases: A potential pitfall for environmental lawyers. *Ecology Law Quarterly,* 2(1): 91–117.

Broughton, R. 1972. Aesthetics and environmental law: Decisions and values. *Land and Water Law Review,* 7(2): 451–500.

Caldwell, L. K. 1970. Authority and responsibility for environmental administration. In *Society and physical environment,* ed. S. Z. Klauser. American Academy of Political and Social Science. pp. 107–116.

Craik, K. H. 1970. The environmental dispositions of environmental decisionmakers. In *Society and physical environment,* ed. S. Z. Klauser, American Academy of Political and Social Science. pp. 87–92.

Cutler, M. 1972. A Study of litigation related to management of Forest Service administered lands and its effect on policy decisions, Part Two: A comparison of four cases. Unpublished Dissertation, Department of Resource Development, Michigan State University.

Douglas, W. O. 1965. *A wilderness bill of rights.* Little, Brown.

Glacken, C. J. 1967. *Traces on the Rhodian shore.* University of California Press.

Hendee, J. C. et al. 1968. *Wilderness-users in the Pacific Northwest: Their characteristics, values and management preferences.* U.S.D.A., Forest Service Research Paper PNW-61, Pacific NW Forest and Range Experimental Station, Portland.

Leopold, A. 1949. *A Sand County almanac.* Oxford University Press.

Leopold, L. B. 1969. *Quantitative comparison of some aesthetic factors among rivers.* U.S. Geological Survey Cir. 620. U.S. G.P.O.

Leopold, L. B., and Marchand, M. O. 1968. On the quantitative inventory of the riverscape. *Water Resources Research,* 4(4): 700–717.

McKecknie, G. E. 1974. *ERI manual: Environmental response inventory.* Consulting Psychological Press.

Musk, S. 1976. William O. Douglas. *Ecology Law Quarterly,* 5(2): 229–232.

Nash, R. 1967, *Wilderness and the American mind.* Yale University Press.

Passmore, J. 1971. *Man's responsibility for nature.* Scribners.

Pepper, S. C. 1937. *Aesthetic quality: A contextualistic theory of beauty.* Scribners.

Rees, R. 1975. The scenery cult: Changing landscape tastes over three centuries. *Landscape,* 19(3): 39–47.

Reich, C. A. 1966. The law of the planned society. *Yale Law Journal,* 75(8): 1228–1270.

Sive, D. 1970. Securing, examining and cross-examining expert witnesses in environmental cases. *Michigan Law Review,* 68: 1175–1198.

Author/Subject Index

Court Case/Law Index

ABOUT THE AUTHORS

The co-authors are Richard C. Smardon, Ph.D., Director of the Institute for Environmental Policy and Planning at the SUNY College of Environmental Science and Forestry, and James P. Karp, Professor of Law and Public Policy with the Syracuse University School of Management. Dr. Smardon has co-edited two books — *Foundations for Visual Project Analysis* (Smardon et al., 1986) and *The Future of Wetlands: Assessing Visual-Cultural Values* (Smardon, 1983), held a national conference in landscape analysis (Elsner and Smardon, 1979), has written a number of articles on law and aesthetics, and has been an expert witness in federal court and environmental hearings. He has also taught a course in visual landscape analysis for several years at SUNY/ESF and teaches aesthetic analysis short courses to the U.S. Corps of Engineers (six courses — 150 professionals) and for the New York State Public Employees Federation (two courses — 70 professionals). Dr. Karp has co-written a book on land-use law, has published articles dealing with the legal aspects of the National Environmental Policy Act, land-use ethics, the regulatory "takings" issue, and law and aesthetics, and has taught courses on environmental and land use law at Syracuse University for 20 years.